No One
Listened

No One Listened

Two children. A horrific act of violence.
No one to trust except each other.

ISOBEL AND ALEX KERR

with Andrew Crofts

HARPER
element

In loving memory of our Mum

This book is based on the authors' experiences.
In order to protect privacy, some names, identifying
characteristics, dialogue and details have been
changed or reconstructed.

HarperElement
An Imprint of HarperCollins*Publishers*
77–85 Fulham Palace Road,
Hammersmith, London W6 8JB

The web address is www.thorsonselement.com

and *HarperElement* are trademarks
of HarperCollins*Publishers* Ltd

First published by HarperCollins*Publishers* 2008

1

A catalogue record for this book
is available from the British Library

ISBN-10 0-00-727245-6 (hardback)
ISBN-13 978-00-727245-7 (hardback)
ISBN-10 0-00-727246-4 (paperback)
ISBN-13 978-00-727246-4 (paperback)

Printed and bound in Great Britain by
Clays Ltd, St Ives plc

Mixed Sources
Product group from well-managed
forests and other controlled sources
www.fsc.org Cert no. SW-COC-1806
© 1996 Forest Stewardship Council
FSC

Chapter One

Alex

Normally my sister Isobel would have got home from school before me, but that afternoon she'd been held up because she couldn't find her PE kit in the changing rooms and she and a friend had stayed behind to look for it. I'd been let out of class a few minutes earlier than usual and I'd walked straight home, just as I always did. If Isobel had left at her normal time and got home before me, she would have let herself into the house before the police arrived to stop her and she would have seen everything. Maybe he would even have attacked her as well.

The day it all happened was the 11th of January, 2002. It was a little after three-thirty in the afternoon so it was already on the verge of growing dark as I crossed the busy main road that ran between our home and our school. I was thirteen and Isobel was fifteen and we had been walking to and from school on our own for a good few years by then. There was nothing unusual about the journey, nothing to alert me to the waiting danger or to the horror of what had just happened behind our locked front door. I was thinking about normal, routine things like the homework I had to do and the after-school activities planned for that evening, and I was wondering what was for dinner.

The first thing I noticed as I came into our quiet road was that Mum's red Vauxhall Nova was parked outside the house. She wouldn't normally have got home from her job as a school teacher for a couple of hours yet and she hadn't said anything about being early when she set off that morning, so that puzzled me.

I turned into our front garden and walked the few paces up to the house, then pulled out my front door key, just as I always did, without even thinking about it, ready to let myself in. As I lifted the key to the lock, a movement in the street behind made me turn and I saw a police car drawing up at the kerb, its vivid markings making it stand out amongst all the other parked cars. I paused for a second and watched as a young uniformed policeman, dressed in a bullet-proof vest and looking a bit like one of those SWAT teams you see breaking into people's houses in television dramas, got out of the driver's door. There didn't seem to be any great sense of urgency in his movements so I turned back to the door and inserted my key in the lock. The policeman called out, making me jump.

2

'No, no lad,' he shouted. 'Stop there. Don't go in. Wait over there a minute.'

He walked up behind me and nodded towards the low wall that separated our front garden from next door's. There wasn't anything particularly dramatic in his tone as he gave me those instructions; it all seemed a routine matter to him, although I found it odd that I was being stopped from going into my own house. Isobel and I had always been brought up to be respectful of authority figures so I did as he told me without question, leaving my key still in the lock, unable to work out what was going on and unsure what to ask. It's always been my habit to stay quiet in new situations where I am unsure of myself, and wait to see what happens rather than launch in with lots of questions, demanding to know what was going on, which is probably what Isobel would have done if she had been in my shoes at that moment.

Under my curious gaze the policeman composed himself and then politely rang the doorbell, as if he was just paying a visit. I wondered if perhaps Mum and Dad had been arguing again and neighbours had rung to complain about the noise or to express their concern for Mum's safety. I decided I wasn't going to interfere, in case it was Dad who came to the door; I would leave it to the policeman to sort it out.

Dad had often threatened to hang himself or set fire to the house with us all in it. It might sound melodramatic

3

but I believed anything was possible as far as he was concerned. Maybe this time he had actually carried out one of his threats and Mum had had to call the police. Isobel and I were so worried about his threats to set fire to us that before we went to bed at night we used to try to find all the matches in the house and hide them – which was pointless really as we had no idea what Dad kept inside his room. We had never been allowed inside the upstairs bedroom where he spent most of his days and nights; we didn't even have any idea what it looked like in there.

A few seconds after the policeman rang the bell, the door opened and Dad was standing there, holding it wide open and giving the officer a clear view right through to the kitchen at the back of the house. I was over to the side so I couldn't see past them. Dad didn't seem at all surprised to find a uniformed policeman standing on his doorstep; it was as if he had been expecting him. He's a big guy, quite scary-looking, with a mean expression permanently set on his face. Whatever the policeman was able to see from there was enough to make him step back in shock and fumble for his radio, bringing it up to his mouth.

'There's been a blue murder,' he announced to whoever might be listening at the other end.

I was momentarily puzzled by the phrase. 'Screaming blue murder' just meant screaming at the top of your

4

voice, as far as I was aware, but maybe this was police code for something else – or had I not heard him correctly? The policeman certainly looked very shaken and it was more because of his agitation than anything else that I guessed someone was dead in the house. My throat felt tight, but I continued to sit where he had told me, not saying a word, just watching and waiting, trying to work out what was going on and what I should do about it. That was how I reacted to most things. The policeman seemed to have forgotten I was there, or at least he didn't look in my direction. He stepped back from the door and peered anxiously down the road.

For a few minutes nothing happened and then the eerie quiet of the afternoon was shattered by screeching tyres and brakes as another squad car arrived and disgorged four more officers. I could hear further vehicles arriving behind them, stopping wherever they could, filling the street. Now there was a real sense of urgency buzzing all around me as I sat on the wall and waited for someone to tell me what I should do. I kept wondering where Mum was, but at the same time not wanting to think about the possible answer to that question. Please no.

Dad was still standing in the doorway as if he had been expecting the police all along and he didn't protest as one of the policemen read him his rights. 'You do not have to say anything. But it may harm your defence if you do not mention when questioned something which you later rely on in court.' Dad didn't struggle as they searched him; he raised his arms to let them pat down his jeans and t-shirt top. They removed a knife from his jeans pocket, handling it carefully as if it was something precious.

'Can I say something to my son?' Dad asked them, glancing over towards me for the first time.

'You should have thought of that before,' the senior officer said and I was quite relieved. I couldn't imagine that I would want to hear anything he might have to say to me at that stage. I never wanted to hear anything he said, in fact. It felt good to have the protection of the policemen, but I just wished I understood why they were swarming all over us now when they had never done anything to help us before, on any of the occasions when Isobel had called them because Dad was being violent.

I watched from the wall as they led Dad out of the house. Several policemen formed a kind of ring around me and I got the impression that they thought I might try to go with him, but they needn't have worried; I wasn't intending to go anywhere, certainly not with Dad. They led him to the second police car and bent him down so he could slide into the back seat. I watched as the shiny bald crown of his head disappeared inside. By that stage seven more police cars had arrived, as well as five unmarked cars, two ambulances and a paramedic car. It was hard to imagine where they could all have come from to get there so quickly. Had they just been sitting around waiting for something to do? The whole street was jammed solid with vehicles.

None of the police said anything to me, all of them apparently too busy trying to work out what they should be doing. I was just waiting for Isobel to get there because she would know what we should do; she would talk to them and find out what was going on. I could always rely on Isobel. Where on earth was she? A few minutes later, I was filled with relief when I saw her familiar figure turning into the road.

Chapter Two

Isobel

The greatest mystery is why Mum and Dad ever got together in the first place because Alex and I never saw the slightest sign of any bond of affection or attraction between them. Even when couples have been worn down by years of money worries, job worries and family worries, you can usually see some remnants of the love that must once have been there – but not with our Mum and Dad. You could see that Mum wanted to please him, but only because she was frightened of what he would do if she didn't, and because she wanted a quiet life more than anything else. He, on the other hand, could never hide his loathing of her for even a second and took great pleasure in making her life as difficult as possible.

If there was any sort of romance or love story in their background, neither of them ever mentioned it to Alex or me, and there's no one else we can ask because there are no other family members who knew them when they were young. Our family was never very good at talking about emotions or soul-searching. We all just got on with the business of daily life, pushing unpleasant thoughts to the backs of our minds in the hope they would go away if we ignored them for long enough.

The only source of information we have about the past is Jillian, who was Mum's good friend at the school where she taught for twenty-three years, and one of the very few people to whom she ever confided any of those sorts of secrets. Mum didn't believe in sharing personal information with anyone unless she had to. She kept everything locked inside her head, probably trying to forget most of it herself. Several teaching colleagues who had known her for twenty years or more didn't even realise she was married, although they knew all about Alex and me and our achievements. She wouldn't have encouraged conversations about her marriage and there certainly wasn't anything nice she could say about Dad. I know she wouldn't have wanted to let anyone else know that her personal life was a horrible nightmare.

As far as we could see, Mum and Dad were totally unsuited to one another, and Dad was totally unsuited to family life in any form at all. He should probably never have married and he should certainly never have had children. Of course we didn't realise that when we were young; we assumed lots of fathers behaved the way he did. Our friends' dads were at work most of the time so we didn't have much contact with them; our social world

9

was largely made up of other children and their mothers, so the fact that our Dad remained locked inside his bedroom most of the time didn't seem particularly odd to start with. It was just the way things were done in our house.

We do know that when Mum and Dad first met, her parents weren't at all happy about the match. Maybe that was part of the attraction for Mum – her one and only act of rebellion against Granddad, who was the big authority figure in her life. She had come from a very disciplined background and it may be she wanted to prove to my grandfather, who was in the military police, that she could make her own decisions, that she wasn't going to be under his thumb all her life. If that is the case, it was a very bad decision and one she must have regretted bitterly. But once Mum had made a commitment to something there was no way she would ever go back on it. She had agreed to marry Dad and to stay with him 'for better and for worse', and she never for a second wavered from that path even though the places it led her were always 'worse' and never 'better'. Maybe she just wanted to have children and Dad was the first person to propose to her. I'll never know now.

Nan and Granddad lived in a bungalow in Torquay and we would go with Mum to visit them every half term and during the holidays, but Dad never came with us. They wanted nothing to do with him and I imagine he wanted nothing to do with them either. There must have been something about him right from the beginning that made it obvious he wouldn't make a good husband for Mum, or for anyone come to that. Neither Granddad nor Nan ever said anything about him in front of us; in fact I don't remember his name ever being mentioned in their company. As far as they were concerned, it was as if he didn't exist.

Even once he'd retired from the army, Granddad was still incredibly strict and humourless, constantly barking out orders and finding fault with everything we did, as if he was inspecting us on the parade ground. By the time we knew him he was already an old man who spent most of his time sitting in a chair puffing on his pipe and glowering at us if we made a sound, but it was easy to imagine how fierce he must have been with Mum when she was young. We were never allowed to play when he was around; we had to sit still and keep quiet. We could only have fun if we went out somewhere with Mum and Nan, or played outside with the other kids in the area with whom we had made friends during our visits. Alex and I were always quite good at making friends in new places, never troubled with shyness.

Granddad didn't seem to care much for any of us, and Alex and I certainly didn't like him. Maybe he was disappointed with the way Mum's life had turned out, but he didn't seem to make any effort to improve things for her,

11

apart from letting us come to stay with him in the holidays. If he was as irritated by our invasion of his peace and quiet as he seemed to be then I suppose that was a sacrifice we should be grateful to him for making.

Nan was Mum's stepmother. Her real mother had died very young, while Mum was still a teenager, but as far as Alex and I were concerned Granddad's wife was our real grandma; she was the only one we ever knew and no one told us that our real grandma was dead until we were much older. It was another of those things that wasn't talked about. Our family was full of secrets like that; things that were just never mentioned because they were felt to be too personal and private or possibly even too painful. Alex and I knew instinctively not to ask questions, that Mum didn't want to talk about any personal things. None of it really mattered to us as long as she was around anyway. Children only really care about their own little worlds and because she took care of everything in our lives we never had any reason to delve into the shadows of our family history.

By the time we were old enough to want to understand more about the past, it was too late because Mum and Nan and Granddad were all dead. As long as we were small we didn't have to question why anything was how it was because Mum made sure everything worked out okay. We knew her world revolved around us and that she would do anything for us, so there was no need for soul searching, no need to try to poke our noses into corners of our family business that she obviously preferred to ignore. We had enough to occupy and stimulate our minds as it was. Children are usually happy to accept life at face value as long as they feel secure and loved and know where they stand. We always knew exactly where we stood with Mum.

I was about ten when Granddad died, and Alex was seven. Nan moved to King's Lynn and died not long afterwards herself. It must have been a blow to Mum despite her difficult relationship with her father, because the trips to Torquay had been an escape for her and us, allowing us to get away from Dad and all the problems at home. Although Granddad was a joyless man, he was still a lot nicer to her than Dad, and Nan was always sweet and friendly. Apart from anything else they had provided us with holiday accommodation and there was no way Mum could afford to take us away so often once we didn't have somewhere free to stay.

I think Dad's family background must have been very different to Mum's, although we never met anyone who knew anything about him or his childhood. It was almost as though he had arrived in our house fully formed as a reclusive middle-aged man, with no history and no past that was ever spoken about. Mum never talked about him and we certainly wouldn't have asked him any direct questions. We knew a few basic facts, and we found out a few more at his trial, but nothing that actually shed any light on how he became the man we knew.

He was from the north-east, Newcastle I think, born in 1948, and we have been told he was one of a family of twelve, but we have never met his parents or any of his brothers or sisters so we have no way of knowing if that is true. Even when one of his brothers came to work in Redditch, the town south of Birmingham where we lived at the time, we still didn't get to meet him. I don't know if he and Dad saw each other then, but Dad would never have introduced him to us anyway. He liked to keep each part of his life secret and separate from every other part, as if that gave him some sort of illusion of control. He hated Mum and me, for reasons I have never fully understood, so why would he want to introduce us to his brother? He probably hated his brother as well, although I never remember him even mentioning him. He hated pretty much everyone, except Alex.

Every so often Mum would say something that gave us the tiniest glimpse into the past, but we were too young to find out more. I know that Dad had already been in trouble with the law by the time he met Mum, although I'm not sure what for. I believe he had run away from home and had spent some time in borstal for stealing. He always claimed that that spell in borstal was 'the best time of his life', as if he was remembering happy

14

school days. I can imagine that was true, because he never liked having responsibility for anything, or taking decisions, or looking after himself. Being locked up in an institution that took care of every decision for him would have suited him perfectly. He was never any good at dealing with money or paying bills or any of the mundane chores that the outside world demands of you. So although we never knew the details of the crime he had committed to be locked up in such a place, we got the impression he was a bit of a tearaway from the start. That certainly wouldn't have appealed to a disciplined and authoritative military man like Granddad.

Dad said a few things at his trial about how hard his childhood had been, claiming that was why he was the way he was, but the judge didn't seem to take any notice. Nothing that could have happened to him as a child in the nineteen-fifties could justify what he did that afternoon in January 2002.

I suspect that even as a girl Mum was always bright and hard-working. I expect she was eager to please Granddad to begin with and that he put pressure on her to do her best at school. She went to university a little bit later than most people, when she was already well into her twenties. She never told us what happened in those intervening years, but once she was set on her life's course to graduate and become a science teacher, nothing would distract or deter her.

15

She went from her home in Manchester to university in London and it was while she was there that she met Dad, who had come down from Newcastle around the same time to work as a computer repairman. Maybe they found they had common ground because both of them had escaped from their families and were living alone in a big, strange city. Maybe because she was a bit older than most of the other students on her course she didn't have many friends in the university, and Dad was almost certainly a bit of a loner himself. Whatever the reasons, they moved in together in Finsbury Park, north London, and embarked on their doomed relationship.

Once she had her degree Mum went to work in a school in Wolverhampton and they got married in 1979. They bought a house in Redditch, a town about an hour's drive from Wolverhampton. I've no idea how they came to choose Redditch and why they didn't live nearer to the school where Mum worked, but they were still there when I was born in 1986. I never questioned it because that was just the way things were. All our lives the routine was the same, with Alex and me going to school locally, Mum commuting to Wolverhampton and Dad locked inside his bedroom in the house. The hour's commute meant Mum had to get up early every morning in order to drive herself to work for the start of school, but she would always be back in time to take Alex and me to our evening activities, and she was always there with us during the school holidays. So, apart from her not being around to get us to school in the mornings, she was there for us whenever we wanted her and we had no reason to want things to be any different. Small children are very accepting of the status quo as long as they feel loved and cared for. However bad our parents' relationship was, we had no reason to feel insecure ourselves.

All the driving Mum had to do at the beginning and end of each working day must have been horribly tiring for her, although she never complained about it. She hardly ever complained about anything when we were young, never discussed anything to do with emotions or feelings, just got on with the practical matters of life in the most efficient way possible. It was only as we got into our teens that the strain began to show, the exhaustion wearing away her patience more and more frequently. If we had only known about the pressure she was under during those years we might have taken more care of her, but she never told us anything, just soldiered grimly on.

She definitely enjoyed her work, maybe because she knew she was good at it and had the respect of all her colleagues. We didn't really think about what she might be like as a teacher, but I remember that she always seemed to know everything about her pupils – about their hopes and ambitions and the progress they made towards realising them. She seemed to take a genuine interest and to have their best interests at heart almost as much as she had ours.

We went to her school a few times when there was some special event, like a piano exam we had to attend, and it always seemed to me to have a pretty tough atmosphere. I remember sitting outside her classroom once, hearing the pupils kicking off and making a noise in a way we would never have done at our school. She did say once or twice she wouldn't want to live in Wolverhampton, even though it would be more convenient for travelling, because she would always be bumping into kids in the town centre and they were more than likely to be shouting abuse. I suppose that sort of behaviour happens in most schools but Alex and I never came across it in our own school because we were always in the top sets for everything, where kids tend to be more motivated to learn and better behaved as a result.

Mum was already head of the science department by the time I was aware of what she did for a living, and her friend Jillian was her personal laboratory technician. She didn't talk to us about events at the school much, but I remember the skin on her hands had become stained and thickened over the years from constant contact with a variety of chemicals. It grew so thick eventually that she was able to lift baking trays and casseroles in and out of ovens without even feeling the heat. Her appearance never concerned her; she was too busy all the time rushing to get on with whatever she had to do next, whether it was driving us somewhere, shopping or marking school work, to even think about it. She had a short, easy-to-keep haircut and wore smart, practical skirts and blouses with low-heeled shoes for work. I don't ever remember her dressing up for an evening out; she wasn't the dressy type.

Mum was already working with Jillian and her other colleagues at the time Alex and I were born, so she had been talking to them about us all our lives. They knew all about us even though we knew nothing about them. Her office was covered in pictures of us, and we were never in any doubt how much she loved us and how proud she was of our achievements; it just felt strange to think of her talking about us to virtual strangers.

She can't have talked much to anyone about Dad because they didn't seem to know anything about him. Jillian told us later that Mum had tried inviting a few of her closest work friends back home for supper when she first joined the school, before I was born, but Dad obviously hadn't been keen.

'Once we were all there,' she told me, 'he came walking into the room completely naked. Your poor mother didn't know what to say. It was as if he was doing everything in his power to make us feel uncomfortable and threatened, to make sure that Mum would never ask us or anyone else back.'

I guess he was trying to demonstrate that his house was his private kingdom and that he resented the fact he had to share it with Mum, let alone with complete strangers. He probably felt threatened by the thought of a bunch of teachers talking about the sort of things that interested them, and felt as if he was being deliberately excluded in some way. He wanted to keep Mum all to himself. He was happy enough for her to go out and earn money to keep him but he didn't want her working life encroaching on his territory. Mum must have got the message pretty quickly because she stopped inviting people to the house after that – not that any of them were likely to want to come back once they had experienced the full weirdness of being in a confined space with Dad. We were used to his oddities, like leaving all the doors and windows open in mid-winter, or threatening to hang himself, or walking round naked, or leaving rude messages for Mum on the white board that hung in the kitchen, but other people found it quite intimidating.

Some women would have realised at that early stage that they had made a mistake in their choice of husband and would have got themselves out of the relationship as quickly as they could, but Mum had made a commitment and she was going to stick to it, however hard Dad might make it for her.

They got married in a registry office and from the few photographs that survive it doesn't look as though any of their families or friends attended the ceremony. The only other people pictured apart from the happy couple themselves are their two witnesses, neither of whom we recognise. It's possible they were strangers brought in off the street to make the process legal. It seems that Dad had already cut himself off completely from his family by then and that Granddad was not willing to relent in his disapproval of the match, not even on the wedding day itself. It must have been sad for Mum that it was such a low-key affair but, knowing Dad, it probably suited him right down to the ground.

By going through with a marriage to a man her father hated, Mum had shown that she was willing and able to stand up to him. I imagine in most cases where the parents disapprove of their children's choice of partner, they relent and put a brave face on it during the actual wedding day, but it doesn't look as if anyone in our family was willing to climb down from their high horse and compromise. For Mum it must have seemed like a bleak start to their married life, but maybe she convinced herself that she liked it, that it was her choice too, that she 'didn't want any fuss'. That would have been entirely in character.

She looks happy in those early photos, quite normal really. Dad looks a bit of a sinister presence in the background, wearing a black suit and shades, but maybe that's just with the benefit of hindsight. Maybe because we know how disturbed and dangerous he later became we assume the signs were all there to start with. It's strange for us looking at old pictures of him before he lost his hair and before he started to bulk up and become heavy-looking. To the casual glance they look like a normal young couple starting out on life's journey together.

When they moved to Redditch and bought the house, they put it into their joint names. With that simple and normal marital action, Mum entrapped herself still further. To escape from Dad after that would have meant giving up her home as well as her marriage, an option that became impossible for her to countenance once she had one, and then two children.

Our home was a very normal, three-bedroom, semi-detached Victorian house with an extraordinarily long garden behind it, just like a million others up and down the country – but most of them house perfectly normal, happy families. No one walking past on the quiet street outside and glancing up at our windows would have been able to imagine that there was anything sinister or out of the ordinary developing behind its façade.

Mum didn't have me until she was thirty-five. I don't know why she waited so long or why she finally decided to start a family then, when there must already have been problems in their relationship. Maybe she wanted to get to a certain point in her career first, or maybe she got pregnant by mistake, or maybe she was trying to get pregnant all those years and it just took a long time. We never talked about such personal matters with her, so now we will never know. Whatever the reasons, from the moment Alex and I arrived in the world she was completely focused and dedicated to guiding us to fulfil every ounce of potential we might possess. Perhaps that was when the cracks in the marriage really started to show, when Dad no longer had her undivided attention and he realised he was going to have to share her with two demanding little newcomers.

There are pictures of Dad holding me as a baby and smiling. It seems unbelievable to me that such a scene could ever have happened because I have no memory of a time when he didn't hate me and Mum. In fact by the end he hated almost everyone to some degree. We didn't know the full extent of it until his trial, but even before Alex and I were born Dad was creating trouble in the street and getting a reputation with the neighbours for being a nightmare. There were times when he would wander into people's gardens uninvited and move everything around, digging up and replanting flowers and bushes. No one could work out whether he thought he was being helpful to his neighbours or if he was deliberately trying to annoy them. Few liked to challenge him because he was a frightening-looking man – tall, aggressive and unkempt, with a mean face. Most normal people were intimidated by him. He didn't care what anyone thought of him, but he wanted them to know just how much he hated them. He had a citizen's band radio fitted into his van and he connected it to loudspeakers and drove up and down the street shouting and swearing, broadcasting his views to the world, like a foul-mouthed politician on some bizarre mutation of an election battle bus. He had big bull bars fitted to the front so that he could push and bully his way into parking spaces, making everyone hate him even more. He was anti-social in every possible way.

He particularly terrorised the old lady next door to us, shooting water pistols at her through the fence when she was out in her garden and shouting abuse at her. One night her garage caught fire in mysterious circumstances and the fire brigade had to be called to extinguish it. To my amazement Alex didn't even wake up amidst the clamour of bells and shouting. The fire officers said the fire had definitely been started deliberately but there was no proof it was Dad so nobody had the nerve to accuse him to his face.

There was a family living opposite us whom Mum, Alex and I became very friendly with, despite Dad's antics. Mum asked the couple, Helen and Steve, to be our godparents when we were baptised. They had four children ranging from our age upwards and were a normal happy family, so we always liked going over there to visit. For the first fifteen or so years of my life we all grew up together and I know Mum looked on them as the people she would have wanted us to go to if anything happened to her and Dad, since we had no close relatives. In fact, she told us so on several occasions. Their kids went to the same school as us, and did many of the same after-school activities, so Mum and Helen spent a lot of time together, often combining resources and driving one another's children along with their own. I think Mum confided more to Helen than she did to anyone else in our neighbourhood, although I never overheard them talking about anything very personal.

I was friendly with one of their daughters, who was roughly the same age as me, and when we were young she came to our house for tea a few times. She even stayed to have a bath with me once, but Dad liked to bath us at that stage and my friend didn't feel comfortable with that, which was hardly surprising. She didn't come round much after that occasion, which was fine with me because it meant I got to go to her house instead or to play outside more. Any excuse to get out of the house and away from Dad's silent, scowling presence was always welcome. Even when he was locked in his room we could sense his malevolence all over the house, all of us waiting nervously for him to emerge unexpectedly somewhere, shouting at us to get out of his sight.

25

Chapter Three

Alex

I don't think Dad can ever have been committed to the idea of working for a living, even though he did have a job when he met Mum. We had no idea at the time but at his trial we discovered that as far back as the 1970s he was already having trouble getting on with other people at work, always picking fights, arguing and threatening to leave. He never seemed able to get on with anyone. It was as if he had been meant to be a recluse from the moment he was born.

I guess he had no choice but to join the world of work when he first left Newcastle because he had to support himself somehow, but once he was married and Mum was earning a steady living from teaching, it became possible for him to start withdrawing from life outside the house.

When Isobel was born Mum had every intention of continuing to work because she loved her job and because she already knew that she couldn't rely on Dad to earn enough to keep a family. She had never been the

sort of woman who would have been
home, cooking and cleaning and waiting
and her children to return each evening. Maybe
one of the reasons she had chosen to marry Dad, bec
she knew he would never ask that of her, that he would
be happy for her to pursue a career, if only to get the
house to himself for most of the day and to have money
coming in without having to work for it himself.

Initially, when they were both working, Mum was
prepared to pay for babysitters and childminders to take
care of Isobel while they were out during the day, but it
wasn't long before Dad realised that he could use his
baby daughter as an excuse to give up work and stay
home all the time. Maybe he genuinely thought that he
could be a full-time 'house husband'.

Although Mum realised he had no interest whatsoever
in looking after the baby, at least he would be there in the
house with Isobel, so Mum thought she could go out first
thing in the morning knowing that the baby had an adult
in charge of her. Even then she must have suspected he
wasn't at all the right man for the job, but he was Isobel's
father so why shouldn't he be given the chance to look
after her? Perhaps at that stage they were still kidding
themselves that they were a normal married couple with
a family, making normal, rational decisions about how to
organise their lives in the most efficient way. Or maybe
Mum just didn't think she had any option.

It wasn't long before she realised her mistake. She would come home after a long day at work to discover that Isobel was still exactly where she had left her that morning. Nappies weren't changed, she hadn't been fed, and it was obvious to her that Dad had basically taken no notice of the baby at all. He might have told her that he had given up work with the intention of caring for his first child, but it soon began to dawn on her that he wasn't capable of it. Within a few days Mum had to go back to hiring babysitters just as she had first intended. Dad, however, had got used to the idea of not working by that stage and made no effort to look for another job beyond the odd temporary one when he was in desperate need of cash for something. As Mum rushed around trying to earn enough to pay for his upkeep as well as Isobel's, and then mine, Dad withdrew further and further into his own private world, most of which was contained behind the closed doors of his silent bedroom, unseen by anyone but him.

'It's like having a third child to look after,' Mum would grumble on the rare occasions when she said anything about him at all. It certainly can't have felt as though she had a partner to share her life and her children with.

His inner sanctum had been Mum's bedroom as well when they first bought the house, but by the time Isobel and I were old enough to take in what was happening at night we realised that Mum always slept on the couch in the sitting room. During the day her pillow and duvet would be tucked away behind it, out of sight, and she would make up the bed last thing each night when she was ready to sleep. Her few clothes and possessions were kept in Isobel's room, so that she never had to invade Dad's privacy or risk waking him while he slept the days away.

'It's because I snore, and because I have to get up early,' she would explain if either of us questioned her about it. 'I don't want to disturb your father.'

We didn't question this logic; we just took it as normal. She made no complaint about the situation so we assumed it was okay and she was happy about it. Dad's bedroom became a mysterious world hidden behind a permanently closed door. Half the time when we came back from school we didn't even know if he was inside or not. Because he led such a nocturnal life there would often be no sounds emitting from behind the door during the day at all. He came down to the kitchen to make meals while we were out at school and never ate with the three of us. We knew he had a television in his room but we could never hear it, so I don't know if he ever actually watched it. Not knowing if he was in the house at any given moment made living under the same roof as him all the more scary.

We tried to carry on with our lives as if he didn't live there at all but sometimes he would suddenly appear on the landing or in the kitchen, usually saying nothing and staring straight through us. He had a habit of coming out of the bathroom stark naked and standing at the toilet with the door wide open, as if he didn't know anyone else was there. If we heard him coming in time we would dodge out of his way so we didn't risk incurring his wrath, but unless he deliberately wanted to pick a fight he wouldn't give any indication that he had seen us or that he even knew we existed. Isobel and I would have our showers before leaving for school in the morning, when we could be pretty certain he was fast asleep and wouldn't be disturbed by any noise we might make.

If he did speak to Isobel it was only to tell her how much he hated her. When she was little she didn't reply, but she grew bolder in later years and would sometimes even insult him as long as there were other people around to protect her if necessary. I remember she once told him he was 'gay', just to wind him up. It sometimes seemed as if she was deliberately courting danger, wanting to goad him into doing something terrible. If she had known just how deeply disturbed and danger-ous he must have been through all those years, she would probably have been more careful. We all would have acted differently if we had had any idea we were living with a ticking time bomb. But you don't realise these things when you are too close to them, too used to them.

Our main babysitter in the early years was a kind hippyish lady called Rita, who had long grey hair. Once we were both enrolled at school, Rita would take us in after Mum had left for work and get us to school on time, then pick us up in the afternoon at the end of lessons. We would go back to her house to play until Mum got back from work in Wolverhampton and collected us. Rita was perfectly nice and it didn't bother me that Mum wasn't there because I always had my big sister with me. I didn't want to go back to our house when Dad was the only grown-up there. There was no way of predicting what sort of mood he would be in, even though he always favoured me over Mum and Isobel.

He really hated them and it was as if he was trying to recruit me onto his side in the psychological war he insisted on waging against them. As a small boy I liked the attention when he was being nice to me, but I could never be confident he wouldn't shout at me or do something crazy like opening all the doors and windows in the middle of winter, or egging me on to do something wrong then telling Mum it was all my fault. Life was altogether safer and more predictable round at Rita's house, so I didn't complain. I wasn't the sort of child to complain about things anyway. There was no doubting how dedicated Mum was to Isobel and me.

As we got older and harder to entertain, Rita used to take us back to our own house after school rather than her

31

own. Most days Dad's bedroom door would be closed when we came in and we would have no idea if he was in the house or not. It didn't worry us as long as the door remained closed, because we were used to living our lives without him. Isobel was still at lower school, so she would have been about seven when Rita stopped escorting us to school in the mornings and Mum told us we were old enough to go back and forth alone as long as we were together. I suppose she needed to save as much money as possible since she was supporting the family on one teaching salary. It wasn't that far to walk but we did have to cross the main road, which was pretty scary, and I would hold on tightly to Isobel's hand. From then on, my sister looked after me pretty much all the time that Mum was at work. Even though she was only two years older than me it seemed to come very naturally to her. She hardly ever complained about it because we got on so easily together. I was pretty stubborn about things I felt strongly about, but I wasn't one to argue or throw tantrums or make her life difficult unnecessarily. We didn't have much time for anything like that anyway, because there was always so much to do from the moment we woke up to the moment we fell back to sleep.

Isobel and I would usually be woken up by the sound of Mum going out the front door at seven-thirty in the morning. It would then be our job to take our mongrel, Alfie, out for a walk before we left, so that he would be able to hold on till we got back. We all knew Dad wouldn't be willing to get up and take him out during the day. If anything made Alfie bark, it would drive Dad completely mad.

Sometimes when we got up Isobel and I would come downstairs and find that Mum had overslept and was still curled up on the sofa, completely laid out with exhaustion and we would have to wake her so she could dash out to work.

We have quite a lot of photographs from our childhood, but hardly any of Mum – probably because she was the one holding the camera. Dad would never have agreed to take photographs of her. There are one or two pictures in the old family albums of Dad playing with us when we were young. He looks quite happy and normal in them, but it can't have happened that often because I have no memory of him doing anything nice with us. I think there used to be more pictures of him but he ripped them up during one of his rampages, when he was thumping around shouting: 'I don't want to have anything to do with any of you!'

He destroyed a lot of the pictures of Isobel, too, because he hated her so much. 'She looks too much like your mother,' he told me, as if that was explanation enough.

There are still a lot of snaps that have survived despite his worst efforts, so Mum must have been very handy with the camera. It's more evidence of how proud she was of us and how important we were to her, which was probably why we were able to put up with Dad's lack of love relatively stoically. He wasn't able to undermine our feelings of self-worth because Mum had done such a good job of building them up in the first place.

There's one snap of us all on a beach together, like a normal family, but we don't know where that could be because neither Isobel or I can remember him ever coming on holiday with us. He built a climbing frame for us in the garden too, so there must have been moments when he did the right thing, but such moments became rarer as time passed and life made him more angry.

I was about seven when Granddad died, meaning that we couldn't go to Torquay on holiday any more. Mum still took us to Devon or Cornwall in the summer holidays, but there was never any question of Dad coming along. We certainly wouldn't have wanted him to. We used to spend our time bike riding, swimming in the sea and trying every activity we could find. All of us liked to be busy and stimulated; we were never ones for sitting around and relaxing, whereas Dad did nothing else. When it was just the three of us together we always got on well, all interested in doing the same sorts of things. I nearly always got sunburned because I'm pale-skinned and we were spending virtually all the daylight hours outdoors.

Granddad didn't leave any money to Mum in his will, which she was very hurt about at the time. I expect he wanted to keep his money out of Dad's clutches, so he put it in a trust set up so that Isobel and I and Nan's grandchildren would each receive a few thousand pounds when we turned eighteen. All Mum inherited was his old car, which I think she thought was a bit unfair. It was probably very wise of Granddad considering what happened in the end.

When Dad eventually took against me as well, he would often deny that I was his son, accusing Mum of having had an affair. It was a ridiculous accusation because Mum was the least likely person ever to do such a thing and because I looked just like him. In fact, by then I would have been quite pleased to have found out that I wasn't anything to do with him. He had an unlimited appetite for unpleasantness. He would make things up just to provoke a fight and to give himself an excuse to be vile to Mum or Isobel, and later on to me as well. In the early days he wanted me to join in with him in everything, even his drinking. I can remember the first time he made me drink whisky when I was about eight or nine, but I hated the taste so much I wouldn't take more than a few sips. It was as if he was trying to mould me into being more like him and less like Mum and Isobel, goading me on to be a bit of a rebel.

35

When I was little he liked to take me out into the garage with him while he was fiddling with the cars, making out that we were doing it together although in reality I was just sitting there watching him most of the time. I think he was more interested in separating me from Mum in order to annoy her than in actually trying to teach me anything useful.

I was on my own with him in the house the day he had a stroke. I was just six years old and Mum had taken Isobel to her karate lesson. Dad and I had been messing about with the car in the garage. We came back into the house and as he started to walk upstairs he suddenly collapsed and crashed back down onto the hall floor. I don't think I panicked; I just went over to shake him and call to him, thinking he had fallen asleep. When I found I couldn't rouse him, I sat down on top of him to wait until Mum and Isobel got back. I wasn't particularly scared. I was confident that Mum would know what to do. She always did.

Chapter Four

Isobel

When Mum and I got home on the day of Dad's stroke, she put her key in the lock as usual and pushed the door, but it immediately hit an obstacle, refusing to open wide enough to let us in. Peering through the gap we could see Dad lying across the hallway where he had fallen down the stairs, motionless. Alex was sitting on top of him, waiting patiently, as he always did for everything.

'Dad's asleep,' he told us, solemnly.

'We'll come in the back,' Mum told him and we hurried round the house to let ourselves in through the kitchen.

Mum knew immediately that Dad wasn't asleep and an ambulance must have been called, although I don't remember it arriving. I do remember going to visit him in hospital later, as he recovered. It wasn't until many years afterwards that we discovered that Mum had told our godmother, Helen, that she had hoped he would die that day. She called Helen to come over before she dialled 999 and apparently said she was considering not calling an ambulance for a while, in the hope that he would just slip peacefully away. It would have been a merciful release for all of us if that had happened, but Mum would never actually have been able to do such a thing, however miserable he was making her life by then. If he had died that day maybe we would still have Mum with us today. Things must already have been very bad between them for her to be thinking such terrible thoughts about him. Not all strokes are fatal, though, so we'll never know if it would have done much harm to have left him on the hall floor a bit longer.

He recovered almost completely over the coming months, although his movement never came back completely because he refused to have the physiotherapy that the doctors recommended. He wouldn't have wanted to put himself in someone else's power like that. He needed to be separate from the world and having someone manipulating him physically would probably have felt too personal. He hardly ever spoke to us so it was hard to tell if his speech had been affected, as it can be after a stroke; as far as I'm aware it didn't seem any different.

Once he was back home Dad's stroke made no difference to any of our lives. Mum went back to work, we went back to school and he went back into his bedroom as if nothing had changed. But who knows what pressure the condition was putting on his brain, both before and after it happened? Did he act the way he later did because of the stroke, or did he have a stroke partly because of the stress he put himself under by hating the whole world?

All Mum's efforts were channelled into giving Alex and me the best possible start in life, and she refused to accept that anything was ever important enough to disrupt the relentless and steady routine of our educational and after-school activities. Feeling a bit ill, for instance, was never an excuse for missing anything. We actually had to be at death's door before she would let us use illness as an excuse to stay home or go to bed. Maybe she was fearful that we might have enough of Dad's genetic make-up to make us give up on life if she didn't keep us continually encouraged and stimulated. If that's the case I don't think she needed to worry, because neither of us wanted to be in the least like him.

Dad took no interest in any of Mum's plans for us. In fact he took no interest in us at all, apart from hating me and trying to recruit Alex to his cause of annoying Mum as much as possible. He would seize any chance he could to upset me. Knowing that I was terrified of dogs, for instance, he brought home a mongrel puppy, which we christened Alfie. He was a lovely dog, black with gold-coloured paws and eyebrows. Dad told Alex in advance what he was planning to do, which delighted Alex because he'd always wanted a dog of his own. The plan backfired on Dad because Alfie was so endearing I immediately overcame my fear and loved him as fiercely as Alex did, while having a dog in the house nearly drove Dad mad, particularly when Alfie barked and forced him to come out of his room unnecessarily. He grew to hate Alfie just as much as he hated us and he would lash out and kick or beat him so often the dog became a quivering mass of nerves whenever Dad was around – which annoyed him even more.

I had other pets over the years, which gave Dad more opportunities to get at me. There was the pet rabbit that he let out of the cage and chased away, taking pleasure in telling me that it would never survive in the wild. And there was the hamster he poisoned and cut open, leaving the corpse for Alex and me to find when we got back from school. It lay in the cage, looking as if it had been turned inside out with all its internal organs on display, and I retched at the sight, knowing straight away who must be responsible. If there was anything that I really liked, Dad would destroy it just for the pleasure of making me unhappy. I began to grow a protective layer over my emotions, always expecting the worst and never letting his cruelty get to me in the way he hoped. Even though he couldn't stand it when either of us cried, he still liked to try to make us, just to prove he could. The deaths of the pets was probably more upsetting for Alex, because he was that bit younger than me, but Dad was willing to pay that price.

Bit by bit he taught me that I could never trust him, never hope that he would change or do something nice for me, and I learned to hide my emotions from him at all costs so that he wouldn't be able to see when he got to me. But the less I reacted to his campaigns of hate, the more violently he hated me. I gave up all hope that he would ever change and grow to like me because the disappointments were too frequent to be bearable. It was better to have no hope at all than to be let down every single time.

Chapter Five

Alex

In some ways at the beginning I liked the idea of being special to Dad, of being the only one in the family he was nice to. When he encouraged me to misbehave at school or not bother to go in at all, he made it sound much more interesting and exciting than it ever turned out to be, particularly as he was always generous with his bribes, giving me sweets or money if I did what he wanted. The more he could encourage me to misbehave, the more he knew he would annoy Mum and undermine all her efforts to keep me working hard and in the top classes for every subject. Annoying Mum and Isobel was the primary aim of almost everything he ever did in the house. I never stopped to question why; that's just the way it was.

At the same time I also discovered that however much he might pretend to me that we were allies when we were alone, he couldn't be trusted not to betray me as soon as he had an opportunity. He would encourage me to do something bad when it was just the two of us together, but as soon as Mum came home he would sneak on me and tell her what I had been doing, without confessing that he had suggested it in the first place. He would gloat over how badly behaved her precious little son really was, and how he had managed to sabotage all her good work in bringing me up. I never protested in my defence because I didn't want to provoke his anger and make him hate me as much as he hated the others, and because I was never one for protesting about things generally. I was always pretty philosophical about life, even as a small boy.

I soon learned that everything Dad did was part of some spiteful mind game he had dreamed up in the long hours he spent on his own in his room. If ever he gave us a present there was always a reason, a hidden agenda behind it. He heard Isobel asking Mum for money for something one day and so he put forty pounds in her room for her to find. Not knowing what to say, Isobel spent it and then a week or two later he demanded it back. Since Isobel only received a pound or two a week as pocket money, that took a long time and was something else for him to hold against her, another way to keep control and prove to her what a bad daughter she was.

He gave us both CD players one time, but only so he could smash Isobel's up in front of her and enjoy the look of disappointment on her face. He must have planned it from the start because the one he bought me was far more expensive than the one he intended to destroy. When he first gave it to her Isobel sensed there was something wrong and was hesitant to even touch it for fear that it would prove to be a trap. When he smashed it he didn't even bother to say why, but I knew he wouldn't touch mine. I think he was always hoping to turn Isobel and me against one another, but that never worked.

Whatever he did to us Isobel and I were always a team. We had been together since the day I was born and we understood each other perfectly. No one could ever come between us, no matter how devious and cunning they might be. Although we had our own separate friends, we were often together socially as well. Isobel was always a bit of a tomboy and quite happy to hang out with groups of boys, playing football or climbing trees. She wasn't interested in whatever it was most of the girls wanted to do, which usually meant staying indoors as far as she could see. As we got older Mum didn't mind letting us go out to play with other kids in the area so long as we had finished our homework and so long as we were together. Not that we had very much spare time to just play around, because she filled virtually every waking hour with activities. If we did have a few spare hours, however, playing outside was always preferable to being indoors and worrying about disturbing Dad if we made any sort of noise at all. We didn't often take friends back home either because we could never be sure if he would be there or not, and if he did emerge from his room and find other people in the house he would always make a scene to ensure they felt as uncomfortable as possible.

'Our Dad might be there,' we would warn them on the odd occasions when we did bring friends back to the house. 'If he's there, just ignore him. Don't say anything to him if he talks to you.'

It was like warning children not to pet an unreliable dog in case it suddenly turned nasty and bit them. It was obvious that our friends couldn't understand why we were issuing warnings like this and I dare say they went back home to their own parents with some colourful descriptions of what the atmosphere was like inside our house, with the invisible bogeyman of a father hiding away upstairs, a bit like the wicked giant in 'Jack and the Beanstalk'. Most of the people we met during our after-school activities didn't even realise we had a dad since they only ever saw us out and about with Mum. He would never come to see us playing in a concert or competing in a sports match. Just like Mum, neither Isobel nor I would ever talk about him to other people if we didn't have to.

If Dad did make an appearance when there were other people in the house he would usually appear quite alarming. He seemed to take pride in making himself look as much of a thug as he could, and he wouldn't say much, just looming there, silent and threatening. On the rare occasions when he came to one or other of our activities he would be deliberately aggressive and abusive to everyone else there, as if he wanted to embarrass us and Mum, to teach us a lesson for taking an interest in something that was nothing to do with him and to show us who was in control. He liked to demonstrate his contempt for anything any of us did, to make it look as though Mum was wasting her time rushing around doing things that he thought were pointless and laughable. If you can't see the point in anything then there really isn't any reason to come out of your bedroom, especially if someone else is willing to pay the bills and provide you with food.

Mum would cook big meals when she had the time. Most Sundays she would do a family roast, although Dad still wouldn't want to come down to eat with us. He didn't even eat with us on Christmas Day. It didn't bother Isobel or me because we couldn't remember anything different, and it was always nicer when he wasn't around to create a bad atmosphere anyway, but it must have been hard for Mum. She must have wished she had a normal husband who was part of the family. She pretended not to notice that anything was wrong, keeping herself and us so busy that we didn't have too much time for introspection, but it must have been wearing her away inside.

On weeknights Isobel and I made sure we'd done our homework by the time Mum got home, and sorted out something to eat. We got through a lot of pasta in those years because there was never any time to cook anything more elaborate. There was certainly no space in our lives for just sitting down and relaxing over a meal. Mum drank endless cups of strong coffee throughout the day – sometimes as many as twenty a day – just to keep herself awake. Dad never ate the meals we prepared, of course. From what I could make out, he seemed to survive on takeaway kebabs or chips.

Mum was a great believer in the importance of exams and achieving things academically. During the daily car rides back and forth between after-school activities she would constantly bombard us with questions about school, getting us to go through every lesson and tell her what we had been learning and then she would fire questions at us, testing us on our times tables or our French vocabulary. She was always enthusiastic in the early days before tiredness started to overpower her, wanting to exercise our brains to the full at every opportunity. During half terms and holidays she would give us her own work projects and tests on top of anything our teachers might have set us. We never complained because we were so used to it and we knew she would always let us go out to play as soon as we had finished our work. We enjoyed most of the tasks anyway.

We certainly never had any time to chill out in front of the television as many of our friends did after school. None of this bothered us because we had never had a chance to get into the habit of watching television and whenever we did tune in the programmes seemed boring compared to the pace and variety of our own lives. The only time we might watch anything would be on a Sunday morning, but even then Mum wasn't that keen if there was something else she thought we should be doing, and we weren't interested enough to go against her wishes. About once a week we would catch an episode of *The Simpsons*, which was the only show we really liked.

From as early as I can remember, Mum would enrol us for every after-school activity imaginable. It didn't matter how much it cost (and they were virtually all private lessons), or how many hours of her evening she had to give up to ferry us from one place to another. She was determined that we should be given every possible opportunity to try everything, even if we decided not to follow it up later, and that we would never be unable to do something just because we couldn't afford it. Almost the moment she arrived home each afternoon, having driven for at least an hour back from work, she would be piling us into the little Metro she'd had for years and driving me to one place and Isobel to another.

The activities she enrolled us for covered virtually every skill she could think of. It wasn't just the musical instruments – piano, violin – and singing in the choir; there were also the physical activities like swimming and gymnastics, ballet and karate. If we tried something and didn't like it she would be happy to let us stop, but would immediately suggest something else instead. We must have belonged to every single club within a ten-mile radius of the house. At one stage I tried learning the trumpet but the teacher said I would do better changing to the French horn, which was a big instrument for a small boy to have to lug around with him all day. I joined the scouts but somehow Isobel escaped brownies and girl guides; I think maybe she didn't have enough hours left in her day to fit them in, although she did do woodcraft.

Isobel's favourite activity was running and she was brilliant at long distance and cross-country. She actually enjoyed going through the thickest mud and deepest puddles. She was so good she went all the way up to compete at county level. She was always a real tomboy, preferring football to ballet. Mum was willing to indulge her in anything that she showed an interest in, even though she was the only girl on the football team, until things got too rough and Isobel broke her finger at one match. After that, Mum decided enough was enough.

When we got a little older and started to have minds of our own, one or other of us might announce that we wanted to give up one of our activities. Sometimes Mum would react badly to this. Maybe she didn't like the idea that we were growing up and not totally within her control any more. When Isobel said one evening that she wanted to give up swimming in order to have more time for her running Mum went completely ballistic.

'All the money I've spent on swimming lessons,' she shouted, 'and you want to give it up just like that?'

She seemed to hate the idea of us limiting our options in any way, even though there obviously weren't enough hours in the week for us to do everything properly. I think Isobel's swimming costume got hurled out of the window during that row, which seemed a bit out of proportion. It may just have been Mum's exhaustion and pent-up frustrations about other things that made her explode like that rather than the actual announcement itself. Isobel was determined not to change her mind, although she felt very guilty about letting Mum down and upsetting her.

When I announced I had quit the church choir she went even more over the top. I was around eleven years old and going through a bit of a rebellious phase at the time. I had actually sworn at the choirmaster during the practice that evening, which had resulted in me being ordered out of the room. I stormed off and disappeared for a few hours. The choirmaster phoned home and so

Mum knew exactly what had happened and started ranting on to Isobel about me.

'I'm going to call social services,' she raved. 'I've got to get something done about that boy!'

By the time I finally walked in through the front door she had lathered herself up into a real state of fury, but I stuck to my guns about leaving the choir and refused to go back. I think I might have provoked the whole confrontation deliberately in order to give myself an excuse to leave, so Mum was right to be angry with me, but I was still shocked by the sheer force of her disappointment.

Part of Mum's motivation could have been to get us all out of the house and out of Dad's way as much as possible, which was fine by us. There were certain times of the day, usually in the later part of the afternoon, when he might wake up and emerge unexpectedly from his room, coming down to the kitchen to make himself some food. At those times he didn't want us anywhere around. He believed it was 'his time' and 'his space' and we would have to make ourselves scarce. The mere sight of Isobel or Mum would remind him how much he hated them and didn't want them around.

It was best for all of us if we weren't in the house at that time if we didn't want to risk inciting his anger. If we had a day off sick from school we had to be very careful not to be in the kitchen during periods that he considered to be 'his'. He spent as much of his life behind the bedroom door as possible. Isobel and I never ventured through it – we had barely even glimpsed through the crack when it was opened for him to go in or out – so we had no idea exactly what he did in there to entertain himself all day. We just dreaded the times when he was forced to come out into the real world in order to eat or go to the bathroom.

There were so many things for us to do outside the house that it wasn't a problem most days. As we got better at our various sports and activities Isobel and I were entered into competitions that were further away from home, and before I left the choir we would sometimes go on trips at weekends to sing at weddings in other churches or even cathedrals. Then we got paper rounds, which got us out of the house for a few hours on a Sunday morning and gave us some spending money of our own. Isobel got the round first, being older, and used it as another opportunity to go running, hauling a trolley behind her as she pounded the streets. When her weekend running commitments got too much, she handed the paper round on to me. The people who ran the newsagents were happy with that because it meant they could go on delivering the papers to the same address each week and they knew it was likely I would be reliable because Isobel had never let them down. The Sunday round was the best one to have because we didn't have to get up as early as the weekday people, who had to finish their deliveries before going to school, but we still got paid the same rate. Part of the job was to insert advertising leaflets before delivering them. I managed to convince Mum that it was harder for me to do that because I was left-handed so she used to help me, much to Isobel's annoyance.

Although doing so much meant our days often ended up being a bit of a rush, both Isobel and I were always happy to do whatever Mum suggested. It was the only way of life either of us could remember and large parts of our social lives revolved around the activities because that was where we made many of our friendships.

Compared to most boys my acts of rebellion were pretty minor, like talking in class or swearing at the choirmaster. I did bunk off school for a day now and again, but very seldom. To Mum, however, with her strict regime of education and self-improvement, this was a cardinal sin. She couldn't bear the thought that I was wasting even the smallest opportunity to get a good education. On one of the few occasions I did wander off, she came home early one day to get her car serviced and caught me and my friends outside the school. She marched us all firmly back in through the gates, even though it was nearly the end of the school day by then, which was not good for my street credibility. She almost always came home at the same time, so I couldn't believe my bad luck when I was caught on that occasion.

The school occasionally sent her letters about my general behaviour. She left before the post arrived in the mornings, so Isobel and I would try to intercept as many as we could before they reached her. Mum knew that I wasn't concentrating fully on my work, even though I was still in the top set for just about every subject, and she became more and more exasperated with me the further I dug my heels in and rebelled against authority. At one stage she threatened to move me to her school, knowing how embarrassing it would be to have a mother who was on the staff, and knowing that I wouldn't want to leave my friends. I knew it was an empty threat because she would never have done anything that might have endangered my education, so then she began threatening to send me to boarding school if I didn't behave better. Even though I knew the cost of it would have been completely beyond her means, I never wanted to call her bluff on that one. She could be very determined when she set her mind on something. As well as not wanting to leave my established group of friends, I wouldn't have wanted to be separated from Isobel.

'I'll go to boarding school,' Isobel piped up in the middle of the argument about me leaving the choir, which deflected Mum's wrath away from me for a while. Because of that interruption Isobel got kicked out of the house that night instead of me, even though she didn't have any shoes on at the time.

Mum must have been bottling up so much anger and resentment that when some little thing like the choir incident happened she would completely lose her cool. She even kicked the dog out with Isobel, as if that would teach us all some sort of lesson. Alfie must have thought it was a bit of an adventure to be allowed out for an extra walk without his lead. At moments like that I think the whole world must suddenly have seemed to be against her and she imagined for a moment that she wanted to be rid of the lot of us. Her moods never lasted long, though – not like Dad's endless, snarling misery.

Whenever Dad got to hear about me doing anything remotely naughty or rebellious he would be delighted and would encourage me, deliberately going against everything Mum was saying. He seemed determined to make me more like him and less like her and Isobel. I don't know that his encouragement made much difference to me. I think I would have been behaving the same anyway, but it did give me a bit more courage to be cheeky at school, knowing that it won his approval. Every small boy wants to please his dad, even when he's as weird as mine was. Once or twice I even went back to the house during the day with my friends when we should have been in school, and Dad seemed to approve, which impressed them. But as soon as Mum came home he told her all about it, wanting to rub her nose in how much she had lost control of me, I guess, and how her children weren't always the hard-working little angels she would have liked them to be.

The strain on her during those years must have been enormous, and we didn't know the half of it at that stage. I feel guilty when I look back now, but I was just being a normal, spirited teenage boy. In retrospect I guess her life was hard enough without that additional pressure.

Chapter Six

Isobel

The row started because Alex had got himself thrown out of choir practice and then announced he wanted to leave the choir altogether, but for some reason I was the one who ended up being thrown out of the house by Mum. Things just went completely mad for a few minutes.

As I stood outside on the drive in my socks, holding onto Alfie by the scruff of his neck, I wasn't sure what to do next. Mum was in such a hysterical state that there didn't seem to be any point in trying to get back in the house until she had calmed down. The only person I could think of to turn to for help was my godmother, Helen, who had moved away from our street by then but was still living in the area. I don't think we had mobile phones at that stage – or at least if we did I didn't have one on me, not having expected to be leaving the house quite so abruptly – so I had to knock on one of the neighbours' doors and ask if I could use their house phone.

I don't think they were surprised by the request because everyone in the nearby houses knew about Dad and assumed that our whole family was a bit dysfunctional. I rang Helen, who very kindly came and took Alfie and me back to her house before going to talk to Mum and attempting to calm her down and make her see sense. Helen was a good friend to Mum and one of the few people she allowed to get close to her. I expect Mum was already regretting her outburst by the time Helen got there. These sorts of temper storms always passed quite quickly and we would then return to our normal family routines as if nothing had happened, the hectic pace of our lives helping us to forget any lingering bad feelings. Dad wouldn't usually come out of his room when Mum was kicking off. He had his own demons to fight in private. He had no interest in anything to do with any of us unless it affected him directly, and if Mum sounded upset that probably pleased him since he spent most of his time trying to achieve exactly that result.

I can't remember a time when I didn't know how much Dad hated me. It started because I looked so much like Mum, or at least that was what he kept telling me, but it grew worse as I got older and started speaking out against him more often. He needed to be able to dominate everyone in his life completely, and Mum was mostly willing to let him get away with it in order to protect us and try to maintain a fragile peace in the house. As I entered my teens, however, I became less willing to put up with everything he did in silence. If he was attacking Mum I would often take her side, speaking up for her while she remained silent, and that made him loathe me all the more deeply. Arguments were usually based on him saying how dirty the house was, or that the vacuum cleaner hadn't been put back in the right way, which was infuriating to me. The house was perfectly clean because Mum spent her weekends cleaning it, but nothing she did was ever right it seemed. It drove me crazy that Dad should have the nerve to complain when he sat around at home all day never lifting a finger.

Sometimes his attacks would escalate beyond mere shouting and he became physically violent. He would slap her and throw things at her while she tried frantically to pacify him by agreeing with everything he said, accepting all the criticism without trying to defend herself. Partly out of anger and partly out of fear, I would be screaming at him to leave her alone and threatening to call the police. He found the thought that I would dare to stand up to him almost unbearable and Mum would become desperate that I was winding him up even more by challenging him, but I couldn't just stand by and watch him hitting her without saying anything. Perhaps her approach was more intelligent than mine. Maybe she already sensed just what he might be capable of if he was pushed too far, but to me at the time, with all the reck-lessness and ignorance of youth, it looked as though she was giving in to him, being a complete doormat, and my pride wouldn't let me do the same.

On several occasions as I went to pick up the phone to call the police, Dad pushed me out of the way, threw an ornament at me, or lunged past me and ripped it out of the wall. He didn't always manage to get there in time, however, and when I was eleven or twelve years old I managed to call them out on two separate occasions. Both times I truly believed that Mum was in real danger and needed grown-up help. Once I heard noises from my bedroom and came downstairs to find him punching her and throwing her around the room. I intervened and he swung a punch at me as well. I managed to get a call through to the police but in the few minutes it took them to turn up he had wrecked the house in his frustration and fury.

Even when the police were standing there in the room and she had a chance to tell them what he was like, Mum would never make a formal complaint or agree to press charges, so there was nothing they could do apart from warn him to calm down. On one occasion when he was particularly wild they took him down to the cells for a few hours to give him time to settle down, only allow-ing him home once they felt he was calm again. I remem-ber we were all terrified that they would release him in the middle of the night. Alex and I were literally shaking with fear so all three of us slept in my bed till morning. Locking him up served the purpose at the time but did nothing to help our overall situation. His was a vendetta of hate that would outlast any short-term measures the police might be able to impose.

When he got home after his night in the cells we were out at our swimming practice with Mum and by the time we arrived back he had changed all the locks on the house so our keys didn't work. Mum had to beg him through the letterbox to let us in, trying to avoid provoking a scene on the doorstep that the neighbours would hear. I suppose ultimately he had to let Mum back into the house because she was his only source of income, but he had made his point, showing that he could take control, lock us out and disrupt our lives whenever he chose if we displeased him or challenged him.

On one of the occasions when I called the police Dad ran upstairs and started stabbing himself in the arm with a fork so that when they arrived he could tell them that Mum had attacked him first, and show them the wounds to prove it. When they got there the police left Alex and me sitting on the stairs, just watching and listening and taking it all in. They didn't ask us for our version of what had gone on, but just ignored us as if we were part of the furniture. Maybe they get called to so many domestic disturbances every day that they have a set method of dealing with them, but they never made us feel that they would be able to offer us or Mum any real protection from Dad should we need it. Later, when we were in court for Dad's trial, a policeman read out his notes of the incident that night, talking about 'two young and clearly very disturbed children' being on the scene. If we were so clearly disturbed, why didn't anyone do anything to help us, or even talk to us? Why did no one come back the next day after one of these fights to check we were okay? I suppose by not pressing charges Mum forced them to assume that she had the whole situation under control.

Most of the arguments happened late at night, when Dad would emerge from his room and expect to have the house to himself, or perhaps he would decide to go and waken Mum to raise some grudge he had been mulling over all day. Looking back, Dad was getting through a lot of whisky and I suspect the worst arguments probably happened when he was drunk. Alex was usually fast asleep by the time they started to shout and often didn't wake up, allowing Dad to believe that he could still control him and keep him on his side, even if I was becoming openly rebellious to his tyranny.

If Mum was still up and about when Dad got downstairs it was almost inevitable that he would start picking a fight with her. Most of the time our routines meant that we were able to avoid him, but if something went differently it would make him feel threatened and he would immediately become aggressive. Sometimes, if he had fuelled himself up enough on whisky, he would keep the arguments going all night, forcing Mum to stay awake just so that he could shout at her, and me as well when I came downstairs to investigate. It didn't bother him how long the fights went on for because he could just sleep through the next day, but we were exhausted and needed our sleep. He knew perfectly well how tired Mum got and exploited it sadistically. I think sometimes he picked fights simply to alleviate the boredom of his existence.

As he got older Alex started to be woken by the shouting as well and we would all end up only getting a couple of hours sleep, but however tired we were in the morning Mum would never consider for a second that we should be allowed a day off school. It was almost like a religious belief to her. She would never take a day off work, however ill or exhausted she felt, and she expected the same level of dedication, determination and discipline from us. We didn't even bother to ask because we knew what her answer would be. I think my attendance rate was pretty close to a hundred per cent and Alex only managed to bunk off once or twice before Mum found out and put a stop to it. To be honest we were always pretty keen to get out of the house after a night of rowing anyway. We certainly didn't want to be trapped there on our own with Dad if we could help it. Once we were with our friends at school, or concentrating in lessons, we could forget for a few hours the unpleasant things we had been forced to listen to in the small hours.

Even when Mum was left with bruises or marks on her face and arms from his beatings she would still go to work, telling colleagues that she had walked into a door or some such excuse, and we later discovered from Jillian that no one ever doubted her for a moment. No one at her school had the slightest idea that she was in an abusive relationship. Jillian and a couple of others knew she was married to a man who was odd, but most of them thought she was a single mother and never enquired any further. I suppose she just wasn't the sort of person you would ever expect to be in that position, because she always seemed so vibrant and in control of every detail of her life.

The only people who I believe knew there was violence going on, and suspected that it was much worse than Mum was saying, were my godmother Helen and the lady vicar at our local church. They were the only two people Mum talked to about it and we discovered that both of them tried to persuade her to leave Dad before things got any worse. Near neighbours later testified that they could hear arguments going on all the time, but none of them wanted to interfere because Dad was such a frightening figure and because Mum seemed to be so capable and seemed to want to keep everything private. When our next-door neighbour on the other side from the old lady was asked why she had never called the police during any of the rows she said that it was because she and her husband were having their own marital problems at the time. Mum never wanted to make a fuss about anything. Perhaps if she had been a little less strong-willed and a little more willing to accept help she would still be alive today.

Mum was a keen churchgoer and would attend every Sunday. When Alex and I were both in the choir we spent even more time there, which could be boring at times although we had a lot of friends there. The biggest bonus to being in the choir was that occasionally we would get paid a few pounds for singing at a wedding. Mum was very proud of us because we got to visit all sorts of cathedrals around the country and once even went on a choir holiday to Wales. We both sang solos so I suppose we must have had pretty good voices.

I think Mum had strong Christian beliefs, although she didn't talk about them much, and maybe that was another reason why she believed she had to soldier on with the marriage 'for better or worse'. In her eyes she had made a commitment to my Dad and she was never one to weaken once she had done that. When I started to learn more about religion at school I would sometimes challenge her on her beliefs, like a typical teenager, but she never rose to the bait. Maybe she just went to church because she always had done and she liked the discipline and routine of it.

Although she and Dad hadn't done anything about having us baptised when we were born, she wanted us to be able to get confirmed at the same time as our friends at the church, so we wouldn't feel like odd ones out. She arranged for us to be baptised when I was about twelve and Alex was about ten and that was when she asked Helen and Steve to be our godparents. Dad wasn't remotely interested in any of it and didn't even turn up for the service.

Mum was the strongest person imaginable considering all she had to put up with, but eventually even she found the pressure too much. One night, after one of Dad's all-night attacks on her, she decided to commit suicide. I was fourteen at the time. We had no idea how bad things had got inside her head and we would certainly never have thought she would consider the option of suicide for even a second. I will never know exactly what was going through her mind on the night she made the decision, although I found out a lot more later that she hadn't told us at the time, but it was a decision she took with all her usual pragmatism and lack of emotion.

It must have been a really hard decision for her on a number of levels. Firstly there were her religious beliefs to overcome, and I also don't believe she would ever have taken the idea of leaving Alex and me with Dad lightly. She must have wrestled with her conscience for a long time before deciding to do it.

Perhaps her mind was clouded by the exhaustion she was obviously suffering from at the time. It must have been a relatively quiet fight she had with Dad that night because Alex and I both slept right through it. She must have stayed awake even after he had finally run out of steam and gone back to his room. Everything must have seemed so impossibly bleak as she sat on her own downstairs in the small hours of the morning, in the dark silent house. I found out later, long after the event, that she had serious health problems, although she hadn't told us at that stage, and she maybe thought that by ending things quickly she was sparing us from having to see her suffer and die slowly.

She had some tablets, but I don't know if that was a co-incidence or if she had been saving them up deliberately. We were told later she took eighty-six pills, a mixture of paracetamol and whatever else she could find in the house, which seems an awful lot unless you have been deliberately hording them. Even in her moment of deepest despair she wanted to cause us the minimum amount of trauma possible. She didn't want us to be the ones to find her, so as soon as she had swallowed the tablets she quietly let herself out of the house and went for a walk across the Downs.

It was a bitterly cold morning so maybe it was the fresh air, perhaps combined with the beauty of the rising sun, that shook her out of her black mood and made her realise that she had made a mistake and that she couldn't abandon Alex and me. Whatever it was that changed her mind she turned round and hurried home, determined to get help before the tablets started to take effect. When she got back she rang Helen and asked her to come to the house to help. The sounds of their raised voices woke me. I could sense an air of panic and I came downstairs to find out what was going on. Helen was trying to ring an ambulance on the house phone. She told me the truth about what had happened but we decided just to tell Alex that Mum was feeling ill without going into any details.

'Your phone's not working,' Helen said, unable to keep the tone of panic from her voice.

'Dad ripped it out of the wall the other day,' I told her.

'I'll have to drive your mother to the hospital,' she said.

There was no option but to keep to our usual routine because Mum wouldn't hear of anything else. As usual Alex didn't ask too many questions when he came down, just watching what was going on around him with patient, solemn eyes, so I didn't have to lie to him as we got ready and walked to school as if it was any other day. He was good like that, always willing to wait until things came clear, never in a rush. When we got home that afternoon Mum still wasn't back from hospital. We kept as quiet as we could while we made ourselves something to eat and did our homework, so as not to aggravate Dad and bring him storming out of his room. We knew all the routines to follow until Mum returned. She came home from the hospital later the same day but she was still throwing up constantly and I'm afraid I wasn't very sympathetic.

'How could you do that to yourself?' I yelled, furious with her at the thought of how she had been willing to leave us at Dad's mercy without even preparing us for the shock, and hurt as well. I was so angry I couldn't bring myself to offer to help her even though she was obviously feeling really ill.

'You must be nice to her,' Helen said when she came round, bustling about, trying to keep the mood cheerful.

'Why?' I wanted to know. 'She's brought this whole thing on herself.'

Helen didn't answer. Mum couldn't give me any explanation as to what she had been thinking, still not willing to talk about all the worries that must have been weighing her down by then. Maybe she didn't want to burden me, or perhaps she knew she wouldn't be able to put them into words without making herself cry, which she wouldn't have wanted to do.

'I knew you would both be okay. You're old enough to look after Alex now,' was all the justification she was willing to give when she was finally feeling strong enough to reply to my open hostility.

With the benefit of hindsight I think she was also worried that she would become an invalid and didn't want to get to the stage where we had to look after her, as well as having to cope with Dad's increasing aggression, but Alex and I didn't know anything about the gravity of her illnesses at that stage. She must have believed that if she died social services would become involved and they would make sure we were okay. Again with the benefit of hindsight, I wouldn't be able to share that confidence.

'I'm going to leave when you're sixteen anyway,' she said in another surprise announcement, but then refused to explain what she meant. I didn't challenge her because it sounded as though she really meant it and I wasn't sure I wanted to know any more. At the time I assumed she meant she would make another suicide attempt when I was sixteen, but perhaps she was thinking she would just walk out and leave us. That seems even harder to imagine somehow. The subject was never mentioned again, like so many things in our family. It is hard to grasp just how deeply depressed she must have been, but to try to take her own life was so far out of character that things must have been very bad indeed.

I didn't know what to think; I just knew I didn't want her to go. Despite my bravado with Dad when she was around, I was deeply frightened of him and didn't like being in the house on my own with him – which was one of the reasons why my school attendance record was as good as it was. The only time I can remember being forced to stay at home during a school day was when the arch of my foot collapsed and I literally couldn't stand on it at all, so I couldn't even hobble into work with Mum. I had to rest for a couple of days, unable to leave the house, and I was terrified that Dad would get up and come down to the kitchen and I would get in his way and impinge on his territory. Being alone in the house with him was the worst feeling imaginable, because I never knew what would happen if I accidentally annoyed him. While he was still safely asleep I set myself up in the living room with drinks and everything I would need in order to last without having to come out until Mum or Alex got home.

I tried to avoid ever being on my own with him, because I knew how much he hated me and how spiteful he could be. Two or three times, when Mum was away for any reason, he decided to cook a meal for us. This might sound as though he was making an effort to be a good father but he had a theory that oil was good for us and he would smother the food so thickly in it that it would be inedible. Apparently he had been diagnosed with high cholesterol and believed olive oil would help him to avoid suffering another stroke. He would insist that we swallowed every mouthful of whatever he had prepared and became very aggressive when he saw that we were struggling to finish what was on our plates. We often worried that he might have poisoned the food and that fear made every mouthful an ordeal. Once the meal was over and he had disappeared back into his room we would sit and wait to see if anything happened to us. It was such a rare thing for him to cook for us we felt sure he must have an ulterior motive.

Sometimes his displays of spite would be completely childish. On cold winter days, for instance, when he decided to open all the doors and windows, I'm sure that he deliberately wanted to make us suffer, just to show that he could. Alex and I would have to huddle up close to the airing cupboard to try to keep warm while we did our homework.

I thought I was coping pretty well with all the trouble at home but around about the age of twelve, I began to become obsessed with washing my hands all the time and counting inside my head. I liked the number four the best – even numbers were always my favourites, and four most of all. I decided that I would wash my hands forty-four times a day, since four wasn't enough, and that's what I began to do. Before long, it was driving Mum crazy. We were always running out of soap and my hands were red and painful from all the scrubbing, but I only felt comfortable when I reached the forty-fourth handwash of the day. It was only years later that psychologists diagnosed my handwashing as a symptom of obsessive-compulsive disorder and said it probably resulted from the stress of all the arguments and violence I witnessed at home.

The stress of living with Dad must also have been wearing Mum down as surely as the physical exhaustion of always being on the go and never having a comfortable night's sleep or a relaxed meal. There is a limit to how much tiredness any body can bear before it starts to wear out. But the problems with Dad and the stress of our day-to-day routines were only the tip of the iceberg. Mum had far more than that to contend with, as we were soon to find out.

Shortly after Mum's suicide attempt I did something really stupid and tried to steal some clothes from a shop. I really needed some new stuff and I didn't have the heart to mention it to Mum, knowing how bad she would feel at not being able to give me everything I needed, however hard she tried. She had enough on her plate so I thought I would solve the problem myself. A lot of the other kids at school talked about pinching things from shops as if it was the most normal thing in the world and for a mad moment I thought perhaps I was the odd one out for always working so hard to earn every penny I needed, and maybe I should just take what I needed like everyone else.

I must have been a terrible shoplifter, made clumsy by my guilty conscience and my wildly thumping heart, because I was immediately caught and marched off to the police station. They called home to speak to Mum and Dad took a message, but didn't do anything about it. I can imagine how pleased he must have been to discover that I had gone off the rails and let Mum down so spectacularly. He must have got immense pleasure from telling her the news the moment she walked in the door from work.

Mum deliberately didn't turn up to collect me from the police station for six hours, leaving me to sit all alone in a bare cell listening to the threatening shouts of a load of indignant drunks. She knew exactly what she was doing because I was absolutely petrified as I sat shivering in my cell. There was no way I was ever going to repeat this mistake. As a girl who never liked to be anything but first at everything I did, I had suddenly sunk to being a failed petty criminal, the lowest of the low in the eyes of the security guard, the manager at the shop and the policemen who took me in – at least that was how it seemed to me.

When Mum did finally turn up in the cell I have never been so pleased to see anyone in my life, even though she was furious and started giving me a really hard time the moment she came through the door. In fact she was yelling so loudly the police, who were used to dealing with stroppy fourteen-year-olds, thought it was me shouting at her rather than the other way round and gave me another telling off for being rude to my mother.

Once we had got home and she had calmed down a bit, Mum stopped shouting at me and started blaming herself instead, saying she wasn't a good enough mother to us – which made me feel even worse about what I'd done. Because so many people in my year at school went shoplifting regularly it hadn't actually seemed such a big deal when I set out but it had degenerated into a nightmare, leaving me feeling as though I had failed and let her down as well as myself. The school got to hear about it and we had to go in together to see the headmaster. Because I was a straight 'A' student and had never previously got into any trouble he was a bit surprised and disappointed to hear what I'd been up to.

'Is everything all right at home?' he asked kindly, obviously assuming there must be another reason for my strange behaviour beyond any sudden need I might have felt to refresh my wardrobe. I didn't have time to say a word before Mum jumped in quickly with an adamant denial, so I could hardly contradict her and make it sound as though she was a liar or a bad mother. It could have been a good opportunity for her to come clean and explain that we had some real problems in the family because of Dad's behaviour, and that she had recently been driven to attempting suicide – but even then she couldn't do it, couldn't talk about something so personal. Instead she took all the blame for my fall from grace, telling him it was her fault for being an inadequate mother and not being around enough for us. I doubt that the headmaster was convinced by that because everyone knew how much she did for us, but he let it pass. No further action was taken but I still had to pay a price for my stupidity. I got a reprimand from the police, which still pops up every time I ever go for a job interview even though it should have been wiped from my record as soon as I turned eighteen. I keep being told that it shouldn't happen, but it does. The one time I tried to break the law and it seems to be haunting me forever.

We only found out what was going on inside Mum's head when she had no option but to tell us. The suicide attempt had been a huge shock, and not long afterwards she was forced to tell us that she had cancer. Before that she had decided not to mention it to anyone apart from the doctors who were treating her. It wasn't until the day she was being admitted to hospital for an operation to remove a lump from her breast that she finally told Alex and me what was going on.

'I'm going into hospital today for an operation,' she said over breakfast. 'It's breast cancer. You'll be staying with Helen and Steve for a couple of days. If you have any questions, look in these leaflets.'

I accepted the pile of leaflets she handed over, too shocked to say much. This was the first we had heard about her being ill at all. There must have been numerous doctors' appointments, scans and tests going on over the previous weeks and months, all of which she had managed to keep hidden from us. We had no idea how long she had known or how serious it might be, but it did give us another clue as to why she might have been so stressed and exhausted recently. Even now she only told us the barest facts, without any elaboration. She still wasn't telling us how she felt about her illness or what the prognosis might be. She didn't offer us any grains of comfort, or give us any opportunity to comfort her. Such considerations wouldn't have entered her head. She simply told us the facts and gave us some leaflets to read should we wish to find out more about breast cancer.

Mum was never very physically or emotionally demonstrative, so Alex and I had become the same way. I wish I had given her a big hug that morning when she told us about the cancer, but it wasn't the way we'd been brought up. I never used to go to her to talk about things that were worrying me. She wouldn't have known how to comfort me anyway; she always looked for practical solutions to any problems and would have counselled me 'not to make a fuss' or 'just get on with it'. I suppose working for so many years as a teacher meant she had seen it all and heard it all and knew that none of the problems of childhood were as serious as they seemed to the child in question, but still it would have been nice if we could have talked more about our feelings and worries from time to time.

With hindsight I wonder if bottling up so many emotions and not talking to anyone about her worries was one of the reasons she got ill. At least Alex and I had each other to talk to when we needed to let off steam, although we had both learned from her example early on and tended not to get emotional about many things.

She wrote to her bosses at school, explaining simply that she was going for an operation and telling them how long she would be off work. She had always scheduled any doctors' or dentists' appointments for late in the day so she would cause the minimum amount of disruption to the school timetable, and she behaved in exactly the same way about the operation. She gave them a detailed description of everything that was going on in each of her classes and of the contingency plans she had made to help the replacement teachers who would have to fill in for her, and she passed all her own textbooks on to them. She guaranteed she would be back in the classroom the first moment she was able. I wonder if perhaps she was frightened to stay off work for too long because then she would have had time to think about things. The fact that she had tried to kill herself suggests that there was a depression just waiting to engulf her if she sat still for long enough to allow it to take hold. As long as she was busy and following a hectic routine there was no chance to dwell on how unhappy she was and just how hopeless it all seemed.

As with everything in her life she stuck only to the facts and the practicalities of the situation and ignored any possible emotional consequences. She wanted no sympathy and no special treatment; she could have been talking about a routine but unavoidable visit to the dentist.

In a way her unemotional approach to news that could have been very traumatic made it easier for Alex and me to deal with. Although we were shocked and frightened by the news, we assumed that if she was being so calm about it then there couldn't be too much to worry about. Maybe the operation was no more than a formality, we told ourselves as we set off to school together as usual that morning. She had made it all sound so minor and casual that when we went into the hospital to visit her in the evening we were horrified to see all the tubes and machines around her bed. As we stood there taking it all in, it dawned on both of us at the same time that our mother had just been through a much more serious operation than we had imagined. But by then it was all over, so we could tell ourselves that she would be recovering soon, blocking out any worries or fears that might try to muscle in. So maybe her approach had some merit.

The nurses asked us to help them bath her the next day as she wasn't able to move her arms because of where she had been cut and stitched. It was good to be given a practical task and to be able to help make her more comfortable, but it was shocking to see the long, livid scar across her chest and into her armpit. Somehow, looking at that, I couldn't imagine she would be back to her old self as quickly as she was promising. The terrifying thought flashed across my mind that maybe this cancer was going to kill her, but I quickly shoved it away and refused to let myself think that way. The prospect was just too awful to contemplate.

Chapter Seven

Alex

We have no idea whether Mum's cancer would have come back or whether it would have eventually killed her because less than a year later Dad had murdered her. We know she went back for follow-up treatments after the operation, but she never talked about them, apart from giving us information about the times of her appointments so that we could make practical arrangements to continue our own lives as normal around her absences. We had no idea whether the doctors believed the treatments were working or not. I guess they probably didn't know at that stage either. As usual we didn't ask her any questions; we weren't sure how to phrase them anyway. I suppose we didn't want to know if it was bad news, preferring to think that as long as she wasn't saying anything to the contrary, we could assume she was fine. We were all sticking our heads in the sand like a family of ostriches.

Once she came out of hospital Mum just got on with life in exactly the same way she always had, so we did the same. When she arrived home after the operation she went back to sleeping downstairs on the couch, even though it was too short for her to be able to lie out flat and it must have been incredibly uncomfortable for her with the stitches. The pain caused her to moan in her sleep at night, which got on Dad's nerves and made him shout and curse. Even though he was complaining that she was making a noise and disturbing his peace and quiet, it didn't occur to him to offer her his bed or to do anything that would help her be more comfortable. Fear of upsetting him gave her another reason to keep as quiet as she could about whatever was troubling her. He hated her so deeply by that stage that he was happy to let her suffer as long as she didn't make a noise and disturb him.

'Please take one of our beds,' Isobel and I both begged. 'We'll be fine on the couch.'

But she wouldn't hear of it. The most important thing to her was our schoolwork, which meant we needed to sleep well in order to be wide-awake in the mornings for our lessons. In every way possible she sacrificed her own health, comfort and happiness for us, determined to give us every possible chance of succeeding in life. The only time she would ever agree to use one of our beds was if we were away sleeping at a friend's house.

But even Mum was forced to make a few concessions to the physical effects of the operation. She let us do the shopping for her for a few weeks because she wasn't strong enough to carry heavy bags, but that was the only interruption she would allow to our normal routine. During the week after the operation she was sitting on the couch marking the piles of school books that she had brought home with her, and the week after that she had gone back to teaching part-time to ensure her students missed as little of their curriculum as possible.

Looking back now I wonder if all the stress and worry she had to put up with was a contributing factor in causing the cancer. She lost a lot of weight and became stick thin and constantly tired-looking towards the end of her life. Where once she had taken care to look smart and tidy whenever she went out of the house, she eventually gave up bothering, pulling on whatever clothes came to hand and making no effort with her appearance. Just getting through each day seemed to take all the energy she could muster.

I can't remember her ever spending any money on herself apart from absolute essentials. Although she must have earned a decent salary as a head of department, the expense of paying for all our after-school activities left nothing for her to spend on clothes or luxuries like make-up or hairdressers. She also had to supply Dad with a never-ending stream of alcohol as well as paying the mortgage and food and petrol bills. Every day she seemed to bring him another bottle of whisky, which he would take back into his room to drink alone without a word, escaping from the world into an alcoholic stupor. I don't know if she hoped that giving him everything he demanded would make him be nicer to her, or whether she was just too frightened of him to say no. Maybe she simply believed it was the best chance she had of having a quiet life. Perhaps in the end it had just become a habit.

The lack of spare money was evident inside the house too, where we never had any new furniture or decoration. We couldn't afford to pay a decorator and we certainly didn't have time to do any painting ourselves. Mum kept the place as clean and neat as she could in the time available to her, but she didn't waste any of her precious financial resources on doing anything up. It was as if she was pouring every last ounce of her energy into her job and into our future, draining herself dry in the process. As well as having to pay for her own travel costs every day she also had to pay for Dad to have a car, plus all the household bills. There wasn't any money left to spend on treats or luxuries.

Even when it was obvious how much he hated her and how badly their relationship had degenerated, Mum kept trying to please Dad. She would still buy him Christmas and birthday presents, even though he never did the same for her and never uttered a word of thanks. I guess the harder she tried to please him, the more he grew to despise her. The more he came to depend on her, the more he resented it.

He was continually attempting to find new ways to divide and rule the rest of us, trying to keep control of things. The telephone was one of his weapons. To spite Isobel and Mum he installed a line for me in my bedroom, and then fitted a lock to my door so that they couldn't get to it without him or me agreeing to let them in. It was a stupid, pointless exercise but none of us wanted to say anything and risk another row.

Alfie the dog hated Dad as much as the rest of us, always cowering away under the table whenever he heard his footsteps on the stairs. He even learned to fear Dad's name – Bert – running for cover if he heard it spoken out loud. If Mum, Isobel or I were in the room when Dad came in, however, Alfie would muster all his canine courage to stand in front of us, snarling a warning that he wouldn't allow us to be attacked. Dad hated him for that; he would have preferred to control him and turn him against us.

'I'm going to keep that dog in my room from now on,' he would threaten every time it happened, 'and train it to attack you.'

He never did that, of course, because he didn't actually want the bother of having Alfie in his room with him, so instead he took to teasing and bullying him in the same way he did us. He would bring in the ferrets he kept in the shed outside and encourage them to attack Alfie, trying to teach him who was boss in the house – as if Alfie didn't already know. Dad loved those ferrets and used to let them crawl up inside his sleeves or run around nipping at our heels. However much he intimidated Alfie, though, he couldn't completely break his spirit. Sometimes, if Alfie had particularly angered him he would chain him up outside and beat him with metal poles or anything else he could lay his hands on, leaving him whimpering in pain and covered in cuts.

It was heartbreaking for Isobel and me to watch, but for years we didn't have the courage to intervene, in case he turned his rage on us instead. As the years passed, though, we became braver and angrier. Once we were so incensed after finding Alfie had been beaten and chained again, we went into the garage and stole the offending poles. They felt so heavy and cruel it made us even more furious and for a few minutes we completely lost our cool. We ran upstairs with the poles and banged on Dad's bedroom door with them, shouting abuse at him. We couldn't be sure if he was in there or not, but he usually was. We would never have dared attempt to break down the door, which he kept locked. Luckily for us he didn't bother to respond to our provocation; maybe he enjoyed the idea that he had finally managed to get to us enough to provoke a reaction.

Mum would always try to quieten us down if we ever seemed about to challenge him; she was always looking for ways to prevent a full-scale confrontation. On that occasion our anger only lasted a few minutes before we came to our senses and backed away, hiding the poles near our beds in case he tried to attack us in the night. I think we just wanted to make a noise and express our unhappiness rather than actually break in to his room. I don't know what we would have done if we had burst through or if he had opened it and stormed out to face us down. We both knew his violence was getting worse.

I imagine Alfie received a lot of beatings and kickings while the rest of us were out of the house that we never knew about. I think sometimes the poor creature received the beatings that Dad would really have liked to be doling out to Mum and Isobel. If he ever barked during the day, which most dogs do from time to time, the noise would waken Dad up and he would charge downstairs to do something about it. He never stopped to find out what Alfie might be barking about; he just did his best to intimidate him into silence as quickly as possible. If we were in the house we would be trying to shut him up, our hearts racing with fear that Dad might burst in and attack either us or the dog, constantly straining our ears in case we heard him coming downstairs.

Just as it is with human beings, I think there are some dogs who are natural-born victims, and Alfie was definitely one of them. He was the meekest of animals, always being picked on by other dogs when we took him out for walks and often ending up having to be taken to the vet to get stitches in his wounds after fights. Our main concern when we got home from school was to get into the house quietly without disturbing Dad, but Alfie would be so excited to see us after spending all day alone he would start barking and we would have to shut him up as quickly as possible in case Dad was there.

There were days when we forgot our keys in the morning rush and when we got home in the afternoon we'd ring the doorbell to get in, but Dad completely ignored us. We'd be left outside until Mum got back to let us in, or until we managed to find a window we could wriggle through like cat burglars. On one of these occasions Isobel and I peered through the letterbox after ringing the bell and we could actually see Dad sitting in the kitchen, pretending he couldn't hear us. It was as if he was always trying to teach us a lesson for some reason or other.

Like us, Alfie seemed willing to put up with any amount of abuse from Dad in order to have a quiet life but eventually Dad overstepped the mark, and that was the day I finally stood up to him. I can't remember what Alfie had done to offend him in the first place, but whatever it was it resulted in Dad smashing him repeatedly around the head with a big heavy mixing bowl to 'teach him a lesson'. I was in the room at the time and watched in horror when Alfie finally reacted as Dad raised his hand to strike again by jumping up and biting it hard, taking out a massive chunk of flesh.

I knew that an act of defiance like that could push Dad to do something even more brutal and before I could stop myself I yelled at him, willing to risk bringing his wrath down on my own head rather than see him attacking the dog any more.

'Leave the fucking dog alone,' I shouted, and was surprised to see that he actually stopped in his tracks. It had never occurred to me before that I might be able to influence his behaviour in any way. I might have saved Alfie from getting a worse beating that day, but from that moment onwards Dad saw me as one of the enemy. I was no longer a potential ally to be used and manipulated in his war against the rest of them. If he couldn't control me and keep me on his side then he wanted to destroy me just as much as he wanted to destroy Mum and Isobel. I'd crossed the line.

Chapter Eight

Isobel

Mum was late getting up on the morning she died. I don't think she ever used an alarm in her life, always relying on her own body clock to wake her at the right moment, following years of the same routines. The more exhausted her body became, the harder it must have been for that instinct to work effectively, especially once she was ill with breast cancer. That Friday morning, the 11th of January 2002, it let her down completely. She succumbed to what must have been an overwhelming need to rest and was still deeply asleep on the couch when I came downstairs.

As always I was preoccupied with planning the rest of my day as I got ready to leave, working out what I needed to take and where I needed to be later. I remembered I had a piano lesson after school and I knew I would need to get myself there because Mum wouldn't be back from school in time to drive me. It wasn't a problem; I was fifteen years old now and I'd done it a thousand times before. If she knew she was coming back from work early for some reason she would offer to give me a lift, but she didn't say anything that morning as she rushed around, bleary-eyed, getting her books together and pulling on whatever clothes came to hand. I had no reason to think she would be there when I got home. Something unexpected must have happened to change her plans during the day; a moved hospital appointment, perhaps.

The routines of the school day passed exactly as normal, just the usual lessons and the usual socialising in between. There is nothing lodged in my memory that makes the school day stand out as any different from hundreds of others.

That afternoon, as we got ready to go home, my friend Katrina and I both discovered that our PE kit had gone missing. We kept them in our particular cubby holes on a shelf in the cloakroom and someone had been messing around and moved them. It wasn't that unusual an occurrence – just annoying, since I couldn't go home without it because I needed it for the weekend. We had to keep searching the changing rooms together until the missing items turned up. It was frustrating but stuff like that happens all the time at school.

We were talking to the PE teacher about things in general as we searched. I can't remember how the subject came up, but I remember saying, 'I think my Mum might die soon.'

I had mentioned my fears about Mum to teachers at school before and they had actually called her in to talk about it once, worried that I might have some deep-rooted anxieties. She had managed to brush aside my concerns, as she always did, and leave the teachers with the impression that there was nothing for anyone to worry about. She was good at that was Mum, always giving the outside world the impression that everything was fine in our family when it obviously wasn't. I don't know what made me make that strange little announcement that day, whether it was the suicide attempt, the cancer operation or her promise that she would be leaving as soon as I turned sixteen. Perhaps I was subconsciously preparing myself, trying to get used to the idea just in case any one of these things happened. I certainly wasn't expecting her to be killed and had no idea how prophetic my words would soon turn out to be.

The search for the PE kit made me a bit later than usual leaving the school premises, but I still had enough time to get home and do my homework before it would be time to go to piano, so I wasn't in any particular rush as I made my way across the main road towards our house.

The junction where I turned into our street was about eight houses away from home and the whole road was jammed full of police cars and ambulances and uniformed men rushing around as if they were on important and serious business. Because there were so many of them, at first I couldn't work out which house their attentions were centred on but my instincts told me it was probably something to do with us, because it always was. Whenever there was trouble in the street it was usually connected to Dad. 'What's he done now?' I wondered. Had he hung himself, as he was always threatening? I didn't have time to think about it logically and realise there were far too many people there for it to be just a suicide attempt. There were no fire engines so presumably he hadn't set fire to the house, which was his other regular threat.

As I walked on I noticed Mum's little red Nova, which she had recently traded the Metro for, was parked outside the house and I wondered what she was doing back home. She certainly hadn't said anything that morning about coming back early or I would have remembered. An uncomfortable knot of anxiety was growing inside me. Maybe all these people were here because of something to do with her. It couldn't just be a fight or a suicide bid; it had to be something major for this many people to turn out. I began to recognise the faces of neighbours amongst the policemen and medics milling around in the road. As I got closer to our front garden I realised that everyone was looking at me as if I was something to do with what was going on. Their expressions were strange – a mixture of curiosity, sympathy and shock. It started to feel like a very long walk before I would reach the point where I would be able to find out what had happened.

When I finally got to our front garden I saw Alex sitting on the wall with his usual patient, calm and slightly puzzled expression. He was surrounded by policemen, who seemed to be trying to stop him from going out to the road, even though he was showing no sign of wanting to go anywhere. One of the police cars drew away from the kerb as I got closer, my heart thumping in my ears. I could see a man in the back but I didn't realise till later that it was my father. By that time I must have been in some sort of state of shock as I tried to push my way through the crowd of men and uniforms to get to the house. The door was slightly ajar but I couldn't see inside.

'Where's the dog?' I demanded, unable to understand why Alfie wasn't barking at all these strangers invading his territory. 'Where's Mum? Why's her car here?'

Everyone was getting in my way, trying to block me from getting into the house to try to find out what was going on, but none of them were talking to me or answering any of my questions. They were just staring at me and then looking away in embarrassment when I caught their eyes. It was like a nightmare and I was becoming more and more annoyed and frustrated until eventually I lashed out at one of the policemen who was deliberately standing in my way. He caught my wrist just before my punch landed.

'If you do that we're going to have to put you in a police car,' he warned, 'and we really don't want to have to do that, do we?'

'Where's the dog?' I persisted, growing angry at being treated like this.

'He's in the kitchen,' the policeman said, although he obviously didn't know that.

'There's no door to the kitchen,' I snapped. 'He's not in the kitchen or he would have come out. Don't lie to me.'

I couldn't understand why these people were bothering to lie to me. Why wasn't anyone simply explaining to me what was going on in my own house? Where was Mum? Why wasn't she at work? Why was her car there? Why weren't they letting us past? Nothing was making sense. Why wasn't Alfie making his usual noise? Normally when he was in the dining room he was kept in with a little metal gate Dad had installed. I didn't realise the police had already taken that away because it had a massive dent in it, which they thought was relevant to whatever struggle had gone on. The police must have shut the door on Alfie to keep him contained. Maybe he was intimidated by so much going on around him, so many strange people and voices and noises. He was probably as frightened and confused as Alex and I were and that's why he wasn't barking. The more questions I asked, the more studiously they ignored me and I was becoming increasingly agitated and worked up as I tried to get some straight answers. Why were they all lying to me? Why wouldn't anyone tell me what was happening?

The main thing I wanted was to be able to get into the house. The main thing the police wanted was to shut me up so they could get on with whatever their procedures were. Alex was still sitting on the wall, watching everything going on around him with wide eyes. It didn't look as though he had any more idea what was happening than I did. We caught eyes but didn't say anything to each other at that stage.

The police must have been praying that someone would find a family liaison officer soon so that they wouldn't have to listen to any more of my questions and could get both of us clear of the scene. They obviously didn't know what to do with us themselves – what to tell us, what not to tell us. Maybe they were worried that if they explained to us what had happened they would do it in the wrong way and cause us even more trauma, so they chose to do nothing, to try to ignore the fact that we were there at all, leaving us in a frightening state of limbo.

Someone asked us if we had any relatives they could contact for us and I felt a stab of panic. That was the question police asked when someone had died.

'There are only our godparents,' I said, giving them Helen and Steve's telephone number. 'We don't know any of our relatives.'

After what seemed like an age someone must have come up with the idea of escorting us across the street to the home of a neighbour who lived directly opposite; it was a family who had children at the same school as us, although we didn't know them very well. I think the parents were teachers, like Mum. Their children were sent off upstairs out of the way and we sat down in their living room, where we were left to stare out the window across the street at all the activity going on around our home. It felt as if we were watching a movie about someone else's life, as if it was nothing to do with us.

'What happened?' I asked Alex after everyone else had left us alone.

'There was just one policeman when I got here,' he explained. 'He wouldn't let me go in, then Dad answered the door and the policeman reported a "blue murder" – at least I think that's what he said – and everything went mad after that. They took Dad off in a police car. He wanted to say something to me but they wouldn't let him.'

It was then I realised it must have been Dad I saw being driven away as I came down the street.

'Why was Mum back home early?' I asked, as much to myself as to Alex. 'She didn't say she would be. She would have said. She would have told me she would be able to drive me to my piano lesson. Why was she there?'

He shrugged. He'd told me everything he knew. Alex's isn't one to gabble on if he doesn't have anything constructive or useful to say. We both sank back into our own thoughts.

'What does blue murder mean?' I asked after a minute, but he had no more idea than I did. Then I said out loud the awful words that had formed in my brain. 'Do you suppose he's killed her?'

Alex just stared at me. We were both in a state of shock and neither of us could take anything in but the idea wasn't so preposterous that we could dismiss it out of hand. In a way I think I already knew that Mum was dead, or at least in a critical condition. But if that was so, why wasn't anyone talking to us about it?

Someone came in and told us to stay away from the window. It was yet another thing that didn't make sense at the time but, looking back, I suppose that was the moment when they brought out Mum's body and they didn't want us watching.

It was nearly an hour before the family liaison officer was eventually found and brought into the neighbour's living room to see us. I immediately started firing questions at her, pouring out my anxieties and frustrations, but she told me she would rather wait until our godparents arrived before she answered. There was no changing her mind, so we all sat together in that room, watching the continuing scenes outside, waiting for

Helen to arrive. Gradually the street started to clear as the ambulances and some of the police cars left. Our house had been cordoned off with police tape and secured as a crime scene. It was obvious that nothing further was likely to happen that would require quite so many people in attendance. It was as though the dust was settling, leaving us staring silently at the ruins of our life, still with no real idea what had happened, waiting to be told what we were supposed to do next. I know it sounds crazy but all I could think was that I should have been at my piano lesson. I fretted about whether I should call my piano teacher but I didn't have her number with me.

When Helen arrived she had brought a friend with her; apparently they had been out walking their dogs together when the call from the police came through. We didn't have the sort of relationship with her where she would have hugged us, so she just sat down on the sofa beside us and told us as much as the police had told her.

'He's finally done it,' she said, or at least that was what I heard in my confused state.

'Done it?'

She nodded and I assumed she meant that Dad had attacked Mum but I still couldn't be sure whether she was dead or not. Maybe I was blocking out her words, or maybe Helen just assumed I would understand that was what she meant. She said more but I can't remember anything else about the conversation and neither can Alex.

There was no air of surprise in the room – more like a feeling of resignation. It seemed as though we had all been expecting something like this to happen sooner or later. There had been so many threats and so many years of hatred and anger. No one cried. We just sat silent and numb, trying to let the news soak in, not knowing what to say, what the appropriate reaction might be. Helen had a word with the family protection officer who had turned up and then told us that she would take us back to her house. That didn't surprise us either. Mum had always said we would go to Helen and Steve if anything happened to her. I had imagined she meant if she committed suicide or if the cancer got her, not this. Now, it seemed, the moment had come for everything in our lives to change.

Helen's car was parked in the road and as we came outside into the cold evening air my only thought was that I wanted to get inside our house to see what was going on for myself. It didn't seem right that we weren't involved in whatever was happening to our own mother, that these strangers were taking over our lives and just shipping us out. All our lives we had lived there. All our possessions were in there, and our mother had either just died there or been seriously attacked. I wanted to see for myself what had happened. I said nothing and bided my time, my eyes darting around as I tried to work out the best way to get away from the adults surrounding us. As we got close to the car I broke free and made a dash across the road. I didn't really have a plan but I knew that once I was in Helen's car I wouldn't get another chance. But the policemen who had been left to guard the house were ready for me and there was no way I was getting past them, however hard I struggled or however loudly I shouted at them.

There must have been a lot of blood splattered around inside and they were determined I shouldn't disturb the crime scene. Someone took a firm hold of my arm and helped me into the back of the car next to Alex, locking the doors so I couldn't clamber back out before we had driven away. I was shouting at them to let me go. I felt furious at having my life taken over by other people, but I didn't know what I could do about it. Although I was capable for my age in many ways, I was still only fifteen, and I had Alex to think about as well. Mum had always said she knew I would be able to look after him if she went away, so that was what I must do before anything else. I had to make sure they didn't separate us. We only had each other left now.

Chapter Nine

Alex

The family protection officers followed us to our godparents' house and had a quick chat with us before going home for the night. Among other things, they explained to us that we would need to talk to the police the following day. It's difficult to be sure what else they told us and didn't tell us that evening because I suppose we were in a state of shock. It felt as though I was anaesthetised somehow and events were taking place somewhere far away. All the usual patterns and routines of our lives had suddenly been turned upside down and we were having trouble working out what had happened and what was going to happen next. I had thought I knew exactly what I was going to be doing all weekend, and now everything had changed.

Helen did her best to make it seem as though we were a couple of normal guests who had come to stay the night. She concentrated on the domestic details of who was going to sleep where and what we might like to eat for supper, which helped to fill the silence left by our inability to understand what was expected of us. In the end I was allocated a bunk bed in their youngest son's room and their daughter went to stay with a friend so Isobel could use her room. Helen and Steve were quite well off by that stage, always having worked hard at good jobs. They had four children – three boys and a girl – of whom the oldest was already at university. The house had a very different feel to ours, bigger and more comfortable. It had five bedrooms and was located in a much nicer area but we would still rather have been in our own home, even with Dad lurking upstairs in his bedroom. Uncertainty is an uncomfortable emotion.

Even though we hadn't asked for anything, a doctor came round later and tried to persuade us to take some sleeping pills, but we didn't think we needed them. We'd never liked taking anything like that, and the way he was describing them it sounded as though they were going to be ridiculously strong and not very good for you. We didn't want to be knocked out for the whole of the next day when we needed to try to understand what was going on around us. It felt as though every aspect of our lives was being taken over by strangers and we wanted to make sure we were alert enough to let them know what we did and didn't want to do, and to understand fully what had happened to Mum. I remember I just wanted to stay close to Isobel; I felt safer when she was nearby.

Because we hadn't been allowed into our house we only had the clothes we were standing up in and the few bits and pieces we had brought home from school in our bags. Helen rummaged around in her wardrobes and found some of her son's clothes for me (which was a slight problem as I was about four inches taller than him), but the only things in the house for Isobel to wear were very girlie and Isobel always preferred to dress like a tomboy. Horrified by the frilly pink items she was being offered, she rang one of her friends to ask if she could borrow some more comfortable stuff from her.

I can't remember how I slept that night, so I guess it must have been okay even without the tablets. We were probably completely exhausted by everything that had happened in the previous few hours. If I did lie awake at all it was because I was trying to work out what was going on. The whole evening had been so puzzling. The fact that Helen had been so calm and matter of fact had rubbed off on us, or maybe it was the other way round. I knew that Dad had killed Mum. Everyone had been talking in euphemisms so it had been impossible to work out exactly what they were saying, but that phrase 'blue murder' kept ringing in my head.

I hoped that things would be made clearer the next day, and at least we had the weekend to sort ourselves out before we had to be back in school and trying to concentrate on work. I think I was aware that a thing called a 'care system' existed to look after children who couldn't stay with their parents for whatever reason, but I didn't think for a minute that we would end up there. If Mum really wasn't going to be able to look after us, and if Dad was kept in police custody, I assumed we would stay with Helen and Steve. That was what Mum had always said would happen and it seemed like the obvious solution. If this was going to be our new home we might as well get used to it.

The next day Helen went to the police station to be interviewed first of all, then she came back to collect Isobel and me so we could do our interviews. We were taken to a room in a family protection unit that was furnished like a house rather than a police station, with a sofa for us to sit on. Isobel was interviewed first and I went in after. Only one woman asked the questions, but the session was being filmed and we were being watched by CID officers on monitors in the next room. The woman seemed to be trying to find out what we knew about Mum and Dad's relationship and to ascertain what family life had been like up till whatever had happened between them the previous day.

Initially I wasn't particularly interested in co-operating with them. I felt that whatever had happened was the police's fault because they hadn't done anything on the occasions when Isobel had called them out when Dad was beating Mum up. Isobel, in her usual plain-speaking way, actually told them she blamed them. They were really good at calming her down, explaining that when it comes to incidents of domestic abuse they aren't legally able to do anything unless the victim makes an allegation and lodges a complaint. Mum would never have done that; she would never have wanted to bring other people into her problems if she didn't have to, especially the police. They were good at putting us at our ease and winning us over to their side.

Neither of us found the experience too traumatic once we had settled down and realised the woman interviewing us was willing to joke about a bit. We were still having trouble working out what had happened and the real seriousness of it all hadn't sunk in. I don't think we actually knew how we felt about anything. Perhaps we were a bit numb from the shock; I certainly felt an air of unreality about everything. In a way it felt quite therapeutic to talk openly about what it had been like to live in our house after so many years of guarding Mum's privacy and pretending to the outside world that everything was okay.

The police told us later they were surprised by how relaxed we were that day. I guess they expected us to be more shocked that our own father could do such a thing, but all our lives we had been listening to him issuing threats of one sort or another. We had seen him hitting Mum and Alfie, and we always knew he was consumed with hatred for the world and capable of terrible violence. Perhaps it had always been at the back of our minds that something like this could happen, although we had told ourselves that he would never go that far. Mum's cancer had also prepared us a little for the possibility that she might die. Obviously if we had thought it was likely he would do something as drastic as murdering her we would have tried to persuade Mum to leave him and take us with her, but whatever he had done the day before hadn't changed our feelings towards him. We had always hated him and the way he treated us. He had simply proved that we were right in our assessment of him.

The officers were quite good at making us feel relaxed and comfortable. Isobel says she started giggling when she was asked my full name, because she and Mum used to have a joke between them that it was 'Alexandra'. It didn't occur to her that it might have appeared odd to be laughing at a time like that. Because we still had each other we automatically felt less vulnerable than other children might have done in that situation. Isobel had always been the most important person in my life, and as long as she was there I knew I would be OK. I knew she would always protect me.

I gleaned more information about what had happened when the woman told me that Dad had attacked Mum with a 'sharpened chisel'.

'Did you ever see him sharpening a chisel?' she asked me.

I guess if I'd been able to say that I had, they thought they would stand a better chance of proving that the murder was premeditated. They wanted to know whether he had become annoyed by Mum that day and gone and sharpened it with the intention of attacking her, or whether he had been planning it for ages.

'I think that chisel was mine at some point,' I told them when they showed me a picture of it. 'I know it was in my room on Friday morning because Dad had been using it to fix in a new phone point. I don't know anything about it being sharpened though.'

I knew they were videoing everything we said, but I don't think I realised it would all one day be played out in court in front of Dad and the judge and jury and anyone else who might have turned up. I expect they told me but I wasn't really taking much in at that stage.

It was a bit like being presented with a puzzle to solve, like watching a whodunnit on television. Why Dad would have sharpened the chisel at all was a mystery to Isobel and me as well as to the police. There were plenty of knives in the house and dozens of other potential weapons in the garage, from hammers to iron bars, none of which would need customising for the job. If he had preplanned the murder, why didn't he just leave one of these somewhere handy?

108

Helen gave the police a lot of information that weekend as well. Although she was doing a good job of keeping up a normal façade around us, we realised later when we saw her tapes played back in court how deeply upset she was by the death of her friend. She knew more about what Mum had been living through than anyone else and she let her anger towards Dad spill out to the police in her statement, forgetting that before long she would have to go through the whole thing again, in court, in front of him.

Both Isobel and I owned mobile phones but we had left them inside the house the previous morning, since we weren't allowed to take them to school with us, and the police made it clear there was no way they were going to let us go back for them. Having seen how quick they had been to stop Isobel going anywhere near the front door, we knew they meant it. It was hard to make contact with our friends over the weekend except for the ones whose numbers we knew by heart. I managed to get hold of some of my mates, and when others went to the house the policemen guarding it told them where we had gone. They then came round to visit us with a 'trick or treat' box of sweets and magazines and funny photographs to cheer us up. It was a brilliant gesture that I really appreciated.

By Sunday morning we were able to read all about what Dad had done to Mum on the front page of the local papers. Even though we were both underage the paper openly printed our names and ages, our school and our home address, with pictures of the house in case anyone was still in doubt. Apparently it had been on the television and radio news broadcasts throughout Saturday as well but we hadn't heard any of them, so we found out most of the details about how our mother had died from the newspapers. Helen had to agree to let us read the story because we would otherwise have heard people talking about it at school.

Whereas everyone else seemed keen to avoid telling us anything face to face for fear of upsetting us, the local reporters had no such qualms. Dad, they informed us, had stabbed Mum 'between fifty and sixty times' in the head and upper body with the 'sharpened chisel' that the police had been asking us about. The attack had been so frenzied and ferocious that the forensics people couldn't tell exactly how many times he had struck, but the force of his blows had chipped bones and penetrated her breastplate. I felt sick to my stomach reading it, trying to imagine the terror Mum must have been experiencing during his onslaught. The pain must have been unbelievable. I didn't say anything with Helen in the room but I cried later for the first time since it happened when Isobel and I were on our own. The details were just so horrific. How hard do you have to hit someone to penetrate their bones?

The police weren't happy about our names being published in the press and after they complained to the editor they were withdrawn, but it was too late by then. The papers had been printed and distributed, everyone who had ever known us or ever known anyone who had known us, could read all about it. Complete strangers who had never heard of us before now knew exactly who we were and where they could find us. From then on, in all their future stories, the reporters referred to us as 'the children who cannot be named for legal reasons'. Talk about shutting the stable door after the horse has bolted!

We kept asking the adults who seemed to have taken over our lives if we could go to school as normal on Monday morning. We both wanted to have the comfort of our familiar routine and it was awkward being in someone else's house all the time, even when it was people we knew as well as Helen and Steve's family. We didn't know what to do with all the hours in the day to distract ourselves from thinking about Mum and we wanted to be back amongst our friends and filling our minds with other distractions. But the school authorities said we had to stay away for a day because they wanted to make an official announcement about it at assembly first and they thought it would be difficult for us if we were there. Because we had been mentioned in the paper they thought it was appropriate to tell eleven hundred other people, most of whom had had no idea who we were until that moment, all the intimate details of our family tragedy. The idea struck us as a bit strange but they were adamant that it was the right way to handle things and we were left sitting around the house for another day, wondering what would happen to us next.

When they made the announcement to the whole school, they also said that if any of our friends felt too traumatised by the news they should come forward and they would be offered support. We couldn't quite understand why they thought anyone else would need any support. A few of our friends knew Mum because of our activities, but virtually none of them had ever met Dad. No one was offering any counselling to Isobel and me, so why would they offer it to other people?

Anyone at our school who hadn't seen it on the news or read about it in the papers got to hear about Mum's murder at assembly on Monday morning. We were told later that some of the teachers were actually crying during the announcement, as though they had lost a close friend or their own mother. Maybe they were crying for us rather than for Mum but I'd only been at the school for one term by then so none of them knew me particularly well. I guess they thought they could imagine how it might feel to suddenly find yourself with no home and no parents. The only thing was, Isobel and I weren't sure how we felt. The main sensation was still a sense of numbness and unreality, combined with a niggling anxiety about what would become of us now. I couldn't let myself think about missing Mum. Maybe I was too scared of what might come out if I opened the floodgates. We'd been brought up learning to keep control of our emotions and it seemed safest to continue doing so now for as long as I could.

Many years later, when I read the reports of psychologists who interviewed us in the months after Mum's death, I learned that they thought we were suffering from 'dissociation', which is a side effect of post-traumatic stress disorder. The feeling of emotional detachment we both experienced in the early days was a symptom of the way our brains were trying to protect us from the sheer horror of what we'd been through. It's a phenomenon that is fairly common following huge trauma, and it's something that would continue to affect us in different ways for years to come, making it difficult for us to trust anyone apart from each other. At that stage I just felt that I was watching a movie of events that I wasn't really part of.

Chapter Ten

Isobel

On the Tuesday they let us go back to school, which was a relief to me because I had a running competition that I didn't want to miss that afternoon. It might sound strange, but Alex and I were craving distractions from what had happened and if there was one thing Mum had always drilled into us it was that there was no excuse for missing commitments and letting other people down. We had never been allowed to take days off sick unless we were completely incapable of walking, and we knew that she would never have allowed us to use her death as an excuse to give up on the things that she had worked so hard to help us achieve. Working hard at school and never letting other people down in out-of-school activities were the most important things in the world to her; more important than having a happy or harmonious home, more important than her own peace of mind, in the end maybe even more important than her own life. We didn't know any other way to behave. Mum had never made a fuss about anything in her life, so why would we? To be honest, we wouldn't even have known how to begin.

I took after Mum in a lot of ways, one of which was a ferociously competitive streak. If I was beaten by anyone else in an exam or a race I would become really frustrated and cross with myself. I think that determination to be the best at everything helped to keep me going through those early, confusing and difficult days after the murder, powering my feet through the school gates when most other people would have stayed home and concentrated on trying to straighten out their heads and their emotional lives. I just decided to grit my teeth and get on with things.

The first time we walked into school together after the announcement in assembly, Alex and I could see people were staring at us, which felt strange. We had never been the sort of kids who wanted to draw attention to themselves. It was a bit as though we'd become accidental celebrities. Everyone knew who we were, even if we didn't always know who they were. I suppose that is what life is like for people who appear on television regularly. Random people we didn't know very well would come up to us with concerned expressions on their faces and ask if we were okay. It felt as though they wanted to be close to us just because our family had been in the papers, as if that made us interesting or exciting in some way and they hoped some of it would rub off on them. Some people seemed to like the idea of being involved in anything even remotely notorious.

People have remarked since that Alex and I were very quiet and withdrawn during this period. I suppose they expected us to break down and sob, but it didn't work like that. We had our moments but we kept them private, just between ourselves. In fact, we were more dazed than anything else, trying to sort out our thoughts and feelings, while at the same time trying to keep up with our schoolwork and not be too much of a burden to Helen and Steve. I remember wandering from one lesson to the next that first day, sitting down and hearing the teacher's words washing over me but not being able to focus for long enough on what they were saying to be able to make sense of it or remember anything. My concentration kept wandering off into a sort of no-man's land. It was like living in limbo. My mind was trying to take so much in, trying to sort it and make sense of it. We still didn't really know what had happened on the previous Friday because a lot of what had appeared in the papers had been speculation. How, for instance, had that first policeman known to turn up on the doorstep when he did? Why had Mum come home early from school? What had made Dad finally erupt so dramatically after so many years? When would we be able to go back home? What would happen to Dad now? Would we be his next victims? He had never made any secret of the fact that he hated me just as much as he hated Mum, so presumably he would like to see me dead too. I guess he knew we would be at Helen and Steve's and I did have moments of anxiety thinking he might come to get me.

Over the following days the police kept coming back to interview us whenever they thought of something new to ask, but we had no idea what was going on in their investigation beyond the tiny snippets of information they would let slip. Knowing that we were growing bored of going over the same questions time and time again, they started bribing us to co-operate by offering to get things for us from the house, like our mobile phones. It wasn't that we were being uncooperative; we were just tired of talking in circles without reaching any new conclusions and we longed to go back to being quiet, anonymous and private. I think they knew they were putting us under stress by constantly interrupting our school and home routine with their visits and they felt they should do something for us in return.

We were told we'd had a 'guardian ad liteum' assigned to us. I think that is a legal requirement for any children who find themselves in our position. This guardian's main job was to represent our views and our best interests in court if social services applied for a care order. Apparently our care proceedings were deemed to be complicated and so had to be held at a London High

117

Court rather than a local one, but no one explained any of this to us and our main concerns were about continuing with our daily lives and trying to find a level of normalcy. After school each day we went back home to our godparents' house and continued with all our usual after-school activities, just as we had done when Mum was around. It seemed strange that something so dramatic had happened and so much had changed, yet a percentage of our lives continued more or less as before. It gave us something to cling onto through those traumatic first weeks.

Helen has since told us how surprised she was that neither Alex nor I ever wanted to talk about how we felt and never shed a tear in front of her, but then I never saw her or Steve cry either; they just kept going, even though I know they must have missed Mum almost as much as we did. Like Mum, Helen was a very private woman who didn't like to talk about her feelings, at least not to us.

We saw social workers from time to time, and about a month after Mum died one of them blurted out something about Mum's suicide attempt. Alex hadn't known about this before. I looked at her aghast and thought, 'Oh, thanks very much!' As if poor Alex didn't have enough shocking news to cope, he had the trauma of finding out that Mum had tried to kill herself as well. The woman's lack of tact was unbelievable. Being Alex,

118

he seemed to take it in his stride but I always worry about what goes on beneath the surface with him.

I tried once or twice to get back into our house to retrieve more of my possessions, but whenever I got to the door there was always a policeman standing guard. When they eventually agreed, after a couple of weeks, to let us have some of our own clothes, they still wouldn't allow us back into the house to fetch them ourselves. A policeman was sent in with a list of the things we wanted, but of course he came back with all the wrong stuff.

Gradually we were piecing together more snippets of information about what might have happened that afternoon, although we still couldn't find out the whole truth because Dad was denying he could remember anything. From the moment the police came to the front door he claimed that he didn't recall anything of the incident. His story was that he could remember Mum coming home and he remembered telling her that he was just fixing the phone extension in Alex's room. The next thing he could recall was coming downstairs and finding Mum slumped over the waste bin and another bin in which we kept dog biscuits just near the back door in the kitchen.

'I assumed I must have done something,' he said in his statement, which was later played in court, 'so I rang the police.'

Why would that be his initial assumption if he didn't remember anything? When he saw Mum slumped there, wouldn't his first thought have been that she had fainted or fallen over? Why didn't he go to see what was wrong with her before calling the police? In fact she was lying there with his chisel still sticking out of her from the final blow, so if he had gone to look he would have known exactly what he had done. I felt angry and cheated when I heard he was denying any memory of events. We wanted to know what had happened and felt we had a right to know. Trust him to deny us even that!

We would eventually learn that he made two phone calls to the police that afternoon. The first must have been made just as we were finishing school, while I was searching around the changing rooms for my PE kit and Alex was coming out of his class and getting ready to start his saunter home. We heard recordings of the calls in court and in the first one he told the police clearly that he had killed his wife. I guess he must have expected that an announcement like that would bring them round in force within minutes, but they obviously didn't take the call seriously for some reason. I don't know how many false alarms they get in a day, with people claiming they have committed murders, but there was obviously something about the way he spoke to them which made them doubt he was genuine.

Every minute that he was waiting in the house for the police to arrive must have seemed like an hour as he imagined Alex and me drawing closer and getting out our keys to unlock the front door. After about fifteen minutes his nerve broke and he rang them again.

'My children are due home,' he warned them, 'they're going to be walking through the front door at any moment.'

He must have been able to picture us in the streets outside, getting closer and closer to the house, completely unaware of the scene that would be awaiting us if we weren't stopped. Why did he suddenly care about protecting us? Was he worried we would be traumatised at seeing our mother dead in the kitchen, her blood spattering the walls? He had never cared for a second about traumatising us before. Was he worried that he might attack us as well? Or was he worried we might attack him when we saw what he had done? Why did he not simply deadlock the door so we couldn't get in until the police arrived? Nothing to do with Dad's behaviour ever really made any logical sense and it certainly made no sense at all that afternoon.

Even after the second call the police still couldn't have been taking him very seriously because they only dispatched one man to the scene, and that was the guy who turned up on the doorstep at the same moment as Alex arrived home and put his key in the lock.

As the reality of our bereavement began to sink in, we asked if we could see Mum's body. They told us we would be able to see her after the three post-mortems were over, but then they seemed to forget about it. A month after her death, when preparations for her funeral were under way, we asked again and they said we couldn't see her now because the body had 'decomposed too much', which they thought would be too unsettling for us. I'm sure they could have covered up anything they thought would be too unpleasant for us, but they decided not to. I am also sceptical that she could have decomposed much as I presume the body was frozen or chilled or whatever they do in mortuaries.

Although they didn't intend to let us see her, the police still needed someone to identify the body. Helen and Steve refused to do it but Jillian, Mum's friend from school, agreed, even though she was surprised to be asked, imagining there would be other people from around our area the police would have gone to first.

I think if Alex and I could have seen her dead it would have given us at least a bit of closure. One of the hardest things for us to come to terms with is accepting that we will almost certainly never know what happened to her in the final few minutes of her life. The fact that she just vanished from our lives and the last time we saw her was when she was rushing to get out of the house on time that morning made it seem as though nothing had really ended for us. Seeing the body wouldn't have answered any of the questions that spun round and round in our heads whenever we weren't distracted, but it would still have helped to quieten them. Maybe it would have made everything seem more real. At the very least, I would have liked to stroke her hair one last time and whisper goodbye and that I loved her.

Chapter Eleven

Alex

The police cordons were left round our house even after the last police guard had been withdrawn. Despite the cordons, and despite the story being plastered all over the front pages of the local papers, the newsagent continued to deliver Sunday papers to the doorstep for me to distribute. We only realised that when we saw them stacked up outside on the doorstep in a news picture.

The computer Mum had bought us to help with our homework was taken away so they could check to see if Dad had written anything on it that might help to explain what had been happening between them, or give an insight into his state of mind at the moment when he finally snapped. The only thing they found that interested them was an odd story that Isobel had written about Mum and Dad arguing, which they duly trawled through in minute detail, looking for signs that she was disturbed by whatever had been going on in the family.

After studying it, they decided it just reflected her life. It probably did, but that was because we'd been leading disturbed lives in many ways for years, not because we were actually disturbed ourselves. Mostly we were just angry at the way Dad had treated us all and how he had deliberately sabotaged our family, something he had been trying to do for years before he finally succeeded in destroying everything.

Jillian, Mum's long-time lab assistant, proved to be a great friend to her and to us. Realising that we had been stranded with no money at all with which to pay for Mum to have a funeral, she took a collection at the school. The service was held in our local church about a month after Mum died. I was shocked when I got there to see how packed it was, mostly with people neither Isobel nor I had ever seen before. I think a lot of them must have been Mum's work colleagues; others were probably the parents of children at our school. All these strangers seemed to know who we were as we walked in, which made it even more of a surreal experience. The funeral directors must have announced that it was happening in the paper because Helen had warned us that the press might be there, looking for a follow-up story. Although I don't think they did turn up in the end there was so much happening that was beyond our understanding they may well have been there and we didn't notice them.

The organisers had asked us what songs we wanted sung at the service and whether we would like to say anything ourselves, a tribute to Mum. Neither of us fancied standing up in front of so many strangers and letting them into any more of our family secrets than they'd already been privy to through the media. In the end the head teacher from Mum's school agreed to speak about her, which was kind.

'Make sure you cry,' Helen whispered to Isobel as we walked through the crowd to our seats in the front row, but neither of us did. Not then, not in public. Helen must have thought it would reflect badly on us if we were seen to be coping too well. Not breaking down might have made us look heartless but that was never the way we did things. We were like Mum in that way. Even though it had been a month since the death, the sense of complete unreality and confusion prevailed. Everything felt as though it was completely out of our hands. No one really explained anything to us in words that we could understand. It was as if they didn't want to upset us so they just avoided talking about the subject that was uppermost in all our minds. Even as we walked into the church and took our seats we had no idea what would happen during the ceremony because neither of us had ever been to a funeral before, and we had even less idea what was going to happen afterwards.

Both of us found it hard to cry. Right from the beginning Dad had drummed it into us that we mustn't, that it was wimpish. When he and Mum were having their terrible fights and he was screaming and shouting at us, he would become even angrier if he saw tears welling up in our eyes.

'Don't cry!' he would yell and we would be frightened into straight-faced silence. After a while it became a habit. I don't remember ever seeing Mum cry and we tended to be practical about things anyway, just like her. I remember her falling over on an icy pavement once and cracking her head open badly. I could tell she was in real pain but still she didn't cry. It wasn't till Helen came round and told her that she really needed to get some stitches that she agreed to go to the hospital. It turned out she needed about twenty stitches.

I had a similar experience when I was with Isobel and her friend at the local swings one day. They were playing that game where you go really high and then jump off mid-swing and I wanted to copy them. Eventually they agreed to give me a turn but I was too small to pull it off and fell awkwardly, all my weight landing on my wrist. I didn't cry so they picked me up and dusted me off before going swimming together while I went home to play on my PlayStation. My arm really hurt but I didn't want to make a fuss because I assumed it would get better. By the time Isobel got back from swimming about two hours later I was in bed and my arm had turned black. Mum decided I had better go to the hospital and when the doctors investigated they discovered it was severely broken. I don't believe I shed a single tear through the whole event.

I think if small children never get fussed over when they cry, and maybe even get shouted at or worse, they soon learn that it's not worth doing and give up. You sometimes see pictures on television from orphanages in places like Eastern Europe where the children have been terribly neglected or abused and you very seldom hear them crying. They give up bothering because it never does them any good. Mum wasn't very demonstrative physically, rarely giving us cuddles, but it didn't matter because we were never in any doubt that she loved us. She dedicated her whole life to bringing us up as well as she possibly could, so it never occurred to us to worry about the fact that she wasn't physically affectionate.

We taught ourselves to distance our thoughts from our feelings even further as the years went by. If we hadn't done that we would have been sobbing all the time after Mum died and everything in our lives would have ground to a halt at that moment, probably including our education. We couldn't allow that to happen because that would have been a victory for Dad, who always wanted to show Mum that she was wasting her time with all the things she did for us. We cried quiet, private tears when we were on our own, but our main goal was to just get on with things as best we could.

Helen asked us whether Mum would have wanted to be buried or cremated, but we had no idea.

'What about your grandparents?' she asked. 'Were they cremated?'

We had no idea about that either. We thought cremation was probably the best idea, considering the state Mum's body was going to be in after the murder and the post mortem. Personally, I wasn't quite sure what happened at a cremation and it wasn't until a social worker, who we had never met before, told us at the end of the twenty-minute funeral service at the church that the cremation would follow next that I found out.

'Your godparents don't want to go to the crematorium,' she told us. 'Do you want to go?'

'Yes,' Isobel said firmly.

Both of us wanted to stay with Mum till the very last minute. It didn't seem right to send her off wherever she was going on her own. It was over half an hour's drive to the crematorium. We sat in a black car, following behind the hearse that held her coffin. No one else came on from the church, so it was just Isobel and me and two social workers who had never met Mum, who were there to witness her body departing on its final journey. I stared and stared at that coffin throughout the short ceremony at the crematorium, trying to picture Mum's body inside and wondering what it looked like now. Somehow it was hard to believe that she was in there. When a curtain came across and we heard the trundling sound of her coffin heading down to the furnace, I had a huge lump in my throat and tightness in my chest. I just gripped Isobel's hand as hard as I could to keep control.

The social workers took us back to the church again but everyone else had left by that stage. We found out later that some cousins of Mum's had been there for the service, but they didn't introduce themselves to us so we didn't even find out that they existed until later.

Jillian had put together a book of condolences, full of letters from people who had worked with Mum for years, talking about what an inspiring and dedicated teacher she was, and how much of herself she gave up to help her pupils. The letters were all full of praise for her vivacity and the way in which she brought her subjects to life when she taught; they talked about how she would jump around the classroom, animating otherwise dry topics, always happy and hyperactive. I know you expect people to be polite and say nice things after someone has died, but these letters seemed far more sincere and enthusiastic and affectionate than you would have expected. It was a strange feeling to read about our mother as if she was a completely different person to the woman who lived such a difficult life at home. In the last year or two of her life she had seemed so weary and run down and defeated when she was with us, but she must have come alive the moment she arrived at that school in a way she never could when she was at home and living under Dad's ominous shadow. By the time she got back to us in the evening she would have been working or driving for about twelve hours and what was left of her energy had been drained out of her.

One of the letters talked about how keen Mum had always been for girls to take their education seriously. 'She was passionate about getting girls to believe in themselves and use their abilities to their greatest advantage,' it read. That was definitely what she believed for herself and for Isobel, and she was equally determined that I should be given every possible educational opportunity that she could manage to provide, even though she sometimes doubted I would take as much advantage of my intelligence as I was capable of doing. There were times when teachers had trouble holding my attention.

It was very moving for us to read about the effect she'd had on other people's lives, people we knew nothing about, reminding us that she had lived a whole other life away from the unhappiness and drudgery of her marriage. Away from Dad's vindictive influence she was seen as someone special rather than someone despicable and hated. It made us appreciate even more just how much she had done for us over the years.

Jillian was our only link with Mum's past. She loved to talk about their early days together, and it was her who told us about the time Mum invited her and a few other colleagues to our house for supper and Dad came into the room stark naked. I don't think Mum ever invited anyone back to the house again after that, which was probably exactly the result that he had wanted to achieve. She kept in touch with us, sending Christmas and birthday presents every year. Even now, whenever we make contact with her she is always keen to know every detail of what has been going on in our lives and to support us in any way she can.

But Jillian was just a good woman and a kind friend. She didn't have any real responsibility for us. She didn't really know us at all. She lived miles away and had her own life to lead. Our life now was with Helen and Steve and we began to get used to it, falling into comfortable routines very similar to the ones we had always followed. Initially Alfie had been put into kennels while everyone worked out what to do with him, but Isobel and I kept pleading for him and eventually Helen weakened and let us bring him to their home. She had been reluctant initially because they had two dogs of their own, which they didn't want to upset. As usual it was poor old Alfie who got bullied because their dogs became fiercely territorial and wouldn't let him eat his meals. We were still happy to have him back, something of our old familiar

132

lives returned to us, and we hoped he would settle down eventually.

No one ever suggested for a moment that we should go anywhere else, so we assumed that was going to be our home until we left school. Mum had always said Helen and Steve would look after us if anything happened to her, so Isobel and I didn't give the matter any more thought. All we cared about was that we should be together and should have Alfie with us, and we tried to be as little trouble as possible. We just needed somewhere to do our homework and sleep after school and someone to help us get around to our various activities for a couple of years until Isobel was old enough to drive. Helen and Steve were taking over from Mum; that was what we told anyone who asked. We assured everyone we would be okay as long as we could stay together.

Our school lives and activities were continuing as normal and although it was awkward being a permanent guest in someone else's house, particularly when there was so much going on in everyone's heads that was being left unsaid, we were starting to think of it as our home. We knew that there had been a social worker visiting the house and we had seen her briefly, but no one explained why she was there or what her duties were towards us.

'Do you have any relatives?' this woman asked us one day, about six weeks after Mum died. 'Anyone you might be able to live with?'

She took us completely by surprise. Weren't we going to live with Helen and Steve then?

'No,' we explained, 'nobody. We never met Dad's family. We don't even know their names. And Mum was an only child. Our grandparents are both dead.'

Isobel vaguely remembered some relative of Mum's writing her a newsletter one Christmas, but she had no more information than that, apart from describing where she thought the letter might be. The social worker must have got permission from the police to go into the house because she found the letter and the woman turned out to be a cousin of Mum's. We eventually found out she had three cousins, all of whom had been receiving regular updates about us from Mum all through our lives. She had never mentioned them to us as far as we can remember. We can only think that Mum didn't want too much contact with any of her relatives in case they came to visit and met Dad. Or maybe, like Jillian, they had come to the house and Dad had made it very clear that he didn't want them to come back. It was better for her to keep everyone separate and at a distance from one another than to risk the embarrassment of Dad behaving threateningly and embarrassing her.

Towards the end of February the social worker who had been assigned to us arrived at the house and told us that some people were going to be coming in a couple of hours who wanted to meet us. No one explained exactly why they were coming, but Isobel and I realised that everything was about to change again.

The couple were a lot older than Mum and Dad. They were both overweight, the man only a bit over five feet tall but weighing nearly twenty stone. The woman was taller than him, but she must have been around sixteen stone. They introduced themselves to us but we were both in such a state of confusion and panic that their names went in one ear and out the other. We didn't feel that we could ask them to tell us again, so we just kept quiet and waited, hoping someone would call them by their names and give us a clue. No one did, so the awkwardness continued.

I wasn't really concentrating on the conversations going on around us. I had no idea who they were or what they had to do with us, but I did notice they were telling us about their home as if they were trying to convince us how much we would like it, and it started to dawn on me that we might be going to live with them. No one had even mentioned 'fostering' up till then. I'm not sure I would have known what the word meant. Neither Helen nor Steve had said anything about what would happen to us next, or so much as hinted that we might not be staying with them. We were completely dumb-struck, unable to understand what was going on, unable even to think how to phrase the many questions that were circling round inside our heads.

The visitors asked us what we thought of them, which was an impossible question to answer so we just shrugged and laughed nervously. It was at that stage that we realised they were planning to pack our things and take us with them there and then. They were even agreeing to take Alfie as well, which we later discovered was an unusual thing for a foster family to agree to.

'Will we be able to go to the same school, and keep up all our after-school activities?' I asked, and they agreed that we would. We explained that we would need to be driven to different venues virtually every night of the week and they smiled and agreed that that was absolutely fine.

Isobel and I didn't know what to say after that but we asked for a little time to think about it all and get used to the idea, and this was agreed.

For some strange reason, things kept happening to us on the eleventh of each month. Mum had been killed on the 11th of January and her funeral was held on the 11th of February. On the 11th of March, two weeks after we were first introduced to them, and still not able to remember what they had said their names were, we found ourselves in a car being driven to our new home with our new foster parents.

To this day Helen has never explained to us when she made the decision that we couldn't stay with her, or whether she had never intended it to happen in the first place. I suppose from their perspective they may never have expected to take us on full time. We arrived at a moment when they were shocked and grieving over Mum's death as well. I can see that it is hard to have two new people suddenly arriving in your family without warning, and the sleeping arrangements had been a bit cramped with us and the other three children who still lived at home. It just seemed strange that no one ever explained to us what was being planned for us. Maybe everyone assumed someone else had told us. Isobel and I still feel anger towards Helen when we think back on it. I would certainly behave differently if the children of a friend of mine were orphaned. I'm pretty sure I would have a bit more humanity.

Chapter Twelve

Isobel

We drove for about twenty minutes from Helen and Steve's house, leaving Redditch behind us and heading towards Evesham, some ten miles away. We had no idea where we were going and didn't feel that we could really ask. I was beginning to wonder how we would be able to get back to our school and our activities if we ended up living too far away. Had anyone thought that through? As soon as they had seen us into the house Helen and our social worker left, hardly even stopping to say goodbye after they had handed us over to our new foster parents. We didn't hear from Helen again for a good few months after that, which felt strange because we had seen her almost every day when we'd lived in Redditch, even before we moved in with them. One by one, it seemed, the familiar faces from our former lives were vanishing and being replaced by strangers.

We assumed that Helen didn't come round because she was giving us time to settle in but later she told me that she stayed away because she thought the foster parents were 'weird' and she 'got a bad vibe off the man'. I was pretty shocked when she said that. Surely that was all the more reason to pop back now and then to check that we were all right? I suppose everyone has their own way of dealing with grief. The foster parents had their own social worker, and she was there when we arrived at our new home.

The house was very similar to the one we had been born and brought up in, although they would soon be doing lots of work to extend it at the back. We each had our own bedrooms. There was also a front room that they didn't use very much and Alex and I pretty much colonised it from day one as our own private space and sanctuary. We didn't know what was expected of us or how we should interact with these people whose house and lives we had suddenly been thrust into. We didn't want to get in their way and so we would disappear into the front room together and close the door until it was time to do something specific like eat a meal or go to bed, talking to each other all the time, keeping ourselves separate.

We'd been there about two weeks before we found out that our foster parents' names were Cathy and Pete. It must have made us seem really rude because we were just saying 'oi' if we wanted to attract their attention, too embarrassed to ask after so long. Eventually the penny must have dropped.

'We've noticed,' the woman said, 'that you never use our names. Do you actually know what they are?'

There was no point lying. I think, because we were the first foster kids they had had, they were as much at sea about how to deal with the situation as we were. They had been on holiday the week before they took us on, so the social workers hadn't been able to brief them as thoroughly as they might have done on our background. As a result, they had found out most of the details of our situation from newspaper articles on the Internet, which gave our family history a very negative spin, suggesting that we were all horribly dysfunctional. Cathy kept trying to quiz us about our background in the early days, asking loads of personal questions that we didn't want to answer. I suppose our reluctance to open up was disappointing to them, and may even have seemed rude, but it's just the way we were. As far as we were concerned they were strangers and we wouldn't have dreamed of telling them all about life at home with Mum and Dad just to satisfy their curiosity.

Both of them liked to drink and would consume several bottles of wine between them during the course of an evening. It was a puzzle to us how they had passed the tests needed to be accepted as foster parents, but maybe the authorities had become desperate when they realised our godparents had no desire to keep us, and couldn't find anyone more suitable who was willing to take on two potentially traumatised teenagers and a dog. They had each had children themselves, although not together, and their children were all grown up by then, with their own families. Some of them came to meet us soon after we arrived, but they didn't seem to want to get involved in their parents' latest 'scheme'. It felt as though we were being paraded in front of even more people we didn't know and we couldn't think of a thing to say, so we probably struck them as two pretty dull children.

If the grandchildren were staying at the house we would be used as a baby-sitting service once Cathy and Pete had started drinking in the evening, or if they were throwing a dinner party and didn't want to be disturbed. We used to be able to hear them talking to their friends about us in the dining room, as if we were an interesting case study, which I suppose is pretty much what we were to them. Their guests never came through to introduce themselves though. Maybe we gave off a hostile vibe, but I don't think so. We were just quiet, as always. People who were told our story but didn't actually talk to us themselves must have been left with the impression that we were troubled children from a dysfunctional background, but that wasn't how we felt. We thought we were getting on with our lives reasonably well; we just weren't sure how to ask for the help we needed in order to do better, help that we had grown so used to receiving unconditionally from Mum.

Their drinking didn't usually make Cathy and Pete unpleasant or aggressive, as it used to make Dad, but it did mean that if we talked to them about anything during the evening they would quite often have forgotten about it by the next day. We relied on them a lot to give us lifts to and from our activities, even more than Mum and Helen because of the distances now involved, but they would often forget we had asked them, or would complain that they weren't able to have a drink because of having to drive. Gradually we had to give up our out-of-school activities just because we could no longer be relied upon to get there as regularly as we once had. It made us appreciate even more how reliable Mum had been all those years. Their promises to do all they could to help us keep up our activities went by the wayside quite quickly; it was soon obvious they had underestimated just how much effort would be involved. I think a lot of people underestimate how much effort it takes to be as conscientious a parent as Mum was to us.

'It's so far,' they would complain. 'Can't you join clubs that are more local?'

Of course we could have done that, but then we would have lost all the friends we had made over the years and we would have had no shared history with our new teammates. We would have been cast even further adrift from our past. We already felt isolated by moving so far away, and losing those ties was cutting us even further adrift from our friends and from our past. In the end, however, Cathy and Pete made us feel so guilty about inconveniencing them that it was easier just to give in and stop asking for lifts. Neither of us felt like going out and starting again at new clubs just yet, especially now it took us so much longer to get back and forth to school each day. Within a month of being with them we weren't doing any extra activities at all. We would just go to school in the morning and come back in the afternoon, do our homework and then sit together in the front room, waiting for bedtime.

We thought about contacting our social worker to try to explain how we felt, but we didn't know how to do that. If we asked Cathy and Pete they immediately demanded to know why we wanted to contact her, as if we were planning to report them for not doing their job properly. We never wanted to upset them unnecessarily, so we kept quiet and concentrated all our efforts on our schoolwork instead. They did drive us to and from school, because the bus routes took too long, but they grumbled a lot about that too, even though they'd known from the start that we wanted to stay at the same school. They wanted us to love and respect them as if they were our real parents, but they didn't actually want to make all the sacrifices that a real mother like Mum has to make.

'Why don't you spend more time with us?' they wanted to know. 'Why do you always shut yourselves away in the front room? You're always talking to each other but you never talk to us. We're all one family now.'

When the question was put to us as bluntly as that it was hard to find an answer. We had just been following our instincts, huddling together for comfort and mutual support because that was what we had always done. It had always been Alex and me against the world. We'd had Mum on our team, of course, and Alfie, and our friends at school, but the most constant elements for both of us were each other. We didn't want to sit watching TV with Cathy and Pete every evening while they guzzled their wine. It was a bonus to us that they had a second front room where we could keep ourselves to ourselves.

I think our new parents would have liked us to tell them our problems, maybe give them a hug now and then and allow them to comfort us when we were sad, but we had never done that with Mum and Dad so we certainly weren't going to start with two virtual strangers. They tried too hard to get to know us, but their questions made me uneasy and I hated it when they were critical of Mum. I became very protective of everything to do with our past. I knew how dysfunctional it had all been, but that didn't mean I wanted other people to tell me it was. I didn't want them judging Mum, or even Dad for that matter. I felt criticisms of them were criticisms of us. It was as if they believed Mum was some sort of bad person for allowing the things that happened to happen. While Cathy and Pete probably believed they were attempting to bond with us, their efforts made us all the more silent and insular as we tried to protect ourselves from criticism.

They kept saying things like: 'I can't get my head round why your Mum didn't just leave him.'

It didn't seem to occur to them that we had already wondered the same thing a million times, and we didn't need to be reminded of it every day by someone who had never even met Mum. How do you explain to someone who thinks completely differently that Mum was both proud and stubborn and didn't want to admit to the outside world that her marriage had failed so catastrophically? She would rather have kept on working at things than give up. The foster parents would never have been able to understand that, even if we had been able to find the words to explain it. Mum's greatest concern was always to keep things even and stable so that Alex and I would have as little disruption to our education as possible.

'We can't understand why you were forced to do so many activities all the time,' was something else they kept saying when they couldn't be bothered to drive us somewhere we wanted to go.

But we were never forced to do anything. Mum might have encouraged us, and she might have got annoyed when we gave things up for no obvious reason, but she had never forced us to take part in any activities. We did them because we enjoyed them, and whenever we stopped enjoying them we gave them up. We resented being judged by these two people who still didn't know us at all. Sometimes it felt as though they were jealous of our past family life and wanted to reconstruct us in their own image as their own children. They wanted us to hate our own family and our own past so much we would be grateful for any love and support they might be offering us now. They couldn't understand how we could still love Mum so much when, to their way of thinking, she had let us down and given us much less than they were willing to give.

Alex was my whole family by that stage and I didn't feel either of us needed anyone else emotionally; we just needed food and a roof over our heads and someone to drive us to school so that we could continue to function in the world and finish our educations. It made for an awkwardness in the relationship with our foster parents that none of us knew how to solve. We didn't feel we knew them enough to trust them with all the personal stuff that was going on in our minds and because we had each other we didn't feel the need to share the pain or confusion with anyone else, particularly two complete strangers. They wanted to look after Alex as if they were his parents and they resented the fact that he didn't need them to do that because he had me. I used to tuck him into bed each night and give him a goodnight kiss and I think they felt that should have been their role, but they were still strangers to us. They wanted to become our family, but we just wanted to get on with them in a civil manner; we weren't looking for a replacement for our real family.

It wasn't as though Cathy and Pete didn't try to do the right things at the beginning. They used to take us out for walks with the dog, for example, but they never took us separately, so we were always talking to each other, deliberately avoiding any attempts they might make to bond with us. Perhaps if they had been more experienced at fostering they would have known better how to win us over individually, breaking down the many barriers we had erected around ourselves. They tried very hard in many ways.

In the morning they would make us enormous cooked breakfasts but we just weren't used to it, always having grabbed bowls of cereal as we got ready for school. They also cooked a lot of hearty meat-based dinners, like spaghetti Bolognese, and I had been vegetarian for years, but I didn't feel I could tell them that at first. When they did find out, they seemed to think it was more evidence that Mum hadn't looked after us properly, and told me that if I wanted food that was different from what they were eating, I would have to cook it myself. I could see that they were hurt by our inability to enjoy their hospitality, but we just couldn't eat as much as they did, and preferred to make simple dishes for ourselves.

From time to time we were visited by psychologists who were preparing reports for a care proceedings court case. One of these interviews took place with our foster parents in the room.

'So what is better about your life now that you're in foster care,' the psychologist asked, 'compared to your old life?'

Alex and I said nothing. We were aware that our silence sounded rude because of everything Cathy and Pete were doing for us, but we didn't want to say anything that was disrespectful to Mum's memory. We weren't willing to be led into saying we hadn't always been happy with her, because it wouldn't have been true.

'We get more pocket money,' Alex said eventually, when the silence had become unbearable, which I guess probably made us sound mercenary and ungrateful.

To begin with, Pete was nicer to us than Cathy. He was a bit like a big, cuddly teddy bear of a man, giving us money and organising holidays and treats, but sometimes things that started out being well-meant ended up creating misunderstandings between us. During that first summer, they took us to visit a friend of theirs who had a speed boat that towed 'doughnut boats' around a lake. We had a fantastic day being pulled around, bumping into each other and falling off into the water, screaming with laughter all the time. By the end of the day our arms were covered in bruises. We had a visit from a social worker a couple of days later and I made a joke about the bruises while our foster parents were in the room. I was trying my best to lighten the atmosphere between us all by making little jokes because Alex was finding it harder and harder to pretend that he liked them and was falling more and more silent during social worker visits.

'Look what they've been doing to us,' I laughed, displaying the black and blue patches, before adding that I was only joking.

Cathy and Pete were utterly mortified that I would say such a thing, snapping that I made it sound as though they were abusing us. They completely ignored the fact that I had made it clear I was joking and that the social worker already knew the bruises had come from the boating. She obviously understood that because my comment was never written down in our case notes. However, they brought that incident up over and over again, using it as evidence that we were liars, as they became increasingly disillusioned with us.

A few months later there was an evening when Pete had had a lot to drink and was becoming quite aggressive towards his wife. I was genuinely worried for her, remembering some of the scenes I had witnessed between Mum and Dad when we were small. Cathy was sitting with me and crying because of the way he was behaving, making all sorts of drunken allegations against her.

'Why don't you sleep in the spare room tonight?' I suggested to her, thinking that would give him a chance to cool down.

Somehow that got turned round and reported to the social workers as me 'wanting her to sleep on the sofa in order to replicate the situation we had experienced at home'. This was despite the fact that she admitted she couldn't remember the incident properly the morning after. She certainly didn't mention to them that she had stripped completely naked in front of me before getting into the bed, an event I found extremely embarrassing, not least because she was so grossly overweight.

'You're trying to make our lives hell,' she accused me, 'just like it was in your house.'

The social workers always seemed to believe everything our foster parents told them about us, and never believed anything we said. It was as if we were banging our heads against a brick wall all the time, trying to explain how we felt and what we needed from the relationship. I've got our case notes now and reading about that time, it is obvious that the adults all thought that the breakdown in our relationship with our foster parents was caused almost wholly by us, not them.

By the winter of 2002–3, they had started actively to resent us for not appreciating them enough. Everything about our past seemed to annoy them from then on. They had strong anti-religious views and when they found out that we had been regular churchgoers all through our childhood they talked in a derogatory manner about it. I didn't feel strongly enough about Christianity to believe I needed to defend it, but I didn't like the suggestion that Mum had done something wrong by involving us in church activities. They seemed to be looking down on us, as if believing in God made us stupid, even though we were still children. They could never resist making snide comments about it whenever the opportunity arose. Everyone, I feel, deserves to have their views respected, especially in a situation where you are trying to build a relationship of mutual trust.

It was beginning to feel as if everyone was judging the way we had lived when Mum was alive. There had been the newspaper articles that made the whole family sound really dysfunctional, and then the curious looks we would get at school, and the way social workers we knew nothing about seemed to be organising our lives from behind the scenes without even discussing it with us, and now we had foster parents pronouncing judgements on our past. I was beginning to feel very defensive of Mum. She had put in so many years of self-sacrifice and hard work for us, for her pupils at school and for Dad, that she didn't deserve to be judged by anyone, especially people who didn't know the whole story in the way we did. The more people said things like that, the more Alex and I would protest about how much fun we had all had together over the years, trying to redress the balance in favour of Mum's memory. The more they disrespected our past, the more determined I became not to enjoy anything they might try to do for us now.

At some point we were told we had been assigned a solicitor, who would liaise with our 'guardian ad liteum' in order to represent our views in the care proceedings. That solicitor realised that no one had thought about sorting out Mum's estate, which only consisted of her share of the house but would still give us a lump of money to help us get established in our adult lives. We kept having meetings with people who we assumed would advise us, but nothing happened once the meetings were over. It seemed almost impossible to get anything done and move forward with our lives.

At the same time, I was struggling with my own private grief. My feelings were all complicated and mixed-up: I felt angry with Dad, of course, and with Helen and Steve, Cathy and Pete; I missed Mum terribly and longed for her with a physical pain that was almost unbearable at times; and I felt determined to protect Alex as best I could. Sometimes I had flashbacks to horrible memories of arguments between Mum and Dad, or other terrifying things that had happened at home, and I'd frequently have horrific nightmares about what

Mum must have gone through during her final minutes of life. I kept all this bottled up and just tried to deal with it on my own. I didn't know what else to do. Who would I have talked to?

Years later, I read in my psychological reports from the time that I was suffering from a raft of disorders, particularly post-traumatic stress and obsessive-compulsive disorder, brought on by what I had gone through over the years of living with Dad and the awful circumstances of Mum's death. All of this must surely have been exacerbated by the lack of understanding and consideration I experienced in Cathy and Pete's home. I was having trouble keeping my head above water, without the added stress of continual arguments under their roof.

Chapter Thirteen

Alex

When our foster parents first told us they would give us twenty pounds a week pocket money each from whatever they were being paid by social services to look after us, it sounded like loads of money compared with what Mum had been able to give us. We soon realised, however, that it wasn't that generous because we were expected to buy all our clothes out of it. We also had to pay any bus fares in and out of town if we wanted to see our friends, which meant the money hardly lasted at all. We could only afford to socialise once a week at the most.

We were never quite sure how Cathy and Pete had made their money in the first place, but they talked a lot about stocks and shares they had bought or sold, and property too. He stayed at home all the time but she had an office job in London, which she would disappear off to on the train every day. I think it was something to do with a housing association. Even though they seemed to have a fair bit of money they were always on the lookout for a bargain, buying knock-off trainers and things like that.

Isobel took her GCSEs in May 2002, just four months after Mum's murder, and managed to get all A's and A stars, apparently putting her amongst the top two or three per cent in the country. Whatever foundations Mum had laid in her when it came to working and not allowing anything to distract her had paid off. She revised like a demon in the final month before the exams to make up for all the distractions we had had over the previous months. When the results came through, she went very quiet and I know that she was missing Mum terribly and feeling desperately sad that she wasn't there, because she would have been so proud.

I was doing okay too; the teachers certainly didn't seem to have any worries or complaints about my work. I liked doing schoolwork because it gave my life some continuity and structure when everything else seemed to be uncertain and up in the air. By keeping our eyes on the goals that Mum had set so firmly for us in the early years we were able to shut out the things that were more difficult to deal with, like emotions, for most of the day. I still seemed to give people the impression that I was messing around a bit in class, so even Isobel was surprised when it came to my turn to sit GCSEs and I did much better than predicted. They'd thought I would only get E's but I managed mostly A's and B's with one C.

It was harder to keep friendships going when we were so far out of town. Isobel had started to lose touch with some of her friends anyway because she had chosen to do sciences at A level and most of them had gone for the arts and drama subjects. If you aren't in the same classes as people you inevitably start to drift apart, particularly if you aren't living in the same area as them. Isobel then lost contact with her other friends simply because she was never available when they wanted to go out together, and our foster parents weren't prepared to drive us around just to socialise. We didn't know anyone who lived in the streets around our foster parents' house because they all went to different schools, so we were pretty much on our own whenever we were at home, sitting around the house, feeling bored. It was a new experience for us. Whatever might have gone on at our family home, we had never had time to become bored.

Every so often Cathy and Pete would do enormously extravagant spur-of-the-moment things, like taking us on holidays to Majorca and to Cuba. They did it because they were used to having four holidays a year themselves and once they had taken on the responsibility of looking after us, they had no option but to take us along. It was kind of them to spend the money, but if they had asked us what we would actually have liked to do, I don't think going on holiday with them would have been high on our list. What we really wanted was more help and support so we could continue to live our normal lives in England, seeing our friends and doing all the things we had always done. Family holidays can be stressful even when you go with your own parents, never mind a couple you hardly know and don't particularly like.

I think Cathy felt much the same because once we were on holiday she would almost immediately become irritated that Isobel and I were hanging around them too much, being a bit nervous to go off on our own in a foreign country. We had never been abroad with Mum so I think it is understandable that we were wary.

'Why don't you go off and do something?' she would protest, wanting some holiday time to herself. Ironically, it was the opposite of what she had been saying at home when she was trying to persuade us to spend more time with them.

It was a bit of a Catch 22 situation for her because I dare say the money they earned for having us was what made a lot of their lifestyle possible, but then having two teenagers lurking around was spoiling that lifestyle once she had it. Isobel and I did do some things on our own, like going on a scuba-diving course together, but there were a lot of hours in the day when we were just relaxing around the hotels, like all the other families there.

I can imagine we came across as being a bit ungrateful and resentful at times like that, not able to get into the holiday spirit in the way they might have hoped we would. There was a canal boat holiday too, which forced us all into very close proximity. It took us three and a half days to cover a distance that would have taken us an hour to drive. We had real trouble seeing the point of the exercise. Cathy and Pete would always end up being angry with us for obviously not enjoying ourselves as much as they had hoped we would. I guess we must have been a disappointment to them, but the very fact that they thought we would enjoy it showed they knew as little about us as we did about them.

It was claustrophobic being in the house when Isobel and I had such different expectations of what we wanted from the relationship to Cathy and Pete. We were typical teenagers in many ways and tensions that in an ordinary family would have been balanced with an underlying love, started to flare up through the polite façade we were all trying hard to maintain. There was one occasion when Cathy got so annoyed with Isobel after she had had a few drinks that she chased her upstairs with a wine-glass still in her hand. Thinking she was going to get the glass lobbed at her, Isobel ran upstairs and took refuge in her room, shaking uncontrollably, suddenly having a flashback to all the angry, unpredictable altercations with Dad.

Cathy burst into the room and was so angry she kept hitting Isobel on the arm with the base of the empty glass. Isobel didn't respond, just staying stock still, which seemed to annoy Cathy even more, making her hit even harder until she eventually got bored and went back downstairs. The next morning when Isobel woke up she found she had massive bruising stretching from her elbow to her shoulder. It was so bad her teacher noticed it in school and took her to one side to ask how it had happened.

'I just walked into a door,' Isobel said, not wanting to start a whole load more trouble. There was a social worker due at the house a few days later and Cathy and Pete told Isobel to wear a long-sleeved jumper for the visit so the bruises wouldn't be visible.

From then on we were both walking on eggshells all the time, just as we used to around Dad, aware that we might spark off their anger and resentment at any moment.

Early in 2003, Isobel realised that the solicitor we had hired to sort out Mum's estate didn't seem to be achieving anything. She was sixteen by then, almost seventeen, and she took the decision to sack him and handle everything herself. When she rang to tell him that she didn't want him working on our case any more he actually thanked her, saying that it was so complicated he had felt over-whelmed by everything that needed to be done. I remember wondering how Isobel was going to manage on her own if a qualified solicitor felt overwhelmed but she was getting quite good at that sort of thing. She then had a battle with that first solicitor because he was trying to charge us for his time when he hadn't actually done anything. She stood up for herself and managed to resolve the situation, which I thought was pretty impressive.

She found us a new solicitor in Evesham but it would still be several years before the whole thing was sorted out because there were all sorts of complications. For example, we found out that Mum's direct debits were still leaving her bank account six months after she died and her bank wanted us to repay them. Isobel seemed to spend her whole life chasing things like Mum's birth certificate, marriage certificate and death certificate. The social services wanted to be my financial guardian and trustee since Isobel was still under 18 but we didn't trust them to make the best decisions. There was so much paperwork to wade through and so many phone calls to make, so much waiting for people to come back to us and then chasing them up that it sometimes seemed as though we would never reach the end of the maze, that we would be sorting out the mess Dad made the day Mum died for the rest of our lives. I don't know what I would have done if I hadn't had Isobel to bear the brunt of it.

Chapter Fourteen

Isobel

The antipathy between us and our foster parents was growing all the time and it was becoming increasingly difficult to maintain the charade that we liked one another. I could tell how much I annoyed them, particularly Cathy. If we ever sat next to each other on the sofa, watching telly, she would hold my arm and pinch me or dig her nails in painfully. It was as if she couldn't resist the urge to inflict pain and show me how she felt about me and how frustrated I made her feel, even if we weren't actually arguing about anything at the time. Only later, when I was given our social services files of the time, did I read that she was saying it was me doing that to her rather than the other way round. That made me absolutely furious!

It was when I protested one evening that she was hurting me that she got angry and chased me up the stairs and hit me with her wineglass. It was as if she believed I was making the whole thing up just to make her look bad. I never told any of the social workers about the way our relationship was breaking down, mainly because I had no idea how to get in contact with them without asking our foster parents for the telephone number, a request that had never gone down well in the past. For several months Alex and I didn't even have a social worker assigned to us, and on the rare occasion when someone did turn up they would always talk to us in front of Cathy and Pete, so there was no chance for us to say what was truly on our minds without risking offending them even more.

Most of the time I kept quiet and tried not to argue, bottling up all my frustrations and resentments, hoping that I could keep things peaceful that way. But by just sitting there and saying nothing I probably appeared sullen and rude, and if I got up and left the room in order to remove myself from the temptation to respond, it would look as if I was storming off in a tantrum. I couldn't find a way of handling the day-to-day situation that didn't give the wrong impression and make things worse between us.

It was so frustrating to be dependent on people we didn't really like and who didn't really like us. We were being treated as if we were still small children even though I was now almost seventeen, virtually an adult. Nobody would talk openly and honestly to us about what was going on, and it was only as the date of Dad's trial drew near that we discovered all the adults around us knew something devastating about us that we didn't know and could never have imagined.

Social services and the police had all known about this particular bombshell since looking at Mum's medical reports. Jillian and Helen had also told the police in their interviews. Even our foster parents had known and never said a word, which was very out of character. We later found out that the police had hoped the doctors would tell us the terrible truth, but the doctors had refused and batted the responsibility straight back to them. They then passed the task on to a psychologist who worked at The Priory in London, the place where all the celebrities go to deal with their addiction problems. We had no idea this was all going on and so in January 2003 when we were told we were going to London to see a psychologist we assumed it was just for another routine interview to gather evidence for the care proceedings.

We had only met this man twice before, when social services first needed a psychological report on us for the care courts, so it is hard to imagine why everyone thought he was the best person to break such a distressing bit of news to us. We were told we were going to see him again, but no one said why and we didn't bother to ask. We had grown used to going where we were told without understanding any of the logic behind what was happening. Our foster parents drove us to London in their car and two social workers followed independently. We didn't bother to ask any questions; it never did any good and we didn't know what to ask anyway.

'We need to tell you this now,' the psychologist said when we finally arrived at his office in The Priory, 'because otherwise you will find out in the courtroom. Your mother had Huntington's disease.'

The news meant nothing to us. Neither of us had ever heard of Huntington's, but he went on to explain what it would have meant to Mum and what it might mean to us. The disease, he said, is caused by the degeneration of nerve-cell clusters in the brain. As it takes a hold the affected person starts to make rapid, jerky, involuntary movements and they gradually descend into dementia. Most people don't start to see any symptoms until they are about thirty-five years old. The disease is hereditary and there is always a fifty-fifty chance that any child of a sufferer will also have it. That meant the chances were that either Alex or I would have inherited it, if not both of us. There was a test for it, the psychologist explained, but we weren't allowed by law to take that test until we were eighteen. So we now knew there was a fifty-fifty chance we had a degenerative disease but I wasn't allowed to find out for sure until my eighteenth birthday in a year and a quarter's time, and Alex would have to live with the uncertainty for another two years after that.

Huntington's only happens to between five and eight people in every hundred thousand. Most of those diagnosed only live for between fifteen and thirty years after the onset of the symptoms. There is no known cure. The symptoms usually start with the sufferer making random grimaces and twitches and becoming clumsy. As the dementia sets in they become irritable and difficult, have trouble making decisions, lose their memory and are overcome with feelings of apathy. Images of Mum in the last year or two of her life kept flashing in front of my eyes as I listened to the psychologist's description. Had she had any symptoms of the disease? Or was her short fuse just due to exhaustion and stress?

Ten minutes after we had walked into his office, having informed us of all these stark facts, the psychologist said goodbye. We returned to the cars to drive back out of London as we tried to take in everything we had been told. Thinking back, I guessed that this must have been what had killed our grandmother early, not cancer, and I also realised that Mum must have known she had it. When she became so depressed and tried to kill herself she must already have known that she would soon be an invalid and would probably die prematurely anyway. She must have been afraid she was going to be a burden to us and an increasing source of annoyance to Dad. So by taking her life she wouldn't have been acting as selfishly as we had thought; she might actually have been thinking of what was best for Alex and me all along. Since she hadn't told us about her breast cancer until the day of the operation, it was no surprise that she had kept the Huntington's a secret as well.

Staring at the backs of our foster parents' heads in the car home it was hard to imagine that they had known about the Huntington's for so many months when we hadn't a clue about it. I didn't hold back on telling them how annoyed I was with them. In some ways I had started to feel I could trust them over the previous few months, even if I didn't particularly like them, and now I found they had been keeping a secret like this, I felt massively betrayed and told them so.

'The police and the social workers told us we mustn't tell you,' they explained. 'They said there was no point because you couldn't take the test yet anyway.'

'So why have they changed their minds now?'

'Because it's all going to come out in court.'

In a strange way the news didn't make us feel particularly frightened – just angry. After everything that had happened to us over the previous year it just felt like one more thing we had to contend with, something else we had no power over. In a way I thought that perhaps after so much had happened to us it would be too much of a coincidence for one or both of us to have a life-threatening disease as well. Surely fate couldn't be that unkind to us after we'd lost our mother in such a traumatic way?

So, as usual, I put it to the back of my mind, deciding I would deal with the problem once I was old enough to take the test.

The date of Dad's trial kept being put off as the police tried to build their case against him and his defence lawyers tried to build up medical evidence about him and about Mum to rationalise and excuse what he had done. To us it seemed like one thing after another holding them up. It felt as though no one in the whole adult world was in any hurry to find out exactly what had happened in our house that day and to punish Dad for what he had done. Until the trial happened the whole house belonged to Dad because as her husband he would automatically inherit Mum's half, which meant we owned little more than the clothes we stood up in.

During those thirteen months of waiting in his comfortable remand prison, Dad had had time to think up a sort of defence with his lawyers, but none of it made much sense to anyone else who listened to it. At moments he seemed to be pleading with the authorities to jail him because that would take away all the worries that he had found so difficult to cope with while surviving in the outside world. We could believe that he was being sincere when he asked to be sent down. Jail would suit his personality; he was never a man who wanted to talk to people if he didn't have to. He wouldn't have started any aggro with other prisoners unless someone else

167

picked on him first, and they would soon learn to give him a wide berth. Even when he was living with us he had always behaved as though he was already in a prison, spending most of his days in his 'cell', passing us by on the landing and not even acknowledging us, always seeking out his own space away from us.

'"Give me twenty years" – pleads wife killer,' was the way the headline writers portrayed his plea.

The authorities weren't keen on us attending the court, saying that we shouldn't really miss so much school, but we fought hard to be allowed in. We were both in a good position with our schoolwork and exams and it wasn't going to affect us too much if we missed a few days. We thought that to be reading about the case in the papers and having to go into school knowing that everyone else was seeing and hearing what was said would be much harder than actually hearing it for ourselves. Thank God we did go because there was lots of bad stuff about Mum said at the beginning and we wouldn't have wanted to go back to school until the whole story had been told, and we had got our version across.

We were fed up with being left on the outside of things that were vitally important to us while everyone else got to talk about us as if we had no minds of our own. It was our family and our lives they were all going to be discussing; why shouldn't we be there to listen and put our points of view? When it was decided we could give evidence as witnesses, it seemed even more ridiculous that we should do that and not be allowed to stay and hear what everyone else was saying about us and about our Mum. Eventually they gave in and we were given permission to attend the whole trial.

Our barrister was a lovely woman and was very worried about calling us as witnesses in case the experience proved to be too traumatic for us. Initially the police agreed with her and didn't want us to have to go through the ordeal either, maybe because they remembered how immature we had been when they first interviewed us a year before. In the end it was Dad's barrister who decided we needed to be called. I think he had heard our interview tapes with the police and underestimated how much we had grown up since then, and how good we had become at defending ourselves when talking to adults. The police interview had happened the day after the killing, when we still didn't really understand what was going on. We could be heard laughing and joking on the tapes, which gave completely the wrong impression of how we were going to be presenting our case this time. It had only been in the ensuing weeks and months that even a portion of the truth about what had happened to our Mum began to sink in. In fact we still didn't know the whole story and would learn a shocking amount by listening to the other witnesses in the following days.

I'm the first to admit that I was not the most mature of fifteen-year-olds. As long as Mum was alive I had been able to remain pretty immature because she did everything for us and I never had to take responsibility for anything. Alex was still just a kid. The year since she died had been a steep and painful learning curve for both of us and neither of us were the same children we had been that day.

Dad's barrister must have thought he would be able to make us look like difficult, nightmare children and bully us into crumbling and admitting that our Dad was a wonderful person really and that Mum had driven him to do what he did. But we were pretty sure that no reasonable jury was going to believe that and we were both confident that we could stand up to any amount of questioning.

Our barrister kindly arranged for us to be taken to visit the court a couple of days before the trial started in order to see the layout of the courtroom and meet some of the people who would be there on the day, just to get us used to the environment. I think the police had recommended that we do this as well. Not many people had shown us that much consideration over the previous year.

When the trial opened on 3rd February 2003, we were both very nervous. Our foster parents came along with us and they seemed to enjoy it rather like they might an extended West End show, making jokes and comments about things that had been said in the courtroom all the way home in the car. Two of Mum's cousins made the odd day visit to the court too but they chatted to our foster parents more than to us. The family liaison officer sat through it with us and our social worker came on the days when we were giving our evidence, so they could go off and write another report about us that we wouldn't get to see for several years.

This was going to be the first glimpse we had had of our father for over a year, since he was led from the house to the police car. Even though we were confident we could stand up to questioning from his barrister, we were still as frightened of Dad as we had always been. A fear that has been with you for so many years, day in and day out, doesn't vanish overnight, however much you might be able to rationalise it away in your mind.

When he was brought into the courtroom he looked different to how I remembered him. If anything he looked more frightening than he had when he was shuffling in and out of his bedroom, or sitting in the kitchen glowering at us. He seemed to have bulked up and with his shaved head and angry scowl he looked like a proper skinhead thug. I suppose I was seeing him for the first time as the rest of the world saw him and I was able to understand why all the neighbours had been so wary of him for all those years.

After a load of preliminaries, which seemed to last forever, they started putting their case and I was shocked by how Dad's barrister laid into Mum's memory, making out that it was all her fault that Dad had run amok and killed her. It had never occurred to me that a murder victim could be made to sound as though they had brought it on themselves, as if she had somehow provoked him into killing her, as if he was some bad-tempered old dog that kids should be careful not to tease.

Dad refused to take the witness stand throughout the trial, so instead the police played the tapes of his initial interrogation, so the jury could hear everything he had to say at the time. The problem with that for our side was that our barrister never got a chance to cross-examine him about any of the claims and statements he made. If she had been able to do that she could very quickly have discredited virtually everything he had to say. As it was, his taped words hung in the air unchallenged and we realised we were going to have to work hard to put our side of the story.

Asked by the police interviewers to explain what had driven him to kill her, Dad told them that it was all because of Mum and us and the way we behaved towards him. He told them how much he hated us and how miserable we made his life. He said that the onset of Huntington's had made Mum irritable and forgetful and difficult to live with. This was rubbish; when Mum's doctor came to the stand, he explained that she had only just started developing symptoms such as slight memory loss and twitching. Listening to Dad talking I understood why the social services had been forced to find a way to tell us about the disease; otherwise it would have come as even more of a shock to hear it talked about for the first time by strangers in a courtroom.

Mum, according to him, was always neglecting her duties as a housewife and there was always out-of-date food in the house. When the police looked into that accusation the only out-of-date food they could find were some old packets of crisps I'd chucked up on top of the fridge when Mum gave them to me because I didn't like crisps. Dad also claimed the house was dirty and Mum never cleaned it, which wasn't true – and anyway he was the one who was supposed to be staying at home to look after us while Mum was out at work earning the money to support us all. The house may have been a bit shabby, because Mum chose to spend her time and money on us while he chose to spend it on drink and locking himself in his room, but it was no dirtier or untidier than any other busy family home.

He claimed that he was anxious because he had no money, and that had been another factor driving him to act desperately. But we knew the lack of money was not really at the root of anything because Mum always gave him whatever he asked for, and always had. It may be that he had kept back a few savings from when he had worked for a short time delivering parcels, a job he claimed he took to make himself feel more independent, and that that money had finally run out. But if that was the problem he could easily have found himself another job that would have earned him as much since he had no other calls on his time. There was never anything stopping him from working apart from his own hatred of the outside world and everyone in it.

Another of his claims was that he didn't like me having friends in the house, particularly boys. He tried to give the impression that I was sleeping around, but as I was always a tomboy nearly all my friends were boys anyway, and they hardly ever came to the house because I was afraid of aggravating Dad. They all thought he was weird and preferred to steer clear. I'd only ever invited people back twice when I was about thirteen. Both times I did it because I thought Dad was out and we wanted to work together on school projects. When he came downstairs unexpectedly and found strangers invading space that he saw as exclusively his, he exploded and threw them out of the house, which I found pretty hard to explain to them the next day. In court Dad insisted it was all to do with sex, which anyone who knew me at that age would have known was ridiculous. All I thought about was school work and sport and other after-school activities.

174

Although his barrister was calling us to give evidence in order to discredit us, from our barrister's point of view we were potentially the most effective character witnesses that she could have hoped for. Our evidence seemed to be by far the strongest of all the witnesses'. Hardly anyone else knew anything about Dad since he had spent most of the previous few years in his bedroom. They might have heard the shouting late at night, or heard stories of some of the more outrageous things he got up to, but none of them had had to live under the same roof as him for years on end, witnessing every piece of weirdness and unpleasantness. His lawyer must have been desperate to discredit us in any way he could because without us no one would have any real idea of what went on behind the closed doors of our home.

Since nothing much that had happened in our life in the previous year had made any logical sense to us, it was always at the back of our minds that Dad might possibly be found not guilty for some technical legal reason, and would then be free to walk out of the court at the end of the trial. Because we were terrified of what he might do to us if that happened, we and the social services had always gone to great lengths to keep our new location secret. The judge, however, called our foster mother to the stand and insisted that she gave her full name and address for the whole courtroom, including Dad, to hear. It suddenly seemed even more imperative that he was convicted and didn't get to walk the streets again for a long time.

When it was time for me to give my evidence, I was led out of the court to another small room where I gave evidence into a video camera.

'Did you get in trouble once at school?' his barrister asked me.

I assumed he was referring to the shoplifting incident. 'Maybe,' I admitted. 'Doesn't everyone get into trouble at school sometimes?'

It was as if neither Dad nor his barrister had the slightest idea what normal family life was like or how normal children could be expected to behave. We were two of the hardest-working, highest-achieving kids in our school, despite the fact that Alex occasionally got into trouble for being a bit bolshie. If we had done anything wrong at home, it would have been the kind of things that a normal father would have sorted out with a few strong words. In fact, Dad had always egged Alex on to misbehave as much as possible because he knew it annoyed Mum and made him feel less like the odd one out in the family.

The barrister had a trick of leaving long pauses at the end of each of my answers in the hope that I would stumble on and say something that would help his case. But each time he did it I jumped in with another example of the horrible things Dad did around the house. After a bit he got the point and stopped doing the pausing.

I gave evidence for most of the first day of the trial, then they said that Alex and I had to stay in separate places that night so we couldn't compare notes, so he was sent to a hotel. Once Alex had answered all his questions, it was time for the police tapes of Dad's interrogation to be played to the court.

All through his recorded statement Dad seemed to be obsessed with sex, even though it was a subject that had never come up when we were together as a family. He insisted that I was promiscuous; that Mum had slept with one of her pupils; and that Alex was being interfered with by a neighbour when he was about seven years old. I actually had to ask what the word 'promiscuous' meant, and neither of us had any memory of there ever being a man living next door, let alone a paedophile. Alex had never been abused by anyone; he didn't even know such things happened. When the lawyer sprang those sorts of questions on me for the first time I actually laughed, partly from shock and partly because I thought he must be joking. What was so surprising was that Dad's barrister hadn't even bothered to check if there was a man living next door to us at any point, nor had he approached the school to ask about the other children who were supposed to have been coming to the house for sex with me. If he had, he would have been told that we were all part of the same study group and that we sometimes met to discuss our projects. As it was he made his accusations in front of the whole courtroom and was left looking foolish.

Dad sat completely still in the dock, his face immobile throughout the trial, showing no glimmer of emotion. It almost looked as if he had been sedated and couldn't hear what was going on around him. The stillness added to the eerie feeling of danger and evil that seemed to envelop him. Maybe he was doing it on purpose to intimidate the witnesses. At one point in the proceedings I was staring at him, trying to work out what might be going through his mind behind those dead eyes, trying to see if there was any reaction to anything that was being said about him, when he suddenly leant forward and muttered something to his barrister. The barrister glanced across at me and went up to whisper something to the judge.

The judge listened to whatever it was he had to say and then he too looked across at me. 'If you continue to look at the accused in that manner, young lady,' he warned, 'I am going to have to refuse you entry to the courtroom.'

I've got no idea how I was looking at him, but maybe my hatred showed on my face. It seemed strange to me that Dad had the right to demand that I didn't look at him when he was sitting at the centre of the proceedings, directly in everyone's line of vision. Did he really feel that threatened by me? Was he just trying to demonstrate to the judge and jury what an intimidating child I was, to show how intolerable it must have been to have to live with me? Or was he trying to remind me that he still had some control over me? It seemed particularly unfair since both Alex and I were nervous that as more and more was said against him he might grow angry, lose his self-control and jump up and attack us. He was seated only a couple of metres away from us. It was obvious that the things that were being said were going to be winding him up and he had made it very clear how much he hated us. We already knew he was capable of making a frenzied attack on someone who annoyed him and I had worked out that the woman who was supposed to be guarding us was sitting too far away to be able to get to us in time if Dad did decide to make a lunge. Since he was trying to get away with a plea of 'diminished responsibility' he wouldn't lose much by attacking us in full view of a courtroom; in fact, he might even be confirming in the eyes of the judge and jury that he was insane and should be sectioned rather than sentenced. All these thoughts were constantly coursing around in my brain as I sat listening to the voices of the lawyers and officials droning on, trying not to look at him.

As another part of his explanation to the police about why he had gone berserk with a chisel, Dad started talking about how he had been abused as a child, as if that was a reason for stabbing his wife to death. The court didn't seem to show any interest in this information. I suppose it is likely that he had a difficult childhood, as one of twelve children, but he had never talked to us about it before.

All through the previous year he had been attempting to prove that he was mentally disturbed and various psychologists had spent time with him trying to ascertain if that was the case. None of them, however, could come up with anything beyond 'a mild personality disorder'. They did say he had a touch of obsessive-compulsive disorder, or OCD, which might have explained why he found it difficult to cope with us when we interrupted his routines, but that hardly gave him a reason for murdering someone. He claimed that it was the OCD that caused him to become agitated when the house was messy and things were not in their right places. Since he spent virtually all his time in his bedroom and was seldom in any other room in the house, it is hard to see how that could have been a major problem.

I understand quite a bit about OCD because I had been diagnosed with it myself. I think it is quite common amongst people who feel they don't have control in their own lives and so they become obsessive about the little things they can control. My condition became worse at Cathy and Pete's when my habits and anxieties started to become more complex. I would have to go through an increasing number of routines every time I left the house or before I could go to bed, checking windows and doors over and over again, insisting on turning off electrical appliances whenever they weren't in use, wanting to feel completely secure and free of anxiety before I could hope to relax and sleep. They used to shout at me angrily when they went to use the kettle and found that I had turned it off at the mains since they last used it. It actually used to annoy me as much as it annoyed them, but I couldn't stop myself. Alex was a little bit the same, although he wasn't so obsessive about routines as I was. His main symptom was lining things up neatly in rows. Maybe we inherited it from Dad. I certainly wouldn't think of using it as an excuse for murder, though.

At one point in his police interrogation Dad claimed that neither of us were really his children, as if Mum was sleeping around all through their marriage, which was completely laughable. It did make us wonder, however, if things like that had happened in his family, and that was why he imagined, or claimed to imagine, that we were living a similar sort of life? Maybe he was abused as a child and maybe there were women in his family who had children that didn't belong to their husbands. I doubt we'll ever know now.

It was hard to sit there and listen as Dad came out with one lie after another and not say anything. My instincts were to shout out that it was all untrue but I knew that would just reflect badly on me. At one point he claimed that he never even knew Mum had cancer. I suppose he wanted to show that she cared for him so little she hadn't even told him something as important as that. But I knew he had picked her up from the hospital after her operation, so he was blatantly lying. I remembered the incident clearly because it was so out of character for him to do anything for any of us. Helen just got a phone call telling her not to worry about picking Mum up because Dad had already done it.

All I could do when I heard these lies on the tapes was jot down notes and pass them to our barrister, because we had said our bit by then and we weren't going to get another chance. Because Dad never took the stand himself she never had the chance to cross-examine him about any of the claims he made in his police interview or that his barrister was making on his behalf.

As we listened to all the barrister's arguments, Alex and I were both becoming truly frightened that he would be let off for some technical reason and would be back out on the street as soon as the case was finished. We had been left in no doubt about the depth of his hatred for us and we were sure he would come looking for us as soon as he could. At least if he was imprisoned for a good few years he would have time to cool off and we would have had time to move away from the area and establish lives for ourselves. Surely the judge would be able to see how dangerous he was? Our faith in the authorities had been shaken so badly by this time that we weren't convinced they would be able to protect us if Dad was released. It was a nerve-racking two weeks, to say the least.

Chapter Fifteen

Alex

Although we were allowed to sit in the court during the trial listening to everyone else, we had to sit in another room and talk to a video camera when giving our evidence, which meant that we couldn't see the reactions of anyone else in the courtroom to our answers. The only person we could see was the lawyer who was actually questioning us from the television screen in front of us. I didn't like the idea that Dad would be thinking he could control us and frighten us into giving our evidence from another room. Even though it was true that we were frightened of him, I would have liked to show him I wasn't scared by giving evidence while sitting just a few feet away from him. I would like to have seen his reactions to the things I had to say – although he probably wouldn't have reacted at all because he hardly did to anything else that was said about him.

Later we were told by people who had been in the courtroom while we were being cross-examined that the jury and all the other people listening had seemed to be completely on our side while we were giving evidence. They said that we made them laugh and that our down-to-earth descriptions of our family life made Dad's accusations seem all the more wild and fantastical.

Isobel gave her evidence first and was on the stand – or in front of the camera – for a whole day. I wasn't allowed to listen, either in the court or in the room with her, in case her answers influenced what I said when it came to my turn to be cross-examined the following day. That night we had to be kept separate, with me in a hotel room, in case Isobel tried to brief me on what she had said and what traps I should be wary of falling into. Dad's barrister wanted to be able to spring the allegations he had made against me to my face without me having been forewarned by Isobel. I knew that the biggest danger was that I would become angry about the things Dad's barrister was saying, which would make me look like an unreliable witness, so I was determined to stay calm and get it right. There was too much depending on it.

The following day, while I was in the other room talking to the camera, there was a party of school kids shown into the courtroom, just to have a look around. Isobel got really irritated because they kept giggling and messing about and in the end she shouted at them to be quiet, which got her a telling off from the judge. It was probably pretty boring to them, but to Isobel it seemed as though they were being disrespectful about Mum's murder and our bereavement. In the end the judge had to ask the kids to leave the courtroom because of their behaviour and I dare say it was a relief for them to get out.

When you are so emotionally involved in a case it is incredibly frustrating to see other people treating it casually. An event that had changed our entire lives and devastated our family was just a professional engagement for most of the people in the room, and a gruesome sort of entertainment for the rest. At one point Isobel spotted a member of the jury falling asleep during the medical reports, but she managed to keep quiet about that. To be fair the medical stuff did go on for about a day and a half and was pretty boring, but still it seemed that staying awake should have been the minimum requirement for a jury member in a murder case. Isobel managed to hold her tongue since no one else in the court appeared to be worried about it.

Everything the barrister threw at me over the video link was easily answered. Most of Dad's accusations were patently ludicrous and figments of a delusional imagination, and just by giving a straight account of how things had been at home I was able to make that point. In fact I did so well they asked if Isobel had coached me in what to say the previous night. She wouldn't have needed to coach me in anything even if she'd been allowed to. It was completely obvious what answers to give; all I had to remember was not lose my temper. People told us that we just had to tell the truth and justice would automatically be done. We wanted to believe that was true, but we still weren't completely confident that some technicality wouldn't arise that would give Dad a loophole to escape through.

The only time his defence team came close to making us look delinquent during those video-links was when they asked about Isobel's reprimand for shoplifting. Dad never said anything about it at the time but he must have been storing it up to use against her and now he hoped that by branding her as a thief and a liar in court he could discredit everything she said about him. It was the first and last time she had ever done anything like it, and half her class at school had been caught shoplifting at least once, so it wasn't a very big deal. Isobel had never made any attempt to deny it and bringing the matter up still didn't convince anyone in the courtroom that either of us had ever given Dad any excuse to do what he had done.

Another of his claims was that he was worried he was going to run out of money, but since Mum was his main source of income that didn't make sense either. Why would he kill the person who was supplying him with food and drink and a roof over his head? Then there was all the nonsense about Mum being terrible at looking

187

after the house. The defending lawyer thought he had tricked Isobel by asking if there was any out-of-date food in the house and then springing the evidence of the crisps that the police had found when she denied all knowledge of it. Apparently the jury actually laughed out loud when she explained about chucking the packets up there herself just because she didn't like crisps. Although we couldn't judge, I imagine all our answers came across as normal and believable, because we had no reason to lie about anything, while Dad's arguments were sounding less and less believable as he piled on new complaints.

Even if everything he had said was true and we had been the terrible children he claimed we were, and Mum had been the worst housewife in the world, it hardly explained why he would have felt the need to stab her more than fifty times. The whole trial was like something from *Alice in Wonderland*.

They called Helen to the witness stand and it emerged that she had always referred to him as 'Mad Bert', a fact that his lawyers jumped on to help prove that Dad was suffering from diminished responsibility, that he was indeed 'mad' rather than just plain 'bad'. There had been endless psychiatric assessments done of him in attempts to ascertain the truth, but all the doctors agreed that he was quite sane enough to know what he was doing that day. The defence team wanted to suggest that Dad's state of mind and his behaviour had all had something to do with the stroke he suffered when I was in the house on my own with him. They wanted to show that he had been perfectly fine until that moment. The police, on the other hand, had found plenty of witnesses from the neighbourhood who were willing to talk to them at length about the things Dad had been getting up to from the first day he moved in, many years before he suffered his stroke. Isobel and I were too young to be able to give any reliable evidence about what he was like before that day, although neither of us had any memories of him ever being any different.

Until the trial no one had ever really talked to us about what had happened on the day of the murder. We learned almost everything that had been excluded from the newspaper reports for the first time in court – like the fact that an elderly couple living in a nearby bungalow had heard screams but thought they were coming from children playing out in the street and so did nothing about them. Details like that would bring the scene horribly to life for us, allowing our imaginations free rein to fill in the rest.

The more facts that were laid out in front of us, the more questions came into our minds. Although we were still puzzled as to why Mum hadn't mentioned that she would be coming home early for her hospital appointment on the day she died, we were willing to accept that she might just have forgotten about it in the rush of being late for work that morning, or that the appointment was changed during the course of that day. But if she did go to the appointment, which the hospital had confirmed she did, how come she was in her comfortable 'home clothes' when her body was found? Even though she had grown more careless about her appearance in her final months, she still had certain standards and whenever she went to a hospital appointment she would always wear her work clothes, which were smarter.

Someone came forward to say they had spotted her driving her car down the road at 3.15 pm, not long before Dad made the calls to the police claiming he had killed her. It seems unlikely she could have changed in those few minutes so she must have done it before. She had left the hospital appointment at 2.10 pm, but it wouldn't have taken her an hour to get home, so we can only assume that at some point she had come home and changed into her casual clothes and had then gone out again in the car for some reason. Isobel and I went over it a thousand times from every angle whenever we were alone together, but whatever way we looked at it there seemed to be forty-five minutes missing from the scenario that the police built up of her final movements. When the forensic experts went into the house to try to work out exactly what had happened, there was a newspaper laid out beside the rocking chair in the dining room. Knowing her habits as we did, that suggested to us that Mum had been sitting in there with the dog to keep him from barking and disturbing Dad.

One of the most distressing things of all was an outline picture produced for the jury that showed the site of all Mum's wounds. Dots marked the spots on her shoulders, collarbone, breastbone and chest where the chisel had punctured, as well as all the wounds on her hands and forearms where she had obviously been trying to defend herself. It gave a graphic depiction of her final, desperate struggle for life that I found horribly upsetting. Every time I tried to imagine what Mum must have gone through in the last moments of her life, I felt sick to the stomach and filled with hatred for Dad.

In court the police played the tapes of the phone calls Dad made to them, in which he told them openly that he had killed his wife and that they needed to get there as quickly as possible because we were on our way home from school. It transpired from their investigations that he had gone upstairs after killing her, changed out of his bloodstained clothes and packed himself a going-away bag, presumably expecting the police to be knocking at the door by the time he came back downstairs. It was almost as if the whole point of killing Mum was to get himself put into a cell somewhere, away from all responsibility and free from all decisions. If that was the case, it was difficult to see how the court was going to be able to punish him for what he had done without giving him exactly the outcome that he was after. Both Isobel and I believe that jail must suit him right down to the ground. It's not a punishment at all for someone like him, who had been living voluntarily in a locked room for many years beforehand.

Chapter Sixteen

Isobel

Dad's lawyers had found one character witness for the defence and they obviously believed they had a good chance of redeeming their client's character through this witness's testimony because of a statement he had given to them when they went to interview him. He was an Italian man whom Dad had worked with briefly at a parcel delivery firm the year before. He was being asked to vouch for Dad being a good worker and a good man. The statement he had made gave them confidence that he would be willing to say these things when questioned. They needed something to counteract all the people who had come forward to say Dad was a terrible husband, father and neighbour.

When this witness climbed onto the stand, however, he said the exact opposite to whatever was in the written version of his statement. Instead of saying Dad 'could' have done something, he was saying Dad 'could not' have done it.

'You do realise that lying in court under oath is a criminal offence for which you could be imprisoned?' the barrister reminded him impatiently, obviously furious that the one straw he had been clinging to looked as though it was being snatched away.

But the Italian stood his ground and swore that he would never have said the words that were in the written statement because he absolutely believed the opposite to be true.

'There has been an error here,' he protested, 'I definitely didn't say that. There is no way I would be standing here saying things in support of this man.'

The barrister kept on at him for nearly an hour but the witness refused to change his story even under the threat of being locked up for perjury. With no other witnesses to turn to, Dad's barrister demanded that the original tape of the interview with the Italian be produced in court and compared to the written statement he was working from. The court was adjourned so they could look into it and they discovered, after hours of time had been wasted, that whoever had transcribed the statement into writing had missed out the word 'not', which was clearly audible on the tape, thereby completely changing the sense of what the man was saying. The witness they had hoped would say positive things about Dad had actually ended up saying negative things. The prosecution team would never have called him as a witness so it was an unexpected bonus for them. It seemed that no one who had ever met Dad had a good word to say for him, not even his own character witness. We were very grateful to the Italian for standing his ground because I doubt if anyone would have gone to check the original tapes if he had caved in to the pressure and agreed that the mistake was his.

A lot of the witnesses were obviously nervous when they had to stand up and speak under his expressionless stare. Jillian was actually shaking and her voice trembling while she talked, but she didn't let it deter her. A lot of the stories the witnesses from our street told about him were the first we knew of the things he had done, like disrupting people's gardens and driving around with a loud hailer on the roof of his van, shouting abuse. Although the things that we had to say must have been an eye-opener for everyone else listening in the court-room, we had also learned a lot about our own family history by seeing the goings on in our house through the eyes of others. They'd all heard the arguments and the shouting and seen incidents of one sort or another over the years. Mum's doctor was called and all the reports about her Huntington's were read out at length, so it was just as well we'd been warned about this beforehand.

In marked contrast to everything that was being said about Dad, there was only one witness who had anything bad to say about us. She was a neighbour who claimed that I had bullied her daughter, an event I had no memory of whatsoever. As far as I was concerned the girl and I had always been good friends until we had an argument about something and had stopped talking. Even if she had perceived it as bullying, which I couldn't imagine was possible, there didn't seem to be any reason to bring it up in front of the court that was looking into the murder of my mother. I was so hurt and angry, particularly because it had been said at the end of the trial when I couldn't defend myself, that I followed the woman out of the courtroom and started haranguing her in the corridor outside, which got me told off again.

At the end of the two-week trial there were the closing speeches. By the time Dad's barrister was making his there was very little he could say because Dad had made him look a fool with all his fantasies and lies. But he still managed to make his speech last for a day and a half.

No one was suggesting that Dad hadn't killed Mum; it just seemed to come down to whether or not he was sane when he did it and whether Mum had provoked him in some way. When the speeches were finally all over the jury only went out to deliberate for a couple of hours before they returned. The foreman announced that they were unanimous in their verdict of 'guilty'.

Our barrister warned us that when the judge passed his sentence we must be careful not to react, however strongly we might feel about his decision.

'I always find it hard not to say anything,' she admitted, 'but we have to control our emotions out of respect for the judge.'

Despite our barrister's warning we weren't able to stop ourselves from rising to our feet as we turned to hear what the judge had to say. He solemnly announced that the mandatory sentence for murder was life, and he would be recommending that Dad should serve between twenty and twenty-five years, but he didn't actually set the tariff there and then. As we came out our barrister explained to us what was happening.

'At the moment sentences are being set by the Home Office and there is a backlog of cases waiting to be decided,' she said. 'We may not hear the final sentence for some time.'

The police had told us that they thought he would get at least fifteen years as he had shown no remorse for his actions at any stage, unashamedly using the court as a forum to air all his unpleasant grievances about Mum and us. For the moment it looked as though we were going to have to be content just to know that he had been found guilty and locked up. We could worry about how long he was going to be away for later.

When the case was over the two barristers were chatting together. 'They'll be off for tea and scones now,' one of the policemen said wryly. It seemed strange to think that a case that was so traumatic and life-changing for us was just a job of work for them, something for them to chat about afterwards, comparing notes and discussing how it went as if it had been no more than a tennis match. There seemed to be an enormous distance between what was going on inside our heads and what we read in the papers or heard the professionals discussing around us. For us, this was about getting justice for Mum and also keeping Dad off the streets so he couldn't come after us seeking revenge for what we had said in court.

At the end of the whole proceedings the police told us we had been good witnesses. The fact that I had been unable to stop myself from blurting out in court once or twice didn't seem to matter because the judge even said something complimentary to us at the end, and then wrote us a letter congratulating us on how well we had behaved throughout the proceedings. He said he could see how hard it was for us to keep our mouths shut in the face of some of the things that were being said about us and about Mum.

It would be four years from 14th February 2003 – the day they pronounced him guilty – before Dad was finally given his tariff. Throughout those years we had no idea how long it was going to be before he was back on the street and able to come looking for us. I knew that everyone expected him to get a long sentence, but I had been let down often enough to know that you can never rely on anyone's opinion until it has been proved to be true. When I got the phone call from our victim liaison officer to say the paperwork had come through with the sentence, I was a university student working in a laboratory. I wasn't supposed to take calls in class but when I saw who was calling I answered it anyway, desperate to know that we were safe for a good few years yet.

'I've just got all the stuff from the Home Office,' she told me. 'His tariff has been set at ten years.'

I had been imagining he would still be in for a minimum of another ten years, maybe even twenty and I couldn't believe what I was hearing. That meant that with the time he had already served before coming to trial he might only be in prison for another five years – until January 2012. It seemed as though he might be back at any moment and Alex and I had no hope of any peace of mind.

We had been asked to fill out a victim's impact statement about a year before, which would be put in front of the judges making the decision about the tariff, but it had obviously had no effect on them whatsoever. It was likely that we would still be tied up with lawyers, courts and victim liaison officers, trying to resolve the financial issues between us by the time he came out. That meant we would never have a time when we were free of him. I had hoped there would be at least ten years after everything was settled when we would be able to get on with our own lives before we had to worry about him coming back out again to haunt us.

The length of the sentence just didn't seem to fit the gravity of his crime. As far as I can tell the minimum anyone can serve for murder is nine years. How could it be that the crime he had committed was only worth one year more than the minimum? Ten years might be appropriate for someone who attacked and killed another man in a drunken pub brawl, but is it an appropriate sentence for a man who allegedly sharpened his chisel in advance, which suggests that he premeditated the attack, had no apparent provocation from the victim and continued stabbing over and over again, long after any initial impulse to strike someone would have passed? Why did he then ring the police and admit what he had done, and fifteen minutes later deny that he could remember anything about it? If the court had decided he was in his right mind, it seemed to us that this was about as bad as a murder could be, so why wasn't the sentence reflecting that? The only way I could imagine that it could have been worse would be if he had gone on to murder more people, or had gone on the run rather than turning himself in.

Once Dad had been convicted of murder he could no longer inherit Mum's half of the house, because that would mean that he was benefiting from his crime, and so it automatically passed to Alex and me. But now that we knew the whole truth of what he had done and what he thought of Mum and us, we couldn't see why he should be allowed to keep the proceeds from the other half either. We knew that it had always been Mum who had worked in order to earn the money to pay the mortgage, so why should he have any claim to anything? Since he had deprived us of our mother and we needed all the financial support we could get if we were to continue our educations, as Mum would definitely have wanted us to, we felt he should be made to contribute from his share. So we went to the solicitor who had been helping us and asked if it would be possible to try to get things made fair.

The solicitor warned us that he thought by the time we had been through the whole fight, we probably wouldn't make any money from it, and if we lost we might even end up losing money because of the legal fees, but by that time it had become a point of principle – more about ensuring that he lost everything than that we gained any financial advantage. It didn't seem to us that Dad was really being punished for what he had done, since he had wanted to go to prison all the time anyway. Being shut in a cell and having all his meals provided for him, with no responsibility for looking after himself, is exactly how he likes to live. The thought that he would eventually come out and have a nest egg of money waiting for him, money that Mum had worked so hard for over so many years, didn't seem right. We were also suing Dad under the Fatal Accidents Act for depriving us of the financial support Mum would have continued to give us had she been alive, and for the psychological harm he had done us by killing her. The fight still goes on but the lawyers tell us that if we win we will be the first people ever to have sued a parent successfully.

By the time Dad's sentence was decided he had already shown that he was co-operating with the authorities; he had already served part of his sentence and the Home Office was worried about prison overcrowding. It was decided in some closed meeting somewhere that the only people Dad was a danger to now were Alex and me; he wasn't a danger to the general public and therefore wouldn't need to be locked away forever.

The thought that in a very few years he could be back out on the street is very frightening for us. He isn't allowed to know where we are, and we aren't allowed to know what prison he is in. In a way that is good, but we're worried that if we don't even know what part of the country he is in we might bump into him accidentally once he has been released. Helen is frightened of him coming out as well because she stood up in court in front of him and called him 'Mad Bert', saying how much she hated him. She had told the police all about him during her interviews, when she was still too upset to think through the possible long-term consequences of anything she might say. I dare say she would not have been so bold if the police hadn't already got her words on tape. Saying it out loud when she was just a few yards away from Dad was a very different matter to saying it to a couple of friendly policemen in the security of a cosy police station, probably with a steaming cup of tea in her hand. She had been the witness with the most to say, and she knew it wouldn't be hard for Dad to find her if he decided he wanted to get his revenge once he was out. In the few times I've seen her since the sentence was set, she has professed to be very worried about what Dad might do when he comes out, and I'm not surprised. We all are.

Chapter Seventeen

Alex

Isobel and I lived with Cathy and Pete for twenty months in the end, from March 2002 to November 2003. Exactly a year after we got there Alfie died of leukaemia – again on the 11th, a date that seemed to bring us one disaster after another. It felt as though we had lost an old friend and ally but we were used to absorbing blows like this without great shows of emotion, having been hardened to such things over the years by Dad killing our hamster and rabbit. Cathy and Pete couldn't understand why we weren't crying about it.

'If we didn't cry when our Mum was murdered,' Isobel pointed out, 'we're hardly going to cry over a dog.'

It seemed the foster parents were more upset than us, which led to some tension.

'They don't even care about their own dog,' we heard them say when they thought we were out of earshot, 'so why should we bother doing anything for them?'

It was just one more blow that we had to cope with, not something to make a big fuss about. From the beginning I think both Isobel and I had coped pretty well with everything fate had thrown at us, and we had done it by taking each day as it came, overcoming each obstacle as it appeared. Most of the responsibility fell to Isobel because she was the older of us, and the more outspoken. Some of the people we came across in the system were really helpful, although they never had enough time to do everything that they might have wanted to do for two children trying to organise their lives on their own. The good ones always seemed to be worked off their feet. There was a family protection officer called Stella who gave us a lot of her valuable time and chatted to us about any issues that were worrying us, and the two CID officers who interviewed us the first day after the murder were really conscientious about keeping us abreast of what was going on behind the scenes. But the good people only have a limited amount of hours in their days, and as it became increasingly obvious to everyone who knew us that we were doing fine at school, and that Isobel was there to help look after me, we heard less and less from everyone in authority, until we eventually reached a situation where I never even got to meet my social workers at all.

About six months after Mum's funeral, in August 2002, it suddenly occurred to us that we had no idea what had happened to her ashes. Isobel asked our foster parents where they thought they were.

'You haven't had them yet?' they asked, obviously surprised by the revelation.

They made some enquiries and discovered that the social workers on our case hadn't collected them from the crematorium after the service as they were supposed to. Because there had been no one to chase them up, they had disappeared into the system. It seemed the final insult to Mum's memory and Isobel demanded that something should be done. She was beginning to get very good at standing up to grown-ups and not allowing them to patronise us when we felt strongly about something. They instigated a search and eventually managed to track the urn down for us so that we could arrange to have the ashes buried and we would know that Mum was finally at peace. We never seemed to reach any sort of closure on anything. We just wanted to put our childhoods behind us so that we could concentrate on looking forward instead of back, but there always seemed to be so much unfinished business hanging over us.

We found a nicely kept graveyard in Redditch, which we thought Mum would have liked, and commissioned a headstone with the little bit of money left over from the collection Jillian had taken at Mum's school to pay for the funeral. We held a short ceremony at the graveside with a priest saying a few words. It was very small and private, completely different to the crowd at the funeral, most of whom can hardly have known her at all. The group around the grave included all the people whose lives had been truly affected by Mum's passing. Helen brought one of her sons, the first time we had seen her since we were taken away to Cathy and Pete's, but she only stayed for about ten minutes so we didn't have time to talk.

Cathy and Pete were there too, which didn't feel quite right to Isobel and me, especially when they threw some dirt into the grave in what seemed like an overly familiar gesture. Maybe I was being too critical because by then I already knew I didn't like them, but I kept thinking that they had never known Mum and didn't have a good word to say about the way she had brought us up, so why were they now standing side by side with the people who had loved Mum? I didn't say anything, as usual, but the thought simmered away inside my head.

I suppose they felt they were supporting us, which was part of their job. They had all sorts of ideas about what we should do and how we should behave, none of which we were very receptive to. They tried very hard, for instance, to make us look on them as our natural parents, wanting to integrate themselves into our existing family, even though our family were all strangers to us. They insisted on taking us to meet Mum's cousins, who we had never met before, and they stayed in contact with them after we stopped living with them. They all discovered they had a common interest in drinking wine, a pastime that didn't interest Isobel or me in the slightest.

Just after the burial of Mum's ashes, they agreed to take us back to our family home so we could pick up more of our stuff. At that stage Dad had still not been convicted so the house was legally his. We had been asking for ages if we could go there but the police had been adamant that no one should be allowed into the crime scene, even though they must have found every clue they could possibly need within a week or two of the murder.

We were grateful to Cathy and Pete for giving in to us because they weren't supposed to do it, but I expect they were curious to see where we had come from, having heard so much about our past. Even though the police had forbidden us to go back to the house, no one had thought to take our keys away so it was easy to walk in now that the police no longer had anyone guarding the premises.

It was an eerie and disturbing feeling to open that front door again seven months after the day the policeman told me to stay outside; we stepped back into a ghost house full of memories. Our lives had changed completely since we were last there, and we had had to adapt too. The house smelled terrible because the electricity had been turned off but food had been left to rot

208

in the fridge and on the shelves in the kitchen. A pint of milk that had been left curdling by the sink, some bananas had blackened and turned to ash in the fruit bowl, and wet clothes had been left to rot in the washing machine. It still looked the same, every room bringing back a host of memories and painful emotions, reminding us of what it had been like to live there with Mum, resurrecting the feelings of fear and hatred of Dad that had smouldered beneath the surface all through the years that we had lived our lives within those walls.

Someone had obviously done their best to clear up the bloodstains by the back door, but they had found it impossible to get rid of every trace and we could see reddish brown smudges on doorframes and in corners where it hadn't been cleaned off completely. There were lots of arrows that the forensic team had stuck up all over the place in order to help them identify where the blood had been. There was no question that we were visiting a murder scene as well as the place that had been our childhood home.

We walked through like tourists initially, staring at everything, taking it in, trying to work out what we were feeling. Were we sad or angry? I suppose we initially had that feeling of emotional detachment that the psychologist had explained can result from severe shock. We climbed the stairs and came to Dad's closed bedroom door. All our lives we had been walking past that door, wondering what was going on behind it, whether he was there or not. We didn't say anything, because we both knew the other was thinking the same thoughts. For the first time ever we could be absolutely certain he wasn't in there, but we were less sure if we wanted to go in. After a few seconds' hesitation, we made up our minds and pushed open the door, stepping into Dad's secret inner sanctum for the first time ever. Whenever he went out he had always locked the door behind him, keeping the key on a chain around his neck. It was like an alien landscape, a dingy home within a home, a squalid little bed-sitting room. It was hard to imagine how he could have borne to spend so much time on his own in such a dreary, self-contained bunker. We just stood there, staring around us at his television and his computer screen, and the few kitchen appliances he had kept in there so he could make himself drinks and simple meals from tins without venturing out and risking bumping into any of us. It was as if we had entered the camp of a hated and now defeated enemy and our initial trepidation, instilled by years of his tyranny, deserted us to be replaced by a mindless fury.

All at once, we both went mad with rage. We started throwing things around the room, cutting up Dad's clothes with a pair of scissors and messing everything up, as if we could somehow punish him for what he had done to us, even though he was locked up and miles away. There was no logic to our rampage; it was just a gut reaction to a man who had been so vile to us for so long and had finally robbed us of our mother, our roots and our family.

I ran down to the garage and grabbed a can of spray paint. Cathy and Pete asked what we were doing, but we ignored them. Isobel and I took turns to spray-paint the word 'murderer' on the wall downstairs and then all over the walls of Dad's bedroom. There was a feeling of liberation as we let all our bitterness and anger out, while our foster parents stood by, looking on grimly, saying nothing. Maybe they were pleased to see us rejecting our past life like that; maybe they realised it was an emotional release. Eventually we had spent all our energy and anger and we collected the things from our rooms that we had come for.

As we came back downstairs we noticed that the message light was blinking on the telephone and when we pressed the button we heard a male voice with a Scottish accent. He announced himself as being somebody 'Kerr', so we assumed it was a relative of Dad's, but it wasn't a name we recognised. The voice asked if he was still planning to come up to Newcastle, so news of what had happened can't have travelled that far. It was unusual for Dad to receive any phone calls at all, and we had never ever heard him speak about his family so we had no idea if this was one of his brothers or a cousin. We might as well have been listening to the voice of an alien. The police had never mentioned the message so the man must have called after they had left the house. Isobel and I wondered if Dad had maybe been planning to run away after killing Mum and had contacted this 'Kerr' to see if he could go there, but had later thought better of it. We have no way of knowing for sure.

The police must have gone back for something after our visit and found the mess we had made. They realised immediately that we were the culprits because of what we had written. Once we had calmed down, we began to worry that in our anger we had made a mistake and given Dad an opportunity to press charges against us for damaging his property. It was still his house at that stage. The police came to warn us not to do it again and took our keys off us but fortunately nothing else happened. It seemed strange that we weren't allowed to do whatever we liked in a house that had been our home for so many years but they were adamant we had to stay away.

Eventually the house was sold. I think Dad's solicitor took care of the sale, and we managed to get our share of the money out of him after Dad was convicted, so that we would have a deposit to put down on a house of our own later. I don't know who bought it. I wouldn't have wanted to move into a place that had been the scene of so much unhappiness, pain and horror, but maybe the price was so low someone was unable to resist it. It made us really angry to think that Mum had worked so hard for so many years, paying every instalment of the mortgage and every household bill, while he just sat in his room, hating her and resenting everything she did, and then he ended up getting half the house. The lawyers tried to explain to us that he wasn't technically 'benefiting' from his crime because the house was already in his name, but none of their arguments seemed morally right.

The guardian ad liteum we had been allocated by social services, a woman named Marjorie Woodford, was supposed to look after our best interests, coming up with an education plan and advising on where we should live. Isobel and I liked her because she asked direct questions and was a no-nonsense type. Quite early on, she wrote a report saying that she didn't think our foster parents were suitable for us but social services didn't take any notice. As far as they were concerned, Cathy and Pete were doing lots of nice things for us like taking us on holiday, so they assumed we must be happy to be with them. After a while, however, other people started to question their suitability for the job too. The school wondered why they never bothered to turn up for parents' evenings, and people outside the school wondered why we weren't doing any of our activities any more when we had been so keen and conscientious in the past. We kept hoping that the authorities would decide they needed to move us to someone more suitable, but the months continued to pass without anything changing. The worst part of having your life run by bureaucrats is that you never know what they are doing. Were they working away behind the scenes in our interests? Or had they forgotten all about us, assuming we were okay so they could get on with more obviously pressing cases? We had no way of knowing. All we could do was wait and see what happened.

Cathy began to get feedback from her social worker suggesting that she and Pete were not doing their fostering job properly, which fed the resentments in the house. They didn't like being criticised when they believed they were doing us a favour by giving us a home at all. They were convinced they had gone into fostering with the best intentions, but it certainly wasn't working out the way they had hoped and they believed that was our fault. They had real trouble disguising their annoyance and disappointment with us. In retrospect it was inevitable that we were all heading for some sort of explosion.

Chapter Eighteen

Isobel

Cathy and Pete must have been becoming more and more disillusioned with us as the months went past and we didn't become any more affectionate towards them, or gushingly grateful to them for agreeing to take us in when no one else wanted us. The ill feeling between us was building all the time but the first major explosion came when I brought a girlfriend called Tania home from school. She was having difficulties with her family at the time – her stepdad was beating her up – so she was staying with us quite often and no one had ever said it was a problem.

That particular evening Cathy and Pete had had a lot to drink and had gone to bed before us. I don't think we were doing anything very bad, but we hadn't gone to sleep as early as we might have done, wanting to lie in bed and chatter the way that teenage girls do. We must have been laughing too loudly because we woke them up or stopped them getting to sleep or something that lit the touchpaper and ignited every little pent-up resentment they had stored up inside them.

They exploded into my bedroom, ranting and raving at us to such an extent that we became frightened. It was like suddenly being thrown back into one of the worst rows at home and I just couldn't face it. Alex woke up and came running from his bedroom under the impression that we were being attacked. We both felt we couldn't deal with things and had to get away. The three of us, desperate to escape from what seemed like a very real threat of violence, hurriedly packed our things and ran out of the house. Even though it was the middle of the night we had to take Tania with us since we could hardly leave her on her own in the house with them when they were behaving so weirdly.

Once we were out on the streets in the dark there was nothing for us to do but to keep walking, hoping that something would occur to us. Our foster parents must have called the police almost immediately we left the house, and it didn't take long for them to find three lost-looking teenagers wandering around the deserted streets. They took us back to the police station first, to try to find out more about us and about what had happened to cause us to walk out into the night like that. They were very friendly, just as they had been when we were first interviewed after the murder. We even watched them playing pool for a while as they tried to work out what they should do with us.

Although we had no idea what the alternative might be, we begged them not to take us back to the foster parents. We explained that they were always drunk and that we didn't feel safe in their care, but in the end the police decided they had no option since they didn't want to put us in the cells for the rest of the night. Remembering my failed and short-lived shoplifting career, I was quite glad that we didn't have to go through that, although it wouldn't have felt so threatening with Alex and Tania there.

Eventually we realised it would be fruitless to argue with them any more. If there was one thing we had learned over the previous year and a half, it was that people like us had very little power to change the minds of those who decided our destiny. We could tell them we didn't want to go, that we were frightened, but ultimately the decision would be theirs.

When we got back to the house Cathy and Pete were waiting and they were absolutely furious. As well as being kept awake they had now been made to look like bad foster parents and they were not in a forgiving mood. With folded arms and angry tone, they told our police escorts that they didn't want us back in their house. I guess they'd had enough of us by then and had decided that even if the money was good, fostering a couple of ungrateful teenagers wasn't worth all the grief.

'If they come back here we are going to end up hitting them,' Cathy warned grimly.

To the police I suppose it must have looked like a normal falling out between teenagers and their parents. Maybe they're called out to such incidents all the time, and they didn't know what to do with us in the middle of the night anyway, apart from put us in the cells, so they talked to us all separately until they were satisfied everyone had calmed down a bit then they left Alex and me there and took Tania back to her own family. I don't know what they would have done if Cathy and Pete had actually attacked us once they'd gone.

Because the police had been involved, social services were forced to react and they came round to see us the following day to try to find out what had gone wrong. Cathy and Pete hadn't relented at all and made it clear they wanted nothing more to do with us. We said, as politely as we could since they were in the room with us all the time we were being interviewed, that we would also like to leave. Looking back now I wonder if they were keen to get rid of us before we were taken away from them, but didn't like to say. Maybe they thought it would have looked bad on their record – a bit like resigning from a job before you get fired.

But it wasn't going to be that easy for any of us to escape the situation. It had taken social services a lot of effort to find this home for us, although we didn't realise it at the time. It was going to be even harder to find another placement now that the relationship had gone wrong and future potential foster parents would be able to read on our record how troublesome it had turned out to be. It seemed we had no option. We were going to have to stay where we were for the foreseeable future and just make the best of it. Now that Cathy and Pete knew we wanted to go too and that there was no chance they were ever going to be able to turn us into the loving little family unit they had imagined when they agreed to take us on, it became all-out war.

'I'm not surprised your dad killed your mum,' Cathy announced brutally in the middle of one of our many disagreements, 'with children like you.'

It seemed that in her opinion we were such terrible children we had driven our father to murder our mother, which was pretty much what he had claimed in his defence in court. How could any child be that bad? Her words hit a raw nerve with both of us and we weren't sure how to cope with the feelings of anger that welled up. We still hadn't had any bereavement counselling and we were finding our emotions hard to cope with. I'm not sure why nothing had been organised by then. Initially we had been forbidden counselling until Dad's trial was over, in case we had ideas put into our heads that would jeopardise the chances of him getting a fair hearing. Afterwards I think everyone just forgot because so much time had elapsed and because we seemed to be functioning okay at school and not getting into any trouble apart from rowing with our foster parents. Even then, the rows can't have seemed particularly serious to the police or the social workers compared to the sort of violence they were used to seeing in dysfunctional families. Mostly we were just quiet and distant and not interacting with them as they would have liked. As always our main strategy was to suppress all our anger and anxiety and get on with the daily business of our school lives as best we could.

There was part of us that knew it was ridiculous to say we had caused Dad to kill Mum, but at the same time the words rattled us and stirred some deeply buried feelings of guilt. In our darkest moments we couldn't help but wonder if maybe we should have done more for Mum. Maybe we should have gone to the police more often ourselves, and told them exactly how dangerous we thought Dad was. But then we were used to living with him so he only seemed really dangerous at the moments when they were fighting. Maybe we should have tried harder to persuade her to leave him. If she had been staying mainly for our sakes, perhaps we could have convinced her that we would be okay if we moved out of the house. Maybe we would even have been better off. Could we have saved her life if we had acted differently in any of these ways? The doubts kept on nagging away at us but we had no one we could talk to about them apart from each other.

'Would you like us to arrange for you to talk to anyone?' Cathy and Pete eventually asked once the trial was over. It was the first time anyone had ever suggested that to either of us, and I couldn't see the point by then. Because we hadn't been allowed to have counselling before the trial, we'd got used to managing without it. We had survived through the most painful months immediately after Mum died, when the loss was raw, so why would we want to rake it all up again now? We knew all too well how horrible our home lives had been, so we didn't need to go over and over the gruesome details with some stranger in order to remind ourselves. It seemed to me it would be better to spend the time finding ways to improve our current situation and move forward rather than dwelling on the past the whole time.

'No thanks,' I said. 'I think we'll be okay.'

But they thought different. No matter how much we protested that we didn't need help, they were determined to try to make us show at least some sort of emotional response to everything that had happened to us. When we continued to decline the offer of counselling they told us that they would stop our pocket money if we didn't do as they suggested. Although it sounded a bit like black-mail it did the trick. Alex and I talked about it between us and decided we didn't think it would do any harm, even if it didn't do us any good. We certainly didn't want our pocket money stopped, so we agreed.

Alex went first. His counsellor was a man who had a smart office with nothing in it but chairs and a big plant. Apparently, with the kind of psychoanalysis he practised, you are not supposed to ask any leading questions but just let the patient raise topics if they want. He started by attempting to make a personal connection with Alex by broaching the subject of football.

'I see David Beckham's in the papers again today,' he said cheerfully.

But Alex didn't really know who Beckham was so that didn't get the conversation going. Changing tack, the counsellor started talking about the plant in the corner of the room, but that didn't get them too far either so they ground to a halt. Alex ended up staring out the window at some pigeons for half an hour until the session was over and he could leave having fulfilled his side of the bargain. Cathy and Pete managed to bribe him into going a couple more times before he finally dug his heels in and refused to go any more. Anything he had ever wanted to discuss he had talked about with me or with his mates over the previous two years. He's never had any trouble saying whatever he wanted to his friends, quite a few of whom had known Mum from our activities. His friends even came to him with their problems, knowing that he'd been through a lot himself and would understand more than most people of his age. He couldn't see the point of talking to a perfect stranger about anything.

So I had an idea what was in store for me when it came to my turn. I went in and sat down with the posh-sounding lady I had been allocated.

'You've got an hour to say whatever you want,' she informed me.

I went to eight or nine sessions over the following few months but I never really said anything about any of the worries or bad memories that were stored in my head. I didn't mind talking about things that were worrying me that day or that week, but I didn't want to go over all the old stuff that we had already been over in court and with our foster parents and in our own memories a thousand times.

Alex and I both had plenty of friends at school, even though it was harder to stay in touch with them now we lived so much further away. We didn't tend to use our time with them to delve into our emotions, though; we preferred to escape from our own thoughts when we were out with our friends.

Just after my seventeenth birthday, I got my first proper boyfriend, a boy from school called Martin. He came to the house to stay over for weekends and Cathy and Pete didn't have any problem with the relationship. I guess most parents of teenagers have a dilemma about where to draw the line, unsure whether to be strict and risk alienating their daughter or to be liberal and risk things getting out of control.

But then the thing happened that must be every parent's nightmare, as well as every teenager's – I discovered I had got pregnant. Martin and I had thought we were being really careful and sensible but we took a risk and didn't use a condom just one time, and that was enough. I couldn't believe my bad luck. When the tell-tale symptoms started to arrive I took about ten pregnancy tests, unable to believe my eyes when each one told me the same thing. Positive! I was showing my friends and even poor Alex. He really didn't want to have to think about his big sister in that way but he was my only family and my closest friend by then. We had been through so much together I couldn't have kept this latest development from him.

As the inevitable truth dawned on me I was horrified, partly because there was no way I was ready to have a baby, and partly because I knew it would reinforce the idea that it was us – or at least me – who was the problem in the fostering situation rather than Cathy and Pete. I had conformed perfectly to the stereotype of the damaged child from the dysfunctional background. I had always intended to go to university in order to fulfil all the potential that Mum had worked so hard to bring out in me and becoming a single teenage mum was definitely not part of my life plan.

I was in such a panic when all the tests kept coming up positive that I went to Cathy to confess, even though we weren't getting on well at all by then. She took me to see the doctor, who did another test and confirmed what I already knew. I couldn't keep up the denials any longer. The question then was what options were open to me? I felt instinctively opposed to abortion, not so much because of my religious upbringing but because it seemed wrong to kill a baby just because it wasn't convenient for me to have it. Even with the risk of Huntington's hanging over the unborn child, I felt that emotionally I couldn't agree to a termination. Both my foster parents, however, saw this as the simplest and most expedient way out of the mess and tried to talk me into it. Cathy and Pete were almost as embarrassed as me, believing that it reflected badly on them for allowing me to have a boyfriend in the house, and they just wanted the problem to go away. My stubbornness, as they saw it, served to widen the gap between us even further.

Now that Cathy and Pete knew, and the doctor knew they knew, there was no way we could avoid informing social services of this latest development. When they heard, they were annoyed with Cathy and Pete for letting Martin stay over so much, believing it was irresponsible of them. The social workers then started putting pressure on me, telling me that if I didn't agree to a termination I would have to go to a 'mother and baby' unit. They made the whole thing seem very threatening, but I still wasn't willing to consider an abortion. As far as I was concerned this baby had as much of a right to be born as any other.

The worst thing about the pregnancy would be that it would make it harder for me to stay with Alex and keep an eye on him because I would have to do what was best for the baby as well. In many ways I had taken over Mum's role in making sure he worked hard and didn't let any of the advantages she had won for him slip through his fingers. I wasn't sure that he was quite ready to be left to his own devices by then – he was still only fourteen – but if I had a baby to take care of I might not be able to look after both of them in the way I wanted to. I felt as though I was being torn in two, but I couldn't have said any of this to Alex for fear of making him feel guilty, as if he was a burden to me. He never felt like a burden to me because he was as much of a support for me as I hope I was for him.

I was about two and a half months gone when I woke up one night and found I was bleeding heavily. I was terrified and, not knowing what else to do, I went to wake my foster parents, but they were too drunk to be able to offer any help. I just had to clear up the mess as best I could, having no real idea what was happening. I went to see the doctor the next day and he said it looked as though I had lost the baby in the night and that I should do a pregnancy test in a week to confirm it. After that Cathy and Pete began to voice their doubts as to whether I had ever been pregnant in the first place, accusing me of making the whole thing up. Cathy suggested that I had just invented a pregnancy as an attention-seeking ploy. I couldn't understand why she would say that when I had shown her some of the positive tests and had even been to the doctor with her to have it confirmed. It seemed to me that their arguments had no more logic to them than Dad's mad excuses as to why he had killed Mum.

Because I'd told Martin about the baby, the school called Cathy and Pete in to talk about the situation. By the time of the meeting I had miscarried and Cathy and Pete repeated their new story that I had made the whole thing up, so I was made to look like I was a liar in front of my form tutor, on top of everything else.

When the rumour got back to Martin that I had made up the pregnancy story he was, understandably, angry to think I might have lied to him about something so important. No matter how often I explained the whole thing to him and showed him the tests and offered to get the doctor to talk to him, there were too many seeds of doubt sown in his mind and eventually we split up over it. I wasn't that bothered because things hadn't been going so well anyway, but he was so upset he didn't turn up at school for a while.

I suppose it was only a matter of time before the tensions between Alex and me and the foster parents exploded again, and ironically the inevitable fireworks happened on Guy Fawkes Night. A friend of mine phoned me and as I was chatting to her I heard someone pick up the extension downstairs and start listening in. I thought they'd done it by accident, perhaps wanting to make a call themselves, so I sent Alex down to ask them to hang up. After I came off the phone, Pete started shouting at me 'Why are you always so rude?' I told him I didn't think I was rude; I just didn't want him listening in to my private conversation.

'It's my house and my phone,' he yelled. 'I can do whatever the hell I want. For being so rude, I'm taking twenty pounds off your pocket money.'

'That's not fair!' I complained, and he said he was taking another twenty pounds, so I complained again and he said 'That's another twenty.'

They were just heading out the door to go off to a firework party. Alex likes fireworks so he had agreed to go with them. As the three of them left the house I called after them, 'See you later.'

I didn't mean to say it in a sarcastic tone, but maybe everything I said to them sounded sarcastic by that stage. Whatever the reason, those three casually delivered words were the final straw for my foster father and he flipped, charging back into the house from the car, coming straight at me, obviously furious and out of control. Realising I was in danger of being hit I tried to slam the door in his face but I didn't manage it in time so I turned and ran into the living room and curled up on one of the chairs to protect myself from whatever blows were going to come. All the old fears I had felt when Dad was rampaging against Mum came flooding back. I immediately realised my mistake. I should have run through the house, or upstairs, or anywhere rather than allowing myself to be trapped in a corner, but it was too late to do anything by then. I just had to protect myself as best I could. He was beside me in seconds and as I peered up from beneath my raised arm I saw him lift his fist and I braced myself for the punch.

As his fist came down towards me there was a crash behind him and Alex was there, having run in from the car to come to my rescue. He pushed Pete off balance so his blow just swung through the air and he stumbled backwards into the kitchen before regaining his balance. He spun round and turned his anger on Alex, punching him hard. He might have been fat and out of condition but he was a grown man and Alex, still a skinny young boy, was no match for him without the element of surprise on his side. Pete grabbed Alex by the throat and lifted him clean off the ground and onto the kitchen work surface. Alex was swinging wildly and managed to knock Pete's glasses off, causing his nose to bleed at the same time and incensing him even further. The fight had become frenzied, just as I imagined Mum and Dad's last fight must have been. I had to do something to stop it before it ended in tragedy.

I jumped up from the chair and grabbed the house phone, trying to dial the police despite my shaking fingers, but by that time Cathy had made it back into the house and she ripped the phone from its socket, exactly as Dad used to do during his fights with Mum, cutting us off from the outside world. For a split second my instincts told me to attack her, all the old fears rising to the surface, but I stopped myself just in time.

'I'm going to call them on my mobile then,' I warned her, but she started raining punches down on me, while Pete continued to hit Alex in the kitchen.

'What are you doing?' I screamed at her, unable to believe things had reached such a pitch. My words seemed to bring her to her senses and she paused for a moment. 'Look at him,' I said, pointing at Pete. 'He's going to kill Alex. You have to do something! Stop him!'

She must have realised I was right and that Pete was about to do Alex some serious damage, which would have opened him up to all sorts of consequences and possibly even criminal charges. There was also a risk that in the heat of the battle Alex would grab any weapon that might come to hand and lash out with even more disastrous consequences.

'Get off him,' Cathy shouted at her husband.

Apparently hearing her voice through the red mists of his anger he backed off and for a second I relaxed. The next moment Cathy swung round and slapped me hard in the face then kicked me in the shin. It was as if she was trying to provoke Alex into attacking Pete or her again. Maybe she thought that it would look better when the police came if she could say Alex had attacked first. I shouted at Alex to warn him not to rise to the bait and then I fled upstairs, followed by their angry shouts ordering us to get out of their house and out of their lives once and for all. They screamed that we were to be gone before they got back and then stormed out to the car, presumably to go to their fireworks display as planned.

We quickly grabbed our few most precious possessions and some spare clothes, stuffed them into our school bags and hurried out of the house, our hearts still thumping from the confrontation. There was no way we wanted to be there for a moment longer than we had to be. The terror of being attacked by two large grown-ups like that was, for us, compounded by the flashbacks it brought on to all the horrible fights at home that had

231

culminated in our mother's murder. We were both shaking uncontrollably as we stumbled down the road, with no idea where to head for next.

Chapter Nineteen

Alex

It was a huge relief to get out of Cathy and Pete's house, even though we didn't have a clue where to go next or what would happen to us. We realised once the adrenaline had settled down in our systems that we were hungry and went for a takeaway burger with the cash we had in our pockets. I was feeling, and looking, pretty bruised and battered at that stage but eating made me feel a bit better about life. Surely the authorities would have to do something to help us after this? The police wouldn't be able to just send us back to them now that they had attacked us physically.

Once we'd eaten we still weren't any further on with our plans; we just knew we didn't intend to go back to the house, no matter what. It was cold so we had to keep moving in order to stay warm. We had imagined someone would have come looking for us by then, just as they had the last time we'd run off in the night, and we weren't sure what to do next. What if Cathy and Pete had decided not to ring the police this time and were just going to let us go? Even though I was still only fifteen, Isobel was seventeen by then, so maybe they thought we were old enough to survive on our own. But if that was the case we hadn't got the faintest idea where to start.

The twenty-four-hour Tesco store was the only place we could think of that would still be open, other than pubs and restaurants, and we didn't have any more money. We walked to the supermarket and sat on a bench outside, not wanting to attract any attention by going in but feeling a little safer for being close to people, hoping that something would happen or we would come up with an idea of what to do.

A few hours later Cathy and Pete's social worker rang Isobel's mobile. To begin with Isobel didn't want to tell her where we were, unsure whose side she would be on, but eventually she gave in and at three o'clock in the morning a duty social worker turned up at the store to collect us. For those few hours we had pretty much become street kids. It was frightening to see how easy it was for young people's lives to slip over the edge into chaos.

Straight away she could see the bruising on my face from Pete's punches so she realised she couldn't return us to the house. She drove us to a place which she said was an 'emergency foster home'. We were let into the house by someone who had obviously been woken up to deal with us, shown to some bunk beds and told to go to sleep.

'You'll be picked up at six,' the social worker told us, 'to be taken to school.'

We were quite surprised that they wanted us to go to school after such a traumatic night, but I suppose the alternative would have been that we were hanging around their offices all day while they tried to work out what to do with us. On balance, I think I would probably have preferred not to go in that day. It wasn't that I minded going to school, but it had been a long, hard night and I could have done with a few more hours' sleep.

I was still doing my GCSEs at that stage, with Isobel pushing me very hard. Unlike her I wasn't a natural academic. I preferred subjects that were more hands-on and vocational. Isobel was very strict with me about doing my homework, just as Mum had always been, so I never fell behind but it was a struggle some days. Grown-ups sometimes used to tell her to lighten up on me, warning her that she was putting too much pressure on me, as if they were worried I might crack under the strain. But she knew what I was capable of and, just like Mum, she was determined that I wouldn't miss out on any opportunities in life just because I was finding the work a bit difficult and it would have been easier not to bother. I think some-times other people worried that she put too much stress on herself by taking responsibility for me as well. Some even suggested that it would be better for her if we were separated so that she could concentrate on her own life a bit more and let other people worry about me. But she had no faith that anyone else would keep on at me in the way she did, and she was probably right.

Until shortly before the fight we'd had an experienced social worker, even though we hadn't seen her very often, but her bosses had recently taken her off our case because we were classed as being 'easy' to deal with. Our file had been passed on to a twenty-one year old trainee, a girl only four years older than Isobel. She wasn't on duty that night so it was Cathy and Pete's social worker who turned up for us at six the following morning, after we'd only had three hours' sleep.

In our haste to pack and get out of the house we hadn't thought to pick up any of my school uniform so I had to go to school in the clothes I had been wearing on the streets the night before. It was alright for Isobel because she was in the sixth form and didn't have to wear uniform. We had hardly walked through the door before I was told to report to the headmaster. They kept a skanky spare uniform on the premises that was usually given to the naughty kids who deliberately turned up in their own clothes in order to flout authority, so I was given that – one more embarrassment that I really didn't feel I needed.

The other problem was that we were hungry because we hadn't had time for breakfast before being whisked away from the emergency foster home and we had no money left to buy anything to keep us going. We had tried asking the headmaster if we could have school dinners before because our foster parents hadn't been giving us lunch money. He had always refused permission, but we thought that on a day like this he would make an exception.

'Can we have a school lunch today?' Isobel asked him.

'No,' he said. 'Free dinners are only for people whose parents are on low incomes and social services are responsible for you.'

That, apparently, was the system and he wasn't about to make an exception, not even on a day that was going as badly for us as that one was. In the end our friends shared their lunch with us or we would have been totally starving.

Our young social worker picked us up again at the end of the school day, accompanied by our previous, more experienced one. The trainee must have been finding the whole thing overwhelming and realised she was out of her depth. It seemed ironic that we suddenly had two social workers at once, although we had often had periods when we had none at all for months on end. It was hard to build up relationships of mutual trust in such circumstances or to feel that any of them really knew much about us. They drove us back to Cathy and Pete's house to get the rest of our stuff, including my school uniform.

'We have no idea where we are going to place you tonight,' they admitted as we climbed into the car. 'We've been searching all day and there's nowhere for you.'

That was not what we wanted to hear, but there were other things we had to do before we tackled the accommodation problem anyway. Back at the house, we each packed whatever we could carry into one bag while Cathy and Pete sat in the sitting room downstairs and the social workers hovered between us to avoid any confrontations.

After we left the house, they took us to see a nurse to have my bruises looked at, although they still hadn't come up in their full glory yet. She also treated the bruising on Isobel's shin, where Cathy had kicked her. The evening was wearing on and there still wasn't anywhere for us to go to. The longer it took to find us somewhere to go the more nervous we became that we would be sent back to the foster parents just because they couldn't come up with an alternative.

'Don't worry,' they assured us when we told them our worries. 'You're not going back there, and they won't be allowed to foster again or work with children in any capacity.'

That was a massive relief to us. We were pleased to see that we were being believed for once and action was being taken. I suppose the bruises were evidence enough, but we were so used to nothing being done when we made a complaint that we'd learned not to expect anything.

When they realised we hadn't eaten properly all day the social workers took us to McDonalds for a meal, still having no idea what they were going to do with us afterwards. They were worried about what time they were going to get home themselves by that stage. I suppose they couldn't really leave us till we were safely housed and it would certainly be against the rules to take us home with them. There were times when we could see why individual social workers ended up feeling overworked and under-appreciated. It can be a thankless job.

After a lot more phoning around they finally found us places in a children's home that took new residents at short notice.

'It's in Cheltenham,' they told us. That was even further from our school than Cathy and Pete's had been, but at that stage we didn't feel we could complain.

The trainee drove us for about forty-five minutes to get there and went in with us. She looked so young the people running the home actually thought she was the one who was looking for a place to stay.

'You'll only be here for two weeks at the most,' she assured us once that misunderstanding had been sorted out. In fact Cheltenham was to become our home for the next six months of our lives. Now we knew for sure that we had become 'children in care'; what we didn't yet realise was that from now on the world would view us very differently. Simply by having those two words 'in care' attached to our records we had been branded as low achievers. Basically we were now going to have to prove to the world that we weren't complete losers.

A few days later the police came to talk to us and asked if we wanted to press assault charges against Cathy and Pete. We did consider it but in the end we decided we had enough to think about and didn't want to get involved in another court case if we didn't have to. Since there was no danger of us being sent back there, or of them becoming foster parents again to any other children, we decided it would be sensible to let the whole assault thing drop. We really just wanted to be allowed to get on with our lives.

Chapter Twenty

Isobel

The poor social worker was obviously anxious to get back to her own home by the time we arrived at Cheltenham, so she was very happy to hand responsibility for us over to the staff there. She left, without telling the key workers at the home anything about how we had come to be in her care in the first place. For all they knew we could have been delinquents who had just burned down their family home or been found in a gutter somewhere selling drugs.

They took our details as soon as she had left, wanting to know all sorts of personal details.

'Any tattoos or piercings? Any other distinguishing marks?' Apparently they needed to know things like that so they would be able to put out a description if we disappeared during the night and the police had to come looking for us.

'Have you had those streaks put in your hair?' they asked me.

'No,' I sighed, used to answering this one. 'They're natural.' My brownish-blonde hair looked as though I'd had artificial highlights although I'd never used any product on it except shampoo! It had been like that since I was born.

We were so exhausted by then we just wanted to be shown where we could sleep and left alone. However, they insisted on itemising every single possession we had brought with us in case we accused anyone there of nicking stuff. Our social worker had put padlocks on our bags to help keep our possessions safe, something we had never had to worry about in foster care. It felt as though we were being processed into a prison, as though we had done something wrong rather than been the victims of an attack. The woman taking our details was quite pleasant and chatty and obviously had no idea what we had been through over the previous few days. Her job was just to fire the questions at us and fill out the relevant paperwork. Once she went off duty she was replaced by a night worker who seemed as if she had been in the job for years and believed she had seen and heard it all.

'You kids are all the same,' she told us. 'Don't think you're any different.'

She basically thought that any child who ended up in care was automatically thick and troublesome. We were too tired to protest so we just walked straight past her and went up to bed. We were each given our own rooms.

I fell asleep almost as soon as I climbed under the duvet, but I was jerked awake with my heart pounding a couple of hours later when the bedroom door creaked open and a dark figure tiptoed in and loomed over me.

'Who's that?' I demanded. 'What do you want?'

'Just a routine check,' a strange voice replied. 'Go back to sleep.'

No one had warned us that they would be checking up on us at regular intervals throughout the night. I don't know if they expected us to do a runner, or to try to hang ourselves from the light fittings or what, but it was a strange feeling to know that I couldn't rely on the privacy of that little room, not even for the few hours I needed to sleep. Although it was good to be away from the foster parents, it still felt as though we had taken yet another step backwards in life.

The staff at Cheltenham came and went in shifts, so the people who had signed us in the previous evening had been replaced by the time we woke up and went downstairs in the morning. Again, no one had warned us that would happen. In fact they hadn't told us anything really, so it was baffling to find new faces there when we went looking for some breakfast. And, of course, they knew as little about us as we did about them.

'You're dressed for school!' one of them said, looking shocked that we wouldn't be taking this opportunity to have a day off.

'We always go to school,' I replied. 'Why wouldn't we?'

'No reason, I suppose. Most of the kids here wouldn't bother.'

We didn't ask anything more. We just ate our breakfast and waited until our social worker turned up to pick us up. She was going to have to give us a lift for the forty-minute journey to school since there hadn't been time for the home to organise a taxi service for us.

By the time we got back to Cheltenham after school that afternoon, another shift of new faces had arrived and there were four other kids hanging around. Because our social worker had assured us we would only be there for two weeks I didn't see why I should make any effort to make friends with the others. There was no point if we were going to be moved on again so quickly. We'd hadn't been introduced to any of them anyway and it was quite scary coming into such an alien place, where they all seemed to know one another already and all stood around smoking and shouting most of the time. It was easier just to go to my room and do my homework. So for the next few days I kept myself to myself and only really talked to Alex, as usual. I felt lonely and missed Mum with a terrible aching in my chest.

The rest of our possessions were packed up and moved out of Cathy and Pete's by a private removal firm. There were twenty-three boxes altogether, but no one labelled the individual boxes and it was only after searching them all that I realised out shared laptop computer had gone missing. We made a complaint and requested compensation from the storage company but it turned out that a social worker hadn't filled out the forms correctly so the claim was thrown out. We then applied for social services to get us a replacement computer, but they said it wasn't their fault that it had got lost. We would have been able to claim for it from the storage company if the social worker had filled the forms out correctly but for some reason this didn't count. They also said we wouldn't be needing a computer for long enough to make it worthwhile, since we were close to the end of our schooling. It was a very disheartening introduction to the inhumanities of the care system, where rules were rules and exceptions were seldom made.

After about a week at Cheltenham, Alex was coaxed downstairs by the staff to watch a football match on the telly and he began to talk to the others. Alex never had any trouble making friends in new places, because he was an easygoing character, happy to talk to anyone. By the end of the second week it was obvious we weren't going to be moving on anywhere just yet. I realised I couldn't spend the rest of my life in the bedroom and started to venture downstairs as well.

The home wasn't a big establishment, although it felt big to us because we had only ever lived with two other people at a time. There was an independent unit attached to the home as well, for people who were almost ready to go out into the world and look after themselves but were still under eighteen. Some of the others had police convictions for crimes like car theft and criminal damage, or just for petty things that they had done around the home. It was the management's policy to ring the police every time any of us did anything that was against the rules. I've come across other homes that have the same policy but I don't agree with it because it leads to kids getting criminal records too young, without having done anything serious enough to merit it. Once you have a criminal record it is yet another stigma that you have to live down for years. It's hard enough convincing someone that you're worth anything if you've been brought up in care; if you have a criminal record as well, the obstacles to getting good jobs become almost insurmountable before you start.

The police were always turning up at the home to carry out drug searches, making us all take our coats and jumpers off, and lift our trouser legs up. We were always under suspicion of trying to hide something from them. I had a feeling that most of those searches were illegal since there was never any evidence found that Alex or I had even touched drugs, let alone carried them around. Both of us have naturally dilated pupils, which we grew tired of having to explain every time someone accused us of being high. According to the Police and Criminal Evidence Act an officer does not have the power to search a person unless he or she has reasonable grounds for suspecting that they will find stolen or prohibited articles. As we were never found to be taking or possessing drugs there were no reasonable grounds for suspecting us, other than the fact that we were living in a children's home. The Act also states that before a search can legally commence the officer must make you aware of their name and the name of the police station to which they are attached, the object of the proposed search and their grounds for proposing to make it – none of which was ever done.

I suppose there was good reason for the police to be suspicious of the home in general since every drug dealer in the area seemed to target the kids there, hanging around outside the gates waiting to pounce. I guess it happens in a lot of places like that where everyone knows there are disillusioned kids who are able to get their hands on a bit of pocket money each week but have nothing in particular to spend it on. Drugs are always going to be tempting to people whose lives are shit, and there was a lot of peer group pressure. Kids were told they would be allowed to hang out with the local people they perceived to be cool if they did something for them, like steal goods that could be sold on easily. Often eager to please and wanting to belong, children in care are sometimes easy to lead astray. Drug use would be an inevitable result in many cases. It's like a vicious circle – lots of vicious circles, in fact, most of them overlapping.

The police searches would happen every few weeks and on one of them twenty officers turned up at once to search the building from top to bottom. Even though they never found anything on Alex or me, and the sniffer dogs they brought with them could never smell anything around us, they still wrote down all that went on during the searches and I was really worried that when I went to my first job interview the information would pop up on some computer somewhere telling people that I had been suspected of taking drugs. When your whole life is in the hands of other people you never know what is being logged on your records somewhere to come back and haunt you later. Lots of people worry about our 'surveillance society' but no one suffers from it more than a child who has come into the orbit of the state's care system.

A really nice male social worker took over our case and he seemed surprised by just how much had happened to us in our short lives, and amazed that no one had told us what other types of counselling were available after the first sort had failed. He was the first person who actually realised that our emotional needs might not have been met. By looking at the records he could see that the type of counselling we had tried before wouldn't work and he wanted to make sure we knew what other options there were. As far as he was concerned, he was surprised that we hadn't had a total emotional breakdown by that point.

I wouldn't want to give the impression that everyone in the care system is useless. Some of them are brilliant. There was one male key worker in the home called Paul, for instance, who had been in care himself, with whom Alex formed a very strong bond. Paul was probably the first adult who had achieved that with either of us since Mum died, and he helped Alex a lot by explaining more about the care system and how it worked.

There were several really excellent female key-workers at the home at the time as well. Vanda, Sandy and Jeanette were particularly helpful with my OCD problems and didn't become impatient and shout at me in the way that Cathy and Pete had. For instance, they could see that I got agitated in the evenings, when it came close to bedtime. The kitchen was always locked at night but they would unlock it for me so I could go round making sure all the plugs were turned off before I went to bed. If I didn't go through all those routines I would find it hard to relax and get to sleep. It used to annoy the other kids because they thought I was being allowed into the kitchen to eat something as a special privilege.

Vanda was good at recognising when I was feeling anxious and encouraging me to talk about my feelings. I spent many hours chatting to her about things and she helped me to sort out a few issues. Sandy and another key worker called Debbie were also amazing. Sometimes they realised I needed to get out of the home and they took me out for a drive so I could chat about any worries I might have. They made me realise it was all right to talk about my problems, although I still didn't want to dwell on past issues or go into detail about how much I missed Mum.

The people in that home were also good at treating Alex and me as two individuals rather two halves of one problem, which was how we had got used to being seen by the social workers who had worked on our case up till then. A lot of the time over the previous eighteen months the authorities seemed to assume that I would look after Alex and so they didn't have to worry as long as we had a roof over our heads. In the home it was different and it was helpful to have different people talking to us separately.

Because Cheltenham was only meant to be for short-term care, other kids came and went all the time so we didn't get to make any lasting friendships with any of them. At one stage all of them except one moved on and no one new arrived for a while, so the staff ratio became one to one, twenty-four hours a day. It didn't last long before new kids arrived but it was good while it lasted, more like being part of a family again.

The care workers were very restricted in the punishments they could dole out to kids who misbehaved and sometimes it seemed a bit unfair to me that whenever a kid kicked off and made a fuss about something, the staff would just try to calm them down. Sometimes the other kids caused such a racket that we couldn't sleep at night. Basically it seemed to us they were getting away with misbehaving, while Alex and I never got any reward for keeping quiet and going to school each day. Although they were very nice to us in the home no one from social services ever asked if we needed anything or if there was anything they could do for us because we just got on with life and didn't make a fuss.

When Christmas came a month after we arrived at the Cheltenham, we sort of assumed that Helen and Steve would invite us to their house for the holiday. We had often spent Christmas with them before we went into foster care, when Mum was still alive, and we knew they had been told that we were no longer at Cathy and Pete's, but no invitation was forthcoming. One of Mum's cousins, who we had only ever met two or three times, kindly offered to have us for a few days, but he explained that there would be a lot of family members there who we wouldn't know. When we thought about it we decided that he was probably just being polite and that it would be better if we declined. We assured him that our godparents had invited us, so he wouldn't feel remotely

251

guilty. So in the end we were going to have to stay in the home while all the other kids went to relatives.

It was hard to get into the Christmas spirit under those circumstances, however hard the staff tried to make things festive for us. Exactly the same thing happened again the following year at the next home we were moved to. It would always be a time of year that would remind us of Mum's death anyway, and listening to other people making their Christmas family plans, full of excitement and optimism, would be painful for us.

Alex and I didn't have any spare money that year at Cheltenham, so we each bought the other a CD, which meant opening our presents took about twenty seconds. The staff had cooked us a Christmas lunch, but none of them ate it with us because they were saving themselves for their own family meals once they got home. We could see they were putting on a brave face for us but they were obviously wishing they were already at home as they watched us tucking into the food. We could understand that. After all, being with us was being 'at work' over Christmas for them. If there had been somewhere for us to go they might have been able to close the unit down for a few days and all enjoy the holiday. None of them would have been allowed to ask us back to their houses, even if they'd wanted to, because that would have been against the protocol and breaking the rules. They weren't even allowed to let us know where they lived. I suppose that was for their own protection in case a kid started stalking them or something. It was supposed to be just a job for them and they were not supposed to allow themselves to become emotionally attached to their charges. Any that failed to follow the rules and actually allowed their hearts to rule their heads would be severely reprimanded and maybe even sacked. I suppose the system can't be allowed to have a heart in case it gets broken.

Three months later it was my eighteenth birthday but I didn't feel like celebrating it at all. The main significance of the date was that I was now allowed to take the test to see if I had inherited Huntington's disease from Mum. I talked them into letting me take it a couple of weeks before my birthday, and the results came through a couple of weeks after. Sandy took me to the appointment and was sitting with me when the geneticist gave me the fateful news – the results were positive. I had the disease, just like Mum and just like my grandmother before her. Suddenly my options for the future were radically altered. To start with I knew I wouldn't ever want to have children now, because there was a fifty-fifty chance I would pass the disease on to them and continue it down the line after that, plus there was the fact that I might not be around to see them grow up and might end up being a burden to them. On the positive side, at least I didn't have to worry about saving for a pension because

I was never going to live long enough to need one. I would also not have been eligible to join the police or the army, had I wanted to, but that fact was more relevant to Alex, who at that time was thinking he might like to join the air force.

There were so many thoughts swirling around my head after I got the test results that I couldn't react straight away. The geneticist seemed more worried about the fact that I hadn't cried than she would have been if I had completely broken down. Why did everyone always want to see me bursting into tears about everything? To me it just seemed like one more thing to cope with, something I could do nothing about. Sandy took me out for a drive around the countryside after I heard the news, knowing that I wouldn't want Alex to see me upset and giving me the opportunity to talk in private if I wanted to. All I really wanted to talk about was how having the disease was likely to affect my chances of getting interesting jobs, and my biggest worry was how Alex would cope when I died, seeing as he would then have lost every single member of his birth family. I think perhaps the odd tear escaped down my cheeks as I thought of all the possible problems this new revelation would raise.

When we got back to the unit I told Alex my news in private and he didn't react either – so then they thought that maybe I hadn't told him, that I was keeping it from him to spare him the worry. But it was just that neither of us were particularly bothered. The staff started getting together all sorts of information about the illness for me, but I didn't really want to know. I was happy just to worry about it later and deal with the symptoms when they arrived. There didn't seem to be much point getting all worked up now when it might not strike for another twenty or thirty years.

'Any of us could be hit by a bus tomorrow,' I reminded them, 'but you can't worry about that every day, can you? But that's what you're telling me to do. I could waste my whole life thinking about how I might die, or I could just live every day to the maximum. There are a lot of people in much worse positions than me, people who are already disabled or have a debilitating disease. I can still live a perfectly normal life.'

It seemed like the obvious way of handling it to me.

After the diagnosis, I travelled down to a hospital in London where the doctors were keen to do tests on me because they didn't get to hear of many people my age who were known to have Huntington's. They told me that even if they found a cure for it they wouldn't know when to give it to me because they can't predict when it will start or what will trigger the onset. One day there may be a cure for Huntington's, they told me, perhaps even as a result of studying my progress, but I have to resign myself to the fact that it probably won't be in time for me to benefit from it.

The rules surrounding friendships with care workers of any sort don't always work to the advantage of kids in care. Alex and I had to leave Cheltenham shortly after I got my Huntington's diagnosis, after just six months there. Vanda, Sandy and Paul were allowed to stay in touch with us for the first few weeks to help us to deal with the change, but after that we were supposed to stop contact. I think this is because they feel it would make it difficult for the workers in the next home to form relationships with us and to have authority over us. Vanda kept texting me for a couple of months but then she was told by her boss to stop it. I'm sure there are good reasons for these rules, but it is hard enough to form relationships with other people when you are in the sort of situation most of us were in, without having the ones you do form being artificially cut off every time you are moved somewhere new. It removed the possibility of forming normal, human friendships that could evolve over a number of years, as most good friendships do.

Sandy was able to stay in touch with me because she left her job soon after we were moved from Cheltenham, but I was surprised how much it hurt suddenly to be cut off from the other people I had grown close to, especially at a time when I was adjusting to a new home and a change of environment. It felt a bit like a repeat of the day when Mum died, as a large chunk of our previous life vanished completely overnight. Every time this happened it reinforced the feeling that nothing and nobody can be relied on to stay with you forever. I made a conscious vow to myself that I wouldn't allow anyone in the next place to get so close to me, so I didn't have to go through the feeling of being separated from them again when the inevitable happened. I knew that I would soon be considered an adult and I would have to sever my roots again in order to move out into the world.

That feeling of needing to be self-sufficient in order to protect myself has stayed with me ever since. I try to do everything myself rather than ask other people for help, for fear that I will become dependent on them in some way. In my experience if you ever rely on someone else you end up being let down.

There are so many misconceptions about children like us who end up having to be taken into care, it is hard to know where to start when trying to dispel them. If ever you tell someone that you were 'in care' once you are out in the adult world their next question is nearly always, 'What did you do wrong?' The immediate assumption is always that you were taken into care as a punishment or because your parents couldn't control your behaviour in some way. I suppose in the old days Alex and I would have been able to say we went to an 'orphanage' and then everyone would know it was because we had lost our parents through no fault of our own, but no one uses that word any more. This stigma

257

can have very real effects on applications for jobs and on forming relationships and any number of other life experiences. It marks you out as having come from a certain sort of background, a background that people assume makes it likely you are troublesome at worst and an underachiever at best.

If I don't want to go into the whole story behind how we came to be in care when I first meet someone, it's always best not to mention it at all. I read somewhere that only a tiny percentage of children in care (I think the figure was less than three per cent) are there through their own fault, but if you ask people to guess most would probably think the reverse was true. The vast majority of us find ourselves there because the adults who should be caring for us aren't able to. I would suspect that even that three per cent are misbehaving for a reason that is based on the way the adults in their lives have treated them. I'm not saying all children are innocent little angels; I'm just saying there are always reasons why they behave the way they do.

As long as I was still at school, or living in care homes, everyone always knew that I was the girl whose father had killed her mother. It had been our choice to stay in the school where the first big announcement was made at assembly, but the story would probably have followed us to any other school just because the teachers would have been informed and because the other kids would soon discover we were in care and would want to know why. At least by staying where we were we didn't have to keep explaining ourselves because everyone already knew the basic story.

The other drawback to people knowing about our past is that it sometimes makes them reluctant to talk about their own problems because they believe everything they say sounds petty in comparison to what we have been through. It is hard to know which is the worst option – not being able to talk about your past, or being constantly judged for what happened to you years before.

Chapter Twenty-One

Alex

We were moved out of the Cheltenham unit a few days after Isobel was told she had Huntington's. In fact we had been due to move the next day but the key workers thought she might need a bit more support considering what she had just found out. As it turned out she was fine about it and didn't need any support, but even if she had been traumatised by the news I doubt if a couple of days would have made much difference.

The worst thing about being moved was that we lost touch with the workers who we had been getting on with so well – there was a guy called Paul I was very close to – and with the friends of my own age. I'd made a whole lot of new friends in the Cheltenham area over the previous six months because it's the sort of place where there isn't a lot for the young people to do so they just tend to congregate around the town centre together, talking. The locals were very wary of anyone they knew had come from the unit and if the community officer spotted us out and about he would always stop us and ask where we were going and what we were doing, as if we were bound to be off to do a bit of thieving or drug dealing just because we were in care. When we first arrived the people at the unit had warned us that they gave our pictures to the local shopkeepers as a matter of routine so they would be able to spot us and watch out that we didn't shoplift. I don't know if it was true or not, but it was depressing to think that we were automatically considered to be dishonest and untrustworthy just because we had ended up in their care.

Each place we were put into seemed to be further from our school than the last. This latest one was an independent unit attached to another home, which was progress for us, but it was an hour and a half's drive away. Trying to get to school from there by bus was virtually impossible. We were now cut off completely from our school friends socially because there was no way we could meet up with them in the evenings. You cook and clean for yourself in an independent unit, so Isobel was able to look after me on her own but she still had the staff of the attached home on hand for back-up if she needed them. Most of the time she was the most capable person on the premises anyway since she had been looking after our interests for over two years.

I was fifteen by then and Isobel had just turned eighteen. She never complained about having to look after me

– not that I ever needed much looking after compared to some of the kids we met in care. The only way in which she put pressure on me was in making sure I did my homework properly and going over any oral course work with me. The key workers sometimes worried that she was holding me back from developing my own powers of self-sufficiency by doing so much for me, but neither of us believed that. If Mum had still been alive she would have been doing even more for me, like most other fifteen-year-old boys' mums.

Whatever anyone said to us, we were always united in our determination not to be separated. If we hadn't got each other we would have had nothing at all at that stage. Although they believed Isobel should not interfere in my life as much as she did, when there was something difficult to do they would often ask her to do it for me. For example, after Isobel had left the home, they rang her when a worker I had bonded with died from liver failure and asked her to break the news to me because they thought I would take it badly and they didn't fancy telling me themselves.

While we were in the homes together they always had our review meetings together until the social workers and unit manager decided it would be better to separate us because I never got a chance to say anything. But they had misread the situation. The reason I never had anything to say was because I didn't have much respect for the people at the meetings or the things they were talking about. I believed I would be wasting my breath if I piped up. I've always preferred thinking to talking anyway; sometimes I over-analyse situations to a ridiculous degree. I've always been like this; if I haven't got anything to say I just keep quiet and wait for everyone else to have their say. Just because I'm quiet, however, doesn't mean I don't do a lot of thinking. Sometimes my brain is so busy I have trouble calming it down enough to let me get to sleep at night. It's always buzzing away, developing theories about anything and everything and exploring new possibilities. There had been so much in my childhood that I hadn't understood, and as I grew up I would sometimes get completely lost applying new discoveries to memories that had previously puzzled me. In particular, I kept trying to come up with logical explanations for all the sequences of events the day that Mum died. From time to time I would try my developing theories out on Isobel and she would pretty soon tell me to shut up.

'You're hurting my brain,' she would complain.

When they told us I must go to the next review meeting on my own Isobel was furious, aware that I wasn't as knowledgeable as her about the law and could easily agree to something that wasn't in my interests just because I couldn't be bothered to argue. I had to fill in a form before the meeting, which had a section asking if there was anyone I would like to accompany me on the day. They must have forgotten it was there, or thought I wouldn't notice. I just wrote Isobel's name in. Their faces were a picture of frustration when she came into the room at the beginning of the meeting with a copy of the form to wave at them when they asked her why she was there. There must have been times when we were very exasperating to them.

Isobel was due to leave school in a few months and was thinking seriously about what she was going to do next. She had gone off the idea of going to university when she did some research because the course she fancied – Forensic Science – was only taught at universities that were a long way away. I was going to have to stay in the home for a couple more years while I did my A levels and the thought of being separated by a big distance was hard for both of us. We both knew, however, that if she didn't go to university she would still have to leave the home and she would then have to find a job and support herself immediately, living in a hostel or a council flat or paying rent. That was what happened to most of the other kids we talked to in the home. The girls all seemed to think that getting pregnant and being given a council flat was probably the best option open to them and none of the staff tried to disillusion them and expand their horizons with alternative suggestions. When Isobel said she wanted to go to university the staff told her she was wasting her time because she was bound to fail, that she didn't have it in her and wasn't ready for it. No one seemed to think it would be worth trying to inspire kids like us to have higher expectations for our lives. No one thought to praise or reward us for going to school every day, for instance, in the hope that it would encourage others to follow our example.

I understand that it was difficult for the key workers because their powers of influence were limited. When kids in the home couldn't be bothered to get out of bed in the morning, the staff could hardly haul them out and drive them to school against their wishes, as a conscientious parent might try to do. Whenever we raised the subject with staff at the home they got defensive.

'It's all right for you,' they said. 'You have the work ethic because of how you were brought up by your Mum. Most of the kids here have come from families on benefits and they've never known anything else. That's all they aspire to.'

I don't think they realised quite how hard we'd had to struggle to keep going during the difficult times. Isobel and I thought that as corporate parents the staff at the homes should have been doing the same things for their charges that Mum had done for us, although Isobel tended to voice her opinions more often than me.

If she did decide to go on to university rather than stepping straight out into the world, social services would continue to pay her expenses and she would receive a small income from Mum's pension for as long as she stayed in full-time education. She would then be in a better position to do what she chose in life at the end of it. If she decided not to go she would immediately have to start earning a living and would be able to stay close to the home I was in, but she would lose the money from the pension. Although I think in her heart Isobel always knew that she should go to university and achieve the goals that Mum worked so hard to steer her towards, it was still a daunting prospect for her compared with staying in a familiar area and just getting a job.

She agonised over it for a long time but when she finally had to make the decision it was obvious that the right and brave thing to do was to go as far as she could with her education. Although I had always depended on her a lot, I had also learned to be pretty self-sufficient myself and I was sure I could manage on my own with the foundations that she and Mum had laid for me, and with the key workers from the home our unit was attached to for back-up. Plucking up all her courage, Isobel sent off application forms to six different universities, with no idea whether they would offer her places or if, as the staff at the home predicted, she was just setting herself up for rejection.

Over the following few weeks she was offered places at all six of them, much to the amazement of the staff. I felt so proud of her and sad at the same time to think that Mum would never know how all her hard work had paid off. No one in the care system seems to expect the children in their charge to go on to further education. None of the workers we came across had been to university themselves and none of the other kids felt that it was worth the struggle even to try to convince anyone of their potential. We knew just how hard it was to be taken seriously after we were unable to get a replacement computer when our own was stolen during the move to Cheltenham.

While we were in the independent unit the *Dispatches* television documentary team infiltrated a reporter into the home posing as a care worker, as part of a programme about the way children's homes in the area were run. It wasn't targeted specifically at our home because they took their hidden cameras to several others as well. The reporter befriended us and the other children in order to get us all to talk candidly, but they didn't show any of the footage they took of Isobel and me in the programme. I guess we didn't fit into the pattern of behaviour they wanted to illustrate. They wanted to show kids behaving in a disruptive fashion and illustrate how the system was letting them down but Isobel and I were just getting on with our lives as best we could in the circumstances, which didn't make for interesting television. We were in the room when many of the conversations that later found their way into the programme took place and we knew that the editing process had frequently changed the sense of what was being said to make it more dramatic and in order to illustrate the points that the director wanted to make.

I suspect that some of the footage shown could have damaged the children featured in it. For example, it showed one child threatening to hit another over a stolen fag and a staff member saying, 'It's your fault if you get punched back.' It also showed some staff in the staffroom calling a particular child a 'slag'. It was true that not all the staff in the homes were brilliant, but the film actually made some of the good ones look bad and lost them their jobs as a result. The sacked staff then had to be replaced by agency staff who came and went very quickly and never formed any sort of lasting relationships with any of us. Many of the agency staff were foreign and knew nothing about the educational system in England and were even less able to advise us than the ones who had been sacked. On top of that some of the kids were all able to hear the staff talking about them on the programme via the reporter's hidden camera. Such conversations should have been confidential and hearing them broadcast undermined everyone's faith in the staff even more. We all knew they talked about us amongst themselves, but to actually hear them doing so on television must have been very unnerving for the kids involved.

Isobel had started taking driving lessons while we were living with Cathy and Pete, using her twenty pounds a week pocket money to pay the instructor. She took her test once we were in Cheltenham but failed it the first time because of her reverse parking. She didn't have any money left for more lessons so all she could do was rebook to take the test again, and hope for the best. This time she pulled it off. As soon as she turned eighteen, she got the money that our Granddad had left in trust for her and she decided to use it to buy a car.

When she told the staff at the new home that she was going to get a car, they laughed and said she would have to get a licence first. They couldn't believe it when she produced her licence and they realised that she had already organised it by herself. She was probably the first child in care they had come across who owned her own car. It was a wonderful feeling of freedom when she could finally drive us around and we didn't have to ask other people to do us favours by giving us lifts or bus or taxi fares all the time.

In October 2004, it was time for Isobel to leave the home and start university. It was a huge wrench for both of us, but at least now she had the car, she could drive back and forth to see me some weekends. It was a struggle for Isobel to manage financially without any parents to help, but somehow she still managed to bring me books to help with my A levels. She got a student loan but she had to pay all her accommodation costs out of that, which left her very little spare money from Mum's teaching pension to live on. She was also having to do all the practical things like buying toiletries and cleaning products and finding somewhere to live. Most students would be able to enlist their parents to help with at least some of these chores, but Isobel had to find out about it all as she went along, do it all herself and still make sure I was getting whatever I needed back at the home. I tried not to ask for too many things or to put her under any extra pressure but, like Mum before her, she was determined that neither of us should miss a single opportunity in life and that took an enormous amount of effort on her part. Lack of money was a constant source of worry. As long as I was in the children's home I was given twenty pounds a week to buy food (which meant I mainly lived on pasta and potatoes). The key workers would give me another ten pounds pocket money for myself, but I had nothing spare by the end of the week.

In the five years after Mum died, Isobel and I had thirteen different social workers, many of them kind people who were doing their best but just didn't have the time to do everything. When my last new social worker was assigned to me I met her once but at the time of writing, over a year later, have not seen her since. I know for sure that I would never have made it into higher education if Isobel hadn't pushed me to keep up my schoolwork at every opportunity. No social workers ever asked me how I was doing at school, or what I wanted to do when I left. As it turned out I suppose I have been okay, but only because Isobel has been there for me at every turn. She stepped into Mum's shoes on the 11th of January 2002 and has looked after me ever since. Life would have been very different for me if I hadn't had her.

Chapter Twenty-Two

Isobel

Going to university was the first time that I had ever been separated from Alex for more than a few days. I'd accepted the offer from Staffordshire University and driving up on my own, having done all the preparation myself, was an overwhelming experience. I felt painfully lonely as I watched everyone else being dropped off by their parents, loaded down with pots and pans and various home comforts. The children's home had bought me one pan, one plate, a duvet and a pillow. Knowing nothing about university life it had never occurred to me that I would need all the stuff the others were carting in from their parents' cars.

In the following weeks, whenever I heard one of the other students talking to their parents on the phone, or watched them unwrapping a food parcel from home, I was reminded how alone in the world I was. I needed someone older and more experienced who I trusted to tell me that it was all right to feel the way I was feeling, but there was no one I could talk to since the people I had befriended at the first home weren't allowed to contact me. The only person I could turn to was my little brother, who didn't know anything about university life and had enough problems of his own to contend with. He suddenly seemed a long way away and I missed him badly.

Four weeks after the beginning of term I panicked, afraid that I was going to feel that lonely and unhappy forever, and I drove back to see him. When I got to the home I announced that I had made a mistake and that I was going to quit my course so that Alex and I could be back together again. When the staff at the home and the social workers heard they just smiled knowingly.

'We told you that you wouldn't be able to do it,' they gloated and there was nothing I could say in return.

Not one of them suggested I should go back and give it a proper go – Alex was the only one saying to me, 'Don't give up. You can do it!' But in the end I should be grateful to them because it was their negative comments that drove me to make the decision myself, just to prove them wrong. After two weeks of hanging around the home, listening to them and thinking through the consequences of my actions, I made up my mind to give it another go and got back into my car. Given time to reflect I realised that the alternatives to university were going to be much worse and that I would probably be feeling just as isolated in a council flat or a hostel somewhere. At least at university I had a chance to make a new circle of friends and to get some better qualifications. Once a child grows too old to be in care they have to go out into the world and fend for themselves as best they can. If they get a job and somewhere to live, that is probably as far as they will go. This university place was probably my only chance to go a little further.

Carol, a social worker I respected, once said to me: 'There are times when people in situations like yours decide either to sink or swim. You have obviously decided to swim.'

Her words kept going through my head as I drove back, determined to enjoy myself and make the best of the opportunities that were on offer to me. Even now, whenever I feel as though I'm struggling a bit, I keep telling myself, 'sink or swim, sink or swim.' It's funny how simple little phrases like that can sometimes seem to sum up all the wisdom in the world. I know that at low moments like the ones I experienced in those first few weeks away from Alex there must be many people who decide it is all too much of a struggle and just allow themselves to sink. Maybe if I hadn't had responsibility for him as well as myself I wouldn't have been able to keep swimming for long enough to get through the hard times.

People often ask me if I chose Forensic Science as my degree subject because of what happened to Mum, but I don't think it was specifically that. I had always leaned towards the sciences, which probably was because of Mum's influence, but I knew my biology, chemistry and physics were not strong enough for me to do a pure course in them. I had always been interested in the idea of collecting evidence at crime scenes in order to get criminals convicted, regardless of what happened in our house that day, and when I discovered you could actually do a course on the subject it seemed like a useful and interesting thing to study.

One of the nicest things about going to university in a different city was that I could choose who I wanted to talk to about my past. At university, you can pretty much re-invent yourself and select which bits of your history you want people to find out about. No one knows anything about where you've come from or what your parents were like. It was a very liberating feeling. Once I had made good friends there, I would tell them bits about my background when the subject came up, but not until they had already got to know me for who I was, and weren't judging me based on the fact that my father had murdered my mother.

My biggest problem once I was at university was concentrating on the work. It was a standing joke amongst my friends that within five minutes of a lecture starting I would be off in my own dream world, think-ing of all the things I needed to do to sort out my life and

Alex's: laying plans, compiling lists of phone calls I needed to make to solicitors or writing letters. I suppose that must have been what Mum's life was like as well, always working out how to get the two of us here, there and everywhere at the same time as doing her job to the best of her ability.

Luckily my lapses of concentration in lectures didn't matter too much because I've always been good at teaching myself. I did the same with my GCSEs and A levels, using the books to learn at home if I had missed a lesson due to attending the court case or talking to the police. There was one topic in a module that the majority of my class failed one year because the teacher had forgotten to teach it, but because I'd done it on my own without realising it hadn't been covered in class, I was one of the few who passed. The same happened at university. I found I didn't really need to concentrate in lectures because all the material could be found in the books or notes anyway. People often thought I was quite thick in classes and lectures because if a question was fired in my direction I would hardly ever be able to answer it. Sometimes I didn't even realise it was me they were asking and I would get told off for following flies round the room, my head in a complete dream world. But a month or so before the exams I would simply sit down and learn whatever needed to be learnt, blocking off whole twelve-hour days for revision and becoming frustrated if someone even walked near my room and their footsteps broke my concentration. I became totally stressed, worrying that I was going to fail and would end up letting everyone down, and wasn't able to talk to anyone for days on end. I couldn't bear the thought that I might not come out top of whatever I went in for. Then when the exams finally came round, a sudden calmness would descend. Studying that way had always got me top marks at school and the same happened at university. Everyone was amazed, including me, when I ended up being the only person who started the course in my year to be awarded a First.

If someone in care chooses to go to university the authorities will help them to fund it with grants and loans, but they will make no allowance for the fact that they have nowhere to go during the vacations. With the Christmas holidays looming at the end of my first term I realised that I wouldn't be allowed to stay in my room at the university, but I wasn't allowed to go back to the children's home either now that I had finished school. But I had no money to rent anywhere. I dare say a lot of people in that situation can find some relative or other who will take them in, but we knew from past Christmases that that wasn't a realistic expectation.

Fortunately for me, the home that Alex was living in applied for special permission so I could go back and stay with him during that first holiday. When they asked us what we were going to be doing on Christmas Day we explained we probably wouldn't be having a meal since we didn't have enough money to buy the ingredients. It didn't seem worth cooking a big meal just for two of us anyway, especially as I'm a vegetarian and Alex isn't, so they allowed us to come down to the home and eat lunch with the one other child who was staying over the holidays. They made it clear I could only stay a few days and it must never happen again.

When I returned during the Easter break, I still had nowhere to stay and so social services were forced to find me somewhere or see me homeless on the street. They responded by putting me into a bed and breakfast hotel. They dropped me off outside the place where they said they had booked me in. It didn't look too promising as I walked in but I was grateful just to have a roof over my head. As the first night wore on I soon realised my temporary home was a mixture between a brothel and a doss house. There were about six people sharing the bathroom and all the guests had to be off the premises during the day. The manager kicked us all out into the street at seven the following morning.

I hadn't slept well that night, after being forced to listen to the prostitutes working in the other rooms around me, and when I woke up that morning, which happened to be my nineteenth birthday, I decided I couldn't stay there a moment longer. I rang my social worker as soon as the office opened, but whoever answered the phone told me she was on annual leave and that there was no one else there who could do anything to help. Alex was still at school so the whole day stretched ahead of me with nowhere to go. Even once Alex was back at his flat I was only allowed in as a visitor between ten in the morning and ten at night. There was nothing else to do but sit in the car and wait for the hours to pass. So that was how I spent my birthday that year.

I could have filled those holidays more profitably by getting a temporary job of some sort but if I had done that I would have risked losing all the pension and social services money that I was living on during term time. The holidays were also only three weeks long, which limited the sort of jobs I could have done. I racked my brain for anyone I could contact for help, but I had lost contact with all my old school friends once I went to university, partly because I hadn't wanted to impose myself on them any more than I already had. Eventually I swallowed my pride and rang Helen, who I had hardly spoken to since Alex and I were put into the foster home, and I begged her to meet me in town. She eventually agreed but when I told her I needed help she was initially wary. In the end I begged so hard she gave in and reluctantly agreed that I could sleep on a pull-out bed in the office until term began again. Just having a roof over my head and not having to sleep in my car was good enough for me by that stage.

Although Helen let me stay for the holidays, I soon realised she was only doing it because she believed she had no choice. I felt as though I was in everyone's way and hated having to impose myself like that. She didn't trust me with a door key, so there was one night when I came back from seeing Alex to find she was out and I wasn't able to get into the house. I didn't want to cause a problem by asking them to come back early from wherever they were, so I slept in my car. The staff at Alex's home suspected what was going on and offered to let me stay in the staff accommodation, which was a kind gesture, but I turned it down. I was stubborn and didn't want to admit that I needed their help. In the end I told Helen I was going back to university earlier than I actually could because I felt so guilty about imposing on her, and I spent the last few nights sleeping in my car.

Even though I'd had so many offers from universities, had taken one up and was now doing well, social services still didn't believe Alex when we told them he was going to follow the same path. We had tried to find out in advance what sort of support might be available to Alex if he accepted one of the university offers, but the social workers wouldn't even discuss it, telling him it was a waste of time to think of it because there was no chance he would get in anywhere. When the offers started to arrive they had to think again and it was obvious they didn't have a clue where to start and were learning about it at the same time we were because the student loan system had changed so Alex's entitlements were different than they had been when I had started university.

As Alex's eighteenth birthday approached, we had a very important appointment to make. My heart was in my mouth as I helped him to make the arrangements to take his test for Huntington's disease. Surely fate wouldn't be so cruel as to let both of us have the faulty gene? If we had both had it, the chances were that I would be the first to die, just because I am older, and I worried about who would look after him once I had gone. Mum must have had all these worries in her final years, fretting about who would nurse her when her health deteriorated and who would look after us once she was gone, little knowing she had much less time left than she thought.

I can't describe the overwhelming relief I felt when the results came back and Alex was in the clear. I think I cried more than I did when I'd got my own positive results over two years before. Now I didn't have to worry about him getting ill and we could make concrete plans for his future; I only had to think about myself and how I would deal with the symptoms when they arrived. Honestly, if one of us had to have this horrible disease, I'm happy that it was me rather than Alex. I couldn't have stood nursing him through it if I was in the clear. That would have been too hard.

The other development when Alex turned eighteen was that he bought himself a car with the money he got from Granddad's trust fund. He'd passed the test after his seventeenth birthday. Unfortunately, he hadn't had the car long when he was involved in an accident. It wasn't his fault but his car was a write-off and he couldn't immediately afford a new one. The insurance company said that if he made a claim, he wouldn't be able to get insurance again until he was twenty-one, so he was a bit stuck.

Before he got the car, social services had been paying for him to take taxis to school, at a cost of nearly a thousand pounds a month, but after the accident they refused to fund him any more so it was very hard for him to get to school. Sometimes circumstances just seemed to pile up against us, and I had to keep thinking, 'sink or swim, sink or swim!'

Rather than helping him find a way to get to school more cheaply, they decided he was being rebellious by not going in every day and was therefore not taking his education seriously. No one offered to help him with his university applications, but because I had already been down the same route I knew exactly what he needed to do and we managed without any help from anyone else.

no one listened

So many times over the years I had promised myself I would never rely on social services for anything, having been let down over and over again. This time, however, I really meant it. I knew that if I waited for them to sort Alex out it would never happen. I was going to have to do it myself, just as I had for my own university applications.

Social services did not believe Alex was going to uni until he was actually there, but he still had to leave the home straight after his last A level exam as he had turned eighteen. Even when he started to get offers of places back from the universities in writing, social services still wouldn't believe that it was actually going to happen. In front of him they said they didn't believe it because he was 'too thick' to go to university. Social services actually wanted to chuck him out into a hostel on the day of his eighteenth birthday, even though he was still in the middle of doing his A levels at the time. I pleaded with them for ages before they eventually agreed to let him stay another week, just to finish the exams, but that was all they were willing to concede. Even if we had still been in foster care the same thing could well have happened because they would have stopped paying for his care the moment he turned eighteen, regardless of whether he was still at school or not. It seemed to me that this was yet another barrier to kids in care getting into further education. How hard would it be to do well in your A levels if you had to move into a hostel half way through the exams?

I was so angry about the injustice of it I wrote to Prime Minister Tony Blair to let him know what was happening. I did get a reply, but it was just to say that he was passing my letter on to the Department for Education and Families. They then wrote to say they couldn't do anything because the law actually states that in the period between leaving school and starting at university a person is officially not in education any more, even though his place has been arranged and all the paperwork has been done. It was a horrific example of a heartless bureaucracy refusing to see what was obviously the right thing to do.

It meant that Alex was not entitled to any accommodation or financial support from social services during the summer between leaving school and starting uni. They wrote to say there wasn't anything they could do because legally Alex wasn't back in education until the first day of his university course. So during those summer holidays I had to find somewhere for both of us to stay. University landlords don't want students hanging around during the holidays and the care home certainly wouldn't have us back now we were both over eighteen. There was nothing else to do but bend the rules if we weren't both going to be spending the summer in my car. I managed to sneak Alex in to stay in my student accommodation, without the landlord knowing, because otherwise he would have been completely homeless throughout the summer. There's no way we could have afforded to rent two rooms.

At the beginning of October 2006 I drove him up to Manchester to start his course, having arranged his accommodation myself and bought all the supplies I knew from my own experience he would need. As far as social services were concerned he had come of age and left the system, so he wasn't their responsibility any longer.

Once he arrived at university he didn't bother to tell anyone about his past history, happy to get on with making new friends and moving forward. He settled in much more quickly and easily than I had, perhaps because he'd had a couple of years on his own in the independent unit before moving out, or maybe just because he has such an easygoing nature.

He started on a computing course in his first year, then moved on to forensics in the second year, learning how to acquire data and maintain its integrity. Working with computers and phones and CCTV cameras is one of the biggest parts of police work these days because the technology contains so many clues and so much information. Someone who knows how to find that information and capture it in a way that it can be used as evidence is a valuable commodity. If Sherlock Holmes were at work today he would almost certainly have these sorts of IT skills as part of his portfolio.

If the police raided a house where they thought someone had been downloading child pornography, for instance, they would need to call in a professional with Alex's skills to make sure they didn't switch off anything valuable, or make the evidence inadmissible by not following the right procedures. They need to know how to get into a computer's memory while not opening themselves up to accusations of having tampered with it.

Alex was always brilliant with computers, totally confident about them from the day Mum first brought one home for us. He seemed to know instinctively how to put them together and make them work, without having to read any manuals or ask any questions. I was so proud of the way he was taking off in the world on his own and I knew Mum would have been too. Only occasionally did I allow myself to stop and feel sad that she wasn't there to see it.

Chapter Twenty-Three

Alex

When I bought my first car, it felt great to be able to get myself about and be independent, without having to rely on anyone else. Social services agreed to give me just enough petrol money to be able to drive myself to and from school each day, which was a lot less than I had been costing them in taxi fares. But then I had the accident, which messed up everything.

I was in the car with two friends when the one sitting in the front suddenly had an epileptic fit while we were driving along. As I pulled over to draw into a lay-by, my other friend in the back panicked and yanked on the handbrake, which sent the car spinning off the road and into a lamppost, hitting it dead in the centre of the bonnet. It was a complete write-off even though none of us were hurt. I was insured but the insurance company warned that if I made a claim I wouldn't be able to get insurance again until I was twenty-one. We couldn't afford for me not to be driving for another three years so we had to accept that all my inheritance from Granddad had disappeared in those few seconds of skidding across the road.

I was heartbroken about it, and to make matters worse, social services wouldn't go back to paying for taxis for me to get to school, telling me I had to get a bus. Not only did the bus trip take about two and a half hours each way, but the first bus of the day didn't leave early enough to get me to school on time so it became increasingly difficult to get to my lessons. They suggested that I could move schools to be closer to the home, but I was on the verge of taking my A levels and I thought that even with the travel problems it would be better to stay where I was at such a crucial time. I think they actually hoped I would quit school altogether at that stage and take up an apprenticeship somewhere, but all Mum's early brainwashing about the importance of education had sunk too deeply into my subconscious for me to be willing to give up at this late stage. Not that Isobel would have allowed me to anyway.

As usual Isobel went into battle on my behalf, demanding that they help me out with taxi money for a few more months just so that I could get my exams, but even when faced with her full fury they were still adamant. They would pay for the petrol and that was all.

'But he doesn't have a car any more,' Isobel protested down the phone from her university. 'So what good is a petrol allowance?'

288

'It's your responsibility to make sure he has a car,' they replied. 'All we can do is provide a fuel allowance.'

Luckily for me Isobel had worked as an evening supervisor in a convenience store over the summer and had managed to save a little bit of money so she scraped everything together and bought me an old banger a few weeks later. Although I had missed a good few days at school by that time it was just enough to get me in for the last weeks and I managed to get the A level grades I needed to secure my place at the university I wanted. Yet again Isobel had saved the day simply by refusing to be beaten.

Once I started university and was living in a different town from her, we stopped seeing much of each other during term time, but we still talk every day for at least half an hour, and we always get together in the holidays. We've bought a house together with the money we got from our half of the proceeds from Mum's house, and we've got tenants in and are keeping it as an investment. Needless to say, Isobel arranged all this, just as she's taken care of most of the practical arrangements in our lives since Mum died.

Social services hardly ever get in touch with me now. I think they speak to Isobel from time to time and when she tells them that I'm doing fine, they just say 'Tell him to ring us if he has a problem.' I can't imagine that I ever would now. If I have a problem, I always ring Isobel –

and I hope that she does the same with me. We are so lucky to have each other. I don't think either of us would be where we are today if we had been only children. In fact, I know we wouldn't, because when Mum died and we desperately needed caring adults to look after us, no one listened.

Epilogue

Isobel

B y the time I had finished my degree I knew that I wanted to work in children's homes myself. I was sure I could make a real contribution, knowing what I did about the system from the inside. I believe it often lets down the kids in care and want to do as much as I can to right that situation. This is not due to lack of effort by the workers themselves, but because of the way the whole system is set up. I am told that only one per cent of children brought up in care get to university. It has become an accepted fact, even in the care homes themselves, that further education isn't for 'people like us'.

This was brought home to me again when I was working in a care home after I graduated and there was a young girl who was having some troubles. During a conversation with her I assured her I understood how she felt because I had been in care too. I hadn't actually told the staff of the home much about my personal background at that stage, mainly because they hadn't asked, so when word got back to a senior worker she asked me into her office for a chat. She informed me that she had been in the room when the girl mentioned to another member of staff that I had been in care.

'Really?' the staff member had replied. 'But I thought Isobel had been to university.'

This was a woman who worked in the system and had closed her mind to the idea that someone in care could go to university. Yet most children in care are there through no fault of their own, so why don't more of them get a chance of further education? They're not there because they are bad, or stupid, but just because there wasn't anyone willing or able to look after them. Is it simply because society doesn't expect them to go and so does nothing to help them? Apart from the academic work necessary to be accepted by a university, there are also all the administration skills needed to fill out the right forms, get to interviews and organise accommodation. It is hard enough for a young person with two parents and a supportive family to find their way through the maze. What chance is there for someone who is being looked after by social workers who mostly have no expectations for them at all and possibly know nothing about the further education system themselves anyway?

'Actually,' I said, 'the young person is right. I was in care.'

'Ah,' she said knowingly, 'foster care was it?'

It seemed she simply couldn't believe that any child from a unit like the one we were working in could ever get to university.

'No one from this unit has gone on to further education,' she said emphatically.

It's as if some of the people working in the care industry feel defeated by the enormity of the tasks they are confronted with and have closed their minds to the possibility that kids in their care could do well in life. They have no energy or enthusiasm left for helping them to achieve anything beyond the bare minimum. They have no confidence that they can make a difference to the life of any individual child, so they just fulfil their obligations to keep the children safe and go no further than that. Partly it's because they are all so poorly paid. It is hard to recruit enthusiastic, educated and hard-working people and ask them to work incredibly anti-social hours if you are paying virtually nothing. How are they to support their own families?

When I was working in a home myself after I graduated, I found a child who wanted to go to university. I was immediately enthused and wanted to help her get the right forms and fill them in correctly. When I mentioned it to one member of staff she dismissed the idea.

'She's always saying that but it's never going to happen,' was all they said, just as I imagine they must have said to one another about me and Alex when we kept saying we wanted to go into further education.

But why not? Would they give up that easily if it was one of their own children who wanted to improve themselves and learn new things? Should there not be training courses for staff who are in the corporate parenting role to make sure they understand how to fulfil the basic tasks of modern parenthood, such as preparing the children in their care for university? Children in care are supposed to have certain rights, including the right to an education, but few are given the necessary support to claim that right. Because most of them don't know their rights they don't claim them and a lazy system is happy to allow that to happen.

Alex and me both getting to university is actually a huge victory for Mum. All Dad's attempts to undermine her efforts to make us into high achievers have failed. The foundations that she laid for us were strong enough to resist all the negative pressures that Dad's crime unleashed in our lives and I feel proud to think she would not be disappointed in us. Now it is my turn to try to do the same for other kids.

Maybe some good came out of the tragedy that our family went through, in that Alex and I got to see what life was like for children who had no family to care for them, and that insight has given us both a powerful focus for our lives. Seeing first-hand how hard life is for many young people has convinced us that this is an area where we can actually make a real difference.

We have had our eyes opened to just how many people need practical help in other countries as well as the UK. Because our Christmases had been so sad since Mum died, in 2006 Alex and I decided to do something different during the holiday season, rather than trying to emulate some stereotype of a happy family Christmas Day. We realised that if we didn't make a positive plan it would just be the two of us sitting around watching rubbish television together all day. There had to be something else we could do, we reasoned, somewhere we could go where Christmas wasn't so horribly commercialised that anyone who couldn't join in, like us, was made to feel like a complete outsider.

Initially we thought about just booking a holiday that would get us out of the country but when I started looking into it, I found a programme for volunteers to go to Ghana to help educate people about Aids, about basic rules of hygiene and disease prevention, about eating a healthy diet and about the drugs that were available to help. We instantly knew that was how we wanted to spend the holiday – doing something useful and learning something new at the same time.

The village we went to was on an island in the middle of Lake Volta, one of the biggest man-made lakes in the world. It is so big, around 400 kilometres long and 25 kilometres wide, that you can't see the surrounding shore when you're on the island and the fares for crossing it are so high that most of the locals have never even left the island.

Because they are so cut off from the outside world the villagers are consequently missing out on everything, from education to medical supplies. It was touching how grateful they were to us for going to visit them, even though we were so young and the amount of help we could offer was always going to be small. They imagined we lived in a country much better than theirs and they couldn't understand why we would want to go all that way to see them. Despite their obvious poverty, there were many things about their culture that we thought were infinitely superior to what we have in the West.

While we were there we also volunteered in an orphanage on the mainland, interested to see how the system worked in an African country. We threw a Christmas party and put on a play, then invited donations from wealthy audience members to help raise funds so they could move to bigger premises, and we were struck by how different their attitude towards orphans was to anything we had experienced in England. When a child has to go into an orphanage in Ghana the whole village takes responsibility for its care. The government doesn't pay a penny.

On another occasion, in the village on the island, a woman who was breast-feeding explained to us that it wasn't her baby.

'If a mother dies while her baby is still small,' she told us, 'another woman will automatically take over the responsibility of breast-feeding it.'

To start with it seemed strange to us that in a community where most people didn't have enough to eat and couldn't afford the medical supplies they needed to survive, there could be so much happiness and generosity of spirit, whereas in England, where everyone has so much, there is a lack of people who want to look after children who have lost their families.

There are charities, of course, that try to fill the gap. I have been working as an independent visitor volunteer for an amazing one called National Youth Advocacy Service (NYAS). The charity assigns me a young person who has been drawn to their attention as someone who might benefit from the scheme. I am given an allowance of fifty pounds a month to take the young person out, which is to cover petrol, food, travel and whatever we might decide to do together. I am expected to take them out for eight hours a month, and I try to do it twice a month for the majority of the day. Sometimes we just go out for a bite to eat or to the cinema, or we might go for a drive or to an amusement park. It gives young people who are looked after by social services a chance to get away from the care system. The role basically involves befriending the child and being there for them as well as taking them out and having fun. It shows them that there is someone else out there who cares about their wellbeing, someone independent of social services who hasn't prejudged them based on their record. It provides them with an escape from where they are living for a few hours. NYAS also has advocacy workers who young people can use to represent their views in meetings and ensure their rights are being met.

There is always a desperate shortage of people in England who want to foster other people's children or work with them in care homes. We have designed our society to function around the nuclear family and when someone falls out of that neat pattern, as we did through no fault of our own, few people have the will to help. There are many dedicated, generous and kind people who work in the care system, but not nearly enough. The best ones are all overworked and underpaid, and consequently unable to do as much good as they might otherwise be able to, and they are often slowed down by bureaucracy and paperwork.

Because young people in care are moved around so often it is much harder for them to develop relationships of trust with the workers. Writing reports and risk assessments means they don't have enough time to provide love and care. Sometimes a young person just needs a hug, which the workers are nervous of giving in case they open themselves up to accusations of having a sexual motive. Many of the workers end up disillusioned because of the system.

In most nuclear families, the parents would never allow their children to change schools so frequently and then to be thrown out into the world at the age of eighteen without any further help and support. Why does society find it acceptable that this should happen to vulnerable young people in the care system? There should be an uproar about this, and changes should be introduced so that kids in care get the same opportunities and support as those growing up with their own families.

Perhaps if the units were smaller, with just a couple of children in each, they would be more like families. There needs to be much more emphasis on education and on continuing to support the young people beyond the ages of sixteen or eighteen, to combat problems like loneliness, drug abuse and homelessness. Everyone is too quick to write off young people in care as 'bad' rather than 'damaged', and to criminalise them too young. We need to establish a system that sets goals for them, gives positive rewards, and is much more supportive of those who choose to continue into further education.

no one listened

It is much easier for the world to forget about inconvenient children like Alex and me. But if children in care received better treatment, all sorts of other problems once they are in the outside world might be avoided.

Dyslexia isn't an OBSTACLE

Three
Dimension
Dyslexia

Firdevs Dede

www.threedimensiondyslexia.co.uk

Published in Jan 2015 by Xlibris

Copyright © Firdevs Dede 2015.
Front cover image, 'Destiny' (Digital Drawing) © Firdevs Dede 2011
Back cover photo © Firdevs Dede 2010

Library of Congress Control Number: 2015900411
ISBN: Hardcover   978-1-5035-3364-6
                Softcover   978-1-5035-3365-3
                eBook   978-1-5035-3366-0

www.threedimensiondyslexia.co.uk
www.firdevsdede.blogspot.co.uk
https://twitter.com/DedeFirdevs
firdevs.dede@gmail.com

This book was printed in the United States of America.

Rev. date: 01/23/2015

To order additional copies of this book, contact:
Xlibris
1-888-795-4274
www.Xlibris.com
Orders@Xlibris.com
702294

Contents

Three

Dimension

Dyslexia

www.threedimensiondyslexia.co.uk

I dedicated this book to the well-known dyslexic genius Albert Einstein and all my precious dyslexic students who allowed me to experience what they experience in their daily lives without any boundary. Many thanks for including me in your achievements!

Firdevs Dede, Jan 2015

"If I had one hour to solve a problem and my life depended on the solution, I would spend the first 55 minutes determining the proper question to ask, for once I know the proper question, I could solve the problem in less than five minutes."

Albert Einstein

Three

Dimension

Dyslexia

Vision Statement

Three Dimension Dyslexia's vision is to empower clients to fulfill their maximum potentials in their personal and professional lives with a great satisfaction.

Aim of Three Dimension Dyslexia

Three Dimension Dyslexia aims to equip students with academic writing and reading skills for research purposes duration of an academic year within supportive environment.

Objectives of Three Dimension Dyslexia

1) To facilitate students' critical thinking skills using various reading and writing strategies in order to build up a viable argument via critical analysis and evaluative writing style.
2) To inform students about how to maximise efficiency in choosing appropriate research methods for academic purposes.
3) To promote academic integrity & ethical research practice.
4) To enable students to be an active participant of research community in their specialist area on a global scale.
5) To empower students via coaching and mentoring for increasing self awareness of learning styles, organisational skills, time management skills and presentation skills.
6) To encourage research studies in my publications.

What do my ex-students think of working with me?

'I just wanted to let you know that I have found working with you a pleasure and maybe the first time I have been given the "real" support I needed to my specific needs.'

J.M. from Goldsmiths University, 2013

'Hi Firdevs, I just got my grade back: 80% which is an A* and 30 masters credit. Thanks for your help.'

C.H. from Goldsmiths University, 2014

'Thank you ever so much. You have been a great help and God richly Bless you!'

M.A. from London Met, 2013

'Thank you for the words of encouragement.
When I do get to where I want to be, I won't forget all you have done for me.'

R.S. from Birkbeck University, 2013

'Please also note that these grades have now been officially confirmed as I have received my course transcript which confirms that I achieved a Distinction overall. Thank you so very much for helping me to achieve these grades.'

C.O. from Birkbeck University, 2013

'So glad to have had your support and guidance, throughout my pregnancy and birth of my child. Your patience and encouragement kept me going and I will never forget that.'

S.S. from the Institute of Education, 2014

'Many thanks for your kindness & support during my PGCE year! I realized in the end I was more capable than I first believed.'

L.W. from the Institute of Education, 2014

Foreword

As a visual artist, I am inclined to use the right hemisphere of my brain with the strong preference for visual communication process during intellectual discourses. That is why the natural cognitive profile of dyslexic students captures my interest to get to know their holistic learning style as intuitive thinkers with strong visual, spatial intelligence and problem solving skills. The majority of my dyslexic students are divergent thinkers as they could make connections between many different concepts at the same time. They are better equipped than their non-dyslexic peers to see the inter-relationship between unconnected ideas which is a gift rather than an obstacle within the creative process such as sculpting, producing complex textile images, designing buildings, acting and playing various instruments.

My dyslexic students are not only gifted but determined to stretch their abilities by going extra miles as they like learning through actively investigating each medium they are engaged with. My learners like reasoning from particular to general and discovering 'what' when they acquire knowledge. Over the years of my empirical research in dyslexia, I have developed an individualized teaching strategy which enables my learners to activate left hemisphere of their brain alongside their intuitive learning style. I have been very lucky to meet hundreds of dyslexic students with different talents and strengths since 2002. It has been a great joy to work with my dyslexic students as I have been observing how it feels to be original each time they experience the new way of looking at academic concepts from an unusual perspective by combining the left brain approach with the right brain approach which is always as creative as a monolithic or single-sided approach and I am in tune with.

In this book, I focused on what makes dyslexic people unique by highlighting their strengths and how some of the linguistic problems could be dealt once the new habits are developed with a systematic and comprehensive support program which I carefully design for each individual learner I work with duration of an academic year. I chose a narrative style rather than academic as I would like my dyslexic students to enjoy a book of literature instead of being confronted with another academic book about what dyslexia is.

I believe learning should be fun but not necessarily dull! I wish you all a good reading by enjoying the reading process with a bit of humor attached to the fascinating characteristic of dyslexia. My professional life would have been rather boring if I did not have a chance to work with the most talented dyslexic students of mine. Thank you all for enriching my teaching career with a lot of enjoyment and variety. I care for your success and happiness in your professional and personal lives.

Firdevs Dede, 2015

Chapter 1

Felix is in trouble - Sept 2002

Felix walks slowly in Borough high street wearing walnut colour velvet trousers and a milky colour wool sweater, which he had bought from the second-hand shop a year ago. Felix looks solemn with distress and worrying about being arrested for breaking the law for the 3ʳᵈ time. It's raining heavily. Adults are on their ways to work. Single parents are taking their kids to the local nurseries or child minders. School children look unhappy to start a new day. It's too early for the unemployed people to leave home. They must be indoors avoiding the rush hour before looking for work. The elderly and the sick may be either in the residential homes or hospitals. Cafes, newsagents and supermarkets open their doors almost at the same time. Life in the city has just started. At the bus station, there is a long queue with the traffic jam in the street. Nothing seems out of ordinary except Felix's misfortune. Felix remembers what his defence barrister urged him to do.

> *'The Jury and the Judge will be taking everything into account, Felix. For your own benefit, you should be punctual especially on the 13th of Sept when you'll be hearing the verdict.'*

Felix enters into the Inner London Court reluctantly remembering the details of his troublesome past and how he had broken into an unoccupied premise unlawfully 6 years ago that was when he was made homeless. Felix had walked around the deserted Victorian house he had spotted on his way to the work. Felix was working as a delivery person in the metal scrap factory. His job didn't pay well but didn't involve any paperwork which had suited Felix better than any other unskilled works as he had difficulty with reading and writing. All Felix needed to do was to carry the heavy metals within the different departments of the factory. Felix's low wage was just enough to cover his lodging expenses and a hot meal once a day. In order to cut down his outgoings substantially, Felix had taken a cheese sandwich daily to work for his lunch. When Felix had reached his 16th birthday, his foster parents asked him to leave home. Since leaving his foster home, life has been more complicated than ever for Felix. It didn't take long for police officers to arrest Felix for occupying the squatted premises unlawfully. Felix's trial had followed immediately. Neither the Jury nor the Judge was impressed by Felix's background as an illegitimate child before making their decision on Felix's future. Felix was sentenced twice. The prison had provided a place for Felix to live for a while. The only trouble was that Felix couldn't go out for a walk by the River Thames. That was the downside of being in prison. Felix didn't get on with his inmates as he had never associated himself with the young gangs. The type of crimes they had committed was based on violence and involved drugs and robbery. Most of them come from deprived backgrounds but their life circumstances sound worse than his. Felix wouldn't have committed crime if he wasn't asked to leave his foster parents' home. There is an enormous digital cloak on the wall in the main entrance of the court. Felix gazes at the cloak. The time is 9.50 am. Felix is earlier than yesterday. He walks up the stairs and finds the courtroom number 8 on the 2nd floor. His defence barrister, Mr Goodman is waiting for Felix in the corridor and greets Felix with a gentle expression on his face.

'I'm glad you're earlier than yesterday. How do you feel today, Felix?'

'Rough!'

'There is a strong possibility that you'll be pardoned. I'll see you at lunch time.'

'See you at lunch time, sir.'

Felix enters the glass gallery, which is designed for the offenders to watch their trials separated from the public and legal representatives in the courtroom. Felix looks around to identify the familiar surroundings of the courtroom and recognises his ex-girl friend, Jackie immediately. She sits at the back bench of the courtroom and turns her head round looking for Felix inside the glass gallery. Their eyes meet while she spots Felix in his isolated waiting room. Jackie greets Felix with warmth and waves at him instantly. Felix greets Jackie in an unfriendly way without waving or smiling back to her. The court usher rushes around carrying papers and letting the Jury members in. The Jury members are ready to start a new day to finalise the case. The court clerk looks professional while she checks the details of the court case on her computer. Felix's barrister sits on the bench in front of the courtroom facing the court clerk and the Judge. He looks through his legal papers. The prosecution counsel does the same thing. Everything is scheduled in accordance with the norms of the British Court. The court usher goes out to inform the Judge that the jury members are present. There is a knock on the door from where the Judge will be making his appearance after the usher's voice is heard.

'All rise!'

Everyone stands up. The Judge in black robe wearing a white wig on his head enters the courtroom and greets the barristers formally. After the greeting, everyone sits down in their seats and the court case starts subsequently. It is 10 o'clock. Felix stops thinking about his past. The prosecution counsel stands up and puts forward his submission to the judge.

'Your Honour, I'd like to make a submission in relation to the offender's character. He had committed the same crime twice. This is his 3rd crime. I don't think that he has got a good character. Based on the knowledge of his previous offences he had committed, I believe the offender will cause a serious threat to the society.'

'Are you judging the offender on the basis of his past crimes, Mr Gavel?'

'Your Honour, I see a link between the current crime and the offender's past history.'

'Mr Gavel, I've understood that you are judging the offender based on his previous convictions. As far as I am concerned, the past crimes of the offender should not affect the Jury's decision. Your misleading statement can easily confuse the Jury.'

'Your Honour, I take your point. I have no further comment to make.'

'Thanks, Mr Gavel. Mr Goodman, can we hear your view now?'

'Your Honour, I'd like to make a clear distinction between a crime, which is committed with a deliberate intention of the offender and a crime, which is committed beyond offender's deliberation of misconduct based on his circumstances. The former one puts a heavy penalty on the offender as he was aware of the seriousness of the crime when he was committing the crime. The later one reduces the detrimental factor of the crime he had committed as he had no any other choice at the time of carrying out the crime. I believe my client's crime shouldn't be examined from the point of view, which will be in favour of sentencing the offender. This won't solve the problem he has got in his life; nor do any good to the society.'

'What is your submission, Mr Goodman?'

'I'd like to raise the question, what are we going to get out of this court case?'

'Have you got an answer for the question you've just raised, Mr Goodman?'

'Your Honour, to punish the defender without giving him a chance to correct his misconduct won't prevent him from re-offending the same crime. I am in favour of a corrective punishment, which should bring a constructive solution to the defendant's problem he is facing.'

'I take your point of view, Mr Goodman. Nonetheless, I'd like you to illustrate your view with a tangible example, which should enable the Jury to see your point much clearer.'

'Your Honour, I'd like to suggest that the offender should be given a chance to start some kind of training, which suits his need. Considering the defender's current situation without any qualification, he won't be able to function within the society. That is the main reason he has been driven into the crime scene for several times. Furthermore, he isn't supported by the state to become a legal occupier. The offender hasn't got an access to any support mechanism to resolve his homelessness. That was why he has been repeating the same crime.'

'That is a good point, Mr Goodman. Thank you. Could Jury members retire now and discuss the matter for further consideration? We will hear the verdict after lunch break. Before going away, I'd like to make it clear that it will be Jury's decision, which finalises the court case today. I don't want to influence the Jury in any way. You have heard the statements made by the defence barrister and the prosecution counsel during the last two weeks. Please think carefully about each detail you've got an access. In the light of the evidence and the statements being put forward by the barristers, you're free to make your own judgements. Once you reach the verdict, there won't be any further discussion on this matter. I hope everything is clear. If you wish further clarification, please let me know. Thank you.'

The Jury members don't have any question to ask and leave the courtroom quietly from the back door, which is separated from the front entrance of the courtroom. The jury members start discussing the details of the crime in the back room of the court which is designated to accommodate jury members only for their confidential discussion during the trial period before reaching the verdict.

Jury member number 1:	'What did you make of the defence barrister's statement?'
Jury member number 2:	'I think he has got a good point. The offender should be given a chance to correct his misconduct.'
Jury member number 3:	'I agree with you considering what the offender has gone through in his life, I feel that he should be pardoned really!'
Jury member number 4:	'I don't agree with you. Don't forget, the offender committed the same crime previously.'

Jury member number 5:   'We should stick to the Judge's point of view. We can't examine the offender's current crime based on his prior crimes he had committed. We ought to treat him fairly by examining his recent crime only.'

Jury member number 6:   'How can we differentiate between the current crime and the past crime?'

Jury member number 7:   'Do you think; the two together are overlapped?'

Jury member number 8:   'We cannot isolate the offender's current crime from the crimes he had committed long time ago.'

Jury member number 9:   'Don't you think you've been judgemental?'

Jury member number 8:   'Aren't we here to make our judgements?'

Jury member number 9:   'I suppose you're right. We aren't therapists to counsel him. We are here to judge the offender's misconduct, but we need to be fair on him.'

Jury member number 12:	'We're all trying to be fair. However, our decision shouldn't penalise the vulnerable members of the society. If he commits the same crime over and over again, I wonder what the possible consequences will be in terms of public safety. Don't we have a responsibility for the members of the public at the same time?'
Jury member number 10:	'What kind of responsibility are you implying?'
Jury member number 12:	'I'm thinking about our responsibility for the innocent citizens like us who didn't get involved with any crime.'
Jury member number 7:	'I think you've been too harsh on the offender. He had nowhere to live. It's hard to imagine how I would have coped with homelessness if I were in his place. I've got a feeling I would have committed the same crime. What about you?'

Jury member number 12:	'I wouldn't have broken into unoccupied premises. When he was made homeless, he could have gone to the Citizen Advice Bureaux for getting advice on what to do. Allowing him to get away with his wrongdoing will certainly create a pitfall for the similar cases.'
Jury member number 8:	'If homeless people feel it was their rights to break into any unoccupied property, how are we going to protect property owners' rights? What are the home owners' legal rights for safety? Just imagine a scenario like having a home in this country and being employed abroad for 10 months; supposing you had found your home being occupied by illegal occupants on your return, how would you react to the unpredictable situation? Are you prepared to repair all the damages had caused into your property while it was in the use of some illegal occupiers?'

Jury member number 11:	'I agree with you that the legal occupants' rights need to be protected.'
Jury member number 1:	'Is he guilty or not guilty? Who is in favour of sentencing him?'
Jury member number 2:	'Shall we vote now? Please put your hands up, if you think he is guilty.'
Jury member number 7:	'Eleven of you are in favour!'
Jury member number 12:	'Well, you're the only one, who thinks the offender isn't guilty.'
Jury member number 7:	'I do feel the offender isn't guilty at all.'
Jury member number 11:	'You are in minority. We need to present our verdict in favour of sentencing the offender.'
Jury member number 7:	'I've found the majority's judgement very subjective and I need to express that I am not entirely satisfied with the verdict.'
Jury member number 8:	'Perhaps, we should identify who is going to read the verdict. Is there anyone willing to do that?'
Jury member number 12:	'I can read out the verdict.'

Jury member number 8:	'In that case, the matter has been resolved. We delegate you to read the verdict on our behalf once we come back from our lunch break at 2 o'clock.'
Jury member number 7:	'With the final decision, we are causing more complications to the offender's current life rather than easing his difficult circumstances for him.'
Jury member number 12:	'We aren't here to resolve the offender's personal problems. His personal problems such as homelessness or getting a well-paid job can be resolved by other professions outside this court. We're only here to make a decision whether the offender is guilty or not. In this case, the offender is found guilty.'
Jury member number 7:	'You didn't consider the fact that the offender didn't harm anyone. He had a very good reason for breaking into an unoccupied property which was to provide him a shelter.'
Jury member number 12:	'Are you suggesting that we've been unjust?'

Jury member number 7:	'No, I am not. That's how you've taken it.'
Jury member number 12:	'What you are getting at, then?'
Jury member number 7:	'I felt the need to highlight my point of view. You're judging a person with the same severity you might have judged a murderer or rapist. There is a big difference between a petty crime such as the one we are examining and the detrimental crime such as murder or rape cases. Even some murderers are pardoned under certain conditions. I cannot understand why you don't consider the fact that the offender isn't guilty at all.'
Jury member number 12:	'Do you really think that breaking into someone's home can be treated like a petty crime?'

Jury member number 7:	'It isn't as petty as mugging someone in the street, perhaps. Nevertheless, he didn't burgle an occupied premise. If he burgled someone's dwelling place, this might have caused more problems. The offender didn't assault anyone mentally, sexually or physically and he didn't take someone's life either. Why are you approaching to his case indifferently?'
Jury member number 12:	'Personally speaking, I think I had enough of this case. I've spent 2 weeks in this court. I've got other things going on in my life. I'd like to move on. We can't keep on contradicting each other's points of view. Besides, you're the only one, who insists on the weak hypothesis of the offender's innocence.'
Jury member number 7:	'We are here not only to make a positive impact on the law and order of the society we live, but on the life of a vulnerable person, who will be affected by our final decision.'

Jury member number 12:	'I appreciate that. However, we need to be firm.'
Jury member number 7:	'You've just said that you've had enough of this case. You'd like to move on. Nevertheless, we must resolve the innocent person's life and death issue in a fair way.'
Jury member number 12:	'You're confusing me. You've started addressing the offender with the wrong word.'
Jury member number 7:	'As far as I am concerned he is an innocent person.'
Jury member number 12:	'His innocence hasn't been proved yet.'
Jury member number 7:	'We're considering all the facts including the burden of proof.'

Jury member number 12:	'The offender has accepted the fact that he had broken into an unoccupied property. That's a crime itself. It isn't our problem to defend his innocence. That was his defence barrister's duty to do so. The defence barrister wasn't successful to convince the 11 members of the Jury. I should remind you that we haven't got much time to re-consider all the facts all over again. We need to focus on the verdict. Is he guilty or not guilty? Eleven of us think that he is guilty. We cannot take your point of view into consideration at this stage. It's nearly lunch time. I need to have a proper lunch break. As far as I am concerned, the case is over. Don't you all agree with me?'

The opinion of the jury member number 12 has been accepted by the majority. They all rush out to have their lunch from 1 pm to 2 pm as they agree that the court case will be finalised with the verdict this afternoon and there won't be any further discussion on this matter concerning Felix's future. Apart from one jury member, everyone feels relief that the trial is over and Felix's existence won't bother them any longer. They will soon forget Felix and his case will remain an insignificant matter to occupy their mind with till the rest of their lives when Felix keeps on struggling to survive without any support mechanism.

Felix meets his girlfriend during his lunch break. They go to the court restaurant. Jackie buys pasta for both of them. They sit down facing each other. Felix remembers how he had met Jackie. On one of those miserable days without any money and feeling very hungry, Felix had stolen an egg sandwich from the shelf of the supermarket. Jackie had seen Felix being questioned by a security guard; she rescued him by paying for Felix's sandwich. He was lucky to walk out of the supermarket free without being arrested. Jackie was on her 1st year at the university studying psychology and she thought that Felix suffered from 'kleptomania' which causes sufferers to steal items they don't need. Jackie acted on impulse with the interference of her middle class bias as she had never experienced any motivation for stealing food out of hunger or lack of financial resources. Jackie had kept in touch with Felix in order to analyse Felix's behavioural problems for her case-study while she was writing her thesis on *'Crimes linked to mental health problems'*. Jackie soon discovered that Felix wasn't suffering from kleptomania or any other mental health problem. Far from it, Felix was mentally fit and honest person in general. His petty crime was due to his poverty and physical hunger only. Felix's good character enabled Jackie to treat Felix as a human being rather than a thief. They had started meeting up regularly which bounded them eventually. Their affection for each other had stayed on a platonic level. Jackie wouldn't get involved with anyone intimately as she believed in sexual purity. They wouldn't consider the possibility of getting married either. Felix was homeless and unemployed without any qualification. Jackie was staying at university campus supported by her family. After a while, Felix had left Jackie as he didn't want to spoil her life. Jackie must have heard from one of his inmates that Felix has been arrested for the 3rd time. Felix looks at Jackie with embarrassment.

'How did you find me, Jackie?'

'Well, that shouldn't be your concern, Felix.'

'I'd like to know who told you I am in trouble again.'

'Wouldn't it be better for us to focus on how you're going to get out of trouble, Felix?'

'Jackie, I really don't want you to get involved with my personal life. Everything is finished between us. You ought to consider someone suitable for you or for your class. I am not the right person for you to get involved with.'

'Felix, please do not think that I'd like to get involved with you in any way.'

'What does that mean?'

'We'll be keeping the same rule without considering any intimate relationship. All I want is to get you out of this trap you've fallen into. It isn't your fault to be homeless. I am pretty sure that I would have done what you have done, if I were in your place facing the similar circumstances.'

'I don't want you to get emotional, Jackie. Homelessness is my problem, but not yours. You shouldn't worry about my problems. How is your study going?'

'It's fine. I'm in my final year. I'll be graduating soon.'

'I'm sure you'll be a very successful psychiatrist. I have no doubt about it considering how you have been treating me since we've known each other.'

'Thanks, Felix. Aren't you having your pasta? It's getting rather cold.'

'That's all right. I don't mind eating cold pasta.'

'Let's have our meal in peace now, shall we?'

'That suits me well.'

Felix and Jackie start eating their pasta in silence. Felix finishes his meal earlier. He sits back and gazes at Jackie. She looks beautiful in her elegant white raincoat with the white woollen hat on her blonde hair. Felix feels he has no right to destroy Jackie's high expectations from life. Jackie deserves a decent man with a decent life style. Felix senses that he wouldn't be a good husband to Jackie without having any profession. Jackie is going to be a successful psychiatrist. Supposing Jackie marries to a husband like himself with a criminal record, how will her family cope with Jackie's decision? They all judge Jackie for making such a wrong decision in her life. That'll ruin Jackie's future. Felix can't even read or write let alone finding a proper job. He had never earned a decent salary. Felix hasn't got a place to live. How on earth this beautiful person has fallen in love with a crook like himself! Felix has never fully understood that. He has no time to figure out what Jackie has found in him either. Perhaps, Jackie had pretended that she was in love with him. What Jackie had wanted was to help Felix to get out of his misery he was locked into through unpredictable circumstances. Jackie must have been an angel with her compassionate heart. Felix was sure that Jackie would have treated anyone in genuine need with the same sensitivity. Jackie has been too kind to Felix. When Jackie had visited Felix in the prison cell for a few times, Felix asked Jackie not to come again. He didn't want Jackie to be in a rough place with other inmates around. Having Jackie around as a visitor within a prison environment had nothing to do with any romantic scene one might only get in heavily exaggerated melodramas in movies. Felix told Jackie not to visit him in prison. There was no need for it, he added. Jackie had to stop visiting Felix. Since then, they didn't see each other. Why has Jackie come to the court today? It's absurd for a law-abiding person like Jackie to get in touch with a convict out of kindness. Felix feels tired of life as well as Jackie's intrusive nature. Felix thinks that Jackie looks righteous without getting involved with any corruption which annoys Felix a lot. Jackie finishes her pasta. She smiles at Felix. He ignores Jackie's friendliness and doesn't seem to be moved by her warmth at all. Felix looks away and examines the colourful desserts placed on the glass shelves opposite their seats. Jackie walks up to the counter. She buys pudding for both of them. Jackie carries the dessert plates to the table, where Felix has been watching her with annoyance. Jackie must have felt that Felix didn't have a decent meal for a long time. Jackie had always been a thoughtful person which irritates Felix. Why does Jackie always act in a proper manner? Why does she leave Felix alone? Felix starts hating Jackie for being too good to him superficially when he starts eating his pudding. Although the dessert tastes so good, he stops eating it suddenly. Felix pushes away the dessert plate as he doesn't want to be patronised by anyone. Felix thinks that Jackie has been pretending to be a loyal friend since they have known each other for a while. As far as our human nature is concerned, it isn't possible for anyone to be as good as her. Jackie has been insulting Felix with the superficial mannerism. Felix feels intimidated by Jackie's table manner while she is having her dessert with a small spoon calmly in a proper way. Felix might go to prison for the 3rd time this afternoon. How could Jackie possibly understand what Felix had gone through in life? Jackie comes from an upper-middle class background with the caring parents. Jackie has never experienced homelessness in her life. She had always given the impression that she could understand Felix. She couldn't possibly understand how Felix felt when he was going through his life struggle all alone. Jackie is a very good liar. Felix pushes the dessert plate with his hands in anger for the 2nd time. He doesn't want to allow Jackie to treat him like an inferior person. Felix has got his own pride. How dare she is to intimidate Felix with her disgusting mannerism! Jackie doesn't have any right to interfere with Felix's life.

Jackie realises that Felix is annoyed with her; perhaps, she has been over protective. Felix has been struggling in life but Jackie has also gone through a lot as Jackie's parents had argued with each other while she was a teenager. Jackie couldn't tell Felix how hard her life had been as a child. Felix thinks he is the only person, who has got problems. Jackie gets angry with Felix for being too judgemental about her upbringing. It isn't Jackie's fault to come from a middle class family. No one should be treated responsible for their upbringings. Felix had his misfortune, but Jackie also had her misfortune. How can't Felix understand that? Felix has been too occupied with his own problems and he is unable to notice other people's problems. Jackie thinks that Felix has been so selfish. Jackie has had enough of Felix's childish tantrums. When Felix pushes his dessert with revulsion on his face, Jackie decides to leave without any desire to stay for seeing the end of his trial. In fact, Jackie won't be seeing Felix again.

'I think you aren't happy to see me today, Felix. You have made it clear to me that my presence bothers you, doesn't it, Felix?'

'If you have taken it like that, it is your problem, Jackie. Whatever you think of me is fine by me. What are you up to?'

'I've decided to leave you now. I am not staying to hear the verdict. As a matter of fact, I'll be getting out of your life. I shall never see you again. Good luck to you and goodbye!'

'Goodbye, Jackie! Good luck to you with your finals! Thanks for the lunch.'

Jackie stays quiet. It has been a humiliating experience for Jackie to be treated in a tactless way. Felix's unkindness to her injured pride ruins Jackie's good impression about Felix's moral integrity. His disrespect for Jackie's sensitivity is the last straw, which Jackie finds too hard to ignore.

> 'Go to the hell, Felix! I don't even care what happens to you this afternoon. If you go to jail, it might serve you well. You deserve it! I'll never feel sorry for you. I've got other things to worry about.'

That was what Jackie thought while she was leaving the court restaurant in haste. Jackie gets out of the Inner London Court. It is pouring rain. She walks down the road to take a taxi. Jackie's tears are streaming down from her eyes.

Felix is furious about Jackie's intrusive attempt to restore his life. She had no right to patronise him what to do with his life. He would like to be left alone and resolve his own problems. Felix will be facing the verdict this afternoon on his own. It doesn't really matter whether the Jury will find Felix guilty or not. There is nowhere for Felix to go to. If they find Felix guilty, it'll do justice. At least he wouldn't worry about committing the same crime and getting arrested for the 4th time. Attending the same court case all over again will be more catastrophic than facing his sentence in prison. Felix leaves the restaurant and walks up to the stairs. When Felix enters the main entrance, he looks at the digital clock on the wall. It is 2 o'clock precisely. Felix climbs up the stairs quickly, reaches the courtroom and sees his barrister Mr Goodman waiting for him near the glass gallery for offenders to sit.

> 'Where have you been, Felix? I've seen you going down with a young lady. Who is she?'

'A friend of mine.'

'Where is she now?'

'She has gone.'

'Why didn't she stay to hear the verdict?'

'The friendship is over, sir.'

'I'm sorry to hear that, Felix.'

'There is no need to be sorry, sir.'

'I don't want to interfere with your private life, Felix. I mean not more than I've already got involved with.'

'You aren't interfering with my life, sir. I'm grateful to you that you've taken up my case with confidence in my innocence.'

'Coming to the main issue, Felix, I've no idea what the verdict will be this afternoon. Whatever the outcome is, there will be always a solution for all the problems at the end. If the verdict isn't that cheerful for us to hear today, you shouldn't feel disheartened.'

'Please do not worry about me, sir. I prepared myself for the worst. Even the worst outcome won't do me any harm. If I go to prison, I'll have somewhere to live for a while.'

'Don't be silly, Felix! You'll have a better place than a prison cell to live in. I'll help you for getting an accommodation.'

'Thanks sir.'

Felix doesn't feel that his barrister will be able to help him more than what he has already done for him. Felix is determined to face his destiny without any fear. If Felix is found guilty, it won't be the end of the world. If he is found innocent, that won't solve Felix's problem. Felix enters the offender's gallery and sits down calmly. The Jury enters the courtroom. They all sit down on their benches. The usher calls out.

'All rise!'

Everyone stands up. The Judge with the white wig and a black rope enters the courtroom. The same formality takes place. The Judge and the barristers greet each other. Then, everyone sits down quietly. The usher asks the Jury whether or not they are ready. A lady in a pretty dress stands up.

'I am ready to give the verdict. The offender is found guilty.'

The Judge thanks the Jury for attending the trial. The defence barrister Mr Goodman turns round and looks at Felix with distress. Felix ignores his barrister's sentimentality. Felix is prepared to go to prison for the crime he has committed. The court clerk is going to issue Felix's sentence notice in a week's time. Felix is bailed by his barrister. He needs to wait until next week. Where is Felix going to stay till his sentence notice is issued to him? Felix prefers going to prison sooner rather than waiting for a week as he has nowhere to stay. If Felix sleeps rough outside, police will arrest him again. He can't sleep inside the train station or metro. They are all shut after midnight. If Felix buys one-day bus card and gets on a red double-decked bus for several rides in order to kill the time without any purpose to go anywhere, that wouldn't be a solution. Felix can't stay on the bus after midnight when the last bus journey ends in London. The bus driver will ask him to leave the bus. Felix comes out of the glass gallery without knowing what to do. His barrister is quick to catch up Felix.

'Felix, wait a minute please! I'm terribly sorry for the outcome. I'll try my best to appeal against the decision.'

'I've nowhere to sleep till next week. Is there any free hostel for offenders to stay until I move to prison, sir?'

'That is a good question, Felix. I'm afraid, I haven't got an answer. You're my 1st case of this kind. I'll find out whether or not there is a free hostel for you to stay.'

'How soon will you be able to do that, sir?'

'I don't think I can find anything for you today. We've got a spare room. My wife and I will be happy to keep you as our guest for a week. Would you like to come over to us, Felix?'

'Thanks, Mr Goodman. I appreciate your kindness.'

'I am going back home now. Let's go home together, Felix!'

'Many thanks, Mr Goodman. Shall I carry your briefcase?'

'I can manage, Felix.'

'Do you always carry this heavy briefcase with you, sir?'

'It's only a matter of climbing up and down the stairs while I am at court. I am lucky to drive back home without using public transport.'

'I am sorry to give you trouble, sir. If I had somewhere else to go, I wouldn't bother you.'

'You aren't bothering me. As a matter of fact, my wife and I'll be delighted to get to know you a bit better. You'll like my wife, Felix. She is also a barrister. We've got a cat living with us. You'll have a chance to meet our cat, Fanny.'

'How old is she?'

'Who?'

'Fanny!'

'Fanny is a few-month-old kitten. We've got her from a pet-rescue home for homeless cats and dogs. She has been with us for two months now. Look, the rain is pouring down. Let's run. My car is over there by the gate. Can you see it from here, Felix?'

'Which one?'

'The grey one.'

'Yes, it's there.'

Felix and Mr Goodman start running. The barrister Mr Goodman opens his car's door. He lets Felix in first. Mr Goodman shuts the door from Felix's side. He opens the door from the driver's side and gets in his car. The barrister takes off his white wig carefully leaving his heavy briefcase with his wig on the back seat. Justin Goodman pulls his seatbelt. Felix repeats the same action and adjusts his seatbelt carefully. Felix can't believe he is going to stay at his barrister's home for a week. Felix had two different barristers previously. They were indifferent to Felix's needs. It's the first time in his life Felix has been cared for by a legal person. During the trial, Felix had stayed in a temporary accommodation, which was provided by a charitable trust for the young offenders, who wait for their trials. The police officer, who arrested Felix had found the defence barrister for Felix. It was the same police officer, who also referred Felix to the temporary accommodation to stay. It was a simple hostel for offenders. There was a communal room to watch the small telly with other offenders. There was a kitchen downstairs. They had a hot meal once a day. Their bus fare was given to them to attend their court cases. However, they couldn't extend Felix's stay longer than two weeks there because of the lack of financial resources. Felix feels grateful to his barrister as Mr Goodman is a kind person with full of compassion.

'Are you comfortable, Felix?'

'Yes sir.'

'Call me, Justin.'

'I can't address you with your first name, sir.'

'Why not?'

'You're a barrister.'

'So what?'

'I respect you.'

'Felix, you don't need to be too formal with me. Your case is over. You aren't my client at the moment. You're going to be our family friend. It'll make our lives much easier to call each other with our first names as I do.'

'Can't I call you, Mr Goodman? Will it sound less formal, sir?'

'No, that won't make any difference. Sir or Mr Goodman is more or less the same thing, isn't it?'

Felix feels too rude to call his barrister with his first name. Mr Goodman places a CD on a CD player. The beautiful music suppresses the noise of the rain. Mr Goodman focuses on his driving. They stop talking. Felix listens to the music. All his worries disappear. Thirty minutes later, Mr Goodman stops in front of a beautiful cottage with a very big garden.

'That's where you are going to stay for a week, Felix.'

'It's gorgeous!'

'I'm glad you like our home. Let's get out of the car now.'

Felix and Mr Goodman get out of the car. Mr Goodman takes his briefcase and locks his car. They both enter the garden. It's still pouring down the rain. They walk quickly in the heavy rain without talking much. Mr Goodman rings the door bell and the door is opened by a very attractive woman. She smiles them both.

'Hello darling, we've got a guest tonight. This is Felix.'

'Nice to meet you, Felix! This is Jasmine.'

'Nice to meet you!'

'You two come on in please. It's such a wet day. I'll turn the heating on.'

'It'll be a very sensible thing to do, darling. How are you?'

'I'm fine, thank you. How are you, Justin?'

'I'm starving actually. Felix must be hungry as well.'

'I am not that hungry, sir.'

'I'll get the dinner ready for us. Let's go to the kitchen.'

'Where is Fanny?'

'She's sleeping upstairs.'

'Perhaps, Fanny meets our guest after supper.'

'Once Fanny smells the food in the kitchen, she'll come down to join us, Felix.'

Felix follows Mr Goodman and his wife. They all enter the kitchen on the ground floor. Felix looks around with a delightful curiosity. The kitchen is furnished like a living room. There is a round table in the middle of the kitchen with a white table cloth on. The grandfather-clock is elegantly placed next to the display cabinet, where the dinner-set is displayed. There is a beautiful plant on top of the mantelpiece. There are antique chairs by the windows. The walls are holding the four abstract oil paintings. There is a colourful rug with the geometrical shapes on the floor. There is a CD player on the coffee-table by the mirror. The kitchen has got a pleasant welcoming atmosphere. While Mr Goodman goes to the bathroom to wash his hands and takes off his black court-robe, Jasmine starts laying the table with dinner plates, cutlery and glasses. Felix doesn't know what to do; he can't decide whether he sits or waits for Jasmine to tell him where to sit. Jasmine is too busy with her supper preparation and forgets to tell Felix that he should take a seat as he pleases himself. Felix watches Jasmine's movements. Mr Goodman comes back from the bathroom and lifts the tight-fitting lid of the large heavy-based saucepan to satisfy his curiosity about what dish they've got for dinner.

'Darling, it looks delicious. What is it?'

'It's casserole, dear.'

'Can I help you in any way?'

'Why don't you pour some drink for us all?'

'With my pleasure, dear! What would you like to drink, Felix? A glass of wine, brandy or orange juice?'

'Can I have orange juice please?'

'Certainly!'

Mr Goodman gets the three wine glasses from the cupboard. He pours orange juice for Felix.

'Here it is, Felix.'

'Thanks.'

'Why don't you make yourself comfortable, Felix? Take a seat.'

'Thank you, sir.'

'What are you having, darling?'

'Can I have a glass of brandy, Justin?'

'I'll get you brandy, darling.'

Mr Goodman opens the cupboard and puts the 2 wine glasses back to cupboard. Instead, he gets the 2 small brandy glasses and pours some brandy for his wife and himself.

'Your brandy is ready, darling. Tell me, how was your day?'

'I had an awful day, dear. I've lost the case.'

'We've also lost the case.'

'We?'

'Felix and I have lost the case.'

'Is Felix your client, dear?'

'I've been representing Felix during the last 2 weeks. Felix's trial has come to the end.'

'There'll be some other things to talk about this evening, darling. Could you tell me about yourself, Felix? What do you do in your spare time?'

'I like walking by the River Thames.'

'How often do you go for a walk, Felix?'

'Once or twice a week'

'We like brisk-walking, don't we darling?'

'At weekends, we often go for a long walk. This weekend, you'll join us, Felix.'

'Thank you.'

'Could you start making some salad for us now, Justin?'

'What kind of salad would you like to have tonight, dear?'

'I don't really mind. Just ask our guest what he would like to have.'

'Would you like to have potato salad or green salad to go with your meal, Felix? I can easily boil potatoes. It won't take long.'

'I don't mind. I'll eat anything.'

'Tell you what; I'll make us green salad for tonight. We'll have potato salad tomorrow. How does it sound?'

'Great!'

'In that case, let me put on my apron first.'

'I put your apron into the washing machine, dear.'

'Can I borrow one of yours, then?'

'Yes you can. Take this one with the red poppies on.'

'Thanks, dear. That'll do for the time being. Does this apron suit me better than my court- robe I wear in the courtroom, Felix?'

'They both suit you well. Do you need any help, sir?'

'You are our guest tonight. Jasmine and I can manage together to get the dinner on time. Can't we, darling?'

'Without Justin, I won't get the dinner ready on time. I'm so lucky to have a husband like, Justin. He is very practical. Many barristers can't cook at all, but Justin is a first class chef. We cook our meals alternately. Do you cook, Felix?'

'I don't know how to cook.'

'At your age I didn't have a faintest idea how to cook. I've been cooking since we've been married. I've picked up some of the essential cooking skills from Justin actually.'

'I must admit that you are a better cook than me now, my dear.'

'Am I really?'

'You're an excellent cook, darling.'

'I like your compliment, Justin.'

'I am not paying a compliment, Jasmine. I am serious.'

'I know you've been always genuine even when you're making a polite comment.'

'Felix, we don't argue over anything, isn't it nice?'

'It must be very good to get on well with each other.'

'Tell me about your girl friend now. Did you have an argument with her today?'

'It wasn't an argument. We don't want to see each other again.'

'Have you got a girl friend, Felix?'

'I used to have one, but that is over now.'

'What a shame! I hope you'll resolve your relationship problem with your girlfriend eventually.'

'I don't think so.'

'Try to be optimistic, Felix. Have you finished with salad, darling?'

'Nearly! I need to prepare dressing for salad now.'

'If you wish, I can give you a hand, Justin.'

'I am fine, darling. It won't take a minute or two. You'd better settle in please. I'll join you both as soon as I make the salad.'

'Felix, if you sit over there, we can both see you at the same time.'

'Thanks.'

'I've forgotten to get the napkins out. Let me get them out for us.'

'Here it is! Salad is ready. Where shall I put the salad, Jasmine?'

'Put it in the middle of the table please. We can all help ourselves from there.'

'Where is the casserole?'

'Darling, you sit down please. I'll get the casserole. Napkins are here. You can take one each.'

'Thanks.'

'Can I wash my hands?'

'I'll show you the bathroom, Felix.'

'Thank you.'

Mr Goodman takes Felix to the bathroom. He turns the light on and leaves Felix in the bathroom. Mr Goodman returns back to the kitchen.

'Darling, could you tell me please what Felix's offence is?'

'Felix had broken into an unoccupied property and he was arrested. Felix was referred onto me to represent him as his defence barrister 2 weeks ago.'

'He doesn't look like a criminal.'

'Far from the description you've just made, Felix is a real gentleman.'

'I'm glad you've brought Felix here this evening, Justin.'

'Felix is homeless. He'll be sentenced in a week's time. I asked him to stay with us for a week. I hope you don't mind.'

'I don't mind at all.'

'Thanks darling. You're an angel. On the way home, I was rather worrying that you might get upset about seeing Felix as an unexpected guest this evening.'

'I am concerned with other people's problems as much as you do, darling. Otherwise, I wouldn't be a barrister.'

'I was only pulling your leg. That was all. You've been a fantastic barrister. You always win your cases. I'm surprised to hear that you've lost your case today. Tell me what went wrong, dear?'

'It's a very long story, Justin. I don't really want to go into details while Felix is around. I'll tell you after he leaves us. We need to cheer him up now.'

'You're right, darling. We need to cheer him up.'

Felix gives a knock on the kitchen door gently.

'Please come in, Felix.'

'Have you found the paper towel in the bathroom, Felix?'

'Yes, I've found it. Thanks.'

'Good. Can I have your plate, Felix?'

'Thank you.'

'I hope you like casserole.'

'Yes, I do.'

'Here it is. Have some bread or rice, help yourself with salad please.'

'Thank you.'

'Can I serve your meal, darling?'

'Yes please.'

'Is that enough?'

'Thank you, dear. That's delicious! How long did it take for the casserole to be cooked so well?'

'It took me 3 hours to cook the casserole on a slow temperature.'

'That's why it tastes superb!'

'I am glad you've liked my casserole. Have some rice, Justin!'

'Thank you, dear.'

'Have you got enough rice, Felix?'

'Yes, I've got enough rice. Thank you.'

'You didn't get enough rice. Let me give you some more rice, Felix. We all need to finish this rice tonight. If it stays overnight, it won't taste good tomorrow.'

'Thanks.'

'Shall I pour you some more orange juice, Felix?'

'Yes please.'

'Would you like some more brandy, darling?'

'I've had enough brandy for tonight. Can I have orange juice instead?'

'Brandy is fine, if it's taken only in small quantity. Otherwise, it gets heavier.'

'I know. We can't increase our alcohol intake. It isn't healthy to consume alcohol in large quantity. Considering all the sugar in brandy and wine, we should really avoid having alcohol altogether, Justin.'

'We hardly drink alcohol, Jasmine. Tonight is a special night for us as you're our guest, Felix. I'm glad you don't take alcohol. Have you ever tried alcohol at all?'

'I've never had any alcohol.'

'Keep away from alcohol, Felix. It isn't good for you.'

'My foster parents used to drink wine a lot. They developed liver complications because of their addiction to alcohol.'

'Alcohol can damage one's health. It'll be sensible not to take alcohol. Once people get addicted to alcohol, it's always too difficult for them to beat their drinking habit. It's like having a chocolate bar several times a day. You can easily get addicted to chocolate, if you aren't careful enough.'

'I don't have an addictive personality to start with. I don't smoke, I don't like eating chocolates. I don't even drink tea or coffee that much. I always know when to stop. Don't you think I'm a sensible husband, dear?'

'That's why I've chosen you as my husband. I cannot stand any type of addictions.'

'How lucky I've been to be chosen by you as your husband, darling!'

'I don't understand people with an addictive nature. I need stability and I like people who can resist against any form of temptations so that I can rely on, like you, my dear. With addictive personality, people cannot manage their life fully. Alcohol or any other addiction can easily ruin people's lives.'

'You're right, my dear! That's why I have chosen you as my wife. We both have similar personalities. None of the harmful habits can tempt us. We'd better stay together and resist against all forms of deadly temptations. We can last longer than the people who are tempted easily in life.'

'I like your philosophy, darling. I've just remembered now, we've another guest for supper tomorrow.'

'Steve confirmed that he is coming for supper tomorrow. Did he call you?'

'Yes, he did. Steve is a very sweet person. I am sure you'll like Steve, Felix. He is a dyslexia specialist. We know him for a long time. How long have we known Steve, dear?'

'I have known Steve for 35 years. You must have known him for 10 years.'

'That's right! I met Steve through Justin, Felix.'

'How nice!'

'Steve visits us regularly. Have you got good friends, Felix?'

'I used to have some friends, but I am out of touch with most of them.'

'Life can be so hectic. We don't have many friends either. Steve fits into our hectic lifestyle. He is so funny. We can have a very good laugh while he is around.'

'Steve bought a new frog.'

'Yes, he mentioned that on the phone. Steve's pet frog died a couple of months ago, Felix. Steve was very upset. He has recently bought a new frog similar to the one he had lost.'

'Steve was very attached to his old frog, Felix. When he came over to us for a meal, he often told us about how well his frog was doing at home. Jasmine and I like listening to Steve's expressions he uses for his old frog.'

'He didn't want to get another frog. When Steve visited the pet shop yesterday, he spotted a frog which reminded him his old frog Frederick, Steve couldn't resist the temptation and he bought the frog.'

'In fact, Steve told me he got himself a couple of frogs this time.'

'I must have missed that bit out on the phone, Justin. I remember Steve telling me he bought a new frog but I can't remember him saying he has got 2 frogs.'

'Steve must have bought the second frog after talking to you on the phone. When did Steve ring you, Jasmine?'

'Steve rang me in the morning from work.'

'He rang me at lunchtime. Steve must have changed his mind later on. Anyway, Steve named the new frog after his old frog. Now he has got another Frederick and Frederick's partner Frederica. It'll be nice to see them both in their fish tank with ocean-like atmosphere. Steve reckons his old frog felt lonely on its own in the very big fish tank with plenty of exotic plants.'

'I agree with Steve. Poor Frederic must have died out of boredom. Do you like animals, Felix?'

'Yes, I do.'

'Have you had any pet?'

'My foster parents got me a hamster when I was little. We were good friends while my hamster was around.'

'Don't you have your hamster now?'

'I gave my hamster away when I left home.'

'If we don't have a place to look after pets, life gets complicated. We're lucky, Fanny isn't a demanding pet. She is such a darling cat. Fanny always comes to our bedroom. She loves our bedroom more than any other place.'

'Fanny also likes the kitchen, dear.'

'That's right! Fanny likes the kitchen. Can you hear Fanny's noise? She is scratching the door. When the door is closed, Fanny lets us know that she is behind the door, Felix. Please let Fanny in, Justin.'

'Come on in, Fanny. Have you had a good nap this afternoon? Look, we have got a guest this evening. This is Felix. You'll like him. Sit down there on your chair and watch us while we are having our meal as you always do.'

'Hi Fanny, this is Felix. It's nice to meet you!'

'Fanny is blinking her eyes. That means Fanny is bonded to you, Felix. Our Fanny is very well trained. She never comes near to the dinner table. Fanny always sits down there on her chair and watches us till we finish our meal. Doesn't Fanny always sit there, Justin?'

'Yes, she does. Fanny is a sensible kitten.'

'That chair belongs to Fanny. She likes the rug I have knitted for her. She can smell her own fur left on the rug covering the chair. That's how she got used to her chair, Felix.'

'We feed Fanny with the cat food comes in tin. Fanny doesn't eat what we eat.'

'Fanny is keen to know what we eat as she is a very curious cat. That's why Fanny likes being around while we're having our meals.'

'Fanny is so cute.'

'Isn't she? Let's have our dessert. We'll have some baked apples with custard.'

'You can't get Jasmine's home-made custard from anywhere else.'

'I like custard.'

'I'll get the dessert. Could you make us some tea, Justin?'

'What would you like to drink with your dessert, Felix?'

'I'll have what you are having, sir.'

'I'm going to brew strawberry tea for us all. How does it sound to you both?'

'It sounds great, Justin!'

'I'd like to try strawberry tea, sir.'

'Tea will be brewed while we are having our desserts.'

'That's a good idea. I like strong tea with the strong aroma.'

'The dessert is delicious.'

'I'm glad you've liked it. You can have another one, Felix.'

'That's plenty. Thanks.'

'It was yummy, my dear.'

'What would you like to have tomorrow evening, Justin?'

'I wouldn't mind having baked apple with custard for tomorrow.'

'We can't bore Felix with the same type of dessert, dear.'

'What about pudding then?'

'That's right! I'll make you pudding. I hope you like pudding, Felix.'

'I like all types of desserts.'

'That's good. Can we have our drinks now?'

'Certainly Madam! Let me pour tea for you both.'

'Thanks, dear.'

'Thank you, sir.'

'It's so nice to have herbal tea after supper.'

'I can't do without a cup of herbal tea which takes away all my daily stress.'

'Camomile is very good to get rid of your stress, isn't it Justin?'

'I need bi-neural beats for relaxation before going to sleep.'

'Have you tried bi-neural beats, Felix?'

'I haven't heard anything about bi-neural beats before? What is it?'

'It's a soothing music type, which was revealed by Heinrich Wilhelm Dove, a Prussian physicist in 1839. He believed that beats encourage the brain to fall asleep easily.'

'It's time to go to bed now. It has been a long day for us all, Justin. By the way, you'll be sleeping in the guest bedroom which is next to our bedroom, Felix.'

'Thank you.'

'I'll get you Justin's pyjamas to wear. Have you got toothbrush with you, Felix?'

'I am afraid I left my toothbrush at the hostel this morning.'

'Don't worry. We've got a spare toothbrush. You can have that. Before going to bed, I'll show you the bathroom upstairs where you can wash yourself.'

'Can I help you with the clearing up?'

'I'll do the clearing up. You'd better go with Jasmine. You need to settle in our home. It takes a bit of time to get familiar with the necessary procedures. Jasmine will show you the bathroom, Felix.'

'Thank you, sir.'

'You're welcome. Sleep well. We do our weekly shopping on Saturdays. We might not be here when you get up tomorrow. Please feel at home. We'll see you whenever we see you. For any emergency, you can call me on my mobile number. In the case of fire, please use the front door as fire exit.'

'You are making a mountain out of a molehill. We haven't had any fire here, Justin.'

'In the likelihood of an unexpected disaster, Felix needs to know what to do. If Felix uses the back door, he'll be stuck in the back garden. There isn't a gate opening to the main road from the back garden.'

'I'll take your point, darling. Precaution is better than being unprepared for any disaster in life.'

'I've read plenty of bad news about home fires and losing not only possessions, but many lives.'

'Don't forget the Great Fire of London!'

'That was the biggest disaster we had in this country. The Great Fire of London had continued from the 2nd September 1666 to the 5th September 1666 throughout the central part of London. The fire had ruined the medieval City of London inside the old Roman City Wall. It had destroyed thirteen thousand two hundred houses, eighty seven churches, St Paul's Cathedral and most of the buildings of the city authorities. It is estimated to have destroyed the homes of seventy thousand out of the city's eighty thousand inhabitants.'

'That must be a ghastly experience. Let's hope we won't have it again, Justin.'

'The sensible safety measurements have been enforced by law since then.'

'That's true. We need to get a fire extinguisher.'

'That's a good idea, actually!'

'Every five years we need to get an electricity-safety check, Felix.'

'That must be a sensible thing to do, sir.'

'We also need to get a gas-safety check each year.'

'Have you contacted the engineer to do the routine check soon, Justin?'

'Yes, I've fixed the dates for gas-safety and electricity check.'

'When are they coming?'

'Before the Easter break, they want to finish everything.'

'Make sure, one of us stays at home then. Let me take you upstairs, Felix.'

'Thank you.'

'Goodnight Felix.'

'Goodnight sir.'

Justin starts clearing up the kitchen while he reflects on what went wrong with Felix's trial today. The jury's decision was appalling. Wealthy people without any experience of poverty always act in a judgemental way as they are incapable of understanding how it feels to be homeless and out of work without any support mechanism in a big city like London with 13 million inhabitants. In a small community, people with less advantaged backgrounds are less judgemental or more supportive and treat vulnerable people with compassion and respect. In the big cities, there is nothing but merciless decision makers everywhere even amongst the civilians let alone heartless bureaucrats who are very keen to penalise the vulnerable and trap them even further in the most complicated system of punishment. Justin wonders what will happen to Felix after he comes out of prison. Sending him to prison is not a solution. It only ignores the social problem which could have been resolved by using many resources available in a rich country with a lot of charities and wealthy population. Nothing is worst than marginalising the most needy people and pushing them outside the social system. Who benefits from the cruelty of punishment system? Justin feels so useless not to be able to change the jury's unrealistic decision which will be decreasing Felix's chance to start a new life without being forced to commit crime. For goodness sake, he is homeless. He needs to be helped but not sentenced for his misfortune. Even judge couldn't change the verdict. Justin thought all the injustice decisions are made behind the closed doors of the courtrooms. Many civilians with secure jobs and the places to live, are unaware of the cruelty of the court drama took place in the Inner London Court. If Justin made a film about Felix's trial and showed what went wrong with the jury's verdict in the courtroom, he would have felt more helpful to change the prejudice of many people which may have positive impact on the future generations' life eventually. Justin feels so angry with the unfairness of the legal system. The first time in his professional life, he doubts about the importance of his role as a barrister. He could have chosen something else to help vulnerable people. Justin pours another brandy in his glass and sips it quickly before leaving the kitchen.

Chapter 2

Felix meets dyslexia tutor Steve

Felix likes the luxury he has been experiencing the first time in his life at his barrister Justin Goodman's home. Felix wishes to have similar life style with a beautiful house and a little cat like Fanny. If Felix becomes a barrister, he will have plenty of money to buy a grand house with a big garden. Felix feels upset about hurting Jackie at lunchtime. While Felix was feeling down, he couldn't help reacting against Jackie's superficiality. Justin and Jasmine have been very kind to Felix, but their kindness is different than how Jackie treats him by telling him what to do all the time which Felix finds rather patronising. Felix feels he isn't comfortable with Jackie because of her non-stop interferences with his life. If only Jackie could stop behaving like a detective, their relationship could have been improved. Felix prefers forgetting all the nasty things happened between Jackie and him at lunchtime.

It's going to be Felix's first night sleeping on a very comfortable bed with a clean sheet and duvet. Mrs Goodman has given Felix her husband's silk pyjamas to wear. Felix had never worn silk pyjamas before; he feels like a gentleman when the pure silk pyjamas touching his skin softly. All the luxury Felix finds in his barrister's home makes Felix realise his subconscious desire to become a wealthy man so that he can buy silk pyjamas to wear at night. Felix wonders if Jackie had seen him in Mr Goodman's silk pyjamas, how she would have responded to Felix's elegant appearance. Probably, silk pyjamas won't impress Jackie at all. Jackie's father must have been wearing silk pyjamas at home and it must be natural for Jackie to see a man in silk pyjamas. Felix can't go to sleep not because he is over anxious about going to prison in a week time, but he is over excited for being in a totally new situation which he could have never anticipated. Felix wishes to have silk pyjamas every night and he doesn't want to wear his filthy trousers in bed. Felix studies himself on the wall mirror out of curiosity. He doesn't look too bad. As a matter of fact, Felix looks rather handsome this evening. Why has the life been too harsh on him? Felix wants to have everything in life. He deserves everything with the best quality. Why doesn't he come from a decent family background? Why didn't his paternal parents provide Felix a comfortable family life? Felix can't help detesting his biological parents. Felix knows that some of the disclaimed children make a special effort to track down their biological parents but he had never wanted to find out his biological parents' whereabouts. Felix wonders why his mother had left him as soon as she had given birth to him. Felix speculates on his likeness of his feature and wonders whether he resembles his mother or father more than the other. Who was his father in any case? If he was a decent sort, he wouldn't have left his girlfriend with a child. Felix doesn't have any trace of his biological parents. Felix's name was given by his foster parents. Felix's foster parents didn't tell Felix he was an adopted child till Felix had reached his 11th birthday. It was such a shock to be told that your mum and dad weren't your biological parents but they had adopted you. Felix felt cheated not only by his biological parents, but also by his foster parents. It was such an awful feeling to know that he was an unwanted child. Not to be welcomed to this world by your biological parents must be the worst experience any child could go through. Felix wouldn't disown his own offspring's existence. Felix wasn't guilty but his biological parents were guilty for bringing him into this world. It was their fault to discard him like a piece of furniture, which they didn't want to have any longer. Felix was a discarded baby with flesh and blood. Many babies' birth brings happiness to their parents. For some reasons, his parents weren't enthusiastic about Felix's unexpected arrival. They must have hated him for that. Why didn't his mother have an abortion? His biological mother didn't kill Felix's flesh but she destroyed Felix's spirit. Felix didn't have a biological mum and dad to go to. How fool Felix had been to presume his foster parents as his biological parents till the age of 11. Each birthday was a happy event for Felix to look forward to. After being told about the shocking truth of being an adopted child, Felix hated his birthdays. Felix would prefer not to know the truth. Why did they spoil Felix's childhood by revealing the nasty truth about his misfortune? If Felix adopts a child like himself, he'll never tell the truth to his foster child. Felix will treat his adopted child like his own.

Felix goes to bed with so many unresolved issues in his mind. While he is very upset about his hard luck, he falls asleep. In his sleep, Felix dreams of himself as a judge in the Inner London Court wearing a black court-robe and a white wig. There is an offender and a defence barrister as well. The barrister, the offender and the Judge are all having the same face Felix has got. When the time comes for each of them either to defend or clarify or judge, they all use their own terminologies. Felix feels exhausted with the three different roles at Court. He is defending himself as a defence barrister. The Judge Felix listens to the defence barrister Felix and makes his judgement while he states his decision. The Judge Felix finds the offender Felix not guilty. The defence barrister Felix expresses his satisfaction with the Judge's decision. Innocent Felix, who faced a very difficult trial, is very happy that his innocence has been proved by his barrister and acknowledged by the Judge Felix. They all shake one another's hands at the end of the court case. The Judge Felix is the 1st person to leave the court. The barrister Felix follows him and leaves the court with the fulfilment of doing his job efficiently. Felix leaves the court with the delirious happiness in his heart at the age of 35 as a free man. Felix walks with self-confidence knowing that he had never committed any crime in his life and carries on walking down the road quickly as if he has no time to waste. Felix is going to live his life in full. Felix gets on a bus. The red colour double-decked bus takes him to Waterloo, where Felix walks by the River Thames. Felix gets off the bus and walks down the river. It is there Felix realises he had been matured while he was facing his trial. Felix has grown more than beyond the natural process of maturity as a result of the agony of the unnecessary trial he had faced in his life. Felix would never be the same person after the completion of his trial. Felix is the person, who will be making up for the past years without living his life for himself while he was treated like a criminal. Felix takes a deep breath when he starts gazing at the River Thames. Felix promises himself that whenever he gets upset in life for one reason or another, he will visit here and reminds himself that his trial is over. The River Thames will be the witness of his innocence. This river looks like a human being and listens to Felix's self-promise he made. Felix's unpleasant experience in life has been left behind. Felix feels a need to live the present time more consciously than he has ever done so.

Felix wakes up in the morning and looks around the room, where he slept over night. To his delight, Felix realises that he isn't in a hostel or a squat but he is in Mr and Mrs Goodman's cottage. The room is very peaceful. There is no sign of any irritating noise. Felix gets up and looks at the silk pyjamas on him. He laughs at himself. Felix remembers the supper he had with Justin and his wife Jasmine last night. He makes his bed in haste and takes off his pyjamas. Felix dresses up and goes down to the bathroom. In the bathroom mirror, Felix examines his face once more. It's pleasing to see him afresh as there is no trace of any tiredness left on his face from yesterday. Felix washes his face with the warm water. He leaves the bathroom and goes downstairs to the kitchen. In the kitchen, he finds the kitten Fanny sitting on her chair. Felix strokes Fanny's beautiful fur. Fanny responds to Felix's affection warmly with a purring sound. Felix spends some time by the chair stroking the kitten. Felix looks at the grandfather clock but he can't read the time. Felix looks at the digital clock on the table. It's 10 am. Felix realises that Mr and Mrs Goodman had left a small note for him on the dinner table in front of the vase with the flowers in it next to the digital table-clock.

Good Morning Felix,

We are off to do our weekly shopping.

We've left cereals for you here. Milk, bread, cheese, jam, honey and eggs are all in the fridge. Please help yourself. We'll be back by lunchtime. If you accompany our Fanny, we'll be delighted.

Much love,

Jasmine & Justin

Justin and Jasmine don't treat Felix like an intruder to their private life; they make a special effort for him to feel included in their life. Felix opens the fridge and takes a pint of milk from the fridge. In a small bowl, he puts some muesli and pours milk on top of it. Felix starts eating while he is projecting the whole week ahead of him. Today is Saturday. Felix has got another 7 days to spend here. How is he going to occupy himself? There is nothing to do. He hasn't got any money that will restrict his movement as he can't go out. Jasmine and Justin will be out all day long. Even they stayed at home; Felix wouldn't like to be in their way. After all Felix is a convict with a criminal record. He couldn't understand how Justin and Jasmine trusted him in the first place and left him alone in their beautiful cottage without worrying that he might steal some of their valuables and walk away with them. Felix had never cheated or deceived anyone who put their trust in him. Felix won't let them down. They welcomed Felix into their living environment without treating him like a criminal even they know that he is a criminal in the eye of legal system. Additionally, Felix is an illegible child without knowing who his biological parents are. That is bad enough for anyone with the respectable legible background to overlook Felix's illegible existence with contempt. Felix feels bad about his life circumstances and stops eating his muesli. Felix feels like vomiting as his future looks so dreary. Felix doesn't know where his life will be heading towards; he can't even read or write. He had entertained himself with a beautiful dream last night before going to bed in Justin's silk pyjamas imagining that one day he would be a barrister and live in a large beautiful house with a garden but how Felix is going to achieve his goal without knowing how to read or write properly. Felix finds it almost impossible to understand the news written in the daily newspapers never mind the law books written with a complicated legal language. Felix gets up slowly and clears up the table by putting his bowl and spoon into the dishwasher. Fanny jumps down from her chair and comes very close to Felix. The little kitten starts smelling Felix's trousers. Felix kneels down immediately, picks up the kitten and starts stroking Fanny's beautiful fur affectionately. Fanny continues purring. Felix sits down on a chair with the kitten on his lap. Fanny looks so friendly to Felix.

'Cats don't have any prejudices.' Felix thinks.

Cats are so adorable. How good it would have been, if Felix can take a kitten with him to prison. The kitten will cheer him up when he is in prison. All of a sudden, going to prison looks so scary without knowing what the life will be after completing his sentence. Felix puts Fanny down on the floor and takes his drawing pencil from his pocket. Felix starts playing with Fanny. The kitten loves the moving pencil. She rushes around and tries catching Felix's pencil. Felix forgets about his sentence or his bleak future while Fanny is happy playing with his pencil. He starts laughing at Fanny's manoeuvres from one place to another. The kitten doesn't want to stop. Fanny is very energetic. Felix stops playing with Fanny when she scratches Felix's finger by mistake. There is a bit of blood coming from the scratch. Felix goes to the toilet and washes his finger under the running tap. The bleeding stops. Felix goes back to the kitchen sees Fanny playing with Felix's pencil. She is chewing the pencil. Felix sits next to Fanny. He gently takes away the pencil. Fanny jumps on the pencil. Felix raises the pencil. Fanny stands up on her two feet and tries touching the pencil with her paws. Felix is amused by seeing the kitten standing on her feet like a human being. Felix puts down the pencil on the floor. Fanny jumps onto the pencil. She starts chewing the pencil again. Felix finds a string inside a container on the table. He places the string on the floor and starts pulling the string slowly. The kitten's attention switches from the pencil to the moving string on the floor. Fanny stops chewing the pencil. She looks at the string like a moving animal. Fanny starts moving her body and her moustache slowly. She jumps on the string. Fanny holds the string with her paws. Felix and Fanny are both having fun together. Fanny enjoys Felix's company. Suddenly, Felix hears the door bell ringing. Justin's voice reaches him shortly. They must have come back home from their weekly shopping. Justin enters the kitchen carrying their large shopping bags.

'Hello, Felix.'

'Hello, sir.'

'I see, you are playing with Fanny. She's lucky to have you around today.'

'Fanny likes playing with a piece of string.'

'Fanny loves playing with anything moving. Fanny runs after balls.'

'Hello, Felix.'

'Hello, Mrs Goodman.'

'Call me Jasmine, please.'

'I told Felix the same thing. He can't call me with my first name.'

'Why is that?'

'Felix feels it'll be rude to address someone perhaps older than him.'

'Well, I used to call my mum and dad with their first name. I like informality. Could you call me with my first name, Felix?'

'I'll try.'

'Look Felix, what we've got for you. In this parcel, you'll have underwear; in that parcel, you'll have two wool sweaters. In here, you'll have a pair of cotton pyjamas. There are two pairs of jeans in there. Take them all upstairs to your bedroom. Try them on and see whether they fit on you or not. If they don't, I'll take them back to the shop this afternoon.'

'Thank you ever so much. That's very kind of you!'

'You're very welcome, Felix. Have you had any breakfast?'

'Yes, I have had some muesli.'

'Good. We haven't had a proper breakfast either. We'll be having our breakfast shortly. Please do join us, Felix. I'll be making omelette for us all.'

'Thanks.'

'I'll call you when the omelettes are ready.'

'Thank you.'

Felix picks up the shopping bags from Jasmine. He takes them to the guest room where he slept last night. Felix puts the bags on his bed and opens them all one by one. Felix finds the 7 cotton underpants and 7 vests in one of the bags he opens. Felix has no spare underpants with him. He has no money to buy new ones either. Felix has worn the same jumper for the whole week without having any vest underneath. His jumper got dirty. Felix finds the two beautiful cotton sweaters in the second bag and a pair of jeans in the third bag. Felix puts them on quickly. Felix has been wearing the same old trousers for 3 years. Felix's old outfits are worn out. He decides to throw them away. Felix takes off his jumper and wears one of the new vests. He puts on his new cotton sweater with the geometrical patterns on it. That fits him perfectly well. Felix opens the last parcel. He finds a pair of cotton pyjamas in it. Felix figures out that the pyjamas will fit them without trying them on. Felix puts the cotton pyjamas on the chair next to his bed. Felix's mood is uplifted. Half an hour ago, he was feeling depressed without having any spare cloth to change. Felix has got new outfits now. He puts his old jumper into the plastic bag, which goes into the small bin next to the chair. Felix smiles while he is touching his new sweater. He feels uncomfortable with his socks though as they are filthy and smelly. Felix didn't wear his socks in the morning. Felix's socks have changed the room's odour. Felix throws his smelly socks into the bin. While Felix is tidying up the room, he hears a knock on his door.

'Felix, can I come in?'

'Please do, sir.'

'Hi, Felix.'

'Hi, sir.'

'Your outfits look perfect on you, Felix?'

'Thanks.'

'Jasmine has got a distinctive taste. She buys all my outfits. I never buy anything for myself. To tell you the truth, I wouldn't think you might need new stuff to wear. That was Jasmine's idea. Wear them all in good health, Felix.'

'Thank you ever so much, sir.'

'Don't start, Felix. I dislike the formality. Please call me with my first name.'

'You and Jasmine have been very kind to me. I cannot find a right word to express my gratitude to you both. I am not sure how I would have survived for a week without your help and support.'

'You've been going through a hard time at present. One day, you'll be overcoming all your difficulties, Felix. Let's go downstairs and have our omelette.'

'I'm coming, Justin.'

'That's better. It's good to hear that you've dropped formality.'

The barrister Justin and Felix leave the guest bedroom. They go downstairs. When they enter the kitchen, they smell the omelette. There are 3 dinner plates on the dinner table. Jasmine serves an omelette, two spoonfuls of baked beans, a few slices of grill tomatoes and slices of cucumber for everybody. Mrs Goodman smiles at them.

'Felix, your sweater and jeans look really nice on you!'

'That's very kind of you to buy me new outfits!'

'It's my pleasure. Please have some breakfast now. Fanny looks so happy today. Will it be possible for you to be our pet-sitter for us while we are at work next week?'

'I'll be very happy to look after Fanny next week.'

'That's fantastic! We employ a pet-sitter for Fanny. Our pet-sitter has taken a month off to go abroad for a holiday. She won't be coming till the following week. We've been worrying about Fanny since Barbara is away. Fanny gets very lonely while we are at work. Fanny and her pet-sitter Barbara bonded each other very well. We don't want to change Barbara. That's why we didn't get another pet-sitter while Barbara is away. Fanny likes you as much as she likes Barbara.'

'Felix you've been just on time to cheer up our Fanny for us in the absence of Barbara.'

'It'll be my pleasure.'

'Shall I pour you tea, Felix?'

'Yes please.'

'Milk is here. Please help yourself.'

'Thank you.'

'Let me pour your tea, darling.'

'Thanks dear. The omelette looks appetising.'

'Good appetite everybody!'

'Thanks.'

'Good appetite!'

'In the morning, we quickly had a bit of cereals before rushing out to do our weekly shopping, Felix. On Saturdays, shopping centre usually gets packed up. We prefer shopping early in the morning. We like keeping the rest of the day for us to enjoy.'

'That's good!'

'What would you like me to play for us, Jasmine?'

'Why don't you play *"The Creation"*, Justin?'

'Haydn is one of our favourite composers. Do you like Haydn, Felix?'

'I haven't listened to Haydn's music.'

'Well, many people are not familiar with Haydn's music. We are very fortunate to get to know his music by chance. We often listen to Haydn's master piece. Let me play the great music for you, Felix.'

'It's awesome, I'm sure you'll like it, Felix.'

'It'll be nice to hear something, which I haven't listened before.'

'Listen now!'

They all start having their breakfast with the splendid music playing in the background. None of them dares to ruin the music and they eat their breakfast in silence. The kitten Fanny jumps on her seat and settles in her place as if she knows how important the music is for everybody. From her chair, Fanny watches them all having their breakfast peacefully. Fanny looks as if she enjoys Haydn's music. Half way through the music, Fanny puts her head on her paws and closes her eyes. The kitten starts meditating through the music with her eyes closed.

Felix is very surprised that the lovely kitten, who has been playing with him a few minutes ago with enthusiasm, is so calm and enjoying the music almost with a human-like quality. Felix starts loving the kitten even more. What a cat! Felix thinks. How good it would have been for Felix to be in Fanny's place. To be born as a cat like Fanny must have been blessing from God. Felix almost gets jealous of the comfort Fanny has. How lucky Fanny is to live with the cat lovers Justin and Jasmine! They are both concerned about Fanny's wellbeing. Felix enjoys the present time and pushes the miserable prospect of two years sentence in a prison out of his mind. The taste of omelette with baked beans goes very well. Felix finishes up the food on his plate and sips his tea slowly without any intention to consume it before the music stops. Justin and Jasmine look happy eating their breakfast slowly. Jasmine realises that Felix has already finished up his breakfast; she puts honey jar and jam container in front of Felix without saying a word. Felix takes another toast from the bread tray and opens the honey jar and takes out a bit of honey with his knife. Felix spreads the honey on his toast and bites the toast with delight. Felix remembers that he didn't have honey for a long time. Felix quickly swallows the last crust of his toast with his tea. The 1st side of the CD finishes and music stops. Justin and Jasmine consume their breakfast leisurely.

'How did you find the music, Felix?'

'It was very good.'

'Before I play the other side, let me tell you about Haydn.'

'In the meantime, I'll brew some more tea for us, darling.'

'Thanks.'

Jasmine puts the kettle on. The kettle starts boiling. Jasmine takes the teapot from the table. She throws the tea leaves from the teapot and rinses the kettle in the sink under the running tap. Jasmine opens the cupboard. She takes tea leaves with the tea spoon from the jar and brews the tea leaves in the teapot for 5 minutes. She takes the teapot back to the table. Jasmine pours the freshly brewed jasmine tea into the tea cups. The pleasant smell of herbal tea surrounds the atmosphere of kitchen swiftly.

'Thank you, darling. I was telling Felix how Haydn started composing his own music.'

'Haydn's life story is very interesting, Felix. Shall I pour some more tea for you?'

'Yes please.'

'In the 18th century, Haydn started his musical career while he was still in his teens singing in the choir of Stephen's Cathedral in Vienna. Later on, Haydn spent 8 years of teaching, doing performance as a violinist and a keyboard player at the same time. However, Haydn didn't make music till he had reached a mature age.'

'When was Haydn born, Justin?'

'Haydn was born in 1732.'

'His masterpiece was first performed in 1799, wasn't it, Justin?'

'That's right. *The Creation* was first conducted by Haydn himself in 1799.'

'At the age of 67, Haydn fulfilled his dream. Isn't it a very long period for a musician to wait for giving birth to his masterpiece, Jasmine?'

'It's a lifelong commitment, dear!'

'The beginning of *The Creation* is superb! The representation of Chaos was cleverly handled in the Part 1. The entrance to No: 2 and No: 3 are delicate. I can feel Haydn's greatness whenever I listen to the beginning of his music. Don't you agree with me, darling?'

'Yes I do, dear. I also love the Scene 4 No:12 *And God said: Let there be lights in the firmament of heaven ...*'

'That part is so good. Felix, you need to listen to the 2nd part too. *Scene 1 No:15 And God said: Let the waters bring forth...*'

'Shall I play the part 2 for us now, Justin?'

'Yes please'

Jasmine puts on the 2nd part of the CD. She hits the play button on the CD recorder and they hear the sound of the great music. Mrs Goodman goes back to her seat. She takes a piece of toast from the bread tray and puts the apricot jam on her toast. The pitch of the music increases. The kitten Fanny opens her eyes and looks at them carefully before closing her eyes again to listen to the music coming from the CD player. Felix looks at Fanny. The kitten's ears move in accordance with the musical rhythm without opening her eyes. Felix feels an irresistible laughter. He suppresses his urge for a good laugh and sips his tea quietly.

'The music is lovely and soothing!' Felix thinks.

Felix had never listened to any classical music at his foster home as his foster parents' musical taste was limited to rock and jazz. That was why Felix had never developed a taste for the classical music. Felix always assumed that the classical music was too difficult for him to understand. However, listening to Haydn's music enables Felix to realise that he can develop a taste for the classical music if he puts his mind into it. Why didn't Felix listen to other types of music before? If Felix brings up a child, he will definitely introduce the classical music to his child. Felix's son or daughter should know who Haydn is. Felix's child should be able to make a comment on any classical music in the same way Justin and Jasmine do. Felix was surprised when Mr and Mrs Goodman remembered Haydn's birthday. Felix can't even remember his own birthday let alone someone else's birthday. There was an approximation of his birthday, but no one knew when Felix was born. Felix realises that he came back to the same point once more. Reflecting on his misfortune distresses Felix a great deal. He didn't even know what his biological parents' names were. Felix's happiness is spoiled by remembering his insignificant past. Felix takes another toast from the bread tray and puts some apricot jam on his toast. Felix bites the toast with a great appetite. The firmness of each apricot leaves a very pleasant taste in Felix's mouth while he is chewing his bread with the apricot jam. Felix remembers the taste of the fresh apricot during the summer time. Apricot was one of his favourite fresh fruit. Felix loves the juicy and ripe apricots as well as blueberries. Instead of buying a bar of chocolate, Felix used to buy a small box of fresh apricots or blueberries as dessert with his pocket money when he was in his teens. Felix could finish up all the apricots in a box within an hour or so. Felix feels bad about taking his mind off from the great music and thinking about something totally irrelevant to the great music he was listening to. Justin and Jasmine both close their eyes while they are sipping their tea. They look like they aren't thinking anything else but music only. Getting into a right mood to listen to the classical music should take some time. Felix decides to buy CD with Haydn's music on as soon as he completes his 2 years sentence. If only Felix gets a place of his own, life will be more pleasant. Felix can listen to Haydn's *The Creation* every night before he goes to sleep. If Felix gets into the habit of listening to Haydn's music regularly, he'll be expert on identifying each passage he listens to without much difficulty and remembers the different numbers for the whole composition. Music ends. Felix starts wondering whether or not Mrs Goodman will be re-playing the same music. Justin smiles at Felix with compassionate human warmth in his eyes. Felix feels awkward and ignores Justin's warmth and starts looking at different direction. Felix's barrister immediately turns his attention to his wife by gazing at Jasmine with the same compassionate warmth. Jasmine smiles back to Justin with the delight of being loved by her husband unconditionally. *'That is simply Justin!' He is always full of unconditional love to offer to anyone without feeling awkward about his warmth. Poor Felix doesn't know Justin's sensitivity yet. He gets used to it.'* Jasmine thinks silently.

> 'Everything was excellent, my dear. I've enjoyed it thoroughly. How are we going to spend the rest of the day?'

> 'You tell me, darling. What would you like to do?'

> 'Let's ask Felix. What would you like to do this morning, Felix?'

> 'I haven't got a clue.'

> 'Can I make a suggestion?'

> 'Yes please.'

> 'We'll all go out for a good walk by the River Thames. How does it sound?'

> 'That'll be fine.'

> 'That'll be splendid, dear. Let me go upstairs. I'll make our bed quickly.'

> 'I'll clear up the table, Jasmine.'

'Thanks dear. See you in a minute.'

'See you, darling.'

'Let me help you, Justin.'

'You need to enjoy your first Saturday with us, Felix. Why don't you play with Fanny? Take her to the living room till I finish clearing up. Once Jasmine is ready, we'll get you from the living room.'

'Thanks. Would you like to come with me, Fanny?'

Fanny opens her eyes. She stands up. Felix picks her up affectionately. Felix suddenly remembers that he doesn't know where the living room is.

'Excuse me, where is the living room?'

'It's at the end of the corridor. The first room opposite the front door, you can't miss it, Felix.'

'Thank you. See you later, Justin.'

'See you later, Felix.'

Felix gets out of the kitchen slowly. He walks down the long corridor holding the kitten on his chest. Felix opens the door and enters the living room with Fanny. It is a spacious and very well-furnished room with a fire-place at the far end. There are two beautiful French windows. Felix puts the kitten on the carpet. He looks out of the windows. The garden looks very picturesque. Felix sits on the floor next to the kitten Fanny. Felix realises that he doesn't have either a string or a pencil to play with Fanny. Felix wonders how he is going to play with the kitten. He needs to create a play, which Fanny will enjoy. Felix starts using his fingers like a horse trotting towards the kitten. The kitten Fanny notices that Felix using his finger like a horse which amuses her. The kitten comes very close to Felix's fingers and jumps on his fingers. Fanny starts biting Felix's fingers gently without hurting him. Felix looks around the living room. He wants to find something that will amuse Fanny even more. The long curtains inspire Felix. He runs quickly behind the heavy curtains and hides himself. Felix shows half of his head from the side of the curtain. Fanny sees Felix's half-hidden head. Felix hides his head behind the curtain again. Fanny can't see Felix's head anymore. The kitten stays at the same point without moving anywhere and fixes her attention to the same point where she has seen half of Felix's head for a few second. Felix shows one third of his head from the curtain to the kitten once more. Fanny gets delighted with the game Felix has just invented. While Fanny is looking at the same point, Felix moves to the other part of the curtain. Felix shows one third of his head from the other side of the curtain this time. Fanny looks she is surprised. Fanny starts gazing at the other side of the curtain motionless. Felix changes his place quickly and shows his head from the other side of the curtain. Felix repeats the hide-and-seek game for a while. Fanny starts moving around. The kitten shows the sign of having a great fun. Fanny starts jumping up and down. Felix comes next to the kitten. Fanny tries to scare Felix. Fanny's fur starts expanding. Fanny is in a mood to play with Felix. Felix uses one of his fingers underneath of a small carpet. When Felix moves his finger slowly from one side to another Fanny rushes to catch Felix's finger as if it is a pencil or a bit of string. While Fanny is going to scratch Felix's finger, Felix pulls his hand quickly and hides it under the carpet. Felix moves his hand under the carpet without showing his hand or fingers to the kitten. In this way, Felix can avoid another scratch. Each time the carpet moves, the kitten Fanny jumps on the moving part of the carpet with the expanded fur and enlarged eyes in the same way the frightened cats may appear.

Jasmine climbs up the stairs quickly and enters the master bedroom. Jasmine looks at their bed where she has been sleeping with her husband Justin during the last 10 years. The duvet of the bed looks how they left it in the morning before going out for shopping. Jasmine pats on their pillows softly. The pillows look bigger than they are after being patted. Jasmine covers the pillows with the white duvet. The beautiful monkey is sitting on the bedside chest. Jasmine usually moves the toy monkey from bed to the bedside chest at night before they go to bed. In the mornings, Jasmine places the toy monkey on top of their bedspread after making their bed. The beautiful toy monkey was given to Jasmine by her husband Justin on their 1st wedding anniversary. During the last 9 years, the monkey has been decorating their bed elegantly. Justin never moves the toy monkey anywhere as he leaves Jasmine to be in charge of moving the monkey from one place to another each night and morning. Jasmine thinks how lucky she has been to have a husband, who is very observant to her early attachment to children's toys. There is a little girl within the barrister Jasmine. She has always kept in touch with her childhood through her childhood objects. Jasmine remembers the fact that neither Justin nor Jasmine had any time to consider the possibility of having a child during the past 10 years. They've been very busy to build up their career. Jasmine thinks that if they had a child, she wouldn't have her toy monkey in their bedroom. Probably, the child would have had the toy monkey in his or her bedroom. Jasmine opens the wardrobe. She looks through her thick wool jumpers folded neatly on the second shelf. Jasmine takes her white wool jumper with turtleneck carefully. Jasmine closes the wardrobe. She takes off the grey jumper she has been wearing. Jasmine puts on the white jumper. Jasmine looks at the life-size mirror on the wardrobe. Jasmine's reflection on the mirror pleases her female ego. She walks towards her dressing table. Jasmine picks up her lipstick from her make-up box at her dressing table. She sits down on the chair and puts the lipstick on her lips slowly. The colour of the lipstick looks like her natural lip colour. Justin prefers Jasmine wearing a bit of make-up when they both go out at weekends. Jasmine never likes wearing heavy make-up though. As a matter of fact, Jasmine never wears any make-up at work. Jasmine makes herself more presentable in order to satisfy Justin's male ego wanting to have a glamorous wife when they are socialising outside. Jasmine picks up the hairbrush and brushes her hair slowly. Jasmine thinks she needs to have another hair cut soon. It'll be nice to get her hair restyled with a modern look this time. Jasmine looks at her eyebrows on the mirror. She has bushy eyebrows. Jasmine gets her eyebrows thinned regularly. There is no time for pulling out one or two eyebrows, which have grown from the awkward places. If Jasmine gets some time off for herself this evening, she might thin her eyebrows herself. Jasmine remembers that Steve is coming for supper. Once they come back home from walk, Jasmine must start her supper preparation. She'd better to explore some ideas about what she should cook for supper this evening. Justin enters the bedroom while Jasmine is about to leave.

'Hi dear, you look glamorous.'

'Thanks. Aren't you getting ready, darling?'

'I don't know what to wear really. What do you suggest, Jasmine?'

'The red jumper I bought for you on your last birthday suits you very well, dear.'

'It's thick and keeps me warm.'

'Shall I take our Wellingtons out?'

'Yes please. There is a bit of mud outside. We need to take the short cut through the woods. Why don't you ask Felix whether he would like to wear my spare Wellingtons?'

'Is Felix still in the kitchen?'

'Felix is in the living room as he is entertaining our Fanny.'

'That's fine! I'll get our Wellingtons out. See you later, dear.'

'See you later, darling.'

Jasmine leaves the bedroom. Justin opens the wardrobe and he picks his red jumper from the pile of jumpers on his side in the wardrobe. Justin takes off his shirt and puts on his wool jumper. Justin closes the wardrobe and looks at his image reflecting on the mirror. The barrister Justin finds himself still handsome with a bit of grey hair and a few wrinkles under his eyes. Justin thinks the 10 years of his marriage has flown away like 10 days from his annual leave. Jasmine and Justin have been enjoying their happy marriage life unlike many couples who get on each other nerves after 2 or 3 years of togetherness living under the same roof. Justin considers himself one of the luckiest men in the world as he found his life-long compatible companion. Justin looks at their bed covered neatly with the toy monkey placed between their pillows. Justin remembers the 1st wedding anniversary when he bought the toy monkey for Jasmine after discovering his wife's interest in children's toys. Whenever they go out for shopping, Jasmine always wants to visit children's toy department. One of their shopping days at weekends, Jasmine had spotted the toy monkey she liked a lot as she found likeness with her old monkey toy from her childhood. At that time, Justin was looking for a suitable present to buy for his wife for their 1st wedding anniversary. Justin went back to the same toy department of the shop next day at his lunch break. Justin was working as a junior barrister in those days. Justin bought the toy monkey and kept it in the small room, where he used to change his outfit for his court cases in the Inner London Court. Justin didn't bring the toy monkey home till their 1st anniversary as he didn't want to spoil the surprise factor. It wasn't easy to keep the huge toy monkey in his little interview room shared with other barristers. Justin's colleagues were so curious about the huge parcel Justin had kept for a month in that tiny dressing room at work. Justin hadn't revealed either the content of the parcel or the identity of the person for whom he bought the present as he wasn't quite sure about other barristers' response to unusual presents he had chosen to give to his wife on their anniversary. Justin smiles while he is looking at the huge toy monkey on their bed. That was a very good choice he made years ago. Jasmine was over the moon while she got her present from Justin. If they had a child, it would have been too hard for Jasmine to be deprived from her toy monkey. Although Justin was pretty sure that Jasmine would sacrifice her own attachment to her toy monkey for their child; nevertheless, that wouldn't be that easy. Anyway, they both worked so hard. None of them was prepared to have a career break for child rearing. It was too difficult to become parents as their time was taken up with the hectic life style. They had only 21 days off from work. How could they bring up a child or children if they decided to have children? At the age of 50, there is still time for them to consider having a child but one of them has to sacrifice their professional life. None of them can afford to give up their career. It didn't appeal to any of them to employ a nanny to look after their child when they go to work. If they wanted to have a child, one of them needed to look after their child at least for a couple of years. They have replaced their need for a child with the kitten, Fanny recently. Instead of having a kid, Justin and Jasmine have decided to have a cat. They've even employed a pet sitter for their kitten. However, they wouldn't like their child being left with a nanny at home. Life has been kind to both of them. They've got a beautiful house, a very good job with the satisfactory salaries coming in regularly and fantastic annual holidays on the luxurious holiday resorts since they've been married. They had never missed out any of their annual leaves for doing decoration or for some other do-it-yourself jobs indoors. Justin and Jasmine have built up the most beautiful holiday memories together. If they had a child, they would have never gone to the splendid holiday resorts. Many parents need to spend their money on their children's future. In life, one cannot have everything. We all need to make our choices. When Justin and Jasmine reach their retirement age, they will still have the precious memories of being together. It won't make much difference whether they had a child or not at an old age. The dazzling holiday memories will create the most valuable gifts for them to treasure after retirement. Justin feels good about being a married man. Not only being married, but married to the right person in life has been very important to him.

If Justin had chosen someone else as his wife instead of Jasmine, he wouldn't have been as happy as he has been with Jasmine. His wife has fulfilled Justin's expectation from an ideal wife. Until Justin met Jasmine, he wasn't even considering the possibility of meeting a woman, who could understand him as much as Jasmine does. Since they have been married, they have never had any unresolved issue. They both miss each other's company during the day time when they are at work. The 10 years of their marriage didn't stale their longing for each other and every single day, coming back home from work is a joyful event for Justin. They always find enough time to take their mind off from their daily worries at work. There has been nothing more important than their perfect marriage. How much Justin wished to meet Jasmine in his 20s instead of his late 30s so that he could have enjoyed longer years in Jasmine's company. The longer they live together the better their relationship gets.

Justin remembers the exact date of meeting Jasmine for the 1st time with the vivid memories. Justin had met Jasmine in his office 11 years ago as soon as Jasmine had gone into a mild depression as a result of losing her both parents within short intervals. Jasmine had contacted Justin for a short bereavement therapy. In those days, Justin was working as a bereavement therapist. Justin recalls each detail of Jasmine's appearance on their first meeting. Jasmine looked stunningly beautiful in her elegant black dress she was wearing. The agony Jasmine was going through made her look even more beautiful. Jasmine rang Justin a week ago and made an appointment to see him for a bereavement therapy. The date was arranged. Justin wasn't expecting to meet such a beautiful woman, let alone to be moved by Jasmine's sparkling beauty in pain. He had started listening to Jasmine's worries attentively. While Jasmine was describing the agony of losing her parents, Justin had felt inadequate to heal Jasmine's suffering. There was nothing to stop Jasmine's grief for her loss. She had to go through the pain of loss by herself. Justin could have done anything to make Jasmine happy but that wasn't possible. The misery of facing our loved ones can only be dealt by us. Justin had seen Jasmine for 10 sessions. At the last counselling session, Justin had proposed Jasmine as he was fully certain about his strong affection for her. Strangely enough, Jasmine wasn't surprised by Justin's proposal and she had accepted Justin's marriage proposal straightway. The wedding arrangement was done without unnecessary fuss about it. Justin sold his bachelor flat immediately as one bedroom flat was too small for a married couple. Justin had bought their cottage in Richmond. Jasmine and Justin had moved in their new home before going on their honeymoon. Jasmine's depression was over. Soon after starting a new life, Jasmine was transformed into a new personality with increased morale. She got a new employment in a legal firm as a legal representative. Justin had decided to switch his interest from counselling to law. Justin was qualified as a solicitor before making a living from his counselling profession. Justin's decision to start trading as a freelance barrister was a right move in his professional life. Jasmine and Justin had never looked back since they've been married. The whole world outside their own didn't affect their happiness as they didn't pay any attention to the destructive news appeared on the telly or in the newspapers; as long as they were together, nothing mattered to them. Justin brushes his hair with his comb. He opens his after-shave bottle displayed on the dressing table. Justin sprinkles the after-shave on his face with the 5 o'clock shadow. Justin knows that Jasmine likes seeing him afresh without having a beard. Justin needs to shave his beard even on their vacation. Justin doesn't have time to shave his beard right now as he is in a rush. Justin needs to go down quickly. Otherwise, they'll be late for their weekend walk. Justin leaves the bedroom quickly.

Jasmine puts the Wellingtons out and gets one of Justin's spare raincoats for Felix from the cupboard in the hallway entrance. Jasmine goes to the kitchen and makes fresh coffee. She fills the coffee flask with the fresh coffee to take away. Jasmine opens the biscuit container and gets cookies from it. She places the flask, steel coffee cups and biscuit container inside a large-size picnic bag. Jasmine is ready to go out for a good walk now. She goes to the living room to call Felix.

'Hi Felix, has Fanny given you any trouble?'

'Not really. We've been playing together. Fanny is an adorable kitten.'

'Isn't she? At least, Justin and I both think so.'

'We have played the hide-and-seek game together. Each time I hide myself behind these curtains, Fanny is quick to discover my whereabouts.'

'Fanny is a very intelligent cat. I have no doubt about it. Fanny can stay here while we are out for a few hours. Bye Fanny! We're going out now, Felix. I've got you a pair of Wellingtons.'

'Thank you.'

'It's going to rain today. We'll be better off with our Wellingtons and raincoats. This is Justin's spare raincoat. You can wear it when we are out.'

'Thanks for your kind thought.'

'You're our guest and your wellbeing is our concern.'

Justin comes down and smiles at them both while Felix is wearing his raincoat.

'Are we all ready to go out for a walk?'

'Yes, we're ready, dear. We can leave the kitchen door open. Fanny can go there whenever she wants to have something to eat or drink.'

'That's sorted nicely. Let me carry the picnic bag.'

'Thanks, Justin.'

Jasmine, Justin and Felix put on their Wellingtons. Justin opens the front door and they all go out. Justin locks the door. They start walking through the park. They walk with the same speed without stopping anywhere for half an hour. When they reach the River Thames, it starts raining. There are swans, ducks, geese, pigeons and squirrels around. Jasmine points at the unoccupied bank to sit down for a while. They all sit down. Jasmine takes out the coffee flask, steel cups and the cookies from her picnic bag. Jasmine pours coffee for everyone. The aroma of the coffee in the open air makes them feel happier. They all have their coffee with the cookies in silence watching the River Thames and the wild life with a great joy. Jasmine is the first one to finish her coffee and cookies. She gets a packet of bread out of the picnic bag and starts breaking the bread into small pieces. Jasmine throws bread pieces to swans, geese, seagulls, ravens and pigeons cheerfully. Justin and Felix finish their drinks and cookies at the same time. Jasmine gives them a packet of bread for each to feed the animals. They both join in bird feeding event. Three of them feed the birds affectionately with a passion for wild life. Watching animals' happiness makes their walk even more purposeful. Jasmine, Justin and Felix enjoy their interaction with the birds. They watch the narrow boats on the River Thames. It's a very pleasant walk by the riverside with a therapeutic effect on their moods. They come back home at 2 o'clock feeling relaxed. They have re-charged their weekly batteries with the freshness of a soothing walk by the riverside. Jasmine suggests her husband and their guest Felix to have some time off while she is preparing their dinner for late lunch and supper in the kitchen. Justin and Felix go to the living room where the kitten Fanny has been sleeping on one of the sofas there.

'Look, Fanny is resting now. She must be fast asleep. I'll get the newspapers from the kitchen. We'll have a look at the newspapers. That'll keep us busy till our lunch is ready.'

Justin goes back to the kitchen and picks up the newspapers from the coffee table.

'How are you getting on, my dear? Do you need any help?'

'No thanks, darling. I'm fine at the moment. I'll call you when I need your help. I'll be grilling mackerels for lunch.'

'That's great. When you are ready, give me a shout. I'll make the salad.'

'That'll be helpful.'

'See you later.'

'See you later, dear.'

Justin enters the living room holding the newspapers. Felix is sitting on the sofa, where the kitten Fanny is sleeping serenely. Justin puts the newspapers on the coffee table.

'Times, Guardian, Independent and Observer are all here, Felix. Which one do you wish to read first?'

'I don't know.'

'Well, you choose the newspaper you wish to read first? Have you got any favourite newspaper?'

'Not really.'

'What newspapers do you usually read, Felix?'

'I don't read newspapers, Justin?'

'What is the reason for that?'

'I find it difficult to read newspapers?'

'How difficult is it, Felix?'

'To tell you the truth Justin, my reading isn't that good.'

'I see.'

'I dropped out from school before grasping the basic how to read and write properly.'

'Don't worry about that! Would you like to watch the telly instead, Felix?'

'I don't mind.'

'Let's watch the telly, Felix. I'll have a look at the newspapers later on.'

Justin turns on the TV. The news is presented by the news readers. While Justin is watching the news, his mind is preoccupied with Felix's inability to read and write. Not being able to read and write can delay Felix's progress in life. Justin can't focus on the news. It's a good job that Steve is coming tonight. Steve might be able to help Felix. Jasmine enters the living room.

'Justin, mackerels are already grilled. You can make our salad now.'

'I'm coming, darling. The remote controller is here, Felix. If you wish to watch another programme, you can change the channel. I'll call you when I make the salad.'

'Thank you.'

Justin and Jasmine leave Felix in the living room. They both enter the kitchen. The dinner table is already set pleasantly.

'You look a bit concerned, dear. Is there anything you worry about?'

'Felix is illiterate.'

'Really?'

'Yes, he can't read. I've taken the newspapers to the living room with the hope that Felix would be happy to read them all. Felix said that he has got problems with reading.'

'At his age, it must be embarrassing for him to admit that.'

'That's why I didn't ask him any further question about his inability to read and write. I am worrying about Felix's prospect now. He can't make much progress in life. He'll be stuck.'

'We've got to do something about it, Justin.'

'Steve will be coming at the right time to meet Felix. What Felix needs is Steve's sensible intervention.'

'That's right, darling! Steve will come up with a right solution for Felix's problem.'

'I'll be making a green salad for lunch. Is that OK with you?'

'That's fine, dear. There are plenty of ingredients for salad in the fridge.'

'Great! We've got spring onions, lettuce, tomatoes, cucumber and herbs.'

'We'll have our supper at 8.30 tonight. Steve will be arriving at 8 o'clock. I'll better start supper preparation after lunch.'

'I'll try to get Felix into some kind of fun. Poor Felix can't read newspapers, magazines or any book. I don't think he can enjoy watching telly non-stop.'

'Watching telly all day long will bore Felix.'

'Felix needs to do something that will take off his worries. Otherwise, Felix gets into a deep depression. What do you suggest us to do in the afternoon, Jasmine?'

'Why don't you take Felix to the gym, Justin?'

'That's a good idea actually. Physical exercise will increase Felix's stamina to improve his mood. I'll take Felix to the swimming pool after lunch.'

'Shall I prepare the salad dressing, Justin?'

'Yes please. Salad is nearly ready.'

'The phone is ringing. Can you answer the phone, darling?'

Certainly! Hello, 395 02 26. Justin is speaking'

'Hello Justin, Steve is here.'

'Hello Steve, it must be telepathy! We are talking about you just now. Are we going to see you at 8 o'clock tonight?'

'That's why I'm calling you, Justin. Will it be OK if I come around at 8.40 instead of 8.00 o'clock this evening?'

'I should imagine so. Have you got something else to do, Steve?'

'I have to finish writing a few diagnostic reports for my dyslexic clients. If I get them all done today, I'll have some time off for Sunday to recover from last week's heavy workload. Will it make any difference to you and Jasmine, if I am a bit late?'

'I shouldn't think so. Let me speak to Jasmine about it. Hold on a second.'

'What's the matter, darling?'

'Steve is on the phone. He needs to finish his report writing. He'll be late for supper. Steve wants to come here at 8.40 instead of 8 o'clock. Will it cause any problem for your supper preparation, my dear?'

'I don't think so. I was planning to have our supper at 8.40 in any case. We'll have our supper at 8.50 then.'

'I'll tell him. Steve, Jasmine says it'll be fine, you can come at 8.40. We'll have our supper at 8.50.'

'Thanks Justin. Give my regards to Jasmine. I'll be there at 8.40.'

'By the way, I need to tell you something else. We've got another guest for supper tonight.'

'That means I am going to meet another soul tonight. Is your guest female by any chance?'

'I am afraid not. We've got a male guest. Felix is staying with us for a week.'

'Who is Felix?'

'He is one of my clients.'

'To be honest with you, I prefer meeting an attractive young lady tonight. Never mind! See you later, Justin.'

'See you later, Steve. Felix is a very nice young guy. I am sure you'll like meeting him.'

'I hope so.'

Justin feels his distress has been lifted as he knows that his childhood friend Steve is an expert in his field and can fix any problem with reading or writing. In the afternoon, Justin will be enjoying himself at the gym without worrying about Felix's problems as he is hoping to refer some of Felix's problems onto Steve to resolve.

'Your worries aren't there anymore Justin, am I reading your facial expression fine?'

'It's such a relief to remember Steve's problem-solving skills. I'm sure Steve will find a solution to Felix's writing and reading problems. Let's have our lunch now! Shall I call Felix?'

'Yes please.'

Justin leaves the kitchen and comes back to the kitchen with Felix. They have their lunch in a cheerful mood but without talking much. As soon as they finish their lunch, Justin takes Felix to the swimming pool at the local gym. Jasmine starts her preparation for the supper. While Jasmine's cooking is in progress, she goes to the living room and sits down on the sofa flipping through the daily newspapers. Jasmine reads some of the articles in each newspaper with full attention. She doesn't realise how quickly time passes. Justin and Felix come back home looking content. They find Jasmine in the living room.

'Hi dear, we are back.'

'Hi darling, it's nice to see you back. Have you enjoyed yourselves at the gym, darling?'

'Yes, we've had a fantastic time, haven't we, Felix?'

'Yes, it was so good to swim in the swimming pool.'

'I'm glad to hear that you had a good day. Time is nearly 8 o'clock. What time did you leave home, can you remember?'

It was 4 o'clock when we went to the gym.'

'You must have spent 4 hours there.'

'It was a long time. We didn't only swim but we did some exercises using the heavy machines there. While we were out what have you done with your time, darling?'

'I have been reading newspapers since the cooking is underway.'

'That's good. Let's have some drink. What would you like to drink, Jasmine?'

'Can I have apple juice, dear?'

'I'll get you apple juice. What about you, Felix?'

'I'll have apple juice as well.'

Justin goes to the kitchen; he opens the fridge and takes out apple juice. He pours the apple juice into the crystal glasses. He puts the glasses on the tray and takes the tray to the living room. Justin offers the apple juices first to Jasmine and then to Felix. Finally, Justin gets himself apple juice. They start having a relaxing evening sipping their juice. The kitten Fanny looks serious when they're all drinking. All of a sudden, she leaves the living room.

'Fanny must be going to the kitchen.'

'She must have been thirsty. I am sure Fanny is going to drink water.'

'Can I watch Fanny while she is drinking water?'

'Go on then.'

Felix leaves his glass on the coffee table and rushes to the kitchen and he finds the kitten Fanny drinking water from the water container placed near her chair she usually sits. Felix watches Fanny with wonder. The kitten doesn't stop drinking her water till she gets rid of her thirst. As soon as Fanny stops drinking, she looks at Felix with a surprise as if she isn't expecting Felix to watch her drinking. Fanny starts cleaning her fur. Felix wants to pick up the kitten and stroke her beautiful fur but that doesn't seem appropriate as the kitten Fanny is too busy with her cleaning. Felix sits down on the chair opposite Fanny. He gazes at Fanny while she is cleaning herself carefully with a mysterious calmness on her face. Felix can't help thinking that he has got to have a kitten as soon as he completes his 2 years prison sentence. A kitten like Fanny will definitely make Felix happy as he can watch his kitten's movements all the time.

Justin and Jasmine start discussing about the supper preparation.

'Is there anything that needs to be updated for supper, darling?'

'I left the salad for you to deal with.'

'We had a green salad for lunch. Shall I make potato salad for a change?'

'I was going to suggest beetroot salad, actually.'

'That's a good idea! Steve likes beetroot salad. It'll be a treat for Steve.'

'Why don't you make 2 different types of salads, beetroot and potato salads? Salads will enrich our supper repertoire, Justin?'

'I'd better go back to kitchen and start preparing salads.'

'I have done my bit. There is nothing for me to do until Steve arrives. I'll go upstairs and dress up now.'

'How do I look with my beard, dear?'

'I prefer seeing you without any beard, Justin. If you've got a bit of time left, have a quick shower and shave your beard please.'

'I'll do that for you, Jasmine.'

'Thanks dear. See you later. If you need any help, give me a shout.'

'It's your turn to relax now. Please enjoy the rest of evening without worrying about anything, Jasmine.'

'Thanks dear.'

Jasmine and Justin leave the living room. Jasmine goes upstairs to the master bedroom. She takes off her trousers and pullover. Jasmine wears her dressing-gown. She goes to the bathroom and fills the bathtub with the warm water. She adds strawberry shampoo bubble into the bathtub. Jasmine enters into the bathtub and takes a warm bath. It's refreshing to have a bath after supper preparation. Jasmine gets out of the bathtub and puts her dressing-gown on again. After unplugging the bathtub, she gives a good clean to the bathtub with a bath spray which shines the surface thoroughly. In the bedroom, Jasmine chooses a very nice silk evening dress to wear for supper. She sits down on the small chair in front of her dressing table and styles her hair by different types of brushes for indulging herself with 15 minutes skincare. Jasmine wears a pair of elegant and comfortable shoes. Mrs Goodman looks at her appearance in the mirror with narcissistic pleasure by admiring her own beauty as she thinks dressing up nicely changes a person's appearance as well as boosting her self-confidence. Before leaving the bedroom, her dear companion Justin enters.

'You look glamorous as usual, my dear.'

'Thanks Justin. Have you finished the salads?'

'They are both ready. There is nothing to worry about. I can take a shower now.'

'That's good. It's still 8.30. Steve won't be here until 8.40. You've got 10 minutes left to get ready. I'll wait for you in the living room. I'll be choosing a soothing music to play for Steve. He must have been stressed up with writing the reports and meeting endless deadlines. Steve needs to unwind this evening. See you later, dear.'

'See you later, darling.'

Justin goes to the bathroom. He undresses quickly and goes under the shower. Justin stays under the shower for 5 minutes. He immediately feels afresh and ready for a nice supper to enjoy himself in the company of his guests and his lovely wife. Justin puts on his dressing-gown. Justin shaves his beard within 2 minutes with the electrical raiser in front of the mirror. After shaving his beard, Justin goes back to their bedroom. He opens the wardrobe and takes out his night suit he normally wears for dining with Steve and some other guest who are invited for supper. Justin wears his shoes which go with his evening suit. He brushes his hair and applies some after- shave on his skin. Justin goes downstairs to the living room. Jasmine, Felix and kitten Fanny are all sitting on the same sofa. There is Brahms Violin Concerto No.1 in G Minor, Op.26 in the background. Felix is playing with Fanny. Jasmine is looking through weekend magazines.

'Hello everybody.'

'Hello darling! You look afresh.'

'I had a warm shower, which has taken away all my exhaustion. I feel so good now.'

'It's nice to see that you've shaved your beard.'

'Yes, I've shaved my beard. It's good to make an effort to look good. Felix, we spent at least 2 hours doing heavy exercises in the gym. You must be tired. The warm shower will relax your muscles. You can take a shower now.'

'Can I use the bathroom?'

'Please do, Felix. Your towels are in the bathroom. You know where they are, don't you?'

'Yes, I do. I'll be back soon. See you later.'

'See you later, Felix. You can use my electrical razor to shave your beard. I have left it for you on the sideboard.'

'Thanks Justin.'

Felix goes upstairs to the bathroom. He goes under the warm shower spending 3 minutes without moving. Felix has a choice to make between a warm bath and a warm shower in his hosts' home. Felix remember he couldn't have bath when he was living with his foster parents as there was only tiny shower unit available in their council flat. Felix is absolutely sure that he wants to have the same luxury he has recently found at Justin's cottage.

Justin sits next to his wife. Jasmine leaves the magazine and looks at her husband's eyes. She can see that her husband is a very happy man.

'You look content with your life, dear.'

'I am exceedingly content with my life. I've had a very good time today. What's more our weekend hasn't finished yet. There will be some more time to enjoy before going back to work on Monday. By the way, what would you like to do tomorrow? Have you got any plan to do?'

'Yes, I've got a plan.'

'What is your plan for tomorrow?'

'I was looking through the *Time Out* and I realised that there is a very good exhibition in the art gallery.'

'What is it about?'

'It's about early writing systems.'

'It'll be edifying as well as enjoyable for Felix. I am sure he'll be delighted to come with us.'

'I guess so. The door bell is ringing. Can you hear that?'

'That must be Steve. Let me open the door for him.'

'I'll re-play the CD.'

Justin leaves Jasmine in the living room and goes to the hallway to answer the door. He looks out of the keyhole and sees Steve waiting calmly. Justin opens the door to let Steve in. Justin's childhood mate Steve smiles at Justin with the same expression of his childhood eyes.

'Just on time, come on in, Steve.'

'Thanks.'

'How are you, Steve?'

'I am all right, Justin. You look as handsome as you have always been. I can't fully understand how you can keep up with your elegant appearance? I need a few tips from you?'

'I don't think you need any tip at all, Steve. You look very smart and energetic each time we see you.'

'You must be joking. I worked from 8 o'clock in the morning till 8.30 in the evening. I am shattered.'

'You don't look exhausted at all.'

'I am exhausted, Justin. I was going to postpone tonight's meeting. Then I thought it would be too rude to do that. I hope I won't bore you tonight.'

'We'll cheer you up, Steve. Jasmine is in the living room. Please go there. Let me offer you a drink. What would you like to drink? Shall we have brandy?'

'That's what I need. A glass of punchy brandy will wake me up, Justin.'

'I'll get us all brandy.'

Justin goes to the kitchen and takes the brandy bottle from the shelf; he pours brandy into the three narrow tiny glasses. Justin puts the brandy glasses on the tray; he looks at the dinner table for final touch before leaving the kitchen. Everything looks fine. The salads bowls are placed in the middle of the dinner table and the supper is in the oven. Justin puts the new candle sticks in the candle holder placed next to the salad bowls and gets the bread out. He starts slicing the bread thinly.

Jasmine re-plays the CD. She jumps off the sofa when Steve enters into the living room. She shakes Steve's hand and shows him a comfortable armchair to sit.

'It's good to see you, Steve.'

'It's good to see you, Jasmine.'

'I am glad you've made it. I really appreciate your effort without cancelling our meeting for supper.'

'I was nearly going to cancel this evening's meeting, Jasmine. I feel exhausted.'

'Oh, no!'

'Yes, I'm so tired.'

'You don't look tired to me, Steve.'

'That's what Justin has just told me. Never mind! I'll survive. How is everything in your life?'

'Everything is fine, Steve. Our marriage is in harmony as usual. We went out for a nice walk by the River Thames after the weekend shopping. It was so good to walk in the fresh air. Watching the swans and birds had a really therapeutic effect on our nerves.'

'I wish I was as lucky as you are. I have no time to go for a walk. I have to write reports which ruins my weekends. I'll be sleeping all day long tomorrow to catch up with my sleep. I don't have enough sleep during the week either.'

'That's so bad. You need to take care of yourself. We aren't that young any longer, Steve.'

'You can say that again. The music is so nice. You and Justin have been very kind to me. I don't know what I could have done without you and Justin.'

'We both like your company, Steve.'

'I really look forward to having a cosy evening here at weekends. Both of you make a difference in my bachelor life.'

'Are you serious what you have just said, Steve?'

'I don't say anything I don't mean.'

'Thank you, Steve. I think it's about to time for you to find a nice wife. What do you think?'

'The trouble is I am far too busy to look for a wife. If only I had been as lucky as you and Justin, it would have been blessing for me to share my life with a lovely wife like yourself. I envy Justin for his successful marriage. I wish I met someone as understanding as you are, Jasmine.'

'Well, it's never too late, Steve. You're only 55. There is plenty of time for you to meet someone, who will enrich your life.'

'Do you think so, Jasmine?'

'I am sure, it'll happen sooner or later, Steve. Who can resist someone like you with a strong personality and honesty? I have no doubt that there will be plenty of female candidates, who will be delighted to be taken as your wife. The only trouble is you are too busy to recognise their existence. That's all!'

'Once I get retired, I might have a chance to look around for a suitable wife to accompany me so that there will be something in the horizon for me to look forward to at my old age. That'll prevent me from getting a grumpy old man.'

'Till what age are you planning to postpone your marriage, Steve?'

'I can't afford to stop working before I reach 65. Teaching dyslexic learners is a very demanding job, Jasmine.'

'Talking about dyslexia, I've just remembered that we need to ask you to do favour for us.'

'What is it?'

'We think that our guest Felix is dyslexic and he needs your intervention.'

'How do you know he is dyslexic?'

'Well, Felix is a 20-year-old adult and very intelligent despite the fact that he can't read and write somehow.'

'I see.'

'Felix is only here for a week. He'll be going to prison next week.'

'Why?'

'Felix had broken into an unoccupied property more than once which didn't impress the Jury. He is sentenced for 2 years. Felix is bailed for a week. Justin brought him here as he is homeless. We're trying our best to treat Felix well. Justin and I wanted you to meet Felix as we think that you are the right person to help him with his reading and writing skills. Otherwise, Felix will never get out of the trap he has fallen into.'

'What about his parents?'

'Felix was an adopted child. He was brought up by his foster parents. He never met his biological parents. When Felix reached the age of 16, he was asked to leave his foster home. The poor soul has been struggling since then.'

'What a depressing life-story!'

'I'm terribly sorry to distress you with Felix's life-story but there is no time to make another arrangement for you to meet Felix. That's why we felt the need to discuss Felix's circumstances with you tonight. However, we need to be careful not to hurt Felix's pride. Perhaps, it's better if you approach him. He needs to disclose his difficulty to you directly. Will it be possible for you to attend Felix's need?'

'I am not sure I will be able to help him at all. I am really exhausted, Jasmine. Please don't take me wrong but I wasn't ready to hear Felix's sad life-story this evening.'

'I can understand you very well, Steve. It's too much to expect from you to work at your leisure time. Nevertheless, we haven't got any other solution we could come up with. You're our only hope.'

'Where is Felix now?'

'He's upstairs having a shower. Justin took him to the gym this afternoon just to help Felix to take his mind off from his worries. They both spent 4 hours at the gym.'

'Justin has gone to the kitchen to get me a glass of brandy a while ago. Where is he now? What has he been doing in the kitchen for so long?'

'Let's go to the kitchen, Steve. Justin must be working on his last minute touch. I cooked our dinner, but I left salads for Justin to deal with.'

'What did you cook for me, Jasmine?'

'I cooked celeriac with green peppers, fresh tomatoes, carrots, peas, garlic and plenty herbs.'

'Is that all?'

'We'll have pasta and I'll be grilling mackerel for you. We all had mackerel for lunch.'

'What do you have for dessert?'

'I made pudding with vanilla flavour.'

'That sounds exciting. Let's go to the kitchen now.'

Justin and Jasmine go to the kitchen and they see Justin slicing an enormous pineapple.

'Where is my brandy you have promised to deliver 10 minutes ago, Justin?'

'Sorry to keep you waiting, Steve. I thought it would be nice to have pineapple while we are sipping our brandy. Help yourself with brandy please. Pineapple slices will be ready soon.'

'Thanks Justin. Brandy is delicious.'

'I am glad you like it. This is your brandy, darling.'

'Thanks. That knife is blunt. That's why it has taken you so long to slice the pineapple. Please use the sharper knife, dear.'

'Could you give me the sharper knife please?'

'Here you are, Justin.'

'Thank you. While Felix is still up there, let's tell Steve about Felix's problems, darling.'

'I've already mentioned Steve about Felix's problems.'

'What do you think, Steve? Can you help Felix to read and write fairly quickly?'

'I can't promise anything before I see Felix, Justin.'

'Let me go upstairs and tell Felix that you are here. Pineapple slices are ready. Please help yourselves from pineapples.'

'Shall I light the candles, dear?'

'Yes please.'

'I'll start grilling the fish for Steve.'

'Thanks, Jasmine.'

'I'll be back soon.'

'Please hurry up, Justin.'

Felix comes out of the shower and dries himself with the soft large towel. Felix covers his body with the towel and shaves his beard with Justin's electrical razor. Felix styles his hair with his fingers. He dresses up in the guest bedroom and sits down in the armchair opposite his bed. Felix closes his eyes to relax for a few minutes. He doesn't want to take up his hosts' time unnecessarily and decides to stay in the bedroom until he is asked to come down for supper. It'll be good to be out of their way for a while.

Jasmine grills the mackerel for Steve. She warms up vegetable casserole and pasta. Jasmine places them on the table. Steve nearly finishes his pineapple slices with brandy. His mood is uplifted. Justin gives a knock on the bathroom door to check whether or not Felix is still in the bathroom. There is no reply.

Justin walks up to the guest bedroom, where Felix is resting. He knocks the door.

'Are you there, Felix?'

'Yes, I'm here, Justin.'

'Dinner is ready. We're waiting for you in the kitchen. Could you join us please?'

'Thank you, Justin. I'll be there in a minute.'

Justin goes to the bathroom and washes his hands. Felix comes out of his bedroom. Justin and Felix go down to the kitchen together.

'Felix, let me introduce you to Steve. This is Felix.'

'How do you do, young man!'

'Felix, this is Steve.'

'How do you do!

'Let's start our meal. You must be very hungry, Steve. Sorry to keep you waiting.'

'Well, I only had a sandwich for lunch. That was a long time ago.'

'I've grilled mackerel for you.'

'Thanks, Jasmine. That's very kind of you.'

Felix sits next to Steve opposite Jasmine and Justin at the table. Jasmine serves the meal and everybody starts having their dinner peacefully.

'The mackerel is well grilled, Jasmine.'

'I'm glad you've liked it, Steve. Shall I put some salad in your plate?'

'Don't worry Jasmine, I'll help myself.'

'Beetroot salad will go well with mackerel, Steve.'

'I understand you've made the salads, Justin.'

'That's right. The rest of the meal was prepared by Jasmine while Felix and I were at the gym. I'll be cooking Sunday dinner though. Jasmine should be putting her feet up and rest all day long without doing any cooking for us.'

'I'll get rest tomorrow, dear.'

'I wish I could join you tomorrow night for supper.'

'Please come along tomorrow, Steve. Jasmine and I will be very happy to see you tomorrow night as well.'

'We'll be delighted to have you around for supper tomorrow night, Steve. The question is that whether or not you could make it.'

'That's very sweet of you both. I was only joking. Let's keep our weekly arrangement as it stands. I cannot invite you for a meal. I've been coming over to you for supper each week during the last 10 years without any return.'

'We don't expect you to cook for us, Steve.'

'If you increase the time allowance from once a week to twice a week for a decent meal, it wouldn't be fair on you. Besides, you'll get bored with me.'

'You won't bore us, Steve. On the contrary, Jasmine and I both look forward to seeing you each week.'

'Thanks Justin. Tomorrow I'll be sleeping all day long as I am exhausted.'

'Is it necessary to work at home at weekends, Steve?'

'I'm afraid, it's necessary. At work, I need to work with dyslexic students on a one to one support. There is no time to interpret their diagnostic test results or write any report while I'm teaching. That's why I need to work at weekends. I don't mind. After all, I'm paid for all the additional work I've to do. The only inconvenience is that I have got less time for myself to unwind. However, I always make it up when I take my annual leave.'

'How many days do you get for your annual leave, Steve?'

'I'm free from work pressure for 2 months. I don't work in July and August. I normally recover from my exhaustion during my summer holidays.'

'You're very lucky to get 2 months annual leave. Justin and I only get 21 days for our summer vacation.'

'Working as a dyslexia tutor isn't easy. You need a proper break. Otherwise, you can end up in a hospital with a nervous breakdown.'

'Are you serious, Steve?'

'Yes, I'm serious. Can I have pasta now please?'

'I'll change your plate, Steve.'

'Not necessary. I can use this plate.'

'You need a clean plate. Don't worry about giving me an extra work. It's only one more plate. Washing up is done by the dishwasher.'

'Thanks.'

Jasmine takes the fish plate from Steve. She brings a new plate with pasta and casserole in it. Jasmine offers Felix some more pasta and casserole. Justin helps himself from pasta and beetroot salad. Jasmine puts some potato salad in her plate. While Steve continuous eating his meal, he starts conversation with Felix.

'Felix, tell me how is your experience living with Justin and Jasmine?'

'It's fine.'

'Do you like being a guest here?'

'Yes I do. I am most grateful to Justin and Jasmine for their hospitality, sir.'

'Call me Steve, please.'

'Felix used to call me sir. You're a real sir as you come from a teaching profession, Steve. Maybe you don't mind Felix calling you sir.'

'Felix is not my learner, Justin.'

'Felix might be your learner in the near future, Steve?'

'Still, I prefer Felix calling me with my first name. Felix, can you tell me about yourself please?'

'About myself?'

'Yes, about yourself.'

'I am not quite sure what to tell you about myself. I don't know who I am in any case.'

'We cannot be absolutely sure about ourselves for hundred per cent, Felix. Getting to know ourselves and others in depth is a lifelong task which can't be accomplished till later on in our life-spans. However, you must have a bit of clue about who I am by now.'

'Kind of.'

'I'll summarise myself with one sentence for you. I am a bachelor dyslexia tutor, who has got very good friends like Jasmine and Justin. Is that sufficient enough for you to know a bit of myself on this occasion, Felix?'

'Yes, that's enough for me to accept you as you describe yourself, sir.'

'Tell me about yourself with a few sentences please?'

'I'm Felix. I've recently met Justin and Jasmine. I'm their guest here.'

'You answered my question rather well, Felix. How long are you going to stay here?'

'I'll be staying here for a week.'

'What happens afterwards?'

'I'll be going to prison for 2 years.'

'Is there any good reason for that?'

'I got myself into trouble.'

'I am sorry to hear that. Can you tell me how?'

'I squatted in an unoccupied property for a few days.'

'Are you going to prison for 2 years for breaking into an unoccupied property?'

'I have committed the same crime more than once. That's why my sentence is a bit long.'

'What are you planning to do after you complete your sentence, Felix?'

'I've decided to become a barrister.'

'When did you decide to be a barrister, Felix?'

'Since I've been here, Jasmine. Once I come out of prison, I'll be studying law.'

'Have you heard that, darling? Felix is going to be a barrister like us.'

'Yes dear. I am astonished and delighted at the same time. You'll be a very good barrister, Felix.'

'I hope so. In fact, it's more than a hope. I am determined to be a very competent barrister, Justin.'

'How did you reach this conclusion, Felix?'

'What I have been through in life helped me to make a quick decision about my future career. Additionally, meeting you both enabled me to take you as my role models.'

'Jasmine and I will be always supporting you throughout your studies and afterwards. You'll be one of our colleagues apart from being one of our family friends, Felix.'

'Thanks for your encouragement, Justin. I'll do my best not to disappoint you both.'

'That's a very emotional moment for me to experience. I wish I could do something for you to increase your chance to become a barrister in the near future. Have you done your A levels, Felix?'

'Not yet. I haven't done my GCSEs either. I have no qualifications. I am a drop out, Steve. I dropped out of my primary school. I can't read or write. I am sure, I'll be learning how to read and write once I'll have a chance to study properly.'

'Would you like me to help you with that, Felix?'

'If you could, I'll be most grateful to you, Steve.'

'Right, we need to arrange a day so that I can give you several diagnostic tests to identify your language processing problems. We'll take it from there. When can I see you for diagnostic tests, Felix?'

'I can take diagnostic tests at any time. I'll be available next week while I am staying here.'

'In that case, can I come over to you tomorrow evening, Justin?'

'Come for supper, Steve. Our invitation is still open.'

'Thank you. I can't resist the invitation.'

'Shall we say at 7.00 o'clock for supper tomorrow?'

'It's fine. I'll be completely recovered by then. The test approximately takes 2 hours. From 8.00 to 10.00 o'clock, Felix can take his diagnostic test. I'll be interpreting his test results next Saturday. Then, I can draw a language support programme for Felix to work with me on a one to one basis. What do you think, Felix?'

'Can you visit me in prison, Steve?'

'That's what I'm planning to do so, Felix. When are you leaving here exactly?'

'The following Monday in the morning.'

'We'll both know what to do for your language support programme by then, Felix. I'll get in touch with the prison service. I'll be visiting you in the prison regularly at weekends. I need to adjust my timetable for an extra weekend work.'

'Thank you ever so much, Steve.'

'It's my pleasure. I'll be proud of your achievement when you start gaining academic study skills.'

'That's very kind of you!'

'Let's have our vanilla puddings now, shall we?'

'Yes please.'

'I'll put the kettle on, darling.'

'That's a good idea, dear!'

'What would you like to drink, Steve?'

'Can I have a strong coffee without milk or sugar?'

'What are you having, Felix?'

'I'll have coffee with milk please.'

'What about you, darling?'

'I'll have green tea with lemon please.'

'I'll make strawberry tea for myself.'

Justin starts making tea and coffee for everybody. Jasmine takes out vanilla desserts from the fridge and grinds a bar of chocolate for decorating the puddings. Jasmine brings the vanilla puddings with the grinded chocolate decoration on top. Justin puts tea and coffee mugs. They both sit down at the dining table.

'I like vanilla pudding.'

'That's why I made vanilla pudding today. It's a special treat for you, Steve.'

'Thanks Jasmine.'

'I like all the desserts Jasmine makes. I've got a sweet tooth, Steve.'

'I've also got a sweet tooth, Justin but I'm overweight and I need to lose weight.'

'You used to go to the gym once a week, Steve. Don't you keep up with it?'

'I've no time for regular exercises any longer. I stopped going to the gym ages ago.'

'Can't you do some exercises at home?'

'I feel too exhausted to do any exercise. I've become a coach potato. I put on 1 stone. I need to get rid of the excess fat on my abdomen.'

'Why don't you get a home bike, Steve? It'll put you into a good shape.'

'I've never thought about it. I should consider that as a long term solution for my weight problem. Where do you get a home bike from? Have you got any idea?'

'You can get it from any store which sells sport equipments. You don't even need to go to the store for it. You can get it from a catalogue. Shall I make enquiries about home bikes for you, Steve?'

'That'll save my time and my life, Justin.'

'I'll get back to you once I do a bit of research on home bikes. Their prices and delivery arrangements vary from one store to another. I'll try to get the best one for you.'

'I'll appreciate your offer. Thank you, Justin.'

'You're very welcome.'

'I've finished my dessert and coffee.'

'Would you like some more coffee, Steve?'

'No thanks. I've had more than enough.'

'Are you sure?'

'I am positive. Although it might be too rude to leave you as soon as I've finished my dinner, I need to leave you all now. Do you mind?'

'You can leave us at any time, Steve. Please feel free. You'll be coming here tomorrow evening not only for a supper, but for work as well. You deserve a good night's sleep.'

'Thanks Justin.'

'Please don't forget that this is your home, Steve. You ought to feel at ease whenever you wish to leave us.'

'That's why I've kept in touch with you, Justin. Neither of you is a pushy person. I feel very comfortable here.'

'It's good to know that, Steve.'

'I can come and go here whenever I want to. You and Jasmine don't pressurise me on either staying longer or eating something that I do not feel like eating. That's the key for a good friendship, which we all seemed to have for such a long time.'

'Our friendship is based on a mutual respect for each other's uniqueness.'

'That's true Justin. We're very different from each other. Yet, we have been getting on very well since our childhood. You've never hurt me so far.'

'I feel the same, Steve. You've never irritated me. Somehow we both achieved keeping up with our friendship without breaching our private space since our childhood even we have been seeing each other once a week during the last 10 years or longer.'

'Well, this week you'll see me more than once, Justin.'

'We'll be very happy to see you tomorrow, Steve.'

'Thanks. Let me shake your hand, Felix. It was nice to meet you. I'll see you tomorrow.'

'See you tomorrow, Steve.'

'Let us see you out, Steve.'

'Please don't bother. I can find my way from here to the door.'

'Still, we wish to see you out. In fact, I am going to give you a lift back home, Steve.'

'No, you aren't going to do that. I'll take a taxi. Please don't bother.'

'I'd like to take you back home, Steve. Don't argue with me please.'

'I'll join you as well. It'll be a nice change for me to go out at night.'

'All right dear. Let's take Steve back home together.'

'Felix, just leave everything as they are. I'll do the clearing up once we come back home. You can watch the telly in the living room.'

'Thank you, Jasmine.'

'See you later, Felix. We'll be back in an hour time.'

'See you later, Justin.'

Justin, Jasmine and Steve go out all together. Justin opens his car and they all get into the car. Justin starts driving slowly.

'Steve, we are really grateful to you what you have promised to do for Felix tomorrow.'

'I'd like to work with Felix. He is a good chap. He needs a bit of support and encouragement for his studies. Otherwise, Felix can never manage to hit his target which sounds quite ambitious.'

'I've just wonder whether we've pushed you too much to make a decision, which you wouldn't have made under different circumstances considering how busy you've been with your own workload, Steve.'

'That's totally different matter, Jasmine. I told you I wouldn't promise you anything before meeting Felix. He himself convinced me that he is serious about his future plans. If Felix didn't sound as enthusiastic as he has been, I wouldn't have considered taking him as an additional workload at weekends.'

'From the financial point of view, Steve, I'm prepared to pay for your hours for the language support you'll be offering to Felix.'

'I don't think I'll charge you for Felix's tuitions, Justin. I'll be tutoring Felix free of charge. I can afford to do so. I earn very well from my contractual work. I know Felix can't afford to pay my tuition fee but the reward I will be getting out of teaching Felix will pay me dividends at the end. Please do not worry about the financial aspect of my involvement with Felix's education.'

'I am speechless, Steve. I do not know how to thank you for your generosity.'

'You're welcome. I am going to ask you both a favour for Felix as well.'

'What's that?'

'Can you spare an hour to teach Felix maths and law at weekends?'

'I can teach Felix maths. There is no problem, Steve.'

'Good, Justin. What about you Jasmine?'

'I can teach Felix Law.'

'The matter is settled then. We'll be working as a team all together. Both of you will be teaching Felix maths and law at GCSE level. I'll be teaching Felix English at GCSE level. We'll see how Felix gets on with the pace. My aim is to enable Felix to pass his GCSEs in maths, English and law while he is still in prison. By the time Felix completes his prison sentence, he'll be ready to take his A level exams. That'll guaranty Felix a place at university to do law.'

'That sounds great, Steve.'

'Within a short period, you'll be preparing Felix for his university education.'

'Felix hasn't got much time. He hasn't done much with his life so far. Felix needs to speed up. What Felix needs to have is a fast track language support, which should be done methodologically.'

'Shall I contact the prison service and get their permission for Felix's weekly private tuitions?'

'As you have been representing Felix's case, it'll be a lot easier for you to deal with the legal aspect of getting extra time for Felix to have a weekly tuition regularly. If you could take this up for me, it'll be very useful.'

'No problem, I'm willing to take more responsibilities for Felix's future success.'

'I've understood that we are all clear what we are going to do the following week.'

'We need to arrange an alternate date for private tuitions in maths and law, Justin. I can teach Felix on Saturdays in the morning and you can teach Felix on Sundays. That'll help Felix's progress without overloading his memory. How does it sound to you both?'

'That sounds good. I can teach Felix on Sundays, Jasmine.'

'You both teach him in the morning at weekends. I'll give him an hour language support in the afternoon. I need to visit Felix twice a week.'

'That's very kind of you!'

'Felix will have a target to meet during his language support sessions. Learning English in context will make sense to him and it'll speed up Felix's learning process as he needs to have enough time to grasp each subject very well.'

'Your suggestion has determined our commitment into Felix's learning programme, Steve.'

'I can't believe we're in my neighbourhood. Thanks for giving me a lift, Justin.'

'You're very welcome, Steve. It's very nice to see you tonight. We'll look forward to seeing you tomorrow.'

'Thank you, Justin. Would you like to come upstairs for a quick drink before driving back home?'

'We'd better go back home without taking your time. You need to go to bed straightway, Steve.'

'Are you sure you don't want to have a quick drink, Justin?'

'You need to generate some energy for tomorrow. You'd better go to bed now.'

'Bye Steve.'

'Bye Jasmine.'

'Have a good rest, Steve.'

'Thanks Justin. Have a safe journey back home.'

'Thanks.'

Steve gets off the car and waves at them. Justin and Jasmine wave back at him. Steve opens the front door. He feels dizzy, tired and sleepy. He turns the light on. Steve goes to the bathroom and brushes his teeth quickly. There is no time for Steve to check his frogs Frederick and Frederica in their fish tank. Steve goes to his bedroom and wears his pyjamas before turning off the light. As soon as he puts his head on his pillow, Steve falls asleep.

On the way back home, Justin and Jasmine talk about possible consequences of committing themselves into Felix's learning programme by coincidence.

'Do you think we're throwing ourselves at the deep end of the sea, Jasmine without fully aware of the heavy responsibilities we're going to take up?'

'What do you mean, Justin?'

'I mean a week ago, neither of us was concerned about Felix's problems. He was one of my clients. Now it seemed to me that we got involved with Felix's future.'

'Teaching Felix regularly will increase our workloads. Nevertheless, Felix hasn't got anyone to turn to apart from us. We're the only people Felix has got. It's our moral obligation to help Felix as much as we could. Plus, it'll give us extra satisfaction in life. None of us has worked as a tutor before. It'll be quite challenging for both of us to teach Felix.'

'I agree with you, Jasmine. Nonetheless, I don't want to put too much pressure on you. I feel guilty a bit about bringing Felix with me without even discussing it with you on the phone. It was a sudden decision I had to make. There was no time to call you and ask your view. I had acted on impulse. Things followed from there. None of us could predict what we were going to offer Felix tonight.'

'Please don't feel guilty about getting me involved with Felix's life circumstances. Felix is a very nice person. It's good to help another human being, who is in need. If you had called me from work, I might have felt a bit apprehensive about having a stranger around for a week. I don't think I would have ever wanted to get involved with anyone at this intimate level. It was a good job that I've got to know Felix gradually. If I didn't meet Felix personally, I might have not taken any responsibility of teaching him law regularly. Teaching Felix will be pleasure for me, but not a duty. I'm sure we'll both manage to take a bit of extra responsibility at weekends. It's only for a limited period. We aren't committing ourselves to Felix's need for life. The two years will pass quickly. After that, Felix can manage his own life without our support.'

'You're right, Jasmine. The two years in prison will be the hardest period for Felix to face. After that, life might become easier for him. At least, we hope so.'

'At the end of two years, Felix will still face some more problems.'

'There is no doubt about that as we all face problems in our lives.'

'Once Felix becomes literate, he'll be better equipped how to go about solving his own personal problems such as finding an accommodation or going to university and getting a job afterwards.'

'Thank you for reminding me that. I need to get in touch with the probation officer on Monday. We'll see whether or not we can get Felix on the housing list for a council flat. That'll take two years or more to come through. At least, Felix will have an accommodation after he comes out of prison.'

'That's a very good idea, Justin.'

'It seems to me it'll take more than two years for Felix to function without our help. It is not easy to get to know how the social system works for a start. Studying law will help Felix to familiarise himself with the social structure of the society. Still, there is a lot for Felix to take in. It can't be done in haste. It can't be done without extra help either. We have taken a lot of responsibilities. That's for sure.'

'That's all right. I don't think we can make any fuss about it now. We both realised what we put ourselves through. Either we do it without feeling bad about it or we leave it before committing ourselves further. After all, Felix didn't ask us for help with his reading and writing. It was us to approach Steve to provide help for Felix. Poor Felix doesn't even know that we're going to teach him at weekends. That was suggested by Steve. Knowing how we've got Steve involved with Felix's problems, I don't think, we have got an option to refuse what Steve suggested us to do. Let's face it Justin, it was our fault to get Steve involved with Felix's personal problems. Steve has got more than enough on his plate. He'll be making sacrifices for Felix at weekends. Steve won't be getting paid for his hard work either. We'd better stop discussing how we are going to manage our extra responsibilities. We need to make some sacrifices at the same time. We just hope our commitments to Felix wouldn't be that demanding.'

'I've begun to see our weekends in my mind's eye. We'll be very busy. As you wisely suggested, we need to be optimistic, Jasmine. It's a good job we never had a child of our own. What a big responsibility!'

'You can say that again, Justin. We both agreed to help out Felix for a temporary period. If things go wrong, there is no one there to blame for. We can only blame ourselves. I hope there won't be anything to regret about our decision we have already made. You can be pretty sure that I'll never blame you for bringing Felix home in the first place.'

'That's enough, Jasmine. Problem has been solved. We both agreed to spare some time for Felix during the next two years. Shall we say we're both willing to adjust our decision depending on the new problems which might encounter? How does that sound to you?'

'That's fine dear. We'll have always a contingency plan to make changes.'

'I hope we don't need to divorce at the end of the two year periods. Do you see what I mean, Jasmine?'

'Do you think an extra responsibility might put a strain on our marriage?

'It may, it may not, dear. We can't predict the future. Getting divorced would be the worst case scenario to consider now. I don't think we can go that far. If things go worse, we can always resign from our voluntary responsibilities. Who can judge us for doing that?'

'As far as I'm concerned, no one can judge us. Let's stop thinking about the worst possibility we might face along the line. We can't afford to be too pessimistic at this stage, Justin.'

'I agree with you, Jasmine. Home, home, sweet home as far as the saying goes. Felix must have fallen asleep. It's nearly midnight.'

'I need to do clearing up a bit in the kitchen before going to bed.'

'I'll help you with the clearing up, Jasmine.'

'That'll be very handy.'

Justin and Jasmine get off the car. Justin puts on the burglar alarm for his car. He opens the front door.

'There is no sign of Felix watching telly in the living room. He must be in his bedroom upstairs, Jasmine.'

'We need to be quiet then.'

'Let's go to the kitchen.'

Justin and Jasmine enter the kitchen quietly. The kitchen looks tidy.

'Felix must have done the clearing up. That's very kind of him.'

'Would you like to have some snacks before going to bed, Jasmine?'

'No thanks. I can't have anything till morning.'

'I'll make a cheese sandwich for myself. Otherwise, I can't go to sleep.'

'I'll leave you here. I am sure, I'll sleep like a log tonight. Good night, dear.'

'Good night Jasmine. Thanks for the splendid supper and your thoughtful support. I mean all the extra things you have done for me, dear.'

'Please don't mention that, darling. We're a married couple. We ought to do extra bits for each other from time to time.'

'I know, dear. I still feel guilty for dragging you into taking up obligatory responsibilities.'

'Don't worry! I've enjoyed my evening. It was my pleasure to cook for four of us this evening. That wasn't a great deal. Whether you cook for two people or four people doesn't really matter. It's the same amount of effort. Tomorrow, it'll be your turn to cook for four people, Justin.'

'I'll do my best. Good night dear.'

'Enjoy your cheese sandwich, Justin.'

'Is there any vanilla pudding left, dear?'

'There is one without chocolate topping in the fridge.'

'I'll have it without chocolate.'

'Please finish it up then.'

Jasmine climbs the stairs and goes to the bathroom first. She washes her hands and brushes her teeth. Jasmine puts her evening cream on her face. She goes into their bedroom and draws the curtains before turning the light on. Jasmine sees the kitten Fanny sleeping next to the toy monkey. She moves the toy monkey to the bedside chest. The kitten is woken up by the noise. Jasmine strokes the kitten Fanny with affection. She moves the kitten further down the bed. Jasmine gets her nightdress under the pillow. She takes off her evening dress and puts on her nightdress. Jasmine gets into bed without touching the kitten Fanny. The kitten tucks her head under her front paws. Jasmine falls asleep peacefully. She dreams about herself as a teacher preparing her teaching material for Felix while the kitten Fanny is dreaming about the "hide and seek" play she played with Felix in the morning. The kitten Fanny jumps while she is sleeping. Fanny is woken up by her own jump. Jasmine doesn't notice Fanny's movement as she is fast asleep. The kitten Fanny goes back to her sleep quietly.

In the kitchen, Justin finishes his cheese sandwich. He starts having the vanilla pudding slowly. Justin puts the cheese knife, the dessert dish, and the small plate into the dishwasher afterwards. Justin pours the liquid detergent in the dish washer and turns it on. Then, he turns off the kitchen light. Justin goes to bathroom to wash his hands and brush his teeth quickly before turning off the light in the bathroom. When he enters the bedroom, he turns on the side light standing on the dressing table. Justin sees Jasmine and the kitten both sleeping heavily. He opens the duvet from his side trying not to make any noise. Justin gets his pyjamas under his pillow quietly. The kitten is woken up suddenly. Fanny looks at Justin with a surprise.

Justin strokes the Fanny gently. The kitten tucks her head under her paws again. Justin turns off the light and takes off his suit in rush. He wears his pyjamas and goes to bed without touching either Jasmine or the kitten. Justin starts thinking about Felix's future. While Justin is thinking about Felix's future, he falls asleep. On Sunday morning Justin, Jasmine and Fanny all wake up at 10 o'clock.

'Good morning, darling. Have you slept well?'

'Good morning, dear. Yes, I have slept very well. How about you, Justin?'

'I've also slept very well. Shall we have our breakfast soon?'

'It's a good idea. We must leave home by 11.30. It'll take half an hour to go to the art gallery. If we spend 2 hours there, we'll be here in good time for supper preparation. Don't forget, Steve will be here earlier this evening. You need to finish cooking by 6.00 o'clock.'

'We'll have our lunch in the gallery. That'll save our time.'

'We'll have a light lunch there. What are you going to cook for supper, dear?'

'How about roast chicken with roast potatoes, peas, cabbage, carrots and home- made gravy?'

'I'm sure, Steve will like the traditional Sunday roast, dear.'

'Let's get up then.'

'Look, Fanny is trying to play with us.'

'There is no time to play with you, Fanny. We must go downstairs.'

Justin and Jasmine wear their dressing-gowns. Jasmine goes downstairs to the kitchen; Justin gives a knock on Felix's door gently.

'Are you awake, Felix?'

'Yes, Justin.'

'We'll be having our breakfast soon. Shall we see you downstairs shortly?'

'I'll be down there, Justin.'

'See you soon.'

'See you Justin.'

Justin goes downstairs. Justin and Jasmine lay down the table for breakfast. Justin brews the tea. He gets the bread slices ready to be toasted. Jasmine puts out the cereals, butter, milk, cheddar cheese, feta cheese, olives, jam and honey jars. Jasmine boils three eggs.

'Would you like salami for breakfast, Justin?'

'It'll take a long time to grill salami. Let's leave salami for next Sunday, Jasmine. We'll have more time for an elaborated breakfast.'

'All right dear. I'll get mushrooms instead. We'll have mushrooms with cheese.'

'I'll slice tomatoes and cucumbers.'

'Wait a minute, we've run out of mushrooms. There is none left in the fridge.'

'Never mind, dear, there is some potato salad left from supper. Let's have potato salad instead.'

'Potato salad won't go with cheese, Justin.'

'Why not? I quite like potato salad with cheese and egg.'

'I'll get the potato salad out for you, Justin.'

'Here we are; Felix is here.'

'Good morning, Felix.'

'Good morning, Jasmine.'

'How do you feel today?'

'I feel great. Thank you.'

'Good! Thanks for clearing up the table last night. That's very sweet of you! Justin and I went to bed straight away without worrying about clearing up.'

'I went to bed after clearing up the table.'

'After spending 4 hours in gym, you must have been so tired.'

'I was very tired last night.'

'We both slept through the night like a log, didn't we darling?'

'That's right. We woke up at 10 o'clock in the morning. Actually, time is 10.20 now. We'd better have our breakfast. We'll be taking you out after breakfast, Felix.'

'Shall I pour your tea, dear?'

'Yes please. What I was saying? Yes, we're taking you to the private art gallery, Felix.'

'Would you like your tea now, Felix?'

'Yes, please. Thank you.'

'You're welcome.'

'Which gallery are we going to?'

'The Spring Gallery; have you been there before, Felix?'

'Only once.'

'Apparently, there is a very nice exhibition there. Jasmine spotted the exhibition from *Time Out.* What was the name of the exhibition, dear?'

'It's called *Early Writing Systems*, darling.'

'That's right, it is about writing systems. I imagine the exhibition is going back to the several centuries before Christ's birth. It should be interesting to see. What do you think, Felix?'

'I'm sure it must be very interesting. Although I've got a difficulty with reading and writing, I'd still like to see how the writing systems develop in human history.'

'That's good! How many toasts would you like to have, darling?'

'I'll have only one toast, Justin. I'll be trying some potato salad with cheese. See how it goes.'

'The toasts are here. Help yourself with toasts, Felix. I can toast some more slices if we need any.'

'Thank you.'

Justin, Jasmine and Felix finish their breakfast by 11.00 a.m. They're 10 minutes late than Justin and Jasmine planned for their Sunday outing. When they reach the Spring Gallery, it was 12.00. They all go to the temporary exhibition without looking at the permanent collections.

> '*Early Writing Systems* Exhibition starts from the room 1. It carries on in the rooms 2, 3 and 4. It's a very large exhibition. Shall we start from here, darling?'

> 'That'll be fine. Let me get a catalogue about the exhibition for us all.'

> 'I've got a better idea. I'll get us all audio player, Jasmine. It'll be easier to enjoy the exhibition with the audio tapes.'

> 'Why don't you get the two audio tapes for both of you, Justin?'

> 'Don't you want to have one?'

> 'No dear. I'd like to read the given information myself. I find it hard to enjoy the exhibition by listening to an audio player.'

> 'All right dear. I'll get two audio tapes.'

Justin hires the two audio players and he gives one of them to Felix. Justin and Felix adjust their headphones. Jasmine reads the written information placed next to each item displayed on the shelves. They spend an hour for looking at the exhibition. At 1.00 pm, Justin and Jasmine decide to have a light lunch at the gallery restaurant.

> 'What would you like to have, Jasmine?'

'It'll be nice to have soup with a crusty roll, dear.'

'What about you, Felix?'

'I don't feel hungry yet.'

'Would you like to have dessert or a salad?'

'I'll have a croissant with cappuccino.'

'I'll get you soup and a crusty roll, darling. I'll get Felix cappuccino and a croissant and I'll have salad with tuna sandwich.'

'I'll help you, dear.'

'We need to queue. Let's pick up the trays from there.'

'We've still plenty of time. We don't need to rush, dear.'

'We're fine with the time.'

'Instead of croissant, can I have scone please?'

'Would you like to have clotted cream or butter on your scone, Felix?'

'I'll have jam on my scone please.'

'I'll get you scone with jam, Felix.'

'How can I help?'

'What is today's soup?'

'We've got lentil soup and carrot soup with leeks.'

'What soup would you like to have, dear?'

'I'll have lentil soup please and a small roll.'

'For the young gentleman, a scone with jam and cappuccino, I'll have a tuna sandwich with salad please.'

'Anything else, sir?'

'I'll have a medium size of fruit yoghurt please.'

'What flavour madam?'

'Apricot please.'

'I'll have a glass of orange juice please.'

They all place the ordered items on their trays. Justin pays the bill for their lunch. Jasmine, Justin and Felix sit down in the quiet place of the gallery restaurant. They start having their lunch peacefully.

'How did you find the exhibition, darling?'

'It is fabulous! The exhibition is very well organised. The information given for each period of early writing systems is accurate and very engaging at the same time. I could spend the whole day here without getting bored, dear.'

'It's a very good exhibition. All the information recorded on the audio tape is superb. I've enjoyed listening to the audio tape. How about you, Felix? How do you find the exhibition?'

'It's lovely. I've never seen a picture alphabet before.'

'That was Sumerian cuneiform writing which developed between 4000 and 3000 BC in the Southern Iraq. The language appeared on one-word, one-symbol basis which is totally different than Latin alphabet.'

'It's logo-graphic structure. Sumerian language has got an aesthetic quality. It's a kind of art you can see in the early writing system. It must have been very interesting to learn pictographic Sumerian language in 3000 BC.'

'I wish we still use that pictographic language today.'

'That won't be practical any longer, Felix. Sumerian language will take more time than modern languages for getting the message across. In our modern age, people are too busy to accomplish aesthetically appealing writing systems.'

'Our writing system functions in a pragmatic way, Justin.'

'That's right darling. Modern human beings are more practical than our ancestors from early civilisations.'

'I'm afraid the art of learning beautifully written languages died away centuries ago.'

'It's nice to look back into our heritage preserved for us till now.'

'It'll be good to have one common language for all human beings to use.'

'That will reduce the misunderstanding among the nations but impoverish the richness of a wide range of language systems, Felix. Therefore, I'm for pluralism rather than a monolithic language reduction. It'll be nice to have different language systems. Each language enriches our human capacity. The more languages we speak, the better it is for us to develop intellectually.'

'I agree with you, darling. Unfortunately, I can only speak English. I cannot speak any other language.'

'You can read French, Justin.'

'It'll be nice to speak French as fluently as French people do.'

'That can't happen unless you live in France. We need to spend some time with native speakers in order to pick up the conversational language fluency, Justin.'

'Maybe, in the future we might go to France for a longer stay on our holidays.'

'We'll have a chance to get fluent in French.'

'Let's hope we'll have a long life so that we can do whatever we fancy doing at our old age, Jasmine.'

'We can only do our best to stay longer and healthy by doing more exercises, having regular nutritious meals, keeping up with regular sleeping patterns, taking regular holidays and reducing stress level to the zero point in our lives.'

'That's the key for our prosperity as happy human beings. Well, I have had a very good time today. Shall we make a move now?'

'What is the time, darling?'

'It's 1.30, dear.'

'Driving back home will take another an hour. We'll be at home by 2.30 Justin.'

'I'd like to watch a discussion programme on the telly before I start cooking our supper.'

'What is the discussion about, Justin?'

'I can't remember just now. It's something to do with law.'

'I'll be interested in watching the discussion with you, Justin.'

'It starts at 2.40. We'd better leave now. Otherwise, we'll miss the beginning.'

'Let's go, dear. Thanks for the delicious lunch.'

'I haven't cooked anything.'

'You've paid for our lunch, my dear.'

'That's all right! It's not a big deal.'

'It's a great deal! You've worked hard and earned the money which enabled you to buy my lunch.'

'It's nice to be appreciated by my darling wife.'

'Thank you very much, Justin for taking me out for lunch too.'

'You're welcome, Felix. I hope you've enjoyed our company.'

'I've enjoyed everything, the beautiful exhibition, the lunch and your company.'

'You didn't eat much, Felix. We'll be having our supper at 7.00 o'clock. A scone and cappuccino won't last that long. By the time we go back home, you'll be starving. When we go back, you need to have a proper lunch.'

'Thanks, Jasmine.'

Justin, Jasmine and Felix leave the Spring Gallery cheerfully. Justin drives slowly and peacefully. They all listen to Felix

Mendelssohn's violin concerto. Jasmine thinks about her new case, which she is going to present at the *Inner London* Court on Monday. How quickly the weekend passed. Tomorrow will be the beginning of a new week. Another case will be occupying Jasmine's mind for a few months. Jasmine hopes that she will win her new case successfully. After watching the telly with Justin, she'd better to look through her case. Jasmine needs to refresh her memory for the details. After all, it isn't only Steve who brings paperwork home but barristers bring their cases home as well. Still, Jasmine likes her work more than any other jobs she did in her younger days.

Felix feels so happy that he was taken to the exhibition, which gave him some idea of how written languages were invented. Felix knows that he needs to learn how to read and write properly. Having an access to any written language is essential for him to understand the world culture. Without knowing a written language, Felix missed out on the cultural aspect of life and its intellectual stimulations.

The music stops; Jasmine doesn't re-play the same CD. There is a short silent. They've already reached the nearby area where they live. Jasmine turns back and smiles at Felix.

> 'Here we are, Felix. Today's outing is over. How are you going to spend the rest of the day?'
>
> 'I don't know.'
>
> 'We'll be watching a discussion on the telly for an hour or so. Justin will be starting cooking afterwards. I'll be doing some preparation for tomorrow. I'm just wondering what would occupy you while we're doing our bits and pieces.'
>
> 'I'm not sure what I'm going to do.'

'You can play with the kitten, of course. That wouldn't fill up your whole afternoon though. Would you like to try painting?'

'Painting the walls?'

'I didn't mean home decoration. I meant painting on a piece of paper or a canvas as a leisure activity. When I have nothing to do, I often paint to pass my free time with a pleasant hobby. Have you ever tried your hands on painting?'

'I haven't done painting much but I love drawing. I keep pencils and pens in my pocket all the time. Whenever I buy anything which is wrapped with a plain wrapping paper, I draw on it.'

'How nice! I'll give you one of my sketchpads, you can draw on it. I've got plenty of art materials. You can have colour pencils, acrylic, water colour and biros. After drawing, you can also colour your drawings. You see your afternoon is sorted out, Felix. You'll be very busy with your drawing in the afternoon.'

'Many thanks for offering me your art materials.'

'You're very welcome, Felix.'

'We know that next week, you won't get bored here while you are working as our pet- sitter. When Fanny goes to sleep which she does so often, you'll have something to do at home. It's nice to find out that you'll have an interest in drawing. Jasmine is clever enough to spot one of your talents. By doing that we'll be both very happy to leave you at home without worrying about you.'

'That's right! There won't be any worry about leaving you here on your own. You won't get bored. I can also give you some of my blank canvases. Who knows you might take up painting as a hobby. Personally, I find painting very therapeutic. It works for me. Once I start painting, I feel so good. I've got a felling you'll enjoy painting as well.'

'I think I'll enjoy painting. I'm only worrying about the cost of the canvases and paints. I do not want to cost you too much.'

'Don't worry about money, Felix. You'll be our pet-sitter for us next week. We pay Fanny's pet-sitter for looking after Fanny during the week. You'll get paid for doing the same job for us. Some of the art materials will be considered as an exchange for some part of the payment we intend to make towards your work.'

'I don't think I'll expect any money for pet-sitting. I don't pay anything for my accommodation or food while I'm here. I don't expect you to pay me for being a pet- sitter for Fanny.'

'That's totally different matter, Felix. You're our guest. The guests aren't supposed to pay any money for their lodgings. We'd like to employ you while you are our guest. If you weren't here as our guest, we had to employ another person for Fanny. In a way, you came to us at the right time while we needed someone's help. We're grateful to you that you're willing to be a pet-sitter for our cat. Fanny is more than a cat for us. We treat Fanny like our baby. Fanny's wellbeing is our concern.'

'We make a decent living. We would like our pet to be happy with comfort and deserved attention. From our point of view, the money you'll be earning here will be well spent.'

'Thank you ever so much for that. I wasn't expected to be employed here. It'll be my pleasure to be a pet-sitter for Fanny.'

'We can appreciate the strong bond you and Fanny developed. We know Fanny really likes you. As a matter of fact, we hope that Fanny will see more of you once you complete your two years. You'll be very welcome to come here not only visit us but our Fanny at the same time. She'll be very happy to see you again. Cats never forget the people who treat them well.'

'I agree with Jasmine. Fanny likes you as you build up a special bond with her. I was surprised how Fanny stayed in our bedroom last night. I thought she was going to move to your room. Your room wasn't open. That must be why Fanny came to our bedroom.'

'I couldn't see Fanny this morning. Where is she?'

'Fanny sometimes likes staying in our bed for a longer period in the mornings; especially, on Sundays. How does Fanny know it is Sunday, we cannot figure out.'

'Fanny must have an internal calendar like some of us have got an internal clock. Fanny doesn't come down till noon on Sundays. I'm sure she must be in the kitchen now.'

'Let's go inside.'

'Put the kettle on, darling. We'll have a hot drink. I'll get the canvases ready for Felix.'

'I'll brew tea for us.'

'Thank you.'

Justin and Felix go to the kitchen. Jasmine goes to her stockroom. She picks up the two blank canvases, paint brushes, acrylic paints, a sketchpad, drawing pens and pencils. Jasmine puts the paints, the brushes, the sketchpad, a few pens and pencils into a plastic bag. She puts the medium size canvases under her right arm. She holds the plastic bag with her left hand. Jasmine carries all the art materials to Felix's room. She leaves them all on the small table by Felix's bedside. Jasmine goes to the bathroom. She washes her hands and face under the running tap. Jasmine dries her face and hands with the paper towel. She goes to their bedroom and quickly makes their bed.

While Jasmine is upstairs, Justin brews the herbal tea. He puts the teapot and tea cups on the table. Justin slices the lemon cakes. He puts 2 pieces of lemon cakes in each plate. Justin turns on the small telly in the kitchen. There is an advertisement about convenient food. Time is nearly 2.35. The discussion programme is going to start soon. Justin goes to the hallway and yells.'

'Jasmine, tea is ready. The discussion is about to start.'

'You settle in please. I'll join you shortly.'

Felix finds Fanny sitting on her chair. He starts playing with the kitten. They're enjoying themselves. Justin looks at them both affectionately. He bursts into laughter; Felix starts laughing too. Justin points at the tea and the cake for Felix to eat.

'Felix tea is ready.'

'Thank you.'

Jasmine enters the kitchen cheerfully. She observes Felix's and Fanny's happiness with content. She turns to Justin.

'Tea and lemon cake smell lovely, dear. I'll ignore my weight watch for today.'

'It's not good to eliminate cakes altogether from your strict diet, Jasmine.'

'Let me join you, Justin. Can you remind me again what the discussion is about?'

'It was something concerning the law. I cannot remember what it is exactly. We'll see now.'

'Felix, I left all the art materials in your bedroom.'

'Many thanks. I'll go upstairs.'

'Not now. Have your tea and lemon cake first, Felix.'

'I need to wash my hands. I'll be back soon.'

'All right then.'

Felix goes upstairs. He enters his bedroom first. Felix sees all the art materials placed by his bedside. Felix opens the plastic bag. He is delighted to find a sketchpad inside the plastic bag. Felix reluctantly leaves his bedroom. He goes to the bathroom and washes his hands quickly. Felix goes back to the kitchen and pours tea for himself. He gets a slice of lemon cake. Felix sips from his tea while biting his lemon cake. Justin and Jasmine watch the discussion programme on the telly. The kitten Fanny eats her cat food. Everyone is occupied with something in the kitchen. It's a very pleasant Sunday afternoon. After having his tea and lemon cake, Felix is impatient to start his drawing in his bedroom upstairs. 'Sorry to interrupt you, I've finished my tea. Do you mind if I go upstairs?'

'Not at all, Felix.'

'Have fun, Felix! See you later.'

'See you later.'

Jasmine and Justin turns their attention onto the discussion programme again. Felix leaves the kitchen quietly. Fanny jumps on her chair and starts cleaning herself. Felix climbs up the staircases quickly and goes into his bedroom. Felix takes his sketchpad from the plastic bag. He puts the sketchpad onto the table. Felix gets all the pens and pencils out of the plastic bag. At last, Felix can enjoy drawing. It has been such a long time Felix couldn't find either a plain wrapping paper to draw on or didn't have any time to draw. How long did I have without drawing? Felix asks himself. The last two weeks, during his trial, Felix couldn't draw at all. The two weeks period looks like a lifetime for Felix. He had a pencil ready in his pocket. Felix used his pen and pencil for amusing Fanny yesterday but he didn't use them for drawing. Felix opens the first page of the sketchpad. He starts drawing on the paper. Felix draws the kitten with different postures one after another. Felix has got 10 sketches of Fanny within half an hour. Felix puts all the sketches on the floor and starts gazing at Fanny's movements captured in his drawings. How much Felix loves Fanny and how much Felix loves drawing! When Jasmine and Justin pay Felix for pet-sitting, he'll be able to buy a few more sketchpads to take with him to prison. The two years will be passing so quickly when Felix draws there. Felix might be having hundreds of drawings by the time he'll be out of prison. Felix spends half an hour for drawing Fanny's sketches only but nothing else.

The discussion on the telly finishes. Justin turns off the television.

'How did you find the discussion, Jasmine?'

'It was fine. I would do the same thing if the child was mine.'

'Would you keep your sick daughter at home by depriving her from a proper medical care?'

'I don't think we can look at this particular case from your point of view. I can't say that a mother deprived her daughter from a medical treatment by respecting her child's decision as her teenage daughter didn't want to go through the medical intervention when no one was able to guarantee the sick child that she would be healed. The sick child should be given a legal right not to be used as a guinea pig. She should be given a chance to die with dignity.'

'Guinea pig?'

'Yes, she can be used for medical advancement. The remaining time of the terminally ill child had, was too precious to be wasted for any medical experimentation.'

'Do you think so?'

'Yes, I do. If I happened to face any incurable disease, I wouldn't like losing my life by going through all the unnecessary complicated medical intervention. Why should a child face her mortality in pain? It isn't ethically correct.'

'Nevertheless, the sick child had decided to receive the treatment and she has survived.'

'That's far beyond the matter we're discussing. Yes, the sick child eventually had changed her mind. She had received the unconventional treatment and she has survived. However, there was a possibility that she might have not survived. If she died, it would be her decision. There was no one to blame for. Children are capable of giving their consent for receiving or not receiving medical intervention. Parents shouldn't interfere with their decisions at all.'

'You might be right, dear. Still, I am in favour of trying every possible medication in order to save life.'

'That's what I would stand for as well. Nevertheless, I loathe the idea of restricting a sick person's choice not to receive a medical intervention, if they feel it isn't worth it regardless of their age. At the end of the day, they'll be the ones who will be going through the pain themselves.'

'I think I can see your point, Jasmine. Let me start cooking. What are you up to?'

'I'll be looking through my new case which I'll be presenting tomorrow.'

'What is it?'

'I need to prove my client's innocence for a false allegation.'

'It sounds challenging.'

'It's challenging. However, I've got plenty of supporting materials to prepare my argument in favour of my client's innocence.'

'It's good to hear that, darling.'

'Let me dive into my papers. I'd like to represent my client in the best possible way. I can't afford any pitfall. Everything must be a crystal clear at court with all the hard evidence I've been gathering so far.'

'Good luck to you, Jasmine.'

'Defending your clients' innocence has nothing to do with luck. It's about professionalism. How good you're to represent your client's innocence with all the facts at your disposal to convince the Jury and the Judge; that counts at the end of each case. I never leave anything to chance. It's a matter of justice. That can only come about with the hard work. Without a good lawyer, a suspect's innocence can't be proved. Our clients' life depends on us, Justin. Without us, human rights can easily be abused.'

'I've no objection to your comment, dear. I'd better peel the potatoes first. It's nearly 3.00 o'clock. Otherwise, we can't have the dinner on time.'

'Good luck to you, Justin.'

'What do you mean, Jasmine? Cooking a meal has nothing to do with luck. The result of best cooking depends on how much I put into my cooking.'

'It's the same with law, Justin.'

'Thanks for reminding me.'

'See you later, darling.'

'See you later, my love.'

Jasmine walks away from the kitchen. Her mind is already preoccupied with her case she'll be taking up tomorrow. Jasmine enters their study room. She picks up her briefcase. Jasmine takes her defence papers out of her briefcase and starts reading her papers paying full attention to each detail.

Justin thinks about his wife's analogy between a good cook and a good defence barrister. The link between the two professions is clear crystal to him now. Justin realises that he has never attended his wife's cases at court. He wonders how Jasmine puts her case into a context in a court setting. Justin decides to watch his wife as a defence barrister at court. Justin starts peeling the potatoes. Jasmine is right. There is no luck element in cooking. A good cook must know his art. Otherwise, the result will be a disaster. Justin boils the peeled potatoes in salted cold water for 10 minutes and he preheats the gas oven for 180 Celsius. Justin gets the roasting tin and pours olive oil into the roasting tin. Justin washes the chicken under the running water. He cuts a lemon into the two halves and starts rubbing the chicken with the half of lemon. It takes about 20 minutes to get rid of the smell of the chicken. Justin places the chicken on the tray. He whisks the egg yolk thoroughly and brushes the chicken with the egg yolk, which will be turning the chicken crispy with a very nice brown colour all around. Justin puts the chicken into the oven to be roasted slowly over the next two hours. The chicken will be ready to be eaten by 7.00 o'clock. Justin leaves boiled potatoes to deal with later on. It would only take 45 minutes for the potatoes to be roasted properly. Justin decides to make a noodle soup and he boils the water with the chicken stoke. Then, adds the noodles into the boiling pan with a bit of salt. Justin is ready to think about dessert. He wonders about what dessert he should prepare for Steve. Justin thinks about ice-cream with fresh fruit. He changes his mind quickly as he has got enough time to make a pastry with the apple crumbs. Justin makes the pastry and fills the middle with apple crumbs. He puts the pastry into the electric oven. Justin washes the cabbages and slices them into ring circles. He boils the cabbage slices in a boiling pan. Justin peels the carrots and cuts them into cubes. Justin boils the cube carrots with peas. In the meantime, the noodle soup is cooked. Justin gets another roasting tray for potatoes. He oiled the tray with olive oil and puts all the peeled potatoes into the tray with some butter and dried-herbs on top and leaves the potato tray into the oven. Everything goes well as planned. Justin decides to spend the next an hour reading Sunday newspapers. He fetches the

Sunday Times from the living room and comes back to the kitchen as he wants to keep an eye on his cooking while he is reading newspapers. If his attention is shifted from cooking to reading, there'll be a danger of burning the supper. Justin sets the timer for cooker and starts reading.

Felix draws 20 sketches of Fanny from his imagination and wonders what Fanny is up to just now. He wants to see the kitten downstairs but suddenly changes his mind knowing that Justin is cooking in the kitchen. It would be better to stay out of Justin's way till he finishes cooking. Felix thinks about painting on a canvas. He has never painted on a canvas before. Felix puts one of the canvases on the table and draws Fanny with a pencil in the middle. Then, he starts adding everyday objects such as Fanny's chair, her food container and the TV next to Fanny's chair in the kitchen. Finally, Felix draws Fanny's image on the TV. Felix is pleased with all the objects he has added to the blank canvas. He needs to paint the picture. Felix opens the acrylic paint-box, gets the 3 paint tubes out ready for painting. He squeezes orange paint first from its tube directly onto the canvas without diluting. Then, he opens red paint tube, adds the red paint with his brush into the details of the television, chair and food container. Finally, Felix opens the black paint tube and draws the contours of each image with the tin brush. The painting looks bright and appealing. Felix can't wait to show his 1st acrylic painting to Justin and Jasmine. Felix spends three hours without stopping drawing and painting. He doesn't feel hungry for food even if he skipped his lunch. It's nearly 7.00 o'clock. Felix takes his brushes to the bathroom, washes them under the running tap, dries them up with the paper towel and takes them back to his bedroom.

Justin lays down the table for supper. The chicken and potatoes are roasted very well. Justin puts the candle holders in the middle of the table as usual. There is a very nice aroma coming from the roast chicken and potatoes. Justin places the salad bowl with plenty of tomatoes, cucumbers, spring onions, fresh parsley and mint in it. The kitten watches Justin's each movement. Justin picks up Fanny gently and closes the kitchen door behind. He carries Fanny to the living room and leaves the kitten on the sofa. Although the kitten never touches human food but it'll be too risky to leave Fanny in the kitchen with the temptation of the roast chicken left outside as she may play with the chicken. Justin goes upstairs to the bathroom and washes his hands with soap. He gives a gentle knock on Felix's door before changing his outfit for the evening.

'Are you O.K. Felix?'

'I'm fine, Justin.'

'Dinner is ready.'

Felix opens the door quickly.

'Would you like to have a look at my painting, Justin?'

'Well, this is a beautiful picture. Is that Fanny?'

'It's Fanny. I've got 20 sketches of Fanny here.'

'Let me have a look at them. They're fabulous. You're a talented artist, Felix. You must show your drawings and picture to Jasmine and Steve. I'm sure they'll like your artwork.'

'Thank you, Justin.'

'I'll call Jasmine. I've taken Fanny to the living room. You may wish to join her in the living room. See you later, Felix.'

'See you later, Justin.'

Felix goes downstairs and enters the living room slowly. Felix sees the kitten Fanny sitting on the sofa. He sits next to Fanny and strokes Fanny's beautiful fur. Fanny purrs slightly. Felix laughs at Fanny's delight for being cared affectionately.

Justin finds his wife studying her legal papers and can't decide whether he should go downstairs to the living room or tell Jasmine that meal is ready as he feels hesitant to irritate Jasmine while her focus is intensified on her case.

'Darling, I'm sorry to bother you.'

'What's the matter, dear?'

'The dinner is ready.'

'What's the time please?'

'It's seven o'clock.'

'I'll be downstairs in a minute. Let me finish the last paragraph.'

'See you downstairs, dear.'

'See you, darling.'

Justin goes downstairs to the living room. It's good to see Felix and Fanny sitting next to one another on the sofa.

'How nice to see you both having a good time, Felix.'

'Yes, we're having a good time.'

'Felix, I've completely forgotten that you haven't eaten much during the lunchtime. You must be starving now. Why didn't you come downstairs to have something to eat?'

'I had tea and two slices of lemon cakes.'

'That wouldn't be enough.'

'We'll be having our supper soon.'

'The bell is ringing. It must be Steve. Let me open the door.'

Justin leaves the living room quickly. Before answering the front door, he wants to make sure it's Steve.

'Is that you, Steve?'

'Yes, it's me, Justin.'

Justin opens the front door. Steve enters the hallway carrying a briefcase.

'You're here as a dyslexia specialist tonight, Steve.'

'What are you getting at, Justin?'

'You look a professional person with your briefcase now. I assume all your diagnostic test papers inside your briefcase.'

'Without the test papers, I won't be able to know what Felix's strengths and weaknesses are. My primary reason of coming here this evening is to give Felix several diagnostic tests. Yesterday, I came here to chill out only, Justin.'

'I was only joking, Steve. Please come on in. The dinner is ready. Felix and Fanny are both in the living room waiting for your arrival.'

'Where is Jasmine?'

'Jasmine is in her study to finish up her case preparation for tomorrow. She'll be coming downstairs in a minute.'

'I thought none of you bring work back home.'

'We try not to. Sometimes we can't avoid. Jasmine has been working on her case during the last 3 hrs without giving herself any break.'

'Well, it's not easy to be barrister then.'

'Who claimed it was?'

'I thought you were better off than me for time wise. We're all in the same boat.'

'Jasmine and I like what we are doing. We can't make any complaint about extra work at weekends. I'm lucky this weekend I didn't bring any paper from work. I'll be busy next week though as I'll be starting a new case tomorrow.'

'What do you have for supper, Justin?'

'To start with, we've got noodle soup. The main course will be roast chicken, roast potatoes and boiled vegetable alongside green salad.'

'How about dessert?'

'I know you were going to ask this question. There is no dessert tonight.'

'Why not?'

'I am kidding you, Steve. I've made apple crumble. We'll have it with ice-cream.'

'Fantastic!'

'Are you going to give diagnostic tests to Felix now?'

'Let's have supper first. I've skipped the lunch today as I'd like to lose weight.'

'You must be starving.'

'I can eat like a horse now.'

'I'll take you to the kitchen.'

'It'll be a very sensible thing to do, Justin.'

Justin and Steve enter the kitchen. Steve sits down; Justin gets the cold drink from the fridge.

'You must be thirsty. I'll pour you orange juice, Steve.'

'Thanks Justin.'

'Hi Steve, good to see you.'

'Hi Jasmine, good to see you too. Have you finished your paperwork?'

'I need to add a few more things after supper. Do you mind, if I leave you all after supper to get on with my papers, Steve?'

'Not at all. I'll be occupied with Felix in any case. Diagnostic tests will take two hours to complete.'

'What are you going to do after supper, Justin?'

'I'll watch the telly while everyone is very busy with other things.'

'What are you going to watch on TV? Is anything particularly interesting?'

'There is a program called "*Preservation of Wildlife.*" I like watching anything on wildlife.'

'It's a good programme. I watch it regularly. Where is Felix?'

'He is in the living room. I'll call him now.'

Justin comes back with Felix. They all have their dinner. After supper, Steve and Felix go to the living room. Justin gives Felix several diagnostic tests. Jasmine goes back to her study room and continues working on her case. Justin watches the film about the wild animals on the small TV in the kitchen. At 10.30 pm Steve and Felix come back to the kitchen.

'Hi Justin, Felix has taken his diagnostic tests. I'll be leaving you now.'

'Would you like to have a cup of tea with a slice of lemon cake, Steve?

'No thanks. I've had more than enough for supper. I'm supposed to be on diet.'

'Shall I give you a lift?'

'I've called a taxi. He'll be here in a minute.'

'The door bell is ringing.'

'It must be the driver. I'll see you next week, Justin.'

'Shall we wait for you next Saturday, at the same time?'

'That's right. I'll be here at the same time. Give my regards to Jasmine.'

'Safe journey back home, Steve.'

'Thanks Justin for the superb supper. Goodbye young man. I'll see you next week. Thanks for taking the diagnostic tests for me. I'll give you the test results next week.'

'Thanks for giving me the diagnostic tests. See you next week, Steve.'

'See you next week, Felix.'

'Let me see you out, Steve.'

Justin and Steve leave the kitchen. Justin opens the front door. The taxi driver is outside.

'Taxi is ready, sir.'

'Thanks. Goodnight Justin.'

'Goodnight Steve.'

Steve and the taxi driver get into the taxi. Steve puts his briefcase next to him and feels good about giving diagnostic tests to Felix. He is a nice fellow. Steve meets many dyslexic learners regularly and he is certain that Felix will be overcoming his literacy problem like all his dyslexic learners do. The taxi driver stops in Steve's neighbourhood.

'What's your door number, sir?'

'Number 11'

'Here we are sir, this is your door.'

'Thanks. You keep the change.'

'Thanks sir.'

'Good evening.'

'Good evening, sir.'

Steve takes his briefcase. He gets out of the taxi and opens his flat door with his key. Steve enters his flat. He turns the light on and sits down in a chair by the dinner table. Steve puts his briefcase on the table and opens his briefcase. Steve takes off Felix's diagnostic test papers and scan through them briefly. Steve puts the test papers in a folder. There is no time for interpreting the test results. Steve will have a very busy day at work tomorrow. He'd better go to bed without further delay. Steve goes to bathroom to wash his hands and face. Steve brushes his teeth quickly and goes to his bedroom. He takes out the hanger from the wardrobe. Steve takes off his suit and carefully hangs his suit in the wardrobe. Steve wears his bathrope before going back to the bathroom to take a warm shower. After shower he comes back to his bedroom. Steve looks at his alarm clock, it's nearly midnight. He sets his alarm clock for 7.00 o'clock and wears his pyjamas. He reflects on his evening before going to sleep. Steve feels happy that everything in his life is fine even he didn't have enough time to spend with his frogs tonight. Tomorrow, before leaving home, Steve has got to say goodbye to his frogs Frederick and Frederica. Steve wonders whether the frogs both had enough food to eat tonight. Steve's cleaner knows the exact amount of the food the frogs consume at weekends. She deals with feeding the pet frogs and cleaning the fish tank for them regularly. Thank goodness, Steve doesn't need to worry about looking after Frederick and Frederica. That would be too much for Steve to handle. He couldn't even cook lunch for himself. Steve falls asleep while he is visualising his pet frogs happy and kicking the ball.

Chapter 3

Felix's first week at prison - Sept 2002

Mr Goodman drives Felix to prison. On arrival, one of the prison wardens takes them to Felix's room on the 2nd floor. He unlocks the room. It is a medium-size room. The prison warden leaves them there. Mr Goodman puts Felix's suitcase and the big bag with art materials on the floor. Justin looks around the bare room with a few essentials like a small table, a chair and a single bed; he smiles at Felix with compassion knowing that life in prison won't be pleasant and time passes so slowly.

'Felix, I'll leave you here. The room is quite nice. What do you think?'

'It's OK.'

'As we've already arranged, Jasmine and I will be seeing you once a week.'

'Thanks.'

'You've got my number. If you need anything, do give me a call, Felix.'

'Thanks.'

'I'll call you in the middle of the week to see how you're getting on here.'

'That's very kind of you, Justin.'

'You've got plenty of art materials here in this bag.'

'Yes, I've got plenty of art materials.'

'Painting will keep you busy, Felix.'

'I should think so.'

'Next week, I'll get you a small telly. We've got a spare one. In the evenings, you'll watch the telly to take your mind off.'

'That'll be nice. Thanks a lot.'

'I'd better leave you now; look after yourself, Felix!'

'I'll try.'

'See you next week.'

'See you next week, Justin.'

After leaving Felix in his room at prison, Justin walks down the stairs and passes the long corridor leading to the exit. He stops by the reception and thanks the prison warden for letting him in once more. Outside the car park, Justin opens his car's door and gets in his car. On the way to his office, Justin thinks about Felix's sentence and hopes that Felix's time in prison will be spent wisely. Once Felix settles in, he will get used to the routine. Felix will be having his regular classes every weekend. Justin has got a special permission from the head of the prison. It has been agreed that Felix will be receiving a one to one support at prison. The identity cards for himself, Jasmine and Steve are issued. They'll be able to visit Felix at weekends for private tuitions. Justin decides to give his old laptop to Felix in order to enable him to have an access to Internet. It was a lucky coincidence that Felix wasn't sent to the prison outside London. Otherwise, it would have been more difficult to visit Felix at weekends. As soon as Justin enters his office, his mobile phone rings and he answer the call.

'Hi Jasmine.'

'Hi Justin, where are you now?'

'I'm in my office.'

'Did you drop Felix to prison?'

'Yes I did.'

'How did Felix feel about his new environment?'

'I've taken Felix to his room on the second floor. He's got a medium size room there.'

'Is Felix feeling OK?'

'Prison is prison, Jasmine. It isn't a holiday resort for anyone to stay. Felix needs to put up with the captivity when he is inside for 2 years.'

'You're right. However I can't stop feeling sorry for him.'

'Jasmine, you're a barrister. You've met many people facing life sentences. Why are you concerned about Felix that much?'

'We know Felix personally. Perhaps, we both attached to him. Felix isn't different than Fanny for me.'

'I can empathise with that.'

'If you've taken Fanny to the veterinary surgery to stay for a while, I would have worried about Fanny as well.'

'I feel the same, darling. However, we can't change Felix's circumstances. He has got plenty of art materials. At weekends, he'll start his studies which will occupy him. Supposing Felix is sent to the boarding school for 2 years, will it make any difference?'

'Even the worst boarding school will be better than any prison, Justin.'

'He'll have enough time to be educated well at prison.'

'Being in prison is a tough life. Nevertheless, it'll do him good in the long run.'

'I agree with you. I'll be taking the small telly to Felix next week.'

'That's a good idea!'

'I'll be giving my spare laptop to Felix.'

'I'll get him a mobile phone so that we could keep in touch with Felix during the week.'

'That'll solve the communication problem.'

'Anyway, I've got to stop now. I need to see my client in a few minutes time. Could you do me a favour this evening, Justin?'

'What is it, dear?'

'Could you do a bit off shopping for us on the way back home? I'll be an hour late home this evening. I have to see another client after 5.00 o'clock. She can't see me beforehand.'

'That's all right, dear. What do we need?'

'We'll have spaghetti tonight. It'll take only 10 minutes to cook. We run out of cheddar cheese; get a medium size cheddar cheese for spaghetti. We need a pint of milk for breakfast.'

'I'll be leaving office early this evening. One of my clients has cancelled the meeting. I'll be seeing him tomorrow. I can cook tonight. Don't worry about cooking, Jasmine.'

'Thanks darling.'

'What time will you be coming back home?'

'I'll be at home around 7.00 o'clock.'

'By then, supper will be ready.'

'Aren't you so kind, darling?'

'I can't help it, my dear. It's my nature.'

'I love you, Justin.'

'Me too, see you tonight, Jasmine.'

'See you tonight, Justin.'

Felix opens his suitcase given to him by Jasmine in the morning. He finds two sheets, two duvet covers, and two small pillows with two pillow cases in the suitcase. Felix takes one of the bed sheets out of his suitcase and covers his bed with the clean sheet. Felix puts his pillow on the bed and places the duvet on top of the bed neatly. Felix takes his pyjamas out of the suitcase and puts his pyjamas under the duvet cover. There isn't a wardrobe in the room. Felix leaves his clots in the suitcase. He takes all his art materials out of the large bag. Felix places them all on the table. The room looks like a bit more welcoming than before. Felix has got a bed to sleep and a table to paint on. After leaving his foster parents' home, Felix didn't have a room of his own. Last week was only a miracle Felix had experienced the first time in his life enjoying all the comfort and luxury Justin and his wife had provided for him. Felix's struggle to find an accommodation is over now. At least, for 2 years, Felix won't be worrying about where he is going to sleep. On top of that, he doesn't need to look for a work. Most of his time here will be spent either studying or painting. Felix feels lucky. It's very strange to see his room in prison like a home.

No one can arrest Felix here. It's his legal right to stay in this room and Felix feels safe. At last, he'll be having the freedom of sleeping in a bed with a decent sheet and a decent duvet cover. Felix sits down on the wooden chair. He opens his sketchpad and starts drawing how he feels. He sketches his room with a bed, a table and a chair. Felix adds his suitcase and his bag with art materials into his drawing. Felix draws himself as a happy young man looking out of the window. Outside doesn't look like inviting though. His room looks the symbol of hope, which is free from the chaos outside. The 1st drawing Felix has just produced in the prison is all about the individual freedom he has recently found when he is locked up. Felix entitles his 1st drawing as *"FREEDOM."* Felix is a free man without any obligation to find an accommodation to live or look for a job to support him. Felix's future doesn't look bleak at all. It looks brighter than the sunny days in summertime. Felix knows that he'll be making up the time he has wasted until now. Felix spends 2 hours drawing without giving any break. At 12.00 o'clock, the prison warden comes around and tells Felix that it's lunch time. Felix is given the key to lock his room. Felix locks his room and follows the warden to the dining-room. Other prisoners are already there. One seat is available for Felix to sit. Felix greets young offenders and they all greet back him. Felix sits down. The prison warden introduces Felix to others.

'This is Felix. Today, his 1st day here; be good to him, will you?'

They all say "hello" to Felix. The cook serves the meal for each prison. They have given baked beans and rice with tomato salad. There is a glass of fizzy water for each. Felix starts having his meal. After lunch, there is an announcement that they can play football in the prison yard for an hour. Felix joins the inmates. They all go out to the prison yard to play football. Playing football makes them all united without being threatened by one another's presence. They all run after a football ball.

Felix feels it's good to start his 1ˢᵗ day playing football with his inmates. Felix's football team wins the match. This increases Felix's morale. In an hour time, the prisoners are asked to join several art and craft workshops like sculpture, basket-weaving, woodwork and painting. Felix joins the sculpture workshop as he has never been to any sculpture workshop before. There are carving materials at the workshop. There is a tutor giving instructions to everyone how to handle the tools and various materials. Other inmates start working on their sculptures which are half done. The sculpture tutor introduces himself to Felix.

'Hi, you're new here, aren't you?

'Yes, today is my 1ˢᵗ day.'

'This is Abraham. I'll be assisting you while you are here.'

'Nice to meet you.'

'Nice to meet you. What's your name?'

'Felix.'

'Shall I show you the materials, Felix?'

'Yes please.'

'This area is for wood sculpture. All the tools you need are kept here. Have you sculpted before, Felix?'

'No, I haven't.'

'We've got plenty of clay for moulding. Would you like to experiment with clay or plaster before moving on to wood?'

'I don't really mind.'

'The materials we use here are messy a bit. Please help yourself with one of the work-coat over there.'

'Which one can I use?'

'You can take any of them. The larger size is for tall fellows like me. There are medium and small work-coats as well.'

'I'll get the medium size.'

'That's better. The clay and plaster are over there.'

'Thank you.'

'Are you OK to experiment with clay without any need for my instruction?'

'I think I'll be alright at the moment.'

'I'll be around till 5.00 o'clock. If you need any instruction, give me a shout.'

'Thanks.'

Felix gets some clay from the clay container. He puts the clay on the wooden table as he wants to create a man with his likeness. Nonetheless, Felix doesn't know how to form the clay and starts touching the clay with his hands gently. Then, he makes a small figure with the rough outlines. Felix predicts that he needs to refine the male sculpture using some tools and he asks help from the sculpture tutor Abraham who demonstrates him how to refine the body with a small wooden tool. Felix watches Abraham while he is working on his sculpture. After Abraham's a few touches, the clay looks human with the refined details. Felix likes moulding the clay and spends the rest of the afternoon working on his small terracotta sculptures. At the end of the session, Felix doesn't want to discard them as he wants to keep them all in his room. Abraham allows Felix to take the small terracotta sculptures to his room. Felix feels so happy while he is taking his terracotta sculptures to his room and he places them all on the windowsill in his room with a great satisfaction.

After supper, Felix starts sketching on his sketchbook. Felix draws some figures for his sculptures. Next time, he will be taking his sketches to the workshop to sculpt. Felix's 1st day at prison is spent in a rather pleasant way. He goes to bed at 10 o'clock. Felix has nothing to worry about now. He has already got a room with full of art materials. Everything in his current life looks comforting. Felix thinks about Fanny for a while. How good it would have been, if Felix had a kitten here in this room. Felix spent all day long with Fanny last week. Felix and Fanny had a very good week together. Felix wonders whether the kitten has missed Felix. No she wouldn't, Felix thinks. Fanny has got her pet-sitter Barbara now. Jasmine and Justin will be there in the evenings and at weekends for her. Fanny wouldn't even remember Felix in two years time. Felix wants to visit Fanny after he completes his sentence. Felix thinks about Justin and Jasmine. They've been so kind to Felix. Jasmine gave Felix £100 for looking after Fanny. Felix didn't know how to thank her for being very generous to Felix. Jasmine also gave him all the expensive art materials for free of charge and she bought Felix's outfits. The new suitcase and the bag were given to Felix as presents. The things Felix got from Justin and Jasmine have a sentimental value attached at the same time. Felix feels uncomfortable with the thought of not being able to return their kindness in any way. There are only a very few individuals with unique qualities in this life, who are able to offer so much to the people, who aren't able to return back for what they receive. Without any doubt, Felix will always feel grateful to Jasmine and Justin till the rest of his life. He remembers his dyslexia tutor, Steve. He can't help questioning himself why Steve cares about Felix. No one cared about Felix apart from his foster parents and Jackie before. However, his foster parents' care had stopped at the end of 16 years. Steve, Justin and Jasmine have promised to visit Felix at prison regularly. It'll be better for Felix not to expect too much from others. They're all professional people with their own commitments in their lives. Felix needs to be strong and try hard to stand on his own two feet. The more Felix feels less dependent on others, the stronger he'll become in life.

Felix falls asleep immediately. In his dream, Felix is in his 30s working as a successful barrister in the Court. He visits Jasmine and Justin in their home with an unusual present that is the drawing, named *"FREEDOM"* he had produced at prison on his 1st day. The drawing, which meant a lot to Felix, is given to his barrister for being so kind to Felix. If Felix didn't feel grateful to Justin and his wife Jasmine for all their kindness, generosity and care they had provided for Felix while he was insignificant and needy, he couldn't be parted from his drawing. Jasmine and Justin like Felix's drawing a lot. They frame the drawing and hang it on the wall in their living room, where they sit in the evenings to watch the telly. Felix feels that he will always have an access to his drawing each time he visits them that makes it easier for Felix to feel less distressed in the absence of his favourite drawing. Felix knows that he wouldn't be able to produce the same drawing with the same intensity of longing for the individual freedom. In order to be able to draw 'Freedom', Felix needed to be in prison experiencing mental freedom while his physical freedom was completely restricted. As a wealthy barrister, he will never be able to feel the freedom he had years ago. Freedom at prison was too precious for Felix to experience. Felix is a free and wealthy man now; but the freedom Felix has got is totally different than the freedom he had experienced at prison years ago. Felix's dream with the concept of freedom and the actual freedom was surreal. When Felix was woken up, he was still under the good impression of the beautiful dream about freedom and his drawing.

Jasmine arrives home at 7.00 o'clock and she feels exhausted. Dinner is ready. Jasmine and Justin both sit down and start having their meal in the kitchen.

'Steamed salmon goes very well with the boiled potatoes. It's delicious, Justin. Thanks for sorting out the dinner this evening. Otherwise, we would be stuck with spaghetti.'

'My pleasure, dear. Did you see your client?'

'Yes, I did. She came around at 5.30. It took us an hour to go through her case.'

'What is it about?'

'It's a divorce case.'

'Is it a complicated one?'

'It's a bit. I don't want to go into details.'

'That's fine. I can understand how you feel. I've also got a difficult case.'

'What is it?'

'Attempted murder.'

'I bet you don't want to go into details of your case either.'

'Not really! I am not in a mood for that.'

'How about Felix? Have you heard anything from him?'

'Today is Felix's first day at prison. Give him a chance to get on with his life without too much interference from us. Felix needs to learn how to survive. We won't be always there for Felix.'

'I know but I can't stop worrying about Felix.'

'Felix hasn't got a mobile phone yet. He wouldn't be able to call us.'

'I'll get him a mobile phone tomorrow at lunchtime.'

'You've got the whole week, darling. You can buy the phone on Saturday.'

'I'll be teaching Felix Saturday morning.'

'Would you like to switch from morning to afternoon shift then?'

'No dear. I prefer working in the morning. You'd better teach Felix in the afternoon.'

'If it suits you better, I have no objection.'

'Darling, I'm so tired. Do you mind if I go to bed now?

'Not at all, dear. Leave everything as it is, I'll clear up the mess.'

'Thanks dear. See you at breakfast. Have you fed Fanny by any chance?'

'Yes, I have.'

'Thanks Justin.'

'Don't you want to have dessert?'

'What do we have for dessert?'

'We've got water melon.'

'I'll have a slice, please.'

'I'll get you a slice of water melon.'

'Fanny is here. How was your day, my dear? Have you eaten your meal, Fanny?'

'I told you Jasmine I have fed Fanny, haven't I, Fanny?'

The kitten Fanny comes near to Jasmine. The kitten strokes Jasmine's legs and purrs. Jasmine strokes Fanny's head warmly.

'Look dear, Fanny must have missed me a lot all day long.'

'She did that to me on my arrival. Fanny loves both of us dearly.'

'Do you think Fanny misses Felix as well?'

'Why don't you ask Fanny?'

'You're so funny, Justin.'

'How could I possibly guess whether Fanny has missed Felix or not? You'd better to find out yourself, ask Fanny directly.'

'Fanny dear, did you miss Felix? Yes or no...'

'Miaow...'

'Fanny says yes, dear.'

'I believe you, Jasmine. Here we are! You've got a slice of water melon.'

'Thank you, dear.'

'Justin sometimes I feel Fanny isn't a cat.'

'Do you?'

'Yes, I do. How about you? Do you feel the same?'

'Not really. I don't confuse a cat with a human being.'

'You lack the imagination, Justin. You really do.'

'I can imagine everything else like being a superman myself, for example. However, I can't imagine a cat being a human being. Not tonight in any case.'

'Are you making a complaint about taking over some domestic responsibilities just recently, Justin?'

'If I give you a wrong impression, I'll apologise for that, Jasmine.'

'I'm sorry, darling. For a moment, I've suspected that you've been nasty to me.'

'Have I ever had an argument with you about anything during the last 10 years?'

'No, you haven't dear. It's a bit odd, isn't it? We don't look like we're a married couple.'

'What do you mean, Jasmine?'

'I mean married couples often argue about so many things but we don't. I'm quite concerned about our relationship. I am not sure how healthy our marriage is!'

'Shall we start arguing then? Is that what you want, Jasmine?'

'No, I didn't mean that but I don't want you to build up gradually and burst out your anger unexpectedly.'

'I can clearly see that you've got involved with your client's divorce case more than necessary.'

'I'm sorry, darling. I can't help it. My new client told me about her marital problems. It's a tragic story. She had a very successful marriage life for 10 years. At the end of 10 years, they had a silly argument. That was it. They have both decided to get divorce.'

'Can you see a parallel between your client's marriage life and ours, Jasmine?'

'I do. On the way home, I was rather upset, Justin.'

'For goodness sake, Jasmine! Please stop worrying about our marriage which has been perfect as far as I'm concerned.'

'If things go wrong with our marriage, I'll be affected badly, Justin.'

'So will I. That won't happen to us. If you wish, we can start practising turning our marriage into bit more conventional one. We'll have an argument once a week or twice just for the sake of it, you know. What do you think?

'Great dear!'

'Are you serious, Jasmine?'

'I mean, we have to tell each other what our concerns are without having any fear of hurting each other. If we talk about how we feel, we can save our marriage in the long run.'

'I can see your point of you, dear. I'll tell you whenever you get on my nerve.'

'Please do so, dear.'

'What about telling you my concerns just now, Jasmine?'

'Is it something wrong?'

'Yes, it's something seriously wrong, Jasmine. You're getting on my nerve?'

'Really?'

'Yes, I mean that, Jasmine.'

'What have I done to upset you, Justin?'

'I don't want you to show too much affection to Felix?'

'I hope you aren't jealous about Felix.'

'I'm jealous about your affection to Fanny as a matter of fact. I don't want you to love anyone more than you love me.'

'I'm sorry, darling. You've never told me that you get jealous of my attention I give to others.'

'I've never wanted to hurt you. That's why I've never told you this before, Jasmine. When you show a bit more affection towards anybody including our kitten Fanny, I get upset.'

'How about Steve? Do you get irritated when I treat Steve in a friendly way?'

'I am not sure about that.'

'Go on, tell me, dear. We're trying to help each other.'

'Perhaps, I shouldn't have told you about my concerns in the first place, Jasmine.'

'I'll be very happy to know what hurts you, Justin. We can work on it together. To tell you the truth, I was irritated when you spent four hours in the gym with Felix on his second day here. I had never expected from you to behave such an irresponsible way. You had left me here alone and spent the whole afternoon with a complete stranger. I was angry with you on that day.'

'Were you?'

'Yes I was. I really worried about our relationship at that time. You never left me four hours on my own at weekends before. Let's face the fact that Felix was and still is a total stranger. His presence shouldn't interfere with our marriage. Your first concern should be my happiness but not others, Justin.'

'Why didn't you tell me how you felt at that time, Jasmine?'

'I didn't want to give an impression that I was feeling jealous of your extra attention to Felix. Additionally, I didn't want to spoil Felix's happiness for being cared by us when he desperately needed our attention.'

'But you are hurting me now by telling your past concerns, Jasmine.'

'I'm sorry, Justin. Tonight is the first night without Felix around. We need to clear all our misunderstandings while Felix was our guest.'

'You're right. We need to sort out our negative feelings. Are you still feeling a bit nervous about our relationship with Felix, dear?'

'I've resolved my emotional conflict.'

'How?'

'Today, I deliberately asked you to do something for me. I was testing you actually.'

'Were you?'

'Yes, I was.'

'What was the outcome of the test I've taken without even noticing? In other words, did I pass the test you set for me about my commitment into our relationship?'

'Yes, you've passed the test without failing, Justin.'

'Can you give me the details please?'

'I wanted to measure your loyalty to me and find out whether or not I was important to you. I mean, as much as Felix.'

'When did you decide to test me?'

'Do you remember I called you this morning?'

'Yes, you did. You asked me about Felix's wellbeing on the phone.'

'That was a secondary concern.'

'Was it?'

'Yes, it was a secondary concern.'

'I thought it was a primary concern as you made such a fuss about how much you cared about Felix.'

'I didn't want you to suspect that I was testing your loyalty to our relationship.'

'I see. Tell me more about it.'

'You took Felix to prison this morning. In the afternoon, I wanted you to do something for me on the way back home just to check whether you were willing to do that for me or not.'

'I've got it. If I refused to do that, you would be thinking I didn't care about you. Is that right?'

'Yes, you're right.'

'It was a good job I didn't refuse to do the shopping on the way back home. Otherwise, you might have asked for a divorce now.'

'Not in the first instance but I'll directly ask you to finish our relationship if you're not hundred per cent committed to our marriage, Justin.'

'Please let me know when something is bothering you, Jasmine.'

'That's the thing, dear. We must talk about how we feel. Even a little silly thing will cause a problem in the long run. We need to discuss everything.'

'From now on, I'll let you know how I feel when you hurt me unintentionally. I expect you to do the same. How does it sound to you, Jasmine?'

'That's what I want, Justin.'

'Now, you can go to bed and have a good rest. Do not worry about the worst possibility. We'll overcome all the problems we might face in our marriage.'

'I believe so, Justin. See you tomorrow.'

'See you tomorrow, goodnight.'

'Goodnight, darling.'

Jasmine doesn't take Fanny to their bedroom after having a conversation about jealousy with her husband, she feels such a relief that her marriage isn't in risk. Jasmine takes a quick shower and goes to bed feeling good about talking through their misunderstandings with each other. They had a perfect relationship during the last 10 years. However, their weekly routine was affected by Felix's presence. Jasmine thinks that it's very hard to have someone around on a permanent basis when they're a married couple. It was a sacrifice they had made for Felix last week. Otherwise, Jasmine and Justin would have spent more time together. They wouldn't have worried about how to occupy Felix at weekends. While Jasmine is ready to close her eyes, Fanny enters the bedroom. She jumps on the bed. Jasmine gets up and strokes Fanny affectionately. Fanny purrs and settles in to go to sleep on the same bed with Jasmine.

On Saturday, Jasmine goes to see Felix in prison while Justin is doing their weekly shopping. Jasmine takes an introductory law book, a notebook, two pencils, two pens, a walkman and a mobile phone for Felix. Jasmine shows her ID card to the security guard in the prison and explains to him that she will be providing private tuition to Felix every Saturday. Jasmine is taken to Felix's room by the prison warden. Jasmine gives a knock on Felix's room and Felix opens the door for her.

'Hello Felix.'

'Hello Jasmine.'

'You look very well. It's a nice room. You've got small sculptures on the windowsill. Where did you find the terracotta sculptures?'

'I made them in the sculpture workshop last week.'

'Well done! How often do you go to the sculpture workshop?'

'Once a week. I worked there last Monday, the whole afternoon.'

'That's very good. I brought you a walkman. You might listen to music while you are sculpting or whenever you feel like listening to music.'

'Thanks a lot.'

'I also bought a mobile phone for you. It's rather easy to operate it. There is enough credit on it to keep you going for a while. When you run out of credit, we can top it up for you.'

'Many thanks. You've gone into too much trouble for me.'

'Not at all, you've got only one table and one chair here. Shall we move the chair near your bedside? You can sit on your bed while I'll sit on the chair.'

'I'll move the table next to the bed.'

'Would you like to clear the table first? What have you got here? Let me see?'

'My paintings and drawings.'

'This is a very beautiful picture. I like it. What is it called?'

'It is called *"Freedom."* It's the drawing of my room.'

'How nice!'

'I also like this picture. Is it Fanny?'

'It's Fanny. How is she?'

'She is very well. I've got a feeling Fanny missed you.'

'Did Fanny's pet sitter come back from her holiday?'

'Yes, she is back. They are both in tune again. Fanny had enjoyed your company as well when you were living with us.'

'When I come out of prison, I'd like to visit Fanny.'

'Please do Felix. I'm sure Fanny will be delighted to see you again. Cats never forget the people they like even after a long time. They can easily recognise the people who have been good to them. Now, where are you going to move all your drawings and paintings?'

'I'll put them all on the floor.'

'Next week, I'll bring you a drawing case. You'll keep all your drawings in the case. Shall I give you a hand, Felix?'

'No thanks, I can manage myself.'

'That's better. Let's carry the table together over there.'

'Is it OK? Shall I move it a bit further?'

'That's OK. You sit on your bed please. I'll sit here. We'll start the 1st lesson. Let me see the time. We already spent ten minutes. We'll have fifty minutes left for today's session. There won't be any break today. Will you be OK without taking a break for fifty minutes, Felix?'

'I'll be fine.'

'This is your notebook. These are pencils and pens for taking down notes.'

'Thank you?'

'Tell me what do you know about the legal system in the UK?'

'I know nothing about the legal system in the UK.'

'That's alright. Once a week, I'll be teaching you law, you'll be learning quite a lot about law. Shall we start with the definition of law?'

'Yes, please.'

'Could you tell me what the terminology of law means to you?'

'We need to comply with law.'

'You're correct. How do we acquire about legal knowledge?'

'We need to be told.'

'That's correct too.'

'Who tells us what is lawful and what is unlawful?'

'The Judge or the law book.'

'That's true.'

'Can you describe Judge for me?'

'A Judge is a legal person, who makes decisions about people's conducts within the law.'

'You're right. How do Judges know what is legal or illegal?'

'They study the law.'

'That's correct.'

'How many laws do we have?'

'Criminal law, civil law, copyright law, employment law and immigration law...'

'That's very good indeed. Now, we'll focus on the criminal law.'

'How do you describe crime?'

'Crime means breaking the law.'

'That's what exactly it means.'

'What happens if a person commits a crime?'

'They face legal actions.'

'Such as?'

'Caution, sentence, community work, ban from driving and paying a fine.'

'Very good. Even though, you've felt you knew nothing about the legal system in the UK, you've demonstrated that you're knowledgeable, Felix. I'm impressed by your answers.'

'I am not familiar with the details of legislations in various areas.'

'Even the legal people cannot know all the legislations in dept. We often need to refer to the law books in order to get the precise definition of lawful and unlawful actions. During my sessions, I'll be summarising the essential particulars in law for you to pass your GSCE exams. In order to be fully qualified as a court barrister, you need to study law further. While you're in prison for two years, you'll be prepared to take your GSCE exam in law. I'll be giving you some tests at the end of each session to assess how well you understand each session and what more you need to know. How does it sound?'

'Fine.'

'Will you prepare to take regular tests at each session?'

'Yes, I will.'

'That's good. You can only make a steady progress in your learning, if you commit yourself into your studies. Learning is a two way process. The tutor can't do the learning for you. You're in charge of your learning. I'll be here to provide a tool for you to benefit from. At the end of the day, you're the one who makes the decision whether or not to do a revision after each session. Do you understand what revision means?'

'To look through what you taught me later on.'

'It's more than that. You need to do exercises to reinforce your learning. Without doing regular exercises, you won't be able to learn. How much time can you spare to do exercises during the week?'

'As much as you suggest me to do.'

'I won't be able to tell you how much you need to spend for your private study. You need to find that out yourself. For some people, it'll be enough to spend half an hour each week. For some learners, it's necessary to practice an hour each day. You'll be able to decide how many hours you need for your revision in order to make a good progress in your learning.'

'I'm prepared to do my best.'

'That's good. In this paper, there are 40 legal words for you to master. Your language support tutor, Steve will be able to help you with the legal terminology. You'll be seeing Steve tomorrow.'

'Are you leaving now?'

'Yes, I'm leaving now as our session is finished. I'd like you to study the legal terminology with your language support tutor and make one sentence with each word. It's up to you how many words you'll be learning each week. It is good to see you, Felix. Keep well. I'll see you next week at the same time.'

'Thanks for your help. See you next week, Jasmine.'

'See you next week, Felix. Keep well!'

Jasmine goes back home by underground. On the way back home, her mind is preoccupied with Felix's studies. Visiting Felix at prison regularly and teaching him law will be quite demanding. She has to juggle with her professional life as a barrister, her marriage life and teaching Felix at weekends. Normally, Justin and Jasmine do their weekly food shopping on Saturdays. Today, Justin needed to take the car to do the shopping. Jasmine has to travel by underground. Next week, Jasmine should take over shopping responsibility from Justin.

It'll be too much to expect from Justin to do weekly shopping each week. If they both take their turns for their weekly shopping, none of them feel exploited. Jasmine arrives at home at noon. Justin is back from shopping. They have lunch together. Jasmine tells Justin that she had a good impression about Felix's willingness to study regularly. They're both optimistic for Felix's future as they guess that Felix's reading and writing skills will be improved, he will be on the right track to achieve his GSCEs without much difficulty.

Justin gets the spare black and white TV from the storage room. He puts the small telly on the front seat next to him in his car and leaves home to teach Felix maths at prison. When he arrives at the prison, Justin does the same formality Jasmine did in the morning. Justin declares that he is taking the small TV to Felix in order to occupy him while he is in prison. The warden takes Justin to Felix's room. Justin gives a knock on his door. Felix opens the door and lets Justin in. Justin puts the telly on the floor.

> 'Hello Felix. How are you today?'

> 'I'm fine thank you. How was your journey?'

> 'It was fine. There wasn't much traffic. Jasmine told me you made terracotta sculptures last week. Tell me how did you find here?

> 'I spend most of my time doing artwork here.'

> 'Good. You're pretty much busy then. Where would you like to put the telly?

> 'Over there by the socket.'

> 'What is the socket for?'

> 'I think it's for electric razor.'

'We can't put the telly on the table. It'll take a large part of the table. You can't study or draw on it. There is nothing to put the telly on. Shall I live it on the floor as it is by the socket?'

'Yes, please.'

'Let's plug it on. I've brought you the internal aerial. You can have a better picture quality. That's it. It's working. Until we get you a digital one, you'll put up with the limited choice. There are only four channels. You won't get extra channels.'

'That's fine. Many thanks.'

'You're welcome. You'll be having an hour maths with me once a week. Without wasting much time, shall we dive into maths? Are you ready for it?'

'Yes, I'm ready.'

'Do you like maths?'

'Not really.'

'Regardless you like maths or not, you need to have GSCE in maths before you go to university to do any degree. Many people don't like maths but everyone has to learn the basic at GSCE level. Can you tell me how do we classify numbers?'

'I haven't got a clue.'

'Can you count my fingers?'

'Yes I can.'

'Could you count your fingers please?'

'One, two, three, four, five...'

'That's enough. Can you count up to 100 without getting confused?'

'Yes, I can.'

'That's good.'

'The number you can count up to 100 is classified as cardinal numbers. Can you remember this?'

'I try to remember.'

'The Romans used different numeric system. Can you guess what did they call their numeric system?'

'Roman numbers.'

'Exactly, the Romans used Roman numbers.'

'Can you recognise Roman numbers?'

'Up to 10, I am fine. After 10, I get confused.'

'Many people feel the same. I'll be showing you the basic symbols for the Roman numbers. Can you tell me the symbol for 10 in Roman numeric system?'

'It's X.'

'That's right. X is equivalent to 10. Can you figure out 31 please?'

'I don't think I can.'

'How many 10 in 30?'

'3 tens.'

'What is the symbol for 10 in Roman numeric system?'

'X'

'If you put 3 Xs, what will you get?'

'Three XXX will be 30.'

'That's right! Can you add Roman number 1 next to the three xxx please?'

'XXXI'

'What is the number you've got now?'

'It's 31.'

'That's it. You're correct. Can you figure out 24 now in Roman symbols please?'

'I can try.'

'Can you think aloud please? Use this paper and write down the symbols.'

'There are two 10s in 20. With the Roman symbol, twenty should be XX. Am I correct?'

'That's correct. How about 4? You said you know Roman numbers up to 10.'

'IV is for 4. I can put IV next to XX. Am I correct?'

'That's correct. Could you write it down please?'

'XXIV'

'Could you right the cardinal number next to the Roman number please?'

'XXIV – 24'

'That's perfect.'

'Once you start building up your new knowledge onto the prior knowledge, you can work out something that you didn't know before. As you practise that just now, maths becomes easier when you start using your reasoning skills. Now, I'll be writing the symbols, which you never had a chance to learn. Afterwards, you'll be forming your own numbers. Is that OK?'

'That's fine.'

'According to the Roman numeric values, L stands for 50. Is that clear?'

'Yes. L is 50.'

'C stands for 100. Repeat it please?'

'C stands for 100.'

D stands for 500.'

'D stands for 500.'

M stands for 1.000.'

'M stands for 1.000.'

'Now, Can you figure out 60 in the Roman numeric symbols?'

'L stands for 50. X stands for 10. LX stands for 60.'

'How about 70?'

'If I add another 10 adding to 60, I'll get 70.'

'Can you write it down please?'

'LXX stands for 70.'

'How about 80?'

I'll add another X which will give me 80.'

'Can you show it to me on the paper please?'

'LXXX stands for number 80.'

'That's very good.'

'What is the symbol for 100 in the Roman numeric system?'

'It's C.'

'Can you guess how you can get 90?'

'Not really.'

'That's fine. It's a bit tricky actually. You couldn't guess it. Can you see my function as a maths tutor now? There are things in maths you can easily guess or figure out based on your prior knowledge. However, there are some facts you need to be taught explicitly. Otherwise the mathematical facts won't be accessible to you.'

'Yes, I can see that.'

'If you place X in front of C, that will take away 10. So XC stands for 90.'

'XC stands for 90.'

'You've got it. Now you know the fact of subtraction from the Roman numeric system. Can you tell me what is the Roman symbol of 500? You can check your notes now.'

'D stands for 500.'

'That's very good. Can you apply what you've just learnt into practice now and write me 400 with the Roman numeric?'

'XD stands for 400.'

'If you reason with logic, you're right. However, in maths you can come across some odd facts, which have nothing to do with logical thinking process. In this case, 400 is CD, but not XD. Isn't it confusing?'

'It's very confusing indeed!'

'C subtracts 100, but not 10s. Can you see the difference between X and C in front of the Roman numbers?'

'That's very interesting!'

'It's very interesting. Now, you can figure out the Roman symbols for 400. Can't you?'

'Yes, I can. D stands for 500. C subtracts 100. If I place C in front of D, I'll get CD which stands for 400.'

'That's superb!'

'I've got some exercises for you to do. You've got the whole week to practise what you've learnt today. I'll give you a test on the Roman numeric values next week. Will you be able to do exercises in maths?'

'I've got plenty of time to do exercises.'

'Jasmine told me she gave you some exercises to do in law as well. Can you cope with the extra workload?'

'I'll try my best.'

'Prepare a timetable for your exercises, please. I'd like to see how many hours you spend on each subject during the week. You haven't got a watch, have you?'

'No, I haven't got one.'

'Take mine. It's digital. It makes life easier to read the time. I've got a spare one at home.'

'Many thanks.'

'You're welcome. I'd better leave you now. We've spent an hour altogether. How did you find the lesson?'

'I've enjoyed it.'

'It's good to hear that. Maths isn't that boring after all, is it?'

'No, it isn't. It's fun actually. I like the Roman symbols.'

'That's good. I've brought you a few slices of ginger cake Jasmine baked it today. Have them with your tea later on.'

'Thanks. Could you tell Jasmine that she has gone into too much trouble again?'

'I'll tell Jasmine. We both want you to achieve your goals in life. Steve will be here tomorrow. Could you pass this vocabulary list on to Steve? He'll help you to learn all the numerical expressions.'

'I'll do that.'

'Take care of yourself, Felix. Hope to see you next week.'

'See you next week, Justin.'

Justin leaves Felix's room and walks quickly towards the end of the corridor. Justin says goodbye to the security guard at the desk. He gets into his car in the prison car park. Justin turns on the CD player feeling in a very good mood. Teaching Felix was enjoyable as he was very quick to pick up the Roman symbols. Justin thinks about their supper. It's Jasmine's turn to cook tonight. Steve will be joining them for supper. Tonight will be different than any other Saturdays. Jasmine, Steve and Justin are working part of the support team. Justin and Jasmine never thought that they would pass their skills on to others as tutors. Justin likes his new role as a maths tutor for a dyslexic learner. Steve will be helping Justin and Jasmine to approach Felix's learning need in a dyslexia-friendly way. Justin never met any dyslexic person before let alone teaching a dyslexic learner. It'll be educational for Justin and Jasmine to learn some of the characteristics of a dyslexic learner's profile from Steve each week when they meet to socialise. Socialising doesn't mean to talk about only art, theatre, music but to talk about education as well. Teaching Felix will strengthen their friendship with Steve. Justin and Jasmine will benefit from Steve's expertise. If they weren't friends, it would have cost them a lot of money to consult a specialist dyslexia tutor. How lucky Felix has been in these circumstances. If Steve wasn't a dyslexia specialist, Felix's dyslexia wouldn't be recognised in the first place. Poor Felix might have thought that he had a low IQ. Felix is a brilliant lad. He has figured out the Roman numbers fine today. Even non-dyslexic people found it difficult to differentiate the Roman numbers without getting confused. It's a good sign that Felix will be learning maths quicker than Justin anticipated. Felix has got an aptitude for maths. See, how long it will take for Felix to sit for his GSCE exam in maths. When Justin arrives at home, it is already 3.30 in the afternoon. He rings the bell. Jasmine opens the door for Justin.

> 'You're just on time. There is a very good programme on the telly about dyslexia. Would you like to join me, Justin?'

> 'It'll be beneficial to watch the programme.'

> 'Hurry up dear! There is an advert now. You'll catch the second part.'

> 'I'm coming darling.'

> 'I'll put the kettle on, shall I?'

> 'That's a good idea. Get me a slice of cake as well, please.'

Jasmine rushes to the kitchen and turns on the kettle. Jasmine slices two pieces of ginger cake for both of them. She places the ginger cake slices on the small plates. The kettle is boiled. Jasmine brews the tea. She puts the teapot and tea cups on the table before Justin enters the kitchen.

> 'It's lovely to smell the ginger cake and Jasmine tea, my dear.'

> 'Quick dear, the program is going to start now.'

> 'Let me have my tea and ginger cake.'

> 'Here you are.'

> 'Aren't you going to have lemon slices for your tea?'

> 'I'll get you some.'

'Sit down please. I'll help myself, Jasmine. You watch the programme. I've missed the first part in any case.'

Justin opens the fridge and gets a medium size lemon out of the fridge. He quickly washes the lemon under the running tap and cuts the lemon into the thin slices. He puts the saucer with the lemon slices on the table. He looks at Jasmine. She is watching the telly with full of concentration. Justin puts one slice of lemon into his tea and pushes the saucer with lemon slices near Jasmine's tea cup without saying anything. Justin sips from his tea and bites from the ginger cake. It's delicious. Justin starts watching the programme on dyslexia carefully. For half an hour, they don't talk. Once the programme on dyslexia finishes, Jasmine switches off the telly. She smiles at Justin with curiosity.

'Tell me how did your maths session go?'

'It went very well, dear. Felix is very bright. He absorbs the given knowledge quickly.'

'I thought so. He's a quick learner. I was watching this programme on dyslexia before you arrived. Dr Leslie Turner made a significant remark about the nature of dyslexia.'

'Was it related to how dyslexic people learn?'

'That's right. She pointed out that dyslexic people learn quickly but they also forget quickly.'

'Does Dr Turner suggest any solution for the dyslexic learners' problems?'

'There is more than one solution actually. I've jotted them down here.'

'Let me see. *Holistic learning style*, what does that mean?'

'*Holistic learning style* caters global approach to problem solving rather than linear approach.'

'Did Leslie Turner give any example to illustrate the global approach?'

'Yes, she did. According to Dr Turner, dyslexic people need an overall picture as a guide to their learning. They aren't interested in details to start with.'

'That's good to know. We can adopt the global approach for our teaching material. What else did you pick up from Dr Turner?'

'Dr Turner also suggests that dyslexic people are *inductive thinkers*.'

'What does that mean?'

'*Inductive thinkers* reason from particular to general. In other words, they don't use generalisations in order to reach a particular conclusion. They learn from lots of first-hand experience and practice while they are discovering *"what"*?'

'Well, it was a good job I used the similar approach in my 1st teaching practice today. That's why Felix has understood the mathematical concepts rather well. Felix told me he enjoyed the session.'

'What did you teach Felix today?'

'The Roman symbols.'

'How did you teach the Roman symbols?'

'I let Felix use his initiative to get a first-hand learning experience.'

'Didn't you explain anything to Felix in the first place?'

'I did but not too much. It was just enough for Felix to figure out some of the symbols himself.'

'Was he successful?'

'Felix was successful after he spotted his own mistake. It was a trial and error approach. First, Felix made a mistake. Then, he corrected his mistake. I think this approach suited Felix more than being taught how to solve the problem step by step approach.'

'It sounds you made maths interesting for Felix to enjoy.'

'That was my main intention. I don't think I would enjoy teaching Felix all the facts without getting Felix involved with his own learning process.'

'That would be one way approach only.'

'It would be one way approach, which would only undermine Felix's capacity to expand his skills. It wouldn't work.'

'You've made a good point actually. Dr Turner suggests that dyslexic people learn better while learning is personalised. They know the answer through personal knowledge as they are intuitive thinkers rather than logical ones.'

'I like how Dr Turner describes dyslexic people in terms of their thinking capacity. Intuitive thinkers are more creative than logical thinkers. Felix is excellent in artistic concepts. He paints, draws and sculpts intuitively.'

'No one taught Felix how to draw, paint or sculpt. Yet, he is more skilful then many trained artists, draftsmen and sculptors. I loved his terracotta sculptures. Have you seen them?'

'Yes, they are fantastic. It'll be so nice if Felix opens his solo exhibition in a public gallery. I'm sure many art lovers will appreciate his artistic skills.'

'I'll have a look around. See whether we can get him a solo exhibition at one of the art galleries in London.'

'That'll increase Felix's morale immediately.'

'It'll boost his morale as well as ours.'

'We definitely need to work on Felix's exhibition next.'

'We shall dear. I'll do a bit of research on the Internet.'

'I'll give you a hand.'

'That'll speed up the process.'

'Can you imagine Felix being picked up by art collectors?'

'I can easily imagine that.'

'If Felix earns his living out of his artwork, Felix's financial problems will be solved automatically.'

'That's what we hope to achieve within a short time. Otherwise, in 2 years time, Felix will be stuck again.'

'That's true. He'll go around the circle once more. We need to prepare the base for Felix to build up his own life.'

'Getting qualifications is the most important step Felix needs to take up. If he starts reading and writing, the worst obstacle Felix facing in his life will be over.'

'Felix should learn how to read and write fluently.'

'It's Steve's job to offer Felix a professional help. We can't help Felix with his reading and writing skills. That's beyond our reach.'

'Have you heard anything from Steve today?'

'No, I haven't. Didn't Steve say he'll be here around 8.00 this evening?'

'That's right. I'd better get on with the supper preparation. What are you going to do?'

'I need to have a shower first. Then, I should look at my new case. It's heavy going. If you don't mind, I won't be able to give you a hand for supper tonight.'

'That's perfectly alright, darling. I can manage without any help.'

'Are you sure?'

'Yes, I'm positive, Justin.'

'See you later then. I'll be down at 7.55. I'll set the alarm clock to remind me the time.'

'See you at 7.55, dear.'

'I'll be precisely on time this evening.'

Justin and Jasmine burst into laughter. Justin goes upstairs to have a shower; Jasmine goes to the kitchen to continue her supper preparation.

Steve arrives at the prison with his briefcase soon after Justin left there. Steve is taken to Felix's room by the prison warden. Steve knocks on Felix's door; Felix opens the door and lets Steve in.

'Hi Felix, it's nice to see you.'

'Hi Steve, it's nice to see you too. Justin was here a few minutes ago. He has just left.'

'Have you had a break after the lesson?'

'No, I haven't had one?'

'It'll be good for you to have a short break every an hour. Otherwise, it'll be difficult for you to take in. Do you know the technique called *visualisation?*'

'No, I don't.'

'I'll explain to you how you practise visualisation step by step. Please lie down on your bed now.'

'Shall I take my shoes off?'

'Yes please. You need to feel comfortable.'

'I've taken my shoes off. I'm ready now.'

'Close your eyes. You need to feel out of body experience. In other words, you'll be travelling outside this room in your vision. You can visualise yourself in any pleasant environment you wish to be. Do you have any good memory of being somewhere else, Felix? Where did you go for taking your mind off before you came here?'

'I loved walking by the River Thames.'

'That's it. You visualise yourself by the River Thames for 10 minutes.'

'What am I supposed to do?'

'You try to remember a pleasant environment from your walk.'

'Is that all?'

'Please don't think any other details from your current life.'

'How?'

'Forget about being in this room. Ignore my existence; suppose that I am not here.'

'But you're here.'

'Yes, I'm here physically but I won't be talking to you. I'll be visualising for 10 minutes too. I'll be somewhere else. I'll set the alarm now. We'll hear the alarm going off in 10 minutes time. You'll be coming back to the current reality from your walk by the River Thames when the alarm goes off.'

'Alright, then.'

Felix closes his eyes. He imagines himself walking by the River Thames as a free person on a summer day with the strong sunshine. Felix walks up and down by the River Thames. Then Felix sits on the bench and he watches the swans, the geese and the seagulls in the river. Felix feels so good to visualise himself in another environment where he could normally go when he was out of prison.

Steve closes his eyes and he imagines himself on his last trip to Antibes in South of France. Steve is walking by the sea. It is a sunny day with a nice breeze. Steve wants to swim in the sea and jumps into the sea. He swims slowly till he can't see the shore. It's a real pleasure to be part of the sea, which leads Steve to overcome his daily monotonous routine. Steve feels afresh. The 10 minutes is gone quickly and Steve's alarm goes off. Steve and Felix both open their eyes at the same time. Felix gets up. He puts on his shoes and sits on his bed calmly. Felix smiles at Steve with full of energy.

'How did you find visualisation technique, Felix?'

'I feel like I've been by the River Thames.'

'You can use visualisation technique whenever you feel you need to get out of the present circumstances, which might exhaust you or irritate you.'

'Do you use the visualisation technique in your personal life, Steve?'

'Yes, at least twice a day. Otherwise, I wouldn't be able to survive. Like everyone else, my hectic lifestyle tires me physically and mentally. Now, tell me about your day, how was it?'

'It was very busy.'

'What did you do?'

'I had almost an hour law studies with Jasmine. I had another hour with Justin teaching me mathematics.'

'How did you find both subjects?'

'I quite liked how Jasmine and Justin taught me.'

'How did they teach you?'

'It was different than how our primary school teacher used to teach us. Justin and Jasmine kept asking me questions to find the answers myself. That made learning more interesting. I wasn't told what to do.'

'Did they give you learning materials or exercises to do on your own?'

'Jasmine gave me the vocabulary list for the legal language. It's here. She asked me to pass it on to you in order to help me with it.'

'Let me have a look at it. It's quite complicated. The legal terminology is difficult in any case. What about Justin? Have you got anything from him?'

'Yes, Justin has given me the list of mathematical expressions.'

'This looks very complicated. Although I am not an expert in maths myself, I can get you familiarised with the mathematical expressions.'

'Thanks for that.'

'I'll teach you learning strategies, which will enable you to remember some facts. I'll be designing a language support programme for you.'

'Thanks.'

'In order to be able to design a language support programme for you, I need to test you first. I'll be asking you questions. Please answer my questions. Are you ready for the test?'

'Yes, I'm ready.'

'You'll be going for a walk by the River Thames. You can only take one of the objects I'll be specifying for you now.

> Object 1 is a pair of sunglasses
> Object 2 is a walkman
> Object 3 is a drawing pad
> Object 4 is a scooter

Which object will you take with you, Felix?'

'Can I take 2 objects with me?'

'You can only take one object.'

'I'll take my drawing pad then.'

'That's fine. The next question is what would you do, if you buy a camera with the instruction booklet?

> Option 1 is you'll figure out how the camera works by touching the several buttons on the camera.

> Option 2 is you'll ask the sale assistant to show you how the camera works.

> Option 3 is you'll look at the pictures in the instruction booklet and follow the instructions.

> Option 4 is you'll get panic and you return the camera back immediately.

Which option do you take, Felix?'

'I'll look at the pictures in the instruction book and follow the instructions.'

'That's fine. The next question is supposing you get lost on the way back here from the River Thames you went for a walk while you were visualising a few minutes ago. You've got 4 options. Which option looks more tempting than others?

Option 1 is you'll ask the bus driver to drop you at the nearest bus station.

Option 2 is you'll ask anyone passing by you to give you directions.

Option 3 is you'll try another route and see whether it will be the correct route.

Option 4 is you'll get panic and don't know what to do.

What would you do, Felix?'

'I'll ask the bus driver to drop me at the nearest bus station.'

'Can you remember any phone number?'

'No, I can't remember any number for a long time.'

'That's OK. I'll be telling you my phone number. What strategy will you use to memorise my phone number?' My telephone number is 020 2211 2255.

Strategy 1 is I'll write down the 11 digits and read them aloud 3 times

Strategy 2 is I'll write down the 3 digits and read them aloud 3 times.

Strategy 3 is I'll divide the 11 digits into 2 digits and learn 2 digits at a time.

Strategy 4 is I'll write down 4 digits and associate them with my body organs.

Which strategy will you choose, Felix?'

'I'll choose the strategy 4.'

'Could you tell me how you use the strategy you've chosen?'

'Yes, it's easy for me to remember the numbers in association with my body organs such as:

> 0202 - on two eyes on 2 images
> 2211 - 2 ears 2 sounds, 1 mouth 1 nose
> 2255 - 2 hands 2 feet, 5 fingers, 5 toes

I won't forget the numbers as each of them is related to my head and body.'

'How can you remember all the associations you've made up yourself?'

'I'll draw a human being and put the numbers on the image.'

'That's very good.'

'Well, you've got a learning strategy, which defines you as a visual learner. You're a tactile learner as you enjoy using your hands while you are learning like preferring a drawing pad when you go out to enjoy yourself by the River Thames. You wish to draw a human being while you are trying to remember the digits in maths.

That also qualifies you as a visual learner. You're a kinaesthetic learner as you wish to move around while you're exploring the environment. You're a person who wants specific information for a fast and professional result as you've preferred to ask the bus driver to drop you at the specific destination and you've avoided asking anyone passing by for direction. You didn't get panic. That's very good. You didn't want to take a risk of losing your way completely by giving another go. Based on the test results I'll be preparing your language support plan, which will suit your learning style.'

'When are you going to do that?'

'I need to take your vocabulary lists in law and maths with me today. The first thing in the morning, I'll be preparing your language support plan. I'll be visiting you in the afternoon. How does it sound to you?'

'That's great!'

'We've still got 10 minutes to finish the session. Have you got any question to ask me?'

'How long will it take for me to learn reading and writing fluently?'

'It depends on what you put into your studies. The more effort you make and the time you spend consciously, the quicker the outcome will be. In other words, you need to commit yourself into your studies and never give up.'

'I am prepared to commit myself to my studies as this is the only option I've got.'

'Sometimes, fewer options can bring more success in life. In a way, you're lucky that you've got the limited options during the next 2 years. I need to leave you now. I'll see you tomorrow.'

'Do you want me to do anything this evening?'

'Before I prepare your language support plan, there isn't much you can do. Instead, you can practice the visualisation technique to free yourself from certain worries of the unknown in your learning venture. Tomorrow, you'll be ready to start a new learning day afresh. How does it sound to you, Felix?'

'It sounds fine.'

'Good to hear that. You've got a telly here.'

'Justin brought it for me.'

'How nice! Do you watch television regularly?'

'When I was staying with Justin and Jasmine, I watched the telly a few hours each day.'

'Does it help you to take your mind off from your worries?'

'Sometimes, it does; sometimes, it doesn't. Drawing is the only thing, which always takes away my worries. As long as I've got a drawing pad, I won't worry about anything.'

'How lucky you are! You've got a gift for drawing. I'm hopeless with my hands. I can't draw a straight line.'

'Well, I am hopeless with letters. I can't read and write at the moment.'

'Reading and writing don't require a special talent. You need to get skilled. With painting and drawing, you need to have a special talent, which I lack.'

'If you try hard, you might get better at painting or drawing.'

'I'll get skilled but I won't be able to become a brilliant draughtsman or an accomplished painter. That's for sure.'

'I can't play a musical instrument.'

'You're a visual person. You aren't an auditory person.'

'Do you think I might get skilled in playing a musical instrument?'

'Anyone can get skilled in anything. Anyone can pick up any skill. However, to be excelled in any skill, you need to have a bit of extra something, which cannot be picked up through practice.'

'I'd like to learn to play the guitar though.'

'Some talented people teach themselves how to play the guitar. I met a guitarist who lost 3 fingers and he plays the guitar with his 2 fingers. He is an excellent guitarist. I'd better go now. I'll be having supper with the Goodmans. I shouldn't be late. See you tomorrow at around 3.00 o'clock.'

'See you tomorrow at 3.00 o'clock. Many thanks for your time.'

'It's my pleasure, Felix.'

'Please give my regards to Jasmine and Justin.'

'I'll do that.'

Steve gets out of the prison quickly. He walks to the train station. Steve looks at his watch. His train will be here at any time. Steve enters the platform. He reads the timetable. The train arrives at the platform just on time. Steve gets on the train and sits by the window. The train passes by the countryside with full of trees. Steve thinks he prefers the train journey to the bus or underground journey as he can visualise himself in the countryside when he looks out of the window. Steve feels a need to go away for a week to recover from his daily routine. Steve is happy that Felix has settled in without feeling depressed about the 2 years sentence. Felix has got a lot to do while he is in prison. Steve will be visiting Felix twice a week. The train route with plenty of green areas will definitely cheer up Steve at weekends. It'll help Steve to overcome the feeling of being stuck in a city life travelling on busses with full of passengers. How good it is that there is hardly any passenger on the train. At weekends, the trains aren't busy at all. Steve gets his mobile phone out of his briefcase. He dials the Goodmans's home number.

'Hello, Jasmine is speaking.'

'Hello Jasmine. This is Steve. I've just wanted to let you know that I'm on my way. I'll be there in half an hour time. Would you like me to bring anything for us?'

'We've got everything. There is no need to bring anything.'

'How about a bottle of wine to celebrate Felix's new start?'

'We've got plenty of good old wines. We'll have one of them this evening.'

'That'll be splendid! Is Justin there?'

'Justin is upstairs, in his study room. He is working on his case.'

'Poor Justin! He can't distance himself from his cases even at weekends.'

'None of us can distant ourselves from our professional worries until we get retired, Steve.'

'You can say that again, Jasmine. I've taken the train journey to Felix's place. The scenery is splendid. I feel like I am in the countryside. I'm desperate to take a week off from my heavy workload.'

'Can you do that?'

'I don't think I can. I have to wait till summer.'

'At least, you can enjoy longer summer holidays than ours, Steve.'

'That's true. Never mind, we should stop complaining about our lives. It won't do any good to our morale.'

'Complaining about our work conditions will only decrease our morale, Steve.'

'I am hoping that I'll buy a cottage in the countryside. In my retirement years, I'll enjoy the peaceful county life. I'm sick and tired of the hectic city life, Jasmine.'

'It's a good idea to move out of the city at retirement age.'

'That's a long term plan.'

'Justin is here. Would you like to have a word with Justin?'

'Yes, please.'

'Steve is on the phone, would you like to say hello to him?'

'Yes, please. Hi Steve! How are you?'

'I'm fine, Justin. I've just finished the session with Felix.'

'Good!'

'I'm on the train.'

'What time will you be here?'

'Less than half an hour, I should think.'

'Good. We'll see you soon, then.'

'See you soon, Justin.'

Justin puts the telephone down. He smiles at Jasmine and she smiles back to him.

'Is there anything I can do for supper?'

'You're off today, Justin. How is your case preparation going?'

'I had it enough for today. I still need to work on it. I'll carry on tomorrow.'

'You need to have a bit of break for yourself, Justin.'

'You're right, dear. I need a break. Maybe, we should take our annual leave soon. What do you think, Jasmine?'

'I can't go away during the next 2 months, darling.'

'Tell you what. I'll book our hotel and flight tickets now. At least, we can start imagining that in 2 months time, we'll be having our break for a week. How does it sound?'

'That's perfect.'

'Where are we going for a week holiday, Jasmine?'

'You tell me Justin, where should we go?'

'You always leave it to me. Please you choose where you would like to go this time?'

'Forget about the long flight journey. Let's go somewhere by train. Steve was telling me how much he enjoys train journey as it reminds him of the countryside. Steve's long term plan is to move into the countryside in his retirement.'

'When is he going to retire?'

'There is a long time for his retirement. That doesn't prevent Steve from considering the possibility of getting out of the city.'

'Shall we do that as well?'

'Why not! It'll be nice to move outside the busy city life. We can move to Bournemouth, for instance. What do you think, Justin?'

'Would you like to go there for a week, dear?'

'That'll be nice actually. I missed the sea and the seagulls.'

'I'll book the accommodation and the train tickets tomorrow.'

'Great! Why don't you open one of your old wines for us to celebrate Felix's new start and our decision to have a week holiday in 2 months time, Justin?'

'I'll do that!'

'I'll set the table for our supper. The food is ready.'

Justin goes to the cellar and gets one of the old wines he has been keeping for important days to consume such as their anniversaries and birthdays. Jasmine lays down the table. She goes upstairs to change her dress. Jasmine feels very tired. She had a long day. Teaching Felix on Saturdays wouldn't be easy. Apart from that, she had to cook supper. How much Jasmine wants to put her feet up and read a novel to take her mind off from her difficult cases she has been dealing with. Jasmine loves her profession as a court barrister but she really needs to have more time off from her legal duties. How good it will be, if Jasmine and Justin move to Bournemouth when they get retired. Jasmine likes the fresh sea air, the green land and the friendly seagulls living by the sea. Jasmine imagines herself and Justin in their cottage in Bournemouth far away from their daily routines. They can go out for a long walk every single day in the mornings and in the evenings. They'll get themselves a small boat too. During the summer time, Jasmine and Justin will sail on the sea. They can have their dinner on the boat in the middle of the sea. Coming back home in the dark without having any worry for the next week must be a delightful experience for anyone to enjoy at weekends, Jasmine thinks. They will live like they are on their annual leaves during their retirement years. Life should be like that. Jasmine is already 50 years old and she isn't in her 30s any longer. If Jasmine doesn't enjoy her life now, when will she be enjoying? Jasmine feels a bit depressed that there isn't much time for her and her husband Justin to have a good rest away from their busy work schedules. Jasmine has got a helper each week doing cleaning and washing but doing weekly shopping and cooking regularly were both tiring enough for Jasmine and Justin. Justin is a very good husband. He is doing his bits. Nevertheless, they would have both enjoyed themselves if they had a bit more time off for themselves. Jasmine cannot make a complaint during the next two years. It was Jasmine's own decision to teach Felix law once a week. Jasmine takes a deep breath before she starts dressing up for the evening. Jasmine looks at herself in the mirror. She looks exhausted. It was a long day. Never mind, she enjoyed teaching Felix. Poor thing, he won't be here for supper. Jasmine puts perfume on her wrists. She is ready for tonight's celebration. Jasmine smiles at her reflection on the mirror. She'll be fine tonight overcoming her exhaustion once she is downstairs in their cosy kitchen in the company of her darling husband Justin and their altruistic guest Steve.

Steve arrives at the Goodmans's home on time. He buzzes the door bell. Justin opens the door in his casual trousers and shirt he wears indoors. He has 5 o'clock shadows on his face. Justin looks run down which is unusual as he usually makes a special effort to look good to Steve and Jasmine at weekends.

'Hi Steve, come on in please.'

'You look drained, Justin.'

'I'm a bit tired, Steve. Sorry, I didn't have any time to change. I don't look my best this evening.'

'Don't worry, Justin! We know each other for ages. You don't need to look gorgeous all the time. You're a human being like me. Forget about being smart each time I visit you both.'

'Thanks for your tolerance of my shabbiness.'

'Don't be silly! You don't look shabby at all. Where are we going now?'

'Let's go to the kitchen straightway. You must be hungry.'

'I'm starving. Are we going to have your old wine tonight?'

'Yes, I've taken a bottle of wine from the cellar. I'll be opening it in a minute. We'll have it with the grilled fish.'

'Where is Jasmine?'

'Jasmine must be upstairs. She'll be here soon.'

'I'm here actually. Hi, Steve! Have a sit. You look very well. How are you?'

'To tell you the truth, I am exhausted as always. However, I feel happy today. Felix is on his way to learn how to fly soon with his two wings.'

'You sound optimistic for Felix.'

'I am sure Felix will be flying soon over the mountains of difficulties he has been facing all his life time.'

'We both hope so, don't we Justin?'

'Yes, we hope so. I am the one, who should feel more responsible for Felix's wellbeing than anyone else. I have introduced Felix to you both. If I didn't bring Felix home last week, neither of you would have any responsibility to teach Felix at weekends. I hope you won't regret for the decisions you've made unexpectedly. Otherwise, I'll feel bad about myself for ruining your entire weekends.'

'Ruining our weekends?'

'Both of you have committed yourselves in Felix's success. If you didn't meet Felix, you would have more time for yourselves today?'

'I am not complaining about my life, Justin.'

'You never complain about anything, Steve. I am only revealing you both how I feel. I've spoiled your weekends.'

'Stop feeling guilty! In two years time, Felix will be completely independent. None of us needs to worry about Felix. It's only a temporary arrangement. It isn't a life time commitment, is it?'

'No, it isn't. Nevertheless, the two years' time is long enough to feel overwhelmed.'

'Let's forget about that and focus on what we have got tonight in order to cheer up ourselves. You look fabulous Jasmine! I bet you are the only one, who doesn't feel tired among us.'

'I wish I could agree with you.'

'Do you feel tired then?'

'I do. There is no point in highlighting how tired I am. I'd rather occupy my mind with the soothing atmosphere of a meal time than mourning about anything. Let's have our meal now.'

'Both of you have surprised me tonight. I've never seen any of you making a complaint about exhaustion.'

'We aren't making a complaint about anything, Steve. We only disclose our moods with transparency. That's all!'

'I appreciate that.'

'The grilled fish need to be eaten in a cheerful mood tonight.'

'I can't wait for the grilled fish. Where is it?'

'It is in the oven. Let me get our meal out of the oven.'

'Let me open the wine.'

'Let me enjoy the wine and the fish tonight.'

'That's what you're expected to do tonight, Steve.'

'That's the easy bit. I can thoroughly enjoy myself.'

'Enjoy yourself Steve. Here it is, have a sip from the good old wine.'

'Let me try it.'

'How is the taste of the wine?'

'Superb! It's fruity. I can taste the grapes. Is it produced in 1930s?'

'It's longer than that. It was produced in 1926, actually.'

'Where did you get this old wine?'

'I have inherited it from my dad. The wine is older than me.'

'Was your dad knowledgeable about wine?'

'My dad owned a vineyard in South of France.'

'You're kidding me?'

'No, I am not. I have inherited about 1000 good old wines from my father. I didn't touch them until I got married to Jasmine.'

'You had never offered me any old good wine before? Why was that?'

'I hardly touch the old good wines except for our anniversaries and birthdays.'

'I see. Tonight, I'm honoured to taste the wine which was produced in your father's vineyard out of passion more than anything else, I suppose.'

'You can certainly say that. My dad was very passionate about his wine business. Although he had hardly drunk any wine he had enjoyed owning a vineyard and kept most of the wines produced with the best quality of grapes from his vineyard in his cellar to pass them onto the next generation.'

'In this case, it was you who had inherited your father's wine collection.'

'That's true and I have inherited the old wines from my dad. My dad's ambition was to have a large family with plenty of children. Unfortunately, my mum wasn't able to conceive more than one child. So they only had me. I ended up having a very good stock of wines as I am the only heir.'

'That's very interesting.'

'It's part of my life history.'

'How long did your dad live?'

'He died in his 90s. I was born when he was 50. My dad had a good life. He lived long enough to enjoy himself.'

'I should imagine so.'

'When we met at high school, was your dad still alive then?'

'Yes, my dad was still alive.'

'It's a shame you had never introduced me to your parents.'

'Somehow, they were too busy with their own lives. My mother had a big garden which had taken up most of her time. My dad had two businesses to keep an eye on at the same time. One was his vineyard in South of France, the other one was property letting agency he owned in London. There was no time left for my parents to entertain their guests let alone inviting my friends around for a meal or so.'

'I imagine you were brought up in a big house.'

'It was a country house with a very large land.'

'What did you do with the land and the country house?'

'I sold them out. I had spent most of the money for setting up my business and going around the world before meeting Jasmine.'

'We lost in touch for a few years. Did you go on a world tour at that time, Justin?'

'Yes, that was the time I had taken some time off to enjoy myself, Steve.'

'Why didn't you tell me that?'

'I didn't tell anybody that I was going to go on a world tour. It was so personal. I didn't even tell Jasmine about my 2 years adventure I had around the world.'

'I didn't know you went around the world on your own, dear.'

'I am sorry, Jasmine. I forgot to tell you all about my 2 years adventure abroad. We had so many things to talk about since we got married. There was no time for me to tell you about my world tour. I'll tell you all about it, if you are prepared to listen to a very long story, darling.'

'Yes, I'd very much like to hear about your world tour. Maybe you can tell me all about it on our holiday, Justin.'

'When are you taking your holiday?'

'In two months time, we'll be off to enjoy a week holiday in Bournemouth.'

'How nice! I wish I could go on a week holiday now, actually. I need a break.'

'We all need a well deserved break. Let's have our supper, now.'

'Good appetite!'

'I'll have this superb wine to our good days!'

'To our health!'

'Cheers!'

Jasmine puts the grilled tuna and vegetables with roast potatoes in their plates. They all start having their meals with plenty of salads and a glass of wine. Steve gives tips to Justin and Jasmine about dyslexic learner's need. Steve leaves earlier than usual time as he needs to build up his energy for next day. Justin and Jasmine clear the dinner table quickly and go to bed around 9.00 o'clock.

Felix goes to bed with the good feeling of being cared and loved unconditionally. Felix asks himself whether he could treat someone in the same way Justin, Jasmine and Steve have been treating him. Felix doesn't have an answer to his question. Felix had never been in a situation that he could dedicate his time and energy to another human being. Neither the family Goodmans nor Steve had their own children. That must be the reason they've all taken the role of adopting Felix as their own child, perhaps. Justin brought a telly for Felix. He left his own watch for Felix to wear. Jasmine got Felix a walkman and a mobile phone. Felix would have never accepted all the generosity they have been showering Felix with, if Felix wasn't in need. Then again, why should they have helped Felix, if Felix had everything in his life? They have been good to Felix out of their compassion. Felix felt that he would be grateful to Justin and Jasmine for their generosity and kindness till the rest of his life. Felix makes his mind that he will be in touch with the Goodmans and Steve even long after standing on his own feet without any need for their support. How good it will be for Felix to visit them with presents. Felix closes his eyes. He starts practising the visualisation technique Steve taught him. Felix walks down the River Thames again with his sketch book and pens. By the River Thames, Felix starts sketching what he sees around him. The River Thames and the trees fill up Felix's drawing pad. There are plenty of sketches in Felix's sketch book. Each time Felix draws the River Thames, the trees and the buildings reflect on the river. Felix feels so happy that he concludes his day with what he observes in his environment by the river; he falls asleep with ease.

After having a lively supper with Jasmine and Justin, Steve comes back home. He takes a warm shower. Steve quickly dries up his body and hair. He covers his belly with a large towel. He goes to his bedroom and wears his pyjamas. Steve goes to the kitchen and makes a mug of herbal tea. Steve takes the biscuit tin and his tea to the living room. Steve puts the biscuit tin on the coffee table. He opens the biscuit tin and takes a bonbon biscuit out of the tin. Steve sits down in his armchair next to the coffee table. While Steve is having his tea he starts thinking about Justin's marriage with Jasmine. They both look happy living together. Nevertheless, they are far too busy with their professional commitments. Justin didn't tell Jasmine about the 2 years world tour he went before meeting Jasmine. Justin and Jasmine have been inviting Steve each weekend for supper. Just recently, they've also taken on an additional responsibility of teaching Felix at weekends. There isn't much time left for Justin and Jasmine to enjoy each other's company. How thoughtless Steve has been to accept Justin's invitation for supper each week, which has almost turned into a routine. If Steve had something to do at weekend and he couldn't make it, Justin and Jasmine called Steve and asked why Steve didn't come around for Sunday dinner. Steve felt difficult to turn down the family Goodmans's invitations for supper each week. Steve compares his life with Justin's. Steve has been a bachelor since the world go. If Steve met someone nice to get marry, he wouldn't be able to make his wife happy. She would have been lonely within a marriage life. There isn't enough time left for Steve to have a short break for himself let alone taking care of his wife. If Steve isn't able to make his wife happy, his marriage will suffer in the long run. It was a good job that he didn't rush into a marriage for the sake of it. Justin and Jasmine had different life circumstances. They both had fallen in love with each other and getting married was the extension of their emotional bond they have developed in due course. Steve hopes that Justin's marriage will never suffer as a result of his professional commitments. Perhaps, Steve should give them a break. Instead of visiting Justin and Jasmine each week, he should reduce his visit to once a month. Justin and Jasmine will have some time off for themselves. Steve sips the last drop of his herbal tea from his mug. He chews the last piece of the bonbon biscuit. He loves bonbon biscuits since he was a kid. His mother had bought Steve bonbon biscuits with a chocolate layer between the two biscuits. Steve had eaten bonbon biscuits with warm milk as a child every night before going to bed. When Steve reached his adulthood, he couldn't kick off his childhood habit of having bonbon biscuits each night before going to sleep. It's like having comfort food regularly. Steve takes his empty tea mug to the kitchen. He washes the mug under the running tap. He goes to the bathroom and brushes his teeth. Steve goes to his bedroom with the nice feeling of hot herbal tea and the bonbon biscuits in his stomach. He gets under the clean bed duvet. Steve's helper Anastasia changes Steve's duvet cover and the bed sheet every week for him. It's like having his mother around. Steve's mother looked after him till she was too old to take care of Steve. Since Steve's mother has moved into the residential home, Steve has been hiring a helper to do his cleaning and washing for him once a week. Steve's helper Anastasia has got a spare door key and she is responsible for all the domestic duties Steve has assigned for her such as ironing his shirts, hovering, dusting, cleaning bathroom and toilet regularly. The only thing Steve has to do is to cook his dinner after work. That isn't a big deal. Steve manages cooking easy meal like pasta, rice and some vegetable dishes. Steve thinks about the fish Jasmine grilled for supper tonight. It was good to have a meal prepared by someone else although Steve can grill fish, if he has got more time at weekends. Steve closes his eyes and visualises himself in a seaside resort.

Jasmine wakes up earlier than Justin and their kitten Fanny. She quietly dresses up and goes down to the kitchen. Jasmine makes a pastry filled with vegetables. She knows that Justin likes pastry with tea for breakfast. The smell of the pastry fills the kitchen. Jasmine fills the breakfast table with butter, cheese, tomatoes, cucumber, bread and pastry she has just made. Justin is woken up by the smell of the pastry coming from the kitchen downstairs. Justin smiles with the pleasure of knowing Jasmine cares about him. Jasmine always does that when Justin feels a bit down. Justin's loves Jasmine's pastry which he can't do as he lacks the necessary skill for baking. That is the only thing Justin couldn't accomplish in the kitchen. Making pastry has always been Jasmine's speciality. Justin gets up and changes himself. He goes to the bathroom. Justin takes a quick shower. He shaves himself. Justin feels afresh once he applies after shave on his face. Today, Justin makes a special effort to look good for making up with Jasmine. She has been a very good wife and a life-long friend for Justin. He has no right to let her down with his tiredness. Justin goes to the kitchen. Jasmine is sitting down on one of the chairs and reading a newspaper. On seeing Justine, Jasmine puts the newspaper down and smiles at Justin wholeheartedly.

'Good morning darling. Did I wake you up?'

'I've smelt the pastry, dear. I've got strong sense of smell for food.'

'I'm glad that your sense of smell is strong. Shall we have our breakfast now?'

'I can't wait for it. Let me brew the tea.'

'Would you like salami?'

'I prefer pastry today.'

'I'll have pastry as well.'

'The tea is ready. Let me pour you some tea, dear.'

'Thank you Justin. You look fresh today.'

'Do I?'

'Yes you do. Did you sleep well?'

'Yes, I slept very well, my dear. I was going to suggest you that we should take a long walk by the river. The weather is so nice.'

'What about your case you need to work on, Justin?'

'It'll wait till we come back from our walk. We'll catch up with the beauty of the early morning.'

'If that won't spoil your schedule, I'll be more than happy to go for a long walk with you.'

'We'll have lunch outside by the river.'

'That'll be nice.'

'It'll be good to have whole morning and lunchtime outside without doing anything so that we can take our minds off from our weekly schedule. Yesterday, we missed out on our walk as we needed to teach Felix. We should re-schedule our weekend program. We need to spend more time together. Otherwise, our marriage will suffer.'

'I've got the same worry actually. Let's stick to a new schedule from today onwards. On Sundays, we'll have time off for each other but nothing else.'

'That's what we need to do.'

'Look, Fanny is here.'

'Fanny, come on in, dear.'

'Fanny must have smelt the pastry.'

'She doesn't eat pastry though.'

'I'll put her food in her plate.'

'That's a good idea.'

After having breakfast with high spirit, Justin and Jasmine go out for a long walk. They walk by the River Thames. They feed the birds, swans, ducks and geese with the two bags of wholemeal bread. Justin and Jasmine feel so happy with each other's company as though they were being on their honeymoon again. There is nothing bothering them any longer. They rebuilt their trust for each other's commitments to their togetherness. Justin and Jasmine are in harmony as they have overcome their daily worries which had strained their marriage beyond their control. They enter the boat restaurant over the River Thames and sit down in the open area of the boat with the tables and chairs. They can see the river with the swans and ducks swimming peacefully. The sun is warming up them generously. Justin and Jasmine order their meals. While they are waiting for their meal to arrive, Justin and Jasmine start making plans for their future.

'I like the tranquillity of the river. It's so nice to have a meal on the boat restaurant.'

'It's nice to be very close to the nature.'

'I wish we had a meal on the boat each week, Justin.'

'Nothing is preventing us from taking up the pleasure of having our meal on the boat restaurant. We can come here every week, if this makes you happy, darling.'

'To have a meal on the boat restaurant will be a delightful treat for us. As a matter of fact, I was thinking that we ought to buy not only a cottage in the countryside but also a small sailing boat.'

'What for?'

'We'll have our meals on the boat during the spring and summer time.'

'That had never occurred to me, Jasmine. It's a fantastic idea. Buying a sailing boat should be our mutual target to hit.'

'Hitting our target isn't that simple in practice.'

'What do you mean?'

'From the financial point of view, we can't stretch ourselves to buy a cottage and a sailing boat before selling our cottage in London. We have to wait till we get retired.'

'We can't wait that long. We're already in our 50s. We need to find a solution now.'

'How?'

'Our old wine bottles in the cellar will resolve our financial problems.'

'The old wine bottles!'

'We hardly drink wine, Jasmine.'

'So what?'

'We ought to put the old wines into auction to raise some cash for our short term goals.'

'Put the old wines into auction?'

'I am sure, there will be a lot of wine merchants up there who will be more than happy to buy our old wines with a good price.'

'How much do you reckon we can get for each bottle?'

'I don't know yet. I'll be doing a bit of research on it. If our old wines fetch a good price in auction, we'll have enough money to buy a cottage and a small sailing boat. So we don't need to wait till we reach our retirement age. We'll be too old to enjoy ourselves at the age 70.'

'Do you think it's feasible to ponder around your idea?'

'Yes it's perfectly feasible. We've nothing to lose after all.'

'That's true.'

'When are you going to do research on wine auctions?'

'As soon as possible.'

'I can't wait to hear the good news that we'll be able to sell all our wines and buy our cottage with a sailing boat before reaching our retirement.'

'We need to be practical. We wouldn't be able to consume all those wines even we live another 50 years or so. How much wine did we consume since we got married?'

'For our birthdays and our wedding anniversary, we consumed three wine bottles each year. We have been married for 10 years. We consumed 30 wine bottles so far.'

'We consumed another wine bottle yesterday for the special occasion. 31 wine bottles out of 1000 are considered below average wine consumptions per household.'

'We've still got 969 wine bottles left.'

'We can't consume them during our lifetimes. There is no one to leave our old good wines. We need to sell them and make a good use of the money out of auction sale. How strange it is that we've never thought about it before.'

'We never needed extra money for us to do something with it. That's why we didn't look at the potential fortune we've been keeping in our cellar for years. Look at us we've been working so hard all those years without having an extra luxury in our lives while our good old wines are all staying in the cellar without making any difference in our lives, Justin.'

'You're right, my dear. We must do something about our unused financial resource. We need to turn it into cash.'

'That's what our priority should be, Jasmine.'

'It was good to explore our options when we thought we were stuck in life.'

'It was very good to feel we were stuck. Otherwise, we wouldn't think of turning the gold into a usable asset for us to enjoy. The gold doesn't mean anything unless we benefit from it. After all, a piece of gold is only a piece of metal but nothing more than that. The wine is the same. It is a liquid. It'll have money value if we find the people who are able to appreciate the old and the good quality of wine.'

'You can say that again, my dear.'

Justin and Jasmine spent their Sunday wondering around the possibilities of increasing their lifestyle before it'll be too late for them to enjoy their lives in full. The new ideas for their near future unite Justin and Jasmine under the same objective. They go back home with plenty of inspirations for increasing their well-beings as a happy couple with the potential of making things happen for themselves instead of postponing them for the indefinite time period. Justin and Jasmine realise the limitation of their mortality. There isn't much time left for them to waste. Whatever they wish to do with their lives, it needs to be done soon but not later on. Otherwise, their dreams cannot be turned into reality. The more practical solutions they generate the more happiness they experience by varying their everyday routine with unusual commitments. Without being practical, nothing can be achieved in life that was what Justin and Jasmine have explored on their Sunday outing while they were having their meal on the boat restaurant.

Steve gets up early at around 7.00 o'clock in the morning. He turns on the radio and finds the classical music channel. Vivaldi's *"The Four Seasons"* satisfies Steve's auditory stimulation with the nice tune touching his heart and mind at the same time. He has breakfast with scramble egg, fried mushrooms, fried tomatoes and two slices of wholemeal toasts in the living room. Steve clears the breakfast table. He turns off the radio and opens his briefcase. He takes off the vocabulary lists for Felix's maths and law studies. Steve starts designing Felix's language support plan. He turns the vocabulary lists into small manageable chunks. Steve prepares his lesson plan for Felix's language support session until lunch time without having any break. At lunch time, he stops working and goes to the kitchen. Steve gets the broccoli and courgette out of the fridge. Steve boils the broccoli for 3 minutes. He takes the half-ripen broccoli out of the boiling pan and uses the water as vegetable stock for boiling spaghetti. Steve peels the courgette and cuts it into small cubes. Steve puts the courgette into the frying pan. He sprinkles a bit of olive oil over the chopped courgette. Steve stirs fries the courgette cubes quickly and chops the fresh tomatoes with parsley. He adds them all into the courgette cubes with the broccoli pieces. Steve gives them all a quick stir. The spaghetti is soft and ready to be eaten. Steve turns off the cooker. He puts the boiled spaghetti on a dinner plate. Steve places the vegetable mix on top of spaghetti and puts two spoonfuls of pro-biotic fat free natural yoghurt next to the spaghetti. Steve takes his dinner plate to the living room. He leaves his dinner plate on the table. Steve goes back to the kitchen and gets the grape juice from the fridge. Steve takes a glass from the cupboard. He pours the grape juice into the glass and goes back to the living room. Steve turns on the radio with the music channel. He tucks into his spaghetti with a glass of grape juice. Steve starts thinking about the afternoon session with Felix. It'll be better to leave home a bit earlier than he had planned. Steve can have the whole evening to get ready for the next week. Steve finishes his lunch. He clears the table and goes back to his bedroom. He wears a clean white shirt Anastasia ironed for him and a pair of cappuccino colour velvet trousers with the dark brown velvet jacket which goes well with a pair of light brown socks. Steve combs his hair and picks up his briefcase with the teaching materials. Steve gets the cappuccino colour shoes from the shoe cupboard to wear next. He is ready to leave his home for another teaching day. When Steve arrives at the train station, it is 1.30 p.m. Steve's train arrives on time. He gets on the train and sits by the window. Steve puts his suitcase on the table slowly and starts gazing out of the window. It is such a nice day. He opens his briefcase. Steve takes out the language support material he had designed for Felix. Steve quickly scans through the 5 words he gathered for Felix's weekly spelling programme in law. Felix needs to study hard. He has to practice the spelling procedure "LSCWC" to remember not only 5 words for his law studies but 5 words for the mathematical expressions too. Steve thinks that learning 10 words for each week won't overload Felix's short-term memory. Learning words based on letter recognition as a whole word rather than learning through decoding by letter-sound blending will be easier for Felix to remember as Felix's phonological deficits are so high and no amount of teaching phonemes will help him to use sub-lexical letter and sound correspondence. How non-dyslexic children learn reading at their early stages through oral exercises with phonemes isn't suitable for Felix. He'll get confused with the phonemes. That was why Steve needed to design a language support program which differentiates Felix's individual learning needs based on his phonological deficits. Steve knows that some of his dyslexic learners made little progress when taught phonically and he had to use whole-word methods in order to remedy their lack of phonic awareness.

Steve prepares the following table for Felix's 1st week Spelling Programme. He puts LSCWC and what it stands for on the first row of Felix's practice sheet for the legal terminology in order to remind Felix the steps he needs to follow for reinforcement of his working memory.

Felix's Weekly Practice Sheet for Legal Terminology (Week1)

LSCWC = Look, **S**ay, **C**over, **W**rite, **C**heck

Problematic Words	Mon	Tue	Wed	Thu	Fri
Prosecution pro/se/cu/tion					
Defendant de/fend/ant					

Plea p/lea					
Verdict ver/dict					
Trial t/ri/al					
Jury ju/ry					

Steve had picked up the simple numerical expressions for Felix to practice with as a starting point. The complicated expressions can be built up on this numerical skeleton gradually without putting too much pressure on Felix's short term memory. Steve needs to monitor Felix's progress regularly and adjust his learning materials in accordance with Felix's changing needs. Teaching a dyslexic learner needs to be flexible as it is not possible to get to know the learner's difficulties in details during the 1st diagnostic tests. Language support needs to be updated regularly in line with the learner's motivation, progression and sometimes regression when a certain learning strategy isn't suitable for the dyslexic learner's learning preferences.

Felix's Weekly Practice Sheet for Mathematical Expressions (Week1)

LSCWC = Look, **S**ay, **C**over, **W**rite, **C**heck

Problematic Words	Mon	Tue	Wed	Thu	Fri
Approximation ap/prox/ima/tion					
Capacity ca/pa/city					
Decimal De/cim/al					
Estimate es/ti/mate					

Integer in/te/ger					

In half an hour time, Steve's train reaches its destination. Steve gets off the train and walks for 10 minutes from the train station to the prison, where Felix is staying. When Steve comes to the prison, the prison warden takes Steve to Felix's room again. Steve gives a knock on Felix's door. Felix opens the door. The prison warden goes back to his office. Steve enters Felix's room.

'Hello Felix! I've arrived a bit earlier than yesterday. I hope you don't mind.'

'Not at all.'

'How are you today, Felix?'

'I am very well, thank you.'

'Good! We've got an hour today. I'll be teaching you a spelling methodology which is called **LSCWC.** Have you heard anything about LSCWC before?

'I am afraid I haven't heard anything about LSCWC before.'

'That's all right. I'll explain to you what LSCWC stands for. The letter **L** stands for Look, **S** stands for Say, **C** stands for Cover, **W** stands for Write and **C** stands for Check.'

'Look, Say, Cover, Write, Check'

'Precisely! You know what LSCWC stands for. It isn't difficult to grasp the spelling procedure. I've already prepared a practice paper for you to experiment with LSCWC during the week on your own till you are confident in your spelling practice. Can you spare certain amount of time for your spelling practice each day?'

'How long will it take to practise with LSCWC?'

'It depends on you. Some people need to practise 4 times a week; some people need to practise 7 days a week. Let's say, you practise with LSCWC for 5 days. When I come here on Saturday, I'll give you a spelling test and see how well you learn spelling of new words through practising with LSCWC. Is that OK with you?'

'That's fine.'

'I need to explain to you the procedure you need to follow while you are practising LSCWC. Would you like me to start the session, Felix?'

'Yes, please.'

'First of all, you need to look at the word and find out what makes it difficult for you to spell the word correctly.'

'I'll be looking at the word and see what makes the word difficult for me to spell.'

'Precisely! I'll be teaching you strategies to memorise the pattern of the words.'

'Do I need to have a paper and pen for that?'

'Yes, you need a notebook, black pen and colour pens. I've brought you a notebook for your spelling exercises. Here you are. In this notebook, you'll be analysing the word visually, you can chunk it, you might link it to your known words, you might be looking at the structure of the word, or you might be using colour coding for the tricky bit of the word to remember better. I'll be teaching you each strategy you can experiment with.'

'Thanks.'

'I'll write here the summary of what I've told you now. When you are experimenting with LSCWC, you can refer to.

<u>Strategies to memorise the pattern of the words</u>

1. Visually analyse
2. Chunk
3. Link to known words
4. Look at structure / morphology
5. Colour code the tricky bit

Is that clear to you, Felix?'

'I couldn't understand the morphology bit.'

'That means the structure of a word. I'll be explaining to you in details with examples on the spelling programme. Don't worry about it too much now.'

'OK, then.'

'In your first practice sheets, I've given some examples how you analyse the word. You could do your own analysis in the way it is easier for you to remember. Once you find a way to remember the structure of the word, you need to say the word slowly to yourself in order to hear the sound of the word.'

'I need to say the word to hear the sound of it.'

'That's right! Then, you need to cover the word.'

'I'll do that.'

'When you cover the word, try to visualise it in your mind's eye as well as saying it aloud so that you can hear the sound of the word at the same time. Is that clear?'

'There is no problem. I can visualise the word. You thought me how to do that yesterday.'

'That's good. The last step is to write the word from your memory without looking at the word in your list. Then you can check it whether you remember it accurately or you need to practise with it a bit longer time till you remember it correctly.'

'I'll do that.'

'Each week I'll be giving you a spelling test to check your progress. How do you feel about taking a spelling test each week regularly?'

'I don't mind.'

'At the end of the 2nd week, I'll be giving you dictation with the words you practise spelling strategies to learn. Is everything clear?'

'Everything is clear.'

'Let's have a look at your lists for law and maths now. I minimised the words for each subject to 5 for each week as I do not want to overload your short term memory. Otherwise, you'll get confused. Let's have a look at the legal terminology now. I'll read them to you one by one.'

Legal Terminology

The Prosecution
1) the act of bringing criminal charges against someone
2) the institution & conduct of legal proceedings against a person
3) the lawyers acting for the Crown to put the case against a person

The Defendant
a person accused of crime

To plea
1) an emotional appeal
2) a statement by or on behalf of a defendant
3) an excuse

Verdict

1) the decision made by a Jury about the guilt or innocence of a defendant
2) an opinion formed after examining the facts

Trial
A formal examination of evidence by a judge, typically before a jury, in order to decide guilt in a case of criminal or civil proceedings

Jury/Juries
a group of usually 12 people sworn to deliver a true verdict according to the evidence upon a case presented in a court of law

'That's all for your law studies today.'

'Thanks for reading them all to me.'

'Is there anything that you haven't understood?'

'I couldn't get **evidence**. What does *evidence* mean?'

'You can add that word in your next spelling list. Do you understand **proof**?'

'Not really!'

'Proof or evidence means something tangible like a piece of material that Jury members can be satisfied with while they are making a decision whether a person is guilty or not. Does it make any sense to you?'

'Yes, it does.'

'Very good! Let's have a look at the mathematical expressions now. I'll read them all for you, shall I?'

'Yes please.'

'Here we are!'

Mathematical Expressions

Approximation
A result that is not exact but sufficiently close to be useful in a practical context.

Capacity
Volume, a measure in three-dimensional space, applied to liquids, materials that can be poured. Unit includes cubic centimetres cm, cubic metres m3. A litre is 1000 cm3 – the volume of 1kg water.

Decimal
Relating to base ten

Estimate
To arrive at a rough answer by calculating with suitable approximations for numbers or in measurement by using previous experience.

Integer
Any of the positive or negative numbers including 0, 1, 2, -2, -1

'How did you find the mathematical terminology, Felix?'

'It's OK.'

'Have you got any question to ask me?'

'When is the right time for me to practise LCWC, in the mornings or at night time before going to bed?'

'This is entirely up to you, Felix. Some people prefer working early mornings as they feel alert to take in information. Some people prefer practising LCWC before going to sleep as they condition their mind to remember the given information by sleeping over the words. Sleeping process enables them to reinforce remembering the words through your subconscious. I suggest you practise LSCWC before going to sleep. When you wake up, you can practise with LSCWC once more. Practising LSCWC twice a day will enhance the capacity of your short-term memory. This will guarantee 100 percent rate of recall. You can minimise memory blockage.'

'I'll practise with LCWC twice a day.'

'Good. I've prepared your ILSP. I'll be reading your Individual Learning Support Programme for you. If you agree with the conditions outlined in your ILSP, you need to sign it for me.'

'That's fine!'

'I am prepared to do regular exercises in order to maximise my learning capacity during the language learning programme. I agree to spend --------- hours each week.

I left the blank line deliberately. Could you tell me how many hours you can spend on your private study during the week, Felix?'

'What do you suggest?'

'It depends on you. You can study as much as you like. There is no limit for it.'

'Can I say an hour each day for 5 days?'

'You are prepared to spend 5 hours for your private study. Is that correct?'

'Yes.'

'I've put the number of hours here. Now you can sign the ILSP.'

'Where should I sign?'

'Please sign here, underneath of your name.'

'Why do I need to sign this paper?'

'We are both committing ourselves into the language support programme. This paper will enable us both to stick what we've originally decided to do from the day 1. If you don't practise what you've agreed to do, I am afraid the language support programme won't work. You won't be able to benefit from the programme. The language support programme can only work if you commit yourself into the written contract with 100 percent of good will. Otherwise, it'll be waste of time for you and for me. I'll be photocopying this agreement. Each of us will have a copy to keep. I'll bring your copy next week.'

'Thanks'

'Would you like me to give you a spelling test before you start practising the LSCWC methodology? That will be sufficient enough for both of us to find out whether or not the words in your practice sheet are already in your sight vocabulary.'

'Yes, I'll take the test.'

'Have a look at your list quickly now. When you are ready, please let me know, Felix.'

'I'm ready.'

'Could you write **Trial Jury**?'

'tiral juri'

'Next one is **Defendant**'

'defindind'

'Another one is **Verdict**'

'virdeckt'

'Could you write **Prosecution**?

'pirusequsin'

'Next one is **Plea**?

'pely'

'Let me see the spelling paper. Could you give me your paper please?'

'Here it is.'

'Thanks. I am glad that none of the words are in you sight vocabulary yet. That means, it'll be worthwhile for you to practise with LCWC methodology.'

'How am I going to learn how to spell each word correctly?'

'Let's analyse your errors now.'

'How?'

'I'd like you to spot your errors. This is the list of the correct words. Take the list. On another paper, please write down each word you've spelt incorrectly. You can add the correct spelling of each word next to the misspelt word.'

'Shall I write the correct words first?'

'Write down each word with large letters. So we can see the errors clearly.'

Felix copies the correct words from the list prepared by Steve. Then he writes his incorrect spelling of the words next to the correct spelling of the words. Felix shows the paper to Steve.

Trial Jury   *tiral juri*

'Good. Can you spot what errors you've made, Felix?'

'I add **i** between **t** and **r** in trial.'

'What else have you done?'

'I dropped **i** between **r** and **a** in trial.

'What do you need to remember when you are going to practise the correct spelling of trial?'

'I need to drop **i** between **t** and **r** in **trial**.'

'What else?'

'I need to add **i** between **r** and **a**.'

'If you chunk the word into 3, it'll be easier for you to see the missing word clearly. Would you like to use colour pen now?'

'Colour pen?'

'If you use a colour pen for the missing letter, you will remember the missing letter while you are memorising the spelling pattern of the word.'

Felix chunks the word and uses red colour for **i** in the middle.

tr   **i**   al

'That's better. You do the spelling error analysis yourself now. Please think aloud. So that I can hear what you think while you are analysing your spelling error.'

Felix repeats the same procedure for spelling analysis by copying the correct words from the list prepared by Steve. Then he writes his incorrect spelling of the words next to the correct spelling of the words as follows and shows the paper to Steve when he starts analysing his error aloud.

Jury   *juri*

'I dropped **y** and I added **i** in **Jury**. If I dropped **i** and add **j**, I'll get the correct spelling of Jury like this:

Ju   r   y

I used the red pen to remind me my missing word **y**.'

'That's good. You have got the idea how you are going to analyse your spelling errors and how you are going to work out a strategy to memorise the spelling pattern of each word you have misspelt. I'll leave you the rest of the strategies to work out yourself. It's the end of the session. I must go now. I hope to see you next week, young man. Shall we say at the same time on Saturday?'

'That's fine.'

'How did you find today's session?'

'I've enjoyed it.'

'Good. Keep well, Felix. See you next week.'

'Many thanks for your help. See you next week, Steve.'

Steve leaves the prison building slowly with the full satisfaction of teaching a dyslexic learner knowing that all the learning strategies will be enhancing Felix's learning within short time. After a pleasant train journey back home, Steve decides to prepare his supper a few hours earlier than usual. Steve takes off the marinated chicken from its plastic bag before placing it on an oven tray without any need to wash or marinate the chicken. Nowadays, domestic life has been simplified for bachelors like himself. Steve goes to his living room and turns on the telly while he is waiting for his supper to be cooked slowly. Steve focuses on the programme about the migrant rare birds visiting Britain. The programme is very interesting. Steve feels an urge to go to the countryside on his annual leave once more. Steve likes living in a city with art museums, art galleries and concert halls but he wouldn't mind living in a countryside surrounded with the pleasant wildlife. Watching the wild birds in the countryside instead of seeing them only on the telly must have a mood enhancing effect on anyone's emotional well-being. The smell of the roasting chicken travels from the kitchen to the living room within an hour time and activates Steve's appetite for feeding himself properly. Steve gets up and checks the oven whether everything is fine or not. He opens the oven and pierces the chicken with the sharp fork. It hasn't cooked yet. Steve picks up a glass from the cupboard and opens the fridge. Steve takes out the grape juice from the fridge and pours himself a glass of grape juice. Steve throws away the empty juice cartoon and goes back to the living room with a glass of grape juice. He sits in his armchair opposite the telly. Another programme about small species on earth starts. Steve finds it fascinating to watch a caterpillar making his home on a wide and thick leaf. The caterpillar designs a circle with the chemical produced by his body and starts cutting the circle quickly and carefully without making any mistake at night in the dark. The TV presenter makes a comment that caterpillars prefer making their own home at night as other species couldn't possibly see them. Once the leaf is cut out, a caterpillar is able to stay inside the leaf which is turned into a shelter to protect them from the dangerous specious outside. Steve starts wondering about how caterpillars' minds work. How do caterpillars acquire the skills for building shelters for themselves and survive in the nature? How competent many creatures are to survive without much difficulty! It's only us, human beings who aren't equipped with all the survival skills animals possess by instinct. When it comes to the manual skills, Steve describes himself useless. Steve can't fix a leaking tap. He can't even unblock the kitchen sink let alone designing and building his home. Steve needs to take training how to use tools for construction. Even building a simple hut to stay on a temporary basis might be a very daunting task for him. How skilful the tiny caterpillar is! It must have taken him only a few hours to design and construct his accommodation without any help from anyone. Building a home requires skills to be learnt by human beings whereas caterpillars' building skills are innate. Thank goodness, Steve can afford to employ other people who have already acquired skills in specific areas. Otherwise, it would have been too difficult for him to survive. Steve has spent a very nice evening. He has learnt a lot about some creatures' survival skills. Steve remembers Felix's situation. Felix didn't have a chance to attain much skill for reading and writing. It must be very hard for Felix not to be able to figure out the written language. Felix has been relying on other people's good will so far. This isn't practical. Felix needs to be self-sufficient. He has to learn the necessary skills to understand the written language. Steve remembers meeting many dyslexic learners without enough compensation skills for their survival in a world which is structured by written information. The alarm clock in the kitchen goes off which reminds him of the chicken he left in the oven to be roasted. The dinner must be ready. Steve goes to the kitchen quickly and checks the oven. The chicken looks crispy. He turns off the oven. Steve makes some green salad with slices of tomatoes. Steve puts the two slices of wholemeal bread into the toaster and lays the dinner table in the living room to have his supper. The programme on natural habitat finishes. Steve switches off the telly and sits at the dinner table quietly. How nice to enjoy a well-prepared supper in peace!

Justin has done extensive research on wine auctions during his lunch breaks at the beginning of a new week. He has got plenty of information about the worldwide sales. Justin has just learnt that Sotheby is specialised in the finest wine cellars for the global market. Justin is amazed to find out that a superb private collection of rare and old wine fetched $2.9 million in London in 1998. Outstanding Bordeaux and Burgundy from an important private cellar fetched $6.1 million in New York in Apr

1998. Justin decides to contact one of the wine auctioneers based in London. He dials the wine auctioneer's number.

'Can I speak to Mr Deluxe please?'

'Speaking.'

'This is Justin Goodman. I'm ringing to make enquiries about the wine auctions?'

'Are you interested in buying or selling wines?'

'I'd like to sell my old wine stock.'

'What type of wine do you have in stock, Mr Goodman?'

'The wines were produced in 1926 from the vineyard my dad owned. I've have inherited 1000 wine bottles. My wife and I had consumed 31 of them so far. We have still got 969 wine bottles left. We would like to sell them all. Will you be interested in buying, Mr Deluxe?'

'I certainly will. Where do you keep the wine stoke?'

'They're in our cellar.'

'Would you like me to come around and see the collection of your old wine stoke?'

'When would you like to come around?'

'When is the most convenient time for you?'

'Any evening after 7.00, you could pop in.'

'I prefer visiting cellars at weekends. Will it be possible for me to visit your cellar this coming weekend?'

'On Saturdays, my wife and I give private tuitions. We won't be at home. Could you make it on Sunday instead?'

'Sunday is fine. I can visit you on Sunday.'

'I'll send my details to your e-mail address.'

'That's a good idea. It is nice to hear from you, Mr Goodman. I hope we'll make a business together.'

'I hope so. Would you like to come over to us for a dinner?'

'I'll come for tea at 5.00 o'clock instead.'

'I look forward to meeting you at 5.00 o'clock on Sunday, Mr Deluxe.'

'See you on Sunday, Mr Goodman.'

'See you soon, Mr Deluxe.'

Justin's confidence reaches its highest point after the short telephone conversation with Mr Deluxe. Justin decides to let Jasmine know about the good news straightaway. Justin starts dialling his wife's number from his mobile phone. Jasmine answers Justin's call.

'Hi Justin! Are you OK?'

'Guess what happened?'

'What happened, dear?'

'I called the *"Deluxe Wine Auction"* a few minutes ago. I talked to Mr Deluxe. He is interested in seeing our cellar. He is coming around on Sunday.'

'Great!'

'I invited him for a meal. He can't make it. He could only stay for tea. Is that OK?'

'It's fine, dear. Did you discuss about the auction prices with him?'

'Not yet. Mr Deluxe will be seeing our cellar first. The deal will start afterwards.'

'I hope we'll get a good price for our wine bottles.'

'I have no doubt about it. Apparently, a private collection of rare and old wine fetched $2.9 million in the wine auction in New York.'

'Really! When was it?'

'It was in 1998.'

'The wine prices must have gone up since then. Ours might be even dearer.'

'I should think so. Let's wait and see what Mr Deluxe suggests.'

'You're right, darling. Let's wait and see how it goes. Have you had your lunch?'

'Not yet.'

'Now, you deserve a very good lunch. I shouldn't keep you waiting. See you this evening, Justin.'

'See you, darling.'

Justin is very happy. He starts unpacking his lunch box in cheerful mood while he is visualising their holiday cottage and the sailing boat with the money they are going to get from the wine auction soon. Justin likes the idea of having dinner on their sailing boat in the good weather. What a shame that they didn't start imagining such a beautiful dream long time ago. They should have bought their holiday cottage and sailing boat years ago. It's never too late. Jasmine and Justin will be turning their dream into a possible reality for both of them to enjoy in the near future. Perhaps, they'll celebrate their next wedding anniversary on their boat near their holiday cottage in Isle of Wight or Jersey wherever they feel the location will fit into their dreams. Justin opens the water bottle. He drinks the water in one go. Justin gets an enormous red apple and bites the crunchy apple with pleasure. While Justin is chewing the piece of a juicy apple, he imagines himself on their sailing boat with the splendid sea view. Jasmine will be so happy to have meals on the boat regularly. They might even go for a voyage around the world in their retirement. Something to look forward to, in the horizon will enable them to face their old age without getting depressed about ageing process.

Jasmine entertains herself with the idea of having their holiday cottage and sailing boat somewhere in the seaside resort as soon as she receives a phone-call from Justin. It was good to explore the possibilities of buying a second home by the seaside. If they wait till they reach their 60s or 70s, they might not be able to fulfil their dreams. It might be too late for them to start a new life or build up a new hobby for a seaside adventure. They might not be able to sail on the sea because of their age and age related diseases. They might suffer from arthritis which might prevent them from enjoying the humid climate of a seaside resort. The time was just right for them to enjoy the seaside climate. Jasmine feels she can't wait to breathe the fresh iodine coming from the sea with the breeze and the plenty of sunshine on their summer holidays.

One week passes by so quickly. On Sunday, Mr Deluxe arrives at 5.00 o'clock without any delay. Justin and Jasmine both walk towards the front door. Justin opens the door while Jasmine is standing beside him waiting to meet Mr Deluxe who is in his smart suit smiles at them both. Justin and Jasmine smile back to Mr Deluxe pleasantly.

'Hello, Mr Deluxe.'

'Hello, Mr Goodman.'

'This is my wife, Jasmine.'

'How do you do, Mrs Goodman.'

'How do you do, Mr Deluxe.'

'Please come on in.'

Justin and Jasmine lead their guest to the living room. Jasmine has already prepared the small dining table in the living room for tea.

'Tea is ready, Mr Deluxe. Would you like to sit here?'

'Thanks ever so much. That's very kind of you.'

'I'll bring the teapot.'

'Shall I give you a hand, Jasmine?'

'I am fine, darling. I'll get the tray. Please don't leave our guest alone. I'll be here in a minute. Excuse me, Mr Deluxe.'

'You shouldn't have gone into too much trouble. However, I won't be able to resist the strawberry cake as it looks rather appetising from here. Is it homemade?'

'Jasmine made the cake. She is an excellent baker.'

'I have no doubt about that. My wife is a very good cook too. Unfortunately, we don't have cakes for tea as she is on a strict diet. My wife never bakes me a cake except on our anniversaries. Once a year, it isn't enough for me. Well, there isn't much to do. I won't tell my wife that I would be breaking my strict diet today. She would get upset about it. My wife wants me to lose the fat on my abdomen. When we first met, I had no stomach at all. I've put on weight. No matter how hard I try, I can't reduce the fat on my belly. You look in pretty good shape, Mr Goodman. How do you keep up with a healthy appearance?'

'We don't have strawberry cakes every day. My wife is on a strict diet as well. We only treat ourselves when we have important guests around like you.'

'I liked the compliment you've paid to me, Mr Goodman. I am not that important.'

'You are the only significant name within the wine industry. Anyone who drinks wine knows your company's name.'

'I have been around for a long time. You remind me of my old age somehow. I'm too old, perhaps, to consider the change of direction in my professional life. Tell me about your teaching career. I understood you and your wife both from teaching profession. Teaching is one of the most respected occupations. Do you like your profession, Mr Goodman?'

'I am afraid, I am not a qualified teacher. My wife and I both come from legal professional background. We both make our living as barristers.'

'I beg your pardon. When you mention weekend teaching job on the phone, I automatically assumed that you were from teaching profession.'

'Teaching at weekends is only a temporary occupation we have taken up as a matter of urgency rather than a choice.'

'Do you like teaching?'

'I don't think I can consider earning a living out of it.'

'Why is that?'

'Teaching isn't sufficient to make a proper living out of it. I prefer my legal career as I earn 10 times more than a teacher's salary. Still we cannot afford to buy a holiday cottage and sailing boat even at this mature age. That's why we have both decided to sell our old wines. Otherwise, we would keep them all for the good days ahead of us to celebrate.'

'I can see your point of view, Mr Goodman. My dad was a university lecturer. If my dad wasn't married to my mother who comes from a wealthy background, he wouldn't be able to support us. I am familiar with the limitation of teaching salaries since I was a child. Luckily, I didn't take up my dad's profession. Otherwise, I would end up struggling all my life time.'

'Here we are! You're more familiar to the teaching professions' life struggle than us.'

'Fortunately, we didn't struggle as my mum's income had provided us a steady income on a regular basis.'

'Tea is ready. Shall I pour you tea, Mr Deluxe?'

'Could you please?'

'Would you take milk or sugar?'

'No thank you. I'm on diet.'

'Mr Deluxe is on diet like us, darling. I told Mr Deluxe we don't often have strawberry cakes.'

'No, we don't. We have less fattening cakes instead like ginger cake which doesn't have much fat and cream in it. Shall I give you this medium slice?'

'Yes please.'

'Here you are. This won't do much harm.'

'We hope so. The older I get, the harder it gets to burn the fat.'

'I've no objection to your point of you, Mr Goodman. My husband and I do regular exercises. Still, it's very hard to lose weight once you are over the scale.'

'None of you look over the scale to me. On the contrary you are both slim.'

'We'll be better off to lose at least 1 or 2 stones.'

'In comparison with my weight, I can assure you that you are doing rather well. Keep up with your figures.'

'Thanks Mr Deluxe. It has been rather busy week for us. On Saturdays we teach.'

'Mr Goodman has just mentioned that. I thought you were coming from teaching background. I've understood both of you working as barristers. I haven't got a clue how hard a barrister's life might be. But I assume that being a barrister isn't easier than being a teacher.'

'I find it each profession hard enough to deal with plenty of responsibilities. However, one pays more, the other one pays less. That's the difference at the end of the day. We both work hard as barristers. We get paid for what we do. I am sorry to say that teachers are underpaid for their hard work. Any earning capacity below £40.000 a year I consider inadequate to live on.'

'I agree with you. I was telling Mr Goodman about my dad's earning capacity as a school teacher.'

'Your father must be one of those unlucky people who take up teaching profession for the professional satisfaction without considering financial strains.'

'He was an idealist. Without being an idealist, there won't be anyone left to teach.'

'Idealism is a romantic word in this century. We need to be realistic more than idealistic most of the time.'

'Without having a good earning capacity, I'm afraid; there is no possibility to survive especially when the world economy is facing the worst recession.'

'Thankfully, the recession didn't hit our business in wine industry. We're one of the luckiest professions to enjoy the economic growth and sustainability. Nothing has been changed for us during the last 20 years or so. The wine industry has always been prosperous since last century. Economic crisis do not reduce alcohol consumptions. People always drink wine.'

'When they do not have any financial problems, they drink to enjoy themselves. During the economic crises, people have a good excuse to cheer themselves up. So there is always a reason to be merry and happy.'

'That works well for the people who are in the wine business like me.'

'You must be one of the fortunate people in this world who don't face any financial hardship.'

'I'm lucky to admit that it's true. I'm a fortunate wine expert. I earn quiet a lot of money out of wine auctioning. By the way, the strawberry cake is superb! Mr Goodman told me you baked the cake. You're a very good baker Mrs Goodman.'

'Thank you. Would you like to have another slice, Mr Deluxe?'

'I would most appreciate another one, if I may?'

'Please help yourself.'

'Thanks. I will. I should keep quiet this. If I confess the greatest sin I've committed today, my wife wouldn't forgive me for that. She would feel cheated. We both promised each other not to have sweet dishes let alone dangerously fattening delicious strawberry cakes. We only allow each other to have cakes on our anniversary. We didn't have a birthday cake for years. Instead we have fruit on our birthdays. That's our arrangement for a healthy life style. It gets boring sometimes.'

'We ought to take a lesson from Mr and Mrs Deluxes's wise arrangement for losing weight, Justin.'

'I always confess you when I breach our agreement outside home. I've never been quiet even I know you would get upset about the unwise choice I made.'

'This is the only sin I've committed since we've been married. My wife is my sweetheart. I can't deceive her in any way. That's against my moral values. My wife and I have been happily married for 45 years without any marital problem at all.'

'How nice! Justin and I found each other in life quiet late actually. We've been happily married for only 10 years. We both hope that there'll be plenty of decades we'll be spending together. That's why we're planning to buy our holiday cottage and sailing boat to celebrate our anniversaries on our boat.'

'I own a yacht which is moored in Guernsey. I am a member of the Royal Channel Island Yacht Club. At weekend, my wife and I fly to Guernsey and have a long weekend. We come back on Tuesdays. Today I've postponed my trip to Guernsey because of this business meeting. I usually avoid weekend's work. I dedicate myself to my wife's need to be accompanied on our yacht. She loves the sea life. Otherwise, she would get upset. We don't have a child. We only have each other's company. It's very important for us to have a good quality of life, you see.'

'Aren't Mr Deluxe and his wife so fortunate, darling?'

'That's right! You must be very lucky. It's Jasmine's idea to have a sailing boat. I don't think we can ever afford to buy a yacht.'

'I haven't seen your wine collection yet. You might be lucky enough to keep a fortune in the cellar. Can I see your collection before I'll get another piece of strawberry cake?'

'I can show you the cellar now, Mr Deluxe.'

'I'll follow you, Mr Goodman.'

'Would you like to join us, Jasmine?'

'I'd love to.'

Justin and Jasmine take their guest to the cellar under the staircases in the hallway.

'Here we're, Mr Deluxe. This is our cellar.'

'It's a very good size and well kept. I assume there is no damp in here.'

'We don't have any damp.'

'Wine quality gets deteriorated within the damp condition. I can see that each wine bottle is wrapped carefully with the wrapping paper to keep the light away. Did I guess the reason correctly for wrapping each bottle individually?'

'Although we don't come here that often, we're very careful to keep the right temperature for our wine cellar which gets warmer over the winter and gets cooler during the summer season.'

'Did you get an expert opinion for the cellar's condition?'

'It's only what I had gathered from my father really. I assume he was trained by my granddad.'

'Can I unwrap one of the wine bottles?'

'Please do.'

'The colour of wine is perfect. I wish I could sample the taste of it.'

'I'll open the bottle for you, Mr Deluxe.'

'I don't want to reduce the number of the collection you've got.'

'I think my wife and I would like to say goodbye to our collection. We can finish off the bottle later on together.'

'In that case, let me have my sip upstairs please.'

'Certainly.'

Justin, Jasmine and Mr Deluxe go back to the living room. Justin opens the wine bottle carefully. Jasmine brings the wine glasses and Justin pours wine into Mr Deluxe's glass.

'That's enough for sampling the wine, Mr Goodman.'

'That's only a tiny drop. I'll put some more.'

'It's enough for me. Thanks.'

'You're welcome.'

Mr Deluxe takes the wine glass from Justin. He closes his eyes and sips the wine. Jasmine and Justin watch Mr Deluxe nervously trying to figure out how Mr Deluxe find the quality of wine. Mr Deluxe swallows the 1st drop. He gets another sip from the wine glass. The pleasant expression appears on his face. Mr Deluxe opens his eyes and looks at Justin happily.

'I dare to say that it's superb quality.'

'I'm glad to hear that. Aren't you feeling the same, Jasmine?'

'Yes, it's so good to hear your approval of the wine quality, Mr Deluxe.'

'I need to get the details of the vineyard like when it was produced and the name of the wine producer. Accordingly, we'll get your wine collection ready for auction in our London branch.'

'I'll get all the details for you. I keep my father's record in safe. Shall I email you the details of the wine later on?'

'Please do, Mr Goodman. Let me have another slice of strawberry cake now before asking your permission for me to leave.'

'By no means! Please help yourself with another strawberry cake.'

'I can brew fresh tea for us.'

'Not for me. I'd like to finish my cake without tea. It was very good to meet you both. Hopefully, your collections of wine will fetch a good price. You never know you might be lucky enough to get a small yacht. As a matter of fact, I can sell you my small yacht which is 5 years old only. We've got a bit larger yacht with the swimming pool in it.'

'How much will you be selling your old yacht?'

'I'd like you to enjoy your life. £100.000 will be fine. There is a double size bedroom, a medium size living room, a shower and a small kitchen unit in it.'

'It sounds a good bargain for us.'

'It's a good bargain. We kept it in good condition, it looks brand new actually.'

'Could you keep your yacht for us until we raise enough funds from the wine auction, Mr Deluxe?'

'There is no problem. The cake was delicious, I hope you don't mind me leaving now.'

'Not at all, please feel free to leave us at any time, Mr Deluxe.'

'Thanks. I look forward to receiving the details of your wine, Mr Goodman.'

'I'll be providing the details as soon as I can.'

'Thanks. Let me give you my business card to you now.'

'Shall we exchange our business card?'

'I'll be delighted to have your card.'

'I'll get my business card from the study.'

'Thanks.'

'Can I use the lavatory in the meantime?'

'Yes, of course. I'll show it to you.'

The bathroom is shown to Mr Deluxe. While Mr Deluxe washes his hands and rinses his teeth with running water in the bathroom, Justin and Jasmine get their business cards ready for him. Jasmine puts 2 large slices of strawberry cakes into a small container to give it to Mr Deluxe to take it to his wife. Mr Deluxe comes back to the living room looking happy and cheerful.

'I'd like to thank you both for a splendid day. I wish I came here with my wife. She would be delighted to meet you both.'

'We'd like to meet Mrs Deluxe in the near future.'

'Perhaps, we'll have a chance to meet Mrs Deluxe next time you visit us. I put 2 slices of strawberry cake here for your wife to taste.'

'That's very kind of you. I'm sure my wife wouldn't resist the homemade cake and forgive me for breaking our strict diet today.'

'I'll make apricot cake for the next time.'

'I'll tell my wife what your offer is. I'm sure my wife would like you both to taste her cakes in return.'

'We can't wait for sampling Mrs Deluxe's cakes.'

'Well, we'll fix a date for it. You can come over to our yacht in Guernsey. We'll have a meal and tea with plum cake that is my wife's speciality, actually.'

'That'll be great.'

Mr Deluxe leaves the Goodmans's cottage with the 2 slices of strawberry cake in the container given to him. Jasmine and Justin feel very happy that meeting with the wine auctioneer Mr Deluxe went very well.

'That was good, wasn't it dear?'

'Hopefully, our wines will fetch a good price with the help of Mr Deluxe.'

'I have no doubt about that. What do you think about the offer?'

'Mr Deluxe's small yacht?'

'That's right!'

'It's a brilliant offer. We ought to jump on to it.'

'Buying a yacht before buying our cottage doesn't sound appropriate to me.'

'We won't get any other bargain. You can't get a narrow boat for £100.000.'

'Why do you think Mr Deluxe has been too generous to us, Justin?'

'Mr Deluxe has got a bigger yacht and doesn't need the small one. Instead of giving the yacht away to a charity or so, he'll be selling it to us with affordable price. Mr Deluxe knows that we can't afford to pay 1 million for his yacht. It'll be a token we'll be paying for his small yacht. Nevertheless, it's better than nothing.'

'I hope we'll be able to buy a small cottage with the similar bargain, Justin.'

'We need to start cottage hunting now.'

'Let's wait until we sell the wine collection at the auction, Jasmine.'

'I can't see any harm to do a bit of Internet research and get an idea about the property prices first.'

'I leave that to you, my dear. You're good at shopping online.'

'Shall we consider buying a cottage in Guernsey like Mr Deluxe and Mrs Deluxe?'

'It'll be too far for us to go to Guernsey at weekends. We'd better consider nearest proximity to our cottage in London within a short distance.'

'How about Isle of Wight? Will you be interested in living there at weekends?'

'That sounds more convenient to me.'

'We'll surprise Steve and Felix once we buy the cottage and the yacht.'

'I feel like telling them immediately. We've already made our decision. If we can't buy a large cottage, we'll definitely buy a small one. We won't change our minds for sure.'

'No, we won't change our minds, Jasmine.'

'We definitely want to make a new start.'

'We do. It sounds terrible as if we've already got bored with each other or we're looking for something to take away our boredom from the 10 years marriage life, do you feel like it, Justin?'

'Not really! Like everything else in life, we need to refresh our marriage in order to avoid falling into the pattern of repetitive life style.'

'You're absolutely right, my dear. Each relation needs to be nourished with sincerity and interest for making the relationship even better by overcoming the boredom of routine patterns.'

'I totally agree with you, Jasmine. Let me come back to my reality now. I must prepare my case for next week now.'

'Me too my dear.'

'We'll have an interesting supper tonight. I'll be taking you out for a dinner. None of us needs to cook dinner tonight as Steve won't be here for supper tonight.'

'We'll celebrate our new venture in life together.'

'That's correct! It's our new venture to live like a millionaire with decent holiday cottage and yacht.'

'Let's turn our dream into a reality.'

'We're on our way to hit our target, Jasmine.'

'We should be thankful to Felix.'

'That's right! Without his existence in our lives for a week, we would never be able to reassess our priorities in our relationship.'

'Our marriage has been saved by Felix actually.'

'Felix entered in our life at the right time at the right place.'

'Otherwise, the wine stock would stay in the cellar without being utilised till we reach the end of our journey.'

'That's true, darling. We'll be making most of our wine stock for good.'

Chapter 4

Felix's 1st month at prison - Oct 2002

Felix's 1st month in prison passed very quickly occupied with his spelling practices and attending a few art classes. Felix didn't get bored; it was like being on a boarding school. Felix had always wanted to have an access to a very good schooling as a child. It had never happened. Felix couldn't understand what he was taught at school. His schooling was interrupted regularly by unexpected events took place out of his control. At last, Felix has a chance to overcome irritating interruptions. Felix has got a laptop, a mobile phone, a bed, a table and unlimited supply of art materials now. Felix has even got a small TV in his room. There are plenty of intellectual stimulations. Felix remembers seeing a film about a convict who didn't have anything in his prison cell to stimulate his mind. Felix closes his eyes and imagines the absence of all the things he possesses at present. If all of them will be taken away from him, he'll get depressed more than ever perhaps. Felix can't imagine himself without his gadgets now. They're part of his existence. All his belongings have increased Felix's well-being. Through Internet Felix has got an access to the whole world. Felix forgets the sense of time when he is in the sculpture room. It's so good to have many things to stimulate his mind. Felix has just started reading simple text and he can understand what Justin, Jasmine and Steve teach him. Everything is going well according to the Divine Plan. Without God's help, Felix would have never been able to feel so happy. Felix understands that the early struggle of his life was a preparation for him to enjoy what God has provided for him now. Without the struggle Felix had gone through in life, he would have lacked the satisfaction he gets out of his current life. The sun beams are entering into Felix's prison cell. Felix feels like writing a poem and jots down the following poem in his diary.

My heart is still beating

Sun is shining up there
My heart is still beating down here
in the prison cell
I live my life
with satisfaction
Life is so good
Life is how I live
Life can't be spoiled
with small worries any longer

Felix
20th Oct 2002

Felix enjoys his spelling routine as he is getting better at remembering the words which he couldn't spell previously. After mastering the LSCWC spelling method, Felix's short term memory has been improved tremendously. Felix has got 40 words in his long-term memory now. Within a month, he practised with 5 words in maths and 5 words in law each week. Felix knows that he could easily learn 10 words a week without forgetting them when he practises with LSCWC and do regular revisions twice a day. In the morning, before breakfast time he does revision. At night, before he goes to bed, Felix does another revision which reinforces not only his short-term memory but also his long-term memory. Felix puts 40 colour post-it notes with 40 words chunked and highlighted the tricky bits with colour pens on the walls. When Felix is in his room, he keeps on gazing at colour post-it notes on the wall. Each day Felix's sight vocabulary enlarges by special effort he has put in his learning. Felix has already projected how many new words he will be storing into his long-term memory in a month, in a year time and in 2 years time.

40 new words = 1 month effort
400 new words = 1 year effort

800 new words = 2 years effort

Felix can write an essay with 500 words without having any problem in his English exam at GCSE level. If Felix has got any problem with any new word he is not familiar with, he can look it up in an electronic dictionary and learn its morphology as he knows how to analyse the complicated words and finds his way around remembering them without much difficulty. Each strategy he develops makes Felix's learning process a lot easier. Learning is not a burden now, learning is fun and it should stay as it is. Felix has recently started keeping a diary. He records all the new words he has learnt in his diary. It has been only two weeks since Felix has been keeping a diary. When Felix reads the first entrance in his diary, he feels that he has made such a remarkable progress in his learning. Felix looks through his scribble in his diary.

<u>6 Oct 2002</u>

Today is my first date of having a diary in my entire life. I've never had such a concept of recording what I do on a day-to-day basis in the past. My life has been such a dull existence. I didn't think there was anything important for me to record or think about later on. If I only had any opportunity in life, I would have deleted the records of my painful memories of being unwanted person to start with. What is the use of recording about how I was unloved, unwanted and exploited as a kid and as a teenager? I'd rather to forget the harsh reality of being rejected not only by my own biological parents, by my foster parents, by the community, in short by the society on the whole. I was turned into a scapegoat by the prejudiced people who couldn't cope with my human existence. I still can't understand why I am here without being murdered so far. All I have been experiencing in life that no one wanted me to have my share in life as if I was the only person to be in the way of other people's happiness, their livelihood and their possessions.

If I didn't meet Justin, Jasmine and Steve, I would have hated myself for being around as a nuisance. Just recently, I feel that after all I am not the one who was wrong to be on this earth, it was the other way around actually. It was all the prejudiced people who treated me unfairly and made me excluded from a decent life, my basic human rights to be housed, protected and enabled to have a decent job to sustain my flesh and spirit together. Even the judge didn't do his job properly. He let me go into prison and spend my precious 2 years in the prison without anything for me to do either in prison or afterwards. How could I change the society's conception of me, their prejudices against me? The legal system is completely a sham operation which only defends corruption, unfairness; it doesn't provide any remedy for the needy, unwanted, homeless and unemployed. The legal system is established to punish the most vulnerable with the illogical and unworkable legal system. I hate the legal system for its harshness on me particularly.

If Justin, Jasmine and Steve didn't volunteer themselves to teach me in prison, there is no value of being kept in prison for 2 years which would only regress me but not progress me in any way at all. Keeping a diary is only fun when there is something worthwhile recording in my life; otherwise, it is only reminding myself what I do not want to remember in the first place. Keeping a diary for recording my learning in order to overcome all the obstacles in written language is not painful; far from it, it'll enable me to monitor what I learn and how I learn so that I'll remind myself what works for me. Steve taught me irregular verbs this week. Today, I need to learn more than 5 words as each word has got 3 different ways of spelling like base form, simple past tense and past participle. The irregular verbs I've practised of so far are awake, become, begin, break and build. I'll write them all here for me to remember what I've been practising with.

Base form	Simple past tense	Past participle
awake	awoke	awaken
become	became	become
begin	began	begun
break	broke	broken
build	built	built

I got them all confused at first as they all look alike. I spent a day learning one verb with 3 different ways of spelling. My bedside is full of irregular verbs. When I get them all confused I get angry with myself.

7 Oct 2002

I am still getting confused with the irregular words. I hate irregular words. Why don't we use one word all the time? Irregular words make life so complicated. I hate doing revision on irregular words. My dilemma is I don't want to let down Steve. He won't come again if I don't do well in my spelling test. I must learn 5 irregular words before Steve gives me a spelling test.

8 Oct 2002

I can spell <u>awake</u> and <u>become</u> with three different forms. I had learnt 6 words within 2 days. I hope I won't get confused when I start practising next 2 irregular verbs. I am feeling down. If I can't make it, I'll feel failure this weekend.

9 Oct 2002

Yesterday I practised with <u>become</u> only and I leave the next irregular verb <u>begin</u> to the next day. I hope I will speed up a bit. I haven't got much time left to learn them all. I have to do revision on numerical expression next.

I am left-handed. I cannot write neatly. Steve's handwriting is so neat. I wish I could write as neat as Steve. I'm trying very hard. Writing tires me but drawing doesn't wear me out. Steve told me I don't need to worry about my handwriting. He said that I can use laptop. But, there is a spellchecker in the computer. For my spelling practice, I need to write by hand.

I had learnt two more verbs <u>break</u> and <u>build</u>. I don't get confused with the first irregular verb awake any more. I check my learning each night before I fall asleep.

I had tested myself. I got 5 out of 10. It isn't bad considering the number of verbs I had practised this week. I am doing well. Next time, I'll do even better. I had less time for drawing this week though. My time is taken up by spelling practice and weekly exercises in 3 different subjects. I am determined to pass my GSCEs in English, Maths and Law. I have no any other option.

Felix feels exhausted but determined not to give up while he closes his diary. His future depends on his focal point which is to get him out of the poverty trap he has been stuck for years. Without enduring the hardship of learning with plenty of practice, he'll never get where he wants to be in ten years time. Felix wants to be a competent barrister. It's necessary to keep all his diaries he writes regularly in prison. When Felix becomes a court barrister, he'll have a chance to look back to his starting point to measure his achievement in accordance with where he has started from and where he'll be reaching without giving up in half way through. Learning is a real struggle just like life itself. Felix needs to struggle with both at the same time until he achieves his long term goals. Felix cannot help wondering about Jackie's life. She has never struggled with any subject in her life. She doesn't have any problem with reading and writing. Jackie had never found out that Felix couldn't read and write properly as Jackie wasn't his teacher. Jackie is pretty knowledgeable about mental health problems she has been studying, however, she couldn't guess Felix's problem with the written language. Probably, Jackie doesn't know what dyslexia means. Felix had never heard of dyslexia himself. Thanks to Steve, the dyslexia specialist and thanks to Justin, Felix's barrister. If Justin wasn't kind enough to offer Felix lodging for a week, Felix wouldn't have met Steve under other circumstances. How could Felix meet a dyslexia specialist? Where? Felix thought that he was an unintelligent soul that was how his primary school teacher treated him. She didn't make any bad remark about Felix's intelligence but Felix could easily sense that his primary school teacher hated him because he wasn't quick enough to pick up the sound of the letters. If Steve didn't tell Felix that there was nothing wrong with his intelligence, Felix could still have doubt about his IQ and would have felt that he had low intelligence. On the contrary, Steve thinks that Felix is very intelligent. Steve can't draw and paint. He said he is not good at drawing. How comes? Steve looks very intelligent as he was able to spot Felix's reading and writing problems but he can't draw at all. What a shame! If Felix had given a chance between being good at drawing and reading, Felix would have chosen drawing despite all the difficulties he had faced in his life because of his dyslexia. Now, he has got two possibilities in his life. Felix could be a very good artist and a very good barrister at the same time. The first one is easier to achieve without making much effort for that in Felix's case. The second one is harder to tackle with. As long as Felix knows what problems he has got and what remedies could help him to overcome his problems, Felix won't be defeated by his difficulties.

Felix thought it would have been so good to know that he was dyslexic when he met Jackie. That might have decreased all the difficulties Jackie and Felix had previously. Felix was too nervous that Jackie would discover the truth about him not being able to read and write fluently. If Jackie and Felix knew that Felix had dyslexia, things between them would have developed a bit better. They wouldn't have endless arguments over so many things. Even Felix's depression might be linked with his lexical struggle more than his homelessness. Certainly, being out of pocket had contributed his depression but his problem with dyslexia didn't resolve his housing problem or poverty. Felix was helpless without any access to the written information before his reading program has been introduced to him. Since Steve has been giving him one to one support, Felix's learning has been increased. It looks like something had happened to his mind. Felix has started seeing things better than ever. He could reason now all the things which were puzzling him before Steve's existence in Felix's life. Steve is good at explaining Felix why he finds certain things difficult as he immediately identifies Felix's problems. Once Steve told Felix that he has got an auditory processing difficulty that is why he can't pick up the sound of certain words, Felix could reason his weaknesses and don't get angry with himself but works on his strength instead. Steve had recognised that Felix confuses the letters d, b and p all the time. Their similarities in appearance cause Felix's confusion. According to Steve's explanation, the confusion between d, b and p has been caused by the visual processing difficulties as Felix has got problem in discriminating the confusing letters of the Latin alphabet. The letters of the written text make Felix feel disorientated when the font size printed smaller than 12. Felix can't see the font size below 12 at all. Felix didn't know that before Steve had picked up Felix's difficulty. Steve had given Felix a reading test with various font sizes. The same sentence written with the font sizes of 8, 9, 10 and 11; Up to the font size 12, Felix couldn't read the four sentences. The only sentence, Felix could read was written by the font size 12. From then on, Felix has been using the font size 12 in his writing on his laptop. Felix had typed his discovery about himself on the screen as an experiment using his laptop by writing the same sentence with 4 different font sizes in bold as follows.

I can't read anything written with the font size 8.

I can't read anything written with the font size 9.

I can't read anything written with the font size 10.

I can't read anything written with the font size 11.

Finally, Felix types the sentence which he could read without difficulty as follows:

I can see sentences with the font size 12 without any problem.

Felix was told by Steve that he should ask the examiners to provide the exam questions with the font size 12 during his GSCE exams. Felix had never thought that he had a right to make such a demand for a special font size because he is dyslexic. It was such a relief that Felix was informed about his legal rights as a dyslexic learner. That'll help him to overcome so many technical problems he had been facing during his schooling years. Hopefully, Felix won't repeat his past mistakes in his further education after leaving prison. Felix is looking forward to doing his degree in law as he is not scared of making mistakes. The college doesn't cause him anxiety any longer. With Steve's language support sessions, Felix will be fine. How lucky Felix has been in life just recently! Jackie should enter into Felix's life now, but not before. Time wasn't ripe enough for Jackie and Felix to develop a decent friendship while Felix was suffering from lack of confidence in his reading and writing skills because of his dyslexia.

Felix knows that there is nothing seriously wrong with Felix. It has just happened that he has got some weaknesses as well as strengths like everyone else. Felix was so unlucky that he had only focused on his weaknesses and didn't recognise his strengths before meeting Steve. Felix is able to accept his weaknesses without hating himself for that and he takes pride in his strengths which he wasn't fully aware before. Felix thought everyone could draw and paint. He had never considered such skills as talent or gift. It was the last thing in his life to know that he could be categorised as gifted until Steve had pointed out that. Steve is a nice guy. He doesn't only focuses on Felix's weaknesses; he also brings out the best bit of Felix by highlighting his strengths which Felix wasn't even aware of. If Felix meets Jackie when he comes out of prison, he will be disclosing his dyslexia to Jackie straightaway. He knows that Jackie won't hate him because of his hidden disability. Felix predicts that Jackie will be considerate and start reasoning Felix's short temper he had previously without getting angry with him. Talking through his weaknesses with Jackie will help both of them to work out some solutions for the problems Felix and Jackie had been facing in their friendship. How good it will be if Jackie stills loves Felix dearly and gets married to him. When they produce a baby together, there is a strong possibility that their baby will be born as dyslexic. Steve told Felix that dyslexia is a genetic disorder. Probably one of his biological parents was dyslexic too. Felix will take care of his child's dyslexia and he'll teach him all the coping strategies he has been learning from Steve. Felix will love his son or daughter regardless of their hidden disability. Felix will feel even closer to his dyslexic children more than a non-dyslexic child. Isn't that strange thing to admit to yourself? But, that is true. Felix can't help empathising with a person who suffers from dyslexia like himself that must be something to do with our human nature. Finding out more about his disability has helped Felix to be more philosophical in his life towards all sorts of problems related to his disability. Felix has got a detrimental problem with the sense of direction. He often gets lost and he can't read a road map which doesn't bother him any longer as Felix knows that getting lost or not being able to read a road map is caused by dyslexia. He can easily make fun of his difficulties now. He couldn't do that for years. Felix has developed reasonable solutions to his problem with direction instinctively. Felix remembers the landmarks as he is a painter. He recognises the landmarks better than reading road or street names. Once Felix captures the landmarks in his mind's eye, he never forgets the road or the street he has been before. Dyslexic person's life gets only better if they are more conscious about their difficulties by finding their own way around within the mountains of so many struggles with letters of alphabet, getting lost, lack of time management skills and organisational skills. It is all about trying different things until you get the best solution to your particular problem which might work for you only but not for another dyslexic person.

Felix hated himself because of his difficulty with writing and reading. Once Steve had started telling him all the strange things Felix had never heard before, Felix could see that it wasn't his fault not being able to read and write. It was his teachers' problems not knowing how to teach a dyslexic learner like himself. Felix could have learnt if a teacher had known how to teach him through clear explanations rather than ridiculing or patronising him in a disgusting way. Steve teaches Felix different learning strategies he could benefit from. No one thought Felix reading strategies before. Recognising letters, spelling patterns and the whole word recognition has improved Felix's reading skills. He wasn't aware of self-monitoring or evaluating his learning outcomes. These are completely new concepts for Felix and facilitate his joy of learning which makes Felix feel good about himself.

Felix closes his eyes and visualises himself outside the prison walls; he places himself where he wants to be as a successful profession without any problem with literacy and numeracy. The years must come to the end soon. He'll be older and wiser when he leaves the prison life behind. Felix wonders whether or not anything he will miss from his prison cell. The freedom, perhaps! Yes, it is the freedom of being himself without being judged for that; being respected as he is without facing the challenge of exclusion from everything he wants to have in life. Felix has got a regular contact with Steve, Jasmine and Justin. They all put their energy on his development as if he is their only concern. Felix feels important with the thought of being cared for. He had never had that luxury before he entered this prison. Felix thinks about how it feels to be outside after experiencing care, respect and unconditional love from those people whom he relates to. Felix never thought that he could relate to the people who come from privileged backgrounds. Steve, Jasmine and Justin never suffered from homelessness. They all knew their biological parents. They weren't thrown away as soon as they were born. It's all weird though. Felix hated Jackie because of her privileged background; he likes Steve, Jasmine and Justin who come from exactly the same privileged backgrounds. Jackie looked like she cared for him but she looked too artificial as if she wanted to be good for the sake of being good which bothered Felix more than anything else. That was why Felix couldn't take Jackie's concern about his well-being seriously.

How strange it is to see the difference between obsessive, controlling even possessive care and natural, welcoming care. Felix prefers the latter. Human relationship is so complex. Some people can't notice how harmful their concerns when they start destroying others' freedom or breathing space for sanity. Felix starts running in his mind eye, he runs continuously to the furthest point in which there won't be any restriction to his fragile freedom. In the prison cell, Felix's freedom is restricted to his imagination only as he can't run or go out for a walk physically. He is a convict and not a free man. Felix remembers of people outside his prison cell. How free they all are! Whether or not they are fully aware of how precious the true freedom is in life without being captivated by anyone or a system is a real puzzle for Felix. There is a possibility that there may be some people who are not captured within any legal system but still feel like being trapped in a prison cell when they have nothing to achieve, without any purpose or dream to fulfil or even any expectation from life.

Felix recalls his memories of seeing sickly-looking tramps with malnutrition asking for a change near shopping centre, at bus stops and on tubes in London. How free those tramps outside without knowing how their misfortune will be drifting their day-to-day existence from one place to another! They don't even have anywhere to sleep or any hot meal to eat. They are not expected to be invited for a feast in a friend's home. They don't know how they will survive next hour let alone next day or next month. Felix experienced how it feels to be broke but didn't have the guts to beg for a penny. How humiliating it would have been for him to ask for another person's mercy without returning anything back to them. Felix had never expected from anyone to spare a coin for him to buy him anything to eat even when he was starving to death almost. Apart from Jackie, no one bought him decent food for nothing. Of course, Justin and Jasmine are completely a different kettle of fish as he didn't know them before getting into trouble with legal system. Even when he was living with his foster parents, he was expected to pay for his lodging. Nothing was given to him as a treat; accordingly, he had never taken granted anything he was offered in life. Felix gets depressed again. By the thought of facing confinement for life outside prison cell distresses him and he wants to forget about the negative possibility of being lost in life once more and living the same struggle for survival all over again.

Felix opens his drawing-pad and starts drawing when he is pondering around his feelings about homelessness and unemployment as a threat in future. After a while, his distress disappears. The abstract form on the drawing-pad cheers him up as he feels a completely free man as long as he has got a pad and pencil in his possession. Felix could create freedom out of nothingness without additional possession via his drawings in which he deliberately gets lost without the sense of time and space. That is blessing itself. To be able to forget the concept of time, how to survive, where to live, what he needs to do next, keeps him sane at least when he is experiencing the joy of drawing in a true sense. While Felix is drawing, the condition of his life is in his control but not others. Felix is the one who could execute his life in the way he wants to live and feel. No one else could interfere with his power of shaping his life in his illusion with a pencil and a piece of paper. That is his strength. Felix is the most powerful person when he draws his own life as he knows that no one could compete with his freedom while he is drawing with the drawing instinct without giving a break to accept the external reality of the confusing people who did not do anything but interfere with his freedom of completeness. That's the real struggle for him to overcome. One day, he will be financially free. There won't be anyone who could dare to steel his freedom from him or prevent him from being himself or being in charge of his own life without being oppressed by anyone including the legal system.

Felix feels privileged in life as a good draftsman. He thinks that he will never give up drawing as it is the basic need for his survival more important than food or shelter for him. As long as Felix draws, he will never be impoverished in life; the highest power for him, it is not what you possess in a material sense but what you possess internally to create out of your own life. Felix will never get bored since he has got ability to draw and paint. Felix draws the places he wants to visit and draws the buildings he wants to live in. He even draws the animals he would like to interact with. Animals shouldn't be kept in captivity. In Felix's drawings, all the wild animals are free enjoying their freedom like Felix enjoys his freedom of drawing whenever he wants and wherever he is regardless he is in prison or outside. Felix carries his pen and a piece of paper to exercise his freedom all the time. The four walls of the prison can't restrict his emotional freedom which cannot be taken from him even he faces 2 years sentence in prison. Felix leaves his drawing-pad on the table and leaves the room to go to the canteen for his lunch. He'll be having his lunch as a free man with his unique interpretation of individual freedom which all starts in one's mind and cannot be given to anyone as a gift. We are born free and we will stay free without any need for acknowledgement of others.

Felix looks around the canteen to find familiar faces from his art room. All the inmates are there. Some of them greet him with a friendly manner. He goes to the same seat and sits down opposite a talkative inmate Henry. While they are waiting for a meal, they start chatting with each other to kill the time.

'Hi Felix'

'Hi Henry, are you OK?'

'Yeah, how about you?'

'I'm OK. I've no complaint about anything.'

'You'll start complaining 6 months later being here. The first 6 months you get used to the new environment and there isn't much to make complaint about.'

'How long have you been here?'

'Altogether is 4 yrs.'

'Well, that is a long time!'

'Tell me about it.'

'Why are you here?'

'I shot my mate 4 yrs ago.'

'What was the reason for that?'

'He got on my nerve man.'

'Why?'

'He was racist. He followed me and threatened me that he would be cutting my throat by a blind knife. Instead, I shot him. There is no fear of being killed by him any longer.'

'Cool! You don't regret for what you committed.'

'No regret whatsoever. If I didn't shoot him, I won't be here today.'

'Well, it is one or the other.'

'That's right. You're a smart guy, Felix. You know how I feel. What is your reason to be here, then?'

'I broke into the unoccupied property when I was homeless.'

'Is that all?'

'Yes, that's why I'm here.'

'For how long will you be around?'

'2 yrs.'

'That's nonsense man. I spent all my life in squat; no one picked me up and put me into the jail for squatting. This is outrageous. Have you got a family?'

'No, I have no family.'

'Why is that?'

'My parents didn't want to keep me.'

'Like me then. Have you been in any orphanage at some point?'

'I was raised by my foster parent.'

'Do you keep in touch with them?'

'No, they asked me to leave when I was 16.'

'That's unfair.'

'It isn't pleasant to find yourself into. Never mind, here we are, in a nice comfortable environment without any worry where to stay overnight. More importantly, we are fed and entertained for being kept here. What else could we possibly expect from life? We're luckier than many others who are destined to join us eventually.'

'You speak a posh language. Have you been to college?'

'Not really. I am drop out.'

'How did you pick up such a high language? Do you mix with the people from higher class?'

'From time to time.'

'How often?'

'Well, it's none of your business.'

'Don't get cross with me. I am not trying to put my nose into your life. It's a matter of curiosity. That's all.'

'I don't want to go into too much details of my life.'

'OK mate. I shut my mouth up. I won't ask any personal questions.'

'I'm sorry. I didn't mean that.'

'You look a decent guy, Felix. Do you get scared of me?'

'Why should I scare of you, Henry?'

'I am a murderer.'

'So what? There are plenty of murderers in life. If we start scaring of each murderer, we'd better stop living our lives.'

'Other inmates won't come near me. Just in case, I repeat what I have done before.'

'It's their problem. All I could tell you that I am not scared of you. Your circumstances dictated what you have done. It's a matter of defence for some people what you've done. If you didn't murder him, he would murder you. You defended yourself. The system is awful. You shouldn't be left alone to protect your dignity. Didn't you tell the police that your life was in danger?'

'I asked for help from police for several times. They took no notice. They didn't take it seriously. Who wants to protect the vulnerable, the poor, and the needy? They prefer us to be killed or go into prison. That's the choice we are given. It isn't a matter of misfortune, but it's a matter of choice to be alive or dead. The rest is the decision between taking an action or not taking an action which will lead to face your destiny of being shot and go to the grave peacefully without having any courage to take the justice into your own hand.'

'I'm sorry to hear what you have gone through in life. Will you be OK when you are discharged from here?'

'No, of course not. As a matter of fact, I'll be better off to be inside. His mate will be taking revenge out of me. I need to hide myself all the time. I won't be completely free for life.'

'I wish there was a way to get out of trap you are in now.'

'There isn't any way for us to get out of trap. We're all condemned to face our misfortune for being born into broken family, being mixed with the wrong circle, being bullied by the racist oppressors, being hated for our race, colour, class, social deprivation, you name the rest of it.'

'Surely, it can't be that hopeless.'

'You're completely out of touch with reality, Felix. There is nothing out there for us to hold onto. If there was a hope for us, we wouldn't be here in the first place.'

'I still prefer living with hope rather than without.'

'You'll waste your life if you wait for hope to arrive. Unless, you're a religious person to believe in after life staff; do you believe in God?'

'I believe in God.'

'Who is your God, Felix?'

'It's up there, can't be seen with our eyes.'

'Don't tell me nonsense. If God was there, why doesn't he protect us? Why are we here inside the jail?'

'You're unbeliever, than.'

'That's correct. I don't believe in God.'

'I'm sorry to hear that.'

'Are you sorry for me or for yourself?'

'For you, of course.'

'What for?'

'There is nothing to comfort you with.'

'If I believed in God, would I have anything to be comforted with?'

'I should imagine so.'

'What type of comfort are you talking about?'

'I mean when you face the misfortune, God sees it.'

'Then what happens?'

'He'll help.'

'How?'

'He'll deliver you from the troubles you have found yourself.'

'Did God deliver you from the trouble you found yourself, Felix?'

'I wouldn't be here if God wasn't with me.'

'Because you're alive, you're grateful to God and think that he protected you.'

'Otherwise, I would be in grave.'

'There are believers who lost their lives while they were fighting for God.'

'That's true. I still want to believe in God. I cannot imagine myself denying His existence in my life.'

'You're funny. I am stronger without fooling myself with an illusion.'

'If that's what you want, it's fine by me. We're different. I accept you as you are, please don't question my belief which what I treasure in life. Without God's existence, I would be completely and utterly hopeless. I need Him more than anything else in life.'

'I hope you won't get disillusioned when you discover that there isn't anyone there to protect you.'

'I will never experience that feeling of denial. I do not want to deprive myself from the belief of God who abides within me and accompanies me wherever I go in life, He will be my guardian angel to protect me. That's the comfort of a believer. Otherwise, I would start scaring of everything including you, Henry. I don't scare of you not because I feel stronger to kill you but because of my belief that God will not fill you with that hatred towards me to kill me. I've got a feeling that you've got compassion for me or for any other human being who didn't threatened you or hated you as much the man you murdered.'

'That's strange, but it's true. I don't feel like killing everyone except the man who wanted to murder me.'

'You see, you are not born as a murderer. You're made one because of how you were treated. If your circumstances were different, you wouldn't be a murderer. You would be a decent guy with respectable purpose to live in life. You would save life but not waste it.'

Henry starts crying aloud. Felix's word touches Henry's heart deep down and regrets the first time in his life that he was forced to murder another human being. He feels ashamed of his action. Felix can't make his mind what to do. The murderer who was justifying his reason to kill another human being looks so vulnerable while he is sobbing with regret and agony. Felix looks around, the other tough guys watching the murderer's despair to be forgiven for life. Felix continues talking to Henry and tries to comfort him from the crime he has committed when he was out of touch with his human instinct of wanting to be good rather than bad. Henry leaves the canteen without waiting for his meal to arrive. Another inmate sits next to Felix.

'What is his problem?'

'Nothing.'

'He can't cry over nothing. What did you say to him?'

'I don't want to tell you what I told Henry.'

'The only reason I asked this question that I am a murderer. If what you said to Henry healed him, if he could cry, I might benefit from your words as well. I can't cry. I can't remember when I cried for the last time. I feel inhuman somehow. Please tell me what made him cry, Felix.'

'All I said to him that he is a good guy regardless he is a murderer or not. His circumstances pushed him to murder another human and I do not get scared of him.'

'Don't you scare of murderer, Felix?'

'No, I don't.'

'Why not?'

'I know the fact that you won't murder me.'

'Who guarantees you that I won't?'

'I believe in God.'

'What has got to do with God?'

'God will protect me.'

'If I decide to kill you, no one will protect you even God. It'll be within my power to kill you.'

'You cannot prove your power by killing another human being.'

'Survival depends on power. The fittest is the one who kills but not being killed.'

'Are you from a gang?'

'I am and very proud of it.'

'You can't scare me. That's why you do not have power upon me. If you kill me is your decision. Go on and kill me. If that's what your passion is all about seeing blood and dead body, there is nothing stopping you. I wouldn't let you take the Mickey out of me. I've got dignity. If you manage to kill me, I'll go to heaven straightaway. You cannot win the battle of hatred. I didn't harm you in any way. Just tell me, what have I done wrong to hate me?'

'Nothing so far!'

'Would you like me to stir your killing instinct just to check how far you could go?'

'Calm down man, don't get on my nerve. What's wrong with you?'

'Nothing is wrong with me. It's you who is looking for a trouble. Leave me alone. I'd like to have a meal without being disturbed. Enough is enough. I don't want to hear all the nonsense of being threatened by you. You'll kill me once. That's all. Don't repeat it over and over again with your words. Behave yourself man! One of the reasons you're here is that you need to act as a human being. You aren't a beast in a wilderness. This is a small community. We need to respect each other's dignity. Why are you threatening me? Am I threatening you in any way in return?'

'You can't threaten me. No one can.'

'Leave me alone. What I said to Henry didn't make you cry. You ought to find the way to be in touch with your emotions. That's all you need to do here. Don't try to stay inhuman. We're all vulnerable in life. You could only be a strong person, if you admit your weaknesses but not by bullying or threatening others. That's the wrong way of dealing with your male superiority.'

'Who said that I am superior to you?'

'That's what you are after. Otherwise, you would leave me alone and let me enjoy my meal without being spoiled by your nonsense.'

'I feel that you are acting superior than murderers here.'

'Don't take me wrong. I have no intention of being superior to anyone. I don't crave for physical power or any other type of power. I'd like to spend my time here in peace. I have no time for all the conflicts you have been creating for nothing.'

'Time won't pass quickly if we get on well without having any problem here.'

'If you are looking for a trouble, I won't encourage you to take a wrong action. I'll make a complaint against you. You'll be moved into another jail that wouldn't do any good to your current circumstances. If you force me to make a decision, I'll have no regret but to take an action to get you out of my way. Understand that?'

'Very well, then!'

The meal arrives in metal containers. Felix eats his fish and chips quickly. His appetite has been completely ruined by the episode of his unreasonable inmates. No matter how much Felix tries to avoid trouble, he is driven into the action of telling the truth that he is not looking for polemics in a jail. He wants to keep his distance from the trouble makers. Felix leaves the canteen and goes back to his room. Thank God, he is given a separate room to live without facing the non-stop bullying of his aggressive inmates. Before Felix left his room, he was worrying about homelessness and unemployment outside prison; during his lunch break he faced the other side of coin for his misfortune in jail.

Felix turns his telly on in order to take his mind off; there is a documentary film about dyslexic population in jails in the UK. The statistical information is given by highlighting the urgency for the dyslexic inmates' training in order to equip them with literacy and numeracy skills during their imprisonment. The 80% of the prisoners' population in Britain is dyslexic with no literacy and numeracy skills or very little which won't help them to compete in the employment market once they leave prison. The average cost of keeping a young offender in jail is £36,000 a day that could be used to educate a young offender and enable them to contribute to community as active members instead of forcing them to repeat the similar crimes. There isn't much educational intervention to support young offenders with dyslexia over their repetitive life cycle with criminal record and without saleable skills. The high percentage of youth face discrimination within judicial system as they don't have enough advocate to raise awareness of detrimental consequences for the void in their lives. The young dyslexic offenders are left to learn how to swim with their instinct rather than educational support provided for them on a regular basis to teach not to sink. In many cases, the dyslexic young offenders won't be able to cope with the pressure being imposed on them to figure out how to acquire literacy skills without given any access to support mechanism either during their imprisonment or after completion of their sentences.

The speaker mentions about the well-known dyslexic names such as Winston Churchill, Pablo Picasso and Walt Disney who learnt how to swim without sinking. Felix turns the telly off and compares himself with the successful dyslexics. They have one thing in common which was dyslexia. How they made it despite having problems with the written language. If they managed to excel in their lives, there is a strong possibility that Felix will do well. Felix opens his sketch book and starts drawing abstract forms without thinking about any figure from the real life existence. The drawing expands with circle lines which have got different thicknesses and tonal values. Felix turns the circle lines into abstract forest in which the vertical lines are competing with horizontal lines. The abstract drawing looks like amazing playground which is controlled by Felix's imagination only. There is no any other reality than the circle forest with vertical and horizontal lines which contain different personalities. The tree-like circles have got bird-like creatures in them. Felix starts enjoying abstract drawing more than his figurative drawings as his imagination is not limited to the visible objects and his invisible ideas are all pulled out of his powerful visual memory effortlessly. Felix sticks his 1st abstract drawing with blue-tack on the wall by his bedside so that he could look at it and imagine the forest with the vertical and horizontal athletes running towards the end of the game which leads them all to their target. Felix loved the idea of ruling vertical lines and horizontal ones to run in the forest without any restriction of human form or human concept of alphabet. If Paul Klee takes a line for a walk, Felix takes the lines for a good run. He made it by expanding Klee's concept one step further and turning them into athletes for a running race. It's good to be an artist who cannot be ruled by anybody but their own imagination which unleashes their creative energy within them without any chain. Felix is not limited to his hidden disability. Who cares that he has got problem with distinguishing **b** and **d** or **p** and **q**, as long as he could distinguish between vertical and horizontal lines, he is a powerful person who cannot be beaten up by any letters of alphabet. That is the only thing which matters to him right now at present time.

It was a good break from all the hassle of being patronised by the inmates during his lunch hour. Felix wears his walkman and turns on Rodrigo's guitar concertos to soothe his mind without worrying about bullying, murder, sentence, prejudice and all sort of boring stuff. He looks over his current existence in his body with a bird view. After a while, he doesn't recognise his body as if his whole existence is the sound of the guitar. The music comes from his body after all he is nothing but his emotions which are hidden within his flesh. Now, his flesh has no significance but his emotions are the only concrete reality he is experiencing. Felix starts imagining himself as a guitar player. The abstract auditory forms are invisible and inside his brain. No one could argue that he is feeling the sound of the invisible reality. How simple, how beautiful and how complicated life is with music and visual art! If Felix is given a chance to choose between music and art, probably he couldn't make his mind which is the most important art form for his survival. Felix never produced any rhythmical sound but he always listens to music which uplifts his spirit in the same way how drawing affects him while he is drawing. He prefers to have it both in his life after all we eat bread and drink water which are both essential for our survival why shouldn't we have music and visual art at the same time like Kandinsky as he had very good ear for musical notes whilst he had a very good eye for details in his abstract paintings. How do I know all these stuff? Jackie told me as she has got a very authentic taste for painting. Jackie thinks that painting and music could heal anyone who suffers from all forms of depression. She would like to open a therapy clinic in which music and painting will be explored with her clients. Jackie detests calling sensitive people as patients as she doesn't see them different than the people who don't experience some kind of depression in life. According to Jackie, it's normal to have mood swings from time to time as this is part of human life. If we do not experience mood swing, we might fool ourselves that we are nothing but robots without emotions. Anyone who has got human feelings is bound to feel high or low in accordance with what we experience in life. It's like weather forecast. There is a rainy day and a sunny day in one's life. When it rains, our moods are affected; when the sun shines, our moods affected accordingly. The strong light beams are capable of cheering even the person with the lowest mood. I think I will never be able to deprive myself from the love of music and art. For my sanity, I need to have them both in my life. Music and visual art are inseparable as long as they have got strong influence on my vitality and passion for a new start each day I experience the struggle for survival in my life.

Chapter 5

Felix meets dyslexia tutor Wonder - Oct 2005

Felix had been very busy when he was prepared for his A levels in English, maths and law in 2004 as soon as he came out of prison. Seeing Steve twice a week at weekends for his language support and having regular tuition from Jasmine and Justin had disciplined Felix's stamina during his sentence and afterwards. As soon as Felix was released, he was housed in a council flat in South London. The council flat doesn't look grand, but it solves Felix's homelessness for the time being. In his council flat, Felix displays all his drawings and paintings he had produced in prison on his tiny flat's walls. Jasmine and Justin brought Felix some of the essential furniture like a small bed, a round table, a comfortable chair, a tall bookshelf, a fridge with a small freezer, a gas cooker, different sizes of saucepans, a set of cutlery and two frying pans. It feels strange for Felix to have his accommodation without any need to squat someone else's property any longer. How things developed in his life puzzles Felix; from homelessness to the space which he occupies now reminds him a childhood fairytale. Felix spent many sleepless nights in his council flat when he first moved in as he wasn't able to adjust himself into his current reality without being chucked out. It looks surreal to be accommodated in his furnished flat. Felix has everything now. He has never felt safe before without having a permanent place to live in, he feels satisfied with the security of his council flat. The insecurity of not having anywhere to live permanently damaged Felix's self-confidence deep down. Felix felt the anxiety of being unprotected without any roof over his head for years. He had to struggle to find a shelter to live for a night or two when he was sleeping rough. What a difficult start Felix had! If Felix didn't meet Justin, he wouldn't be able to get where he is at present, in a cosy council flat with all the essential possessions he had longed for when he was homeless a few years backwards. While Felix is reflecting on his past experience of being homeless and without any self identity, his mobile phone rings; Felix picks up the phone immediately.

'Hi Felix! This is Justin. How are you getting on?'

'I'm very well, Justin. I was thinking of my past life when I didn't have anywhere to live. It was only 3 years ago, but it looks like a long time ago.'

'Time is relative. Sometimes, a decade feels a few minutes. Sometimes, a few minutes looks like a decade. I'm sure you won't face homelessness again, Felix.'

'Thanks for your help, Justin. Without you and Jasmine, I couldn't make it.'

'Let's put it this way, our meeting was within our destiny. Your life might have been developed in a different way for better or worse if we didn't meet. One cannot speculate the difference now.'

'I'm sure my life wouldn't be as good as it is now if I didn't meet you both.'

'Meeting us was certainly a turning point for you, Felix. It has worked out well. Let's hope that you'll meet the people who will make even better impact on your life. Be cautious of the negative people who could destroy your future deliberately and cause you regression in life.'

'I know what you mean, Justin. There are many destructive people out there. I need to be careful not to mix with the trouble makers.

'That's what I meant, Felix.'

'How is Jasmine?'

'Jasmine is preparing her case, she's in her office.'

'How is Fanny?'

'Fanny is fine. She is bigger than 3 years ago. You ought to visit us and spend some time with Fanny as well as with us.'

'I'd love to do that!'

'Would you like to come over for a dinner tomorrow?'

'I'll be very happy to see you all.'

'Can you come over at 12.00 o'clock?'

'Yes, I can. See you at 12.00 then.'

'See you at 12.00, Justin.'

Felix switches off his mobile. He goes to the kitchen. He fills up the kettle with tap water and turns the kettle on. While waiting for the water boil, Felix goes back to the living room and gets his diary out of the drawer. Felix writes how he feels in his diary after giving a long break without writing anything.

'I haven't written to my diary for a month as I've been very busy to adjust myself into my new circumstances. After leaving prison, doing A levels for a year and settling in the comfy of my council flat, time has gone so quickly, quicker than before.

Today, the first time in my life, I thought that I must have been strong enough to overcome the problems of being different from many people I've met. It was good to talk to Justin on the phone a few minutes ago. Justin, Jasmine and their friend Steve have been good to me. I know that without their help, I must have been still struggling to find my feet on the ground without stumbling. Meeting them at the right time speeded up my actions to get out of the trap I was placed in. I could have easily chosen not to take their help seriously. Even worst, I might have refused to take their offer in the first place. That would have delayed my progress I've made since I have known them. My council flat is being filled up with the bits and pieces donated by Justin and Jasmine. None of the furniture is chosen by me. None of my belongings represents my identity. A chair, a bed, a bookshelf in my flat all reveals Justin's or Jasmine's taste. I'm so grateful to them that they've provided me with the essential furniture to live. Without having a bed, it would have been very uncomfortable to sleep on the floor as I used to do when I was living rough. Without kitchen utensils, it would have been impossible to cook my meals. Without bookshelf, it would have been untidy to keep my books within cardboard boxes on the floor. To be able to predict another person's needs for a piece of furniture is the sign of human sensitivity and compassion. One day, I'll be able to choose what I need in life with the spending power to buy without any need to accept donation or gift from anybody. Today, I appreciate Justin's kindness for investing their money in me and my future. When I'm fully qualified as a barrister with enough money to buy whatever I want, I shall never forget what Justin and Jasmine have done for me at the time when I needed their financial assistance. True friends are the ones who support you not only emotionally, but financially when they are in a position to do so.

Steve has given me his time so generously. He spent all his weekends to support me during the last 3 years. Now, I've got another language support tutor at university. Having another support tutor freed Steve from his voluntary duties. The groundwork of Steve will always stay with me though. The reassurance Steve has given me will always be there whenever I need his help. Steve's existence in my life is another gift for me from God. Although I'll try my best not to disturb Steve, it's a good feeling to know that he will have an answer for the problems my dyslexia has been causing me.

At university, I have met quite a few people. None of us knew each other's life circumstances. I don't automatically assume that they were brought up by foster parents. It's hard to guess what kind of life-style they have had. I guess they all have better life circumstances than mine. I cannot imagine anyone having worse life story than mine. I assume many of them come from Jackie's backgrounds. The spoiled childhood with all the luxuries of comfort ensures the sustainability of well-being in human life. I'm pretty sure that none of my fellow classmates suffered from any identity problem. They weren't confused about who their biological parents are. Most likely, they weren't jailed for squatting. They don't even know how it feels to be homeless. I've nothing in common with any of the students. I get irritated when they make silly assumptions of having the same life circumstances with me. People are conditioned to think that everyone's life looks alike. That is not true! I am completely different than everyone else. They've never had any experience of maturing through struggle. I'm 24 years old now but it feels I reached my maturity already. How I will feel when I am 64, I haven't got a clue. I've got my youth to focus on without worrying about accommodation or earning my daily bread. I don't have to pay for the tuition fee at university. Justin and Jasmine keep contributing towards my living expenses. In three years time, I'll be able to earn a decent salary out of my skills. I'll be able to go on holiday and book a decent hotel room. I can even travel by aeroplane which I've never done before. Life has never looked as promising as it does now. I hope it'll stay as it is without going downwards again.'

Felix realises that he has forgotten the kettle boiling in the kitchen. He rushes back to the kitchen. When he touches the kettle, it feels lukewarm. Felix switches on the kettle once more. He opens the cupboard and gets himself a tea-bag from the container. He puts the tea-bag into a pretty mug Jasmine gave him as a present. The kettle makes a pleasant noise letting him know that the water has just been boiled. Felix unplugs the kettle and pours the water over the teabag in his mug. He gets biscuits tin from the cupboard and puts the biscuits on a small plate. Felix goes back to the living room with his tea mug and the plate with biscuits. He puts the biscuit plate on the table and sits in his chair. While he bites his digestive biscuit, he sips his tea from the beautiful mug. Felix looks at the design of the mug carefully. The scenery with trees and seaside depicted with the colours of red, blue and yellow looks gorgeous! Felix feels like exploring seaside with plenty of trees. Even the mug we drink our tea should promise us a better future with a strong hope for better days in life. Felix doesn't like the negative logos displayed on the mugs like a political slogan. He hated drinking from a mug displaying destructive mood such as:

'It's for a lazy day' or *'Life is so boring'.*

Life can't be boring for Felix. Far from it, life has been so exciting with full of wonders for a new start since he has been learning in a structured way with the help of Steve, Justin and Jasmine. Learning new concepts is the best enjoyment which couldn't be replaced with anything else in life. Boredom only gets in the way when you stop learning new concepts. Felix plans his day. It'll be exciting to do some revision for his essay writing about interviewing clients. Thanks to Steve, Felix has become an expert how to analyse a pattern of a confusing word. Felix opens his source material **'Correct usage of**

English Grammar in Legal Language' and looks through his notes taken from the book on interview techniques for legal profession.

Interview Procedure

Interview technique needs to be mastered with paying attention on clients' specific need. Knowing interview procedure accurately is the most important part of the legal practice. If it is not done correctly, it will cause misunderstanding and loss of confidence to the legal profession. Without the correct procedure, rapport cannot be built between the clients and their lawyers. A competent lawyer usually fulfils the following stages during the interview process:

1. *Meet, greet and seat stage: this stage is also known information gathering stage in which the lawyer makes enquiries about the nature of the client's problem. Accordingly, aims and objectives of the client's agenda will be established correctly without any misunderstanding of the facts.*
2. *Advising stage: The legal person demonstrates his/her competence in the area of speciality providing adequate legal advice by addressing the client's specific concerns accurately in private.*
3. *Conclusion stage: the interview must be completed with a brief and sufficient recap of what it has been discussed and what actions need to be taken.*

Felix visualises himself in an office environment and interviewing his first client as a lawyer. Felix has never had any chance to work in an office before let alone interviewing anyone for establishing a legal case on his behalf. It feels so unusual to interview a person for identifying his problems. Felix will be sitting in an office to solve other people's problems in three years time. His professional role will be empowering other people.

Felix will be having the necessary knowledge and skills to offer to the people who lack the access to the legal language. Felix was interviewed by a few lawyers when he had problems. They all had different approaches and techniques. When Felix start acting as a lawyer, the scenarios will be changing each time he sees a new client. Felix will be learning from his clients' life experiences. Getting to know what problems they face in their lives will increase Felix's life experience. He'll try to see their struggle without any preconception. Felix remembers reading Professor Richard Nisbett's book entitled 'The Geography of Thought, How Asians and Westerners Think Differently' explaining about human understanding.

> 'When people in one culture differ from those in another in their beliefs, it can't be because they have different cognitive processes, but because they are exposed to different aspects of the world, or because they have been thought different things.'

Richard E. Nisbett, 2004

Felix will be exposed to different aspects of human complexity as he will be able to make connection between the problems his clients face and the origin of their life circumstances. Felix knows that providing legal help to his clients will never solve their personal problems like their weaknesses not being able to function without committing crime in terms of drug dependence. The clients with drug dependency should receive help from the medical people to clear themselves from addiction. Felix was so lucky to keep himself out of drug culture even he was exposed to various drugs some of his class mates were taking when he was in a secondary school. It was a good job that his dyslexia helped Felix to drop out of the school. If Felix had stayed at school, there was a possibility that he might have mixed with the drug addicts and felt the peer pressure to try some of the hard drugs and got hooked on it for life. If Felix was doomed to become a drug addict, Justin and Jasmine wouldn't be able to help him. They wouldn't take the trouble of supporting him financially. Felix would have ended up in the same way some of his class mates have ended up without any way-out from the awful trap they all found themselves into. Addiction to any addictive substance is the most unfortunate weakness in anyone's life. Without beating the habit of addiction, no one can beat the reality of being a failure in life. With any addiction you are bound to suffer from all forms of disillusion in the long run.

Felix goes back to his reflective diary and reads his struggle with the academic writing for his thesis.

> *'I woke up with all the ideas in my mind and not knowing what to do with them. I feel exhausted before even starting my day. I've been doing a lot of reading. I've taken plenty of notes. But putting them together will be the challenging aspect of academic writing, I presume.*

> *I lose tract on the articles I've been reading. Is it my fault or the writers who don't get me into a mood that I could carry on reading their texts without losing a track? My mind has been already clustered with so many expressions which I hardly use in my daily life. The academic terminology has got a special coding system that keeps me out of focus. Wondering about what a writer meant with a particular expression exhausts me. Sometimes, I feel like giving up altogether. Just do something else for 1 hour or 2. Then I get into panic. The deadline is there. I have to meet the deadline. Time is against me. Being under the pressure of the time constraint makes me like I haven't done much. It seems I am not making enough progress to complete my final thesis.*

> *I talked to Steve how often I get distracted by so many other things. Steve's response to my self-observation was that distraction is the natural aspect of our defence mechanism and helps us to keep our sanity's balance*

without getting nervous breakdown. If the mind cannot take in any longer, you need to give a break for some time like doing completely different things than reading and writing. By doing so, you free your brain from clusters of so many concepts related or unrelated to your research topic. I often give myself a tea-break every an hour or so. When I am at home, I put the kettle on and have a snack like a toast with honey on top to go with a mug of tea. A handful of nuts do the trick most of the time to restore my energy. It is a quick fix to see me through another an hour. Then, I always have a large meal with brain food like oily fish to keep me alert at night when I need to work through midnight. A good sleeping pattern is as important as a sensible eating pattern. I must have minimum 8 hrs sleep at night. Otherwise, I cannot function next day. I have to stop writing now. If not, I will never finish my assignment.'

Felix puts his diary in the drawer of his desk and he goes back to his academic reading on **'Correct usage of English Grammar in Legal Language'**. He rereads the paragraph he read before entering his diary.

Aims of drafting

You need to identify your client's concerns with an appropriate legal language which has got the following specifications:

1) *Correct interpretation of your client's instruction what the client wants you to do.*
2) *Accurate language without any ambiguity.*
3) *Brief overview of the client's instruction*
4) *Modern usage of legal terminology – avoid archaic expressions –*
5) *Comprehensible language – keep the draft easy to comprehend –*

Correct interpretation of client's instructions

This requires competent listening skills and recording what it has been said on a face to face transaction in writing precisely. You need to provide your client the 1st draft to check out on its accuracy. If it is not in line with the client's instruction, the 1st draft needs to be redrafted until the client agrees with its contents.

Felix takes notes from his reading. He summarises the important points in his notebook:

'*Effective drafting in legal practice is the essential skill a legal person should accomplish. A legal adviser should ensure that he understands the client's instruction correctly and produces a draft with a clear language accurately for the client to check it out.*'

Felix understands more when he regularly takes down notes. Writing enables Felix to remember the facts a lot easier. The written information is well digested at the end of reading process. Without taking notes, reading any academic text is almost impossible for Felix to assimilate. Academic reading is completely different than reading for pleasure. When Felix reads for pleasure, he never takes notes. It's like having a meal for pleasure without following a strict diet in order to survive. Felix treats academic reading as a necessity for his survival rather than a leisure activity to boost his morale. Felix remembers that he hasn't read any book outside his academic books for his academic studies for a long while. Even writing his diary is turned out to be a tool for enforcing what he learns from his academic studies and helps him develop self awareness how he feels as a student while he is at university. Felix wants to treat himself for a good novel over his Christmas break for a few days without worrying about academic reading. Felix knows that this is not possible. He has to get on with his research as he has to submit a dissertation with 20.000 word count. Christmas break will be consumed by reading and writing. Perhaps, he will postpone his wish to read for only pleasure after graduation. Then, he needs to set up his business. There will be a lot of things to do after leaving university. What a busy life! At least, during the next 5 years, there won't be any time left for him to enjoy reading for pleasure only. All he needs to do is to educate himself constantly in order to increase his competence and knowledge in legal issues and recent legislations.

Felix realises that becoming a legal profession means a life without much pleasure outside legal responsibilities. Being a barrister demands complete dedication of one's life. Felix assumes it must be the same for a medical doctor or an academic lecturer or a researcher. Once you are engaged with any discipline, it is a lifelong commitment which cannot be neglected whenever you feel the pressure of breaking the daily routine which is not possible until you become financially free till you reach your retirement age. Felix needs to find a way out of all the hustle and bustle of academic life. He needs time to enjoy reading for pleasure or taking trips to the places he hasn't been before. To have some time off for drawing, painting and falling in love with a right person will increase his morale. Felix thinks about Jackie. Was he in love with Jackie? He cannot answer it. He doesn't know what it was. Felix wonders where Jackie is now. She must have got married to someone suitable by now. Jackie doesn't know what kind of life Felix has been leading soon after leaving prison as his life has been transformed into completely different episode than what Jackie knew about him when he was a homeless person. Felix looks around his cosy council flat and thanks to his luck. One day, he will be buying a big house like Justin's house. It's worth enduring the struggle of academic life. Without any struggle, he will never have the same life style of the wealthy people. Look at Justin, Jasmine and Steve! They have got wealth which doesn't buy them free time though. Their life is not less hectic than Felix's life. They're all occupied with their duties for survival as well. They cannot afford to give up everything and live less busy life.

Felix could do anything to start a new life without any responsibility, just to have a great fun with drawings and paintings all day long. It'll be good to travel around the world whenever he feels like exploring the external world beside his internal world. Without financial freedom, he has to postpone all his dreams at least for a decade or so. He has to make a good living first. His time will be taken up by his academic studies and working as a full time barrister. After a decade, he might be able to take some time off without any need to work that hard. Felix could imagine himself being a painter with lots of money. He could visualise rising from his bed with the great inspiration to start his new painting; each day will be a new canvas for him to fill up with the vibrant colours. Each night, there will be a pleasure of fulfilling his creative potential without any pressure of finding buyers to sell his paintings. He will store all his paintings in his gorgeous house. He will open his home to public once a year to share the joy of creativity with the viewers without any intention to sell his work. If they don't like what he produces, who cares! It'll be their loss not his concern as his survival won't depend on selling any of his paintings or drawings. As a matter of fact, Felix will be happier to keep all his artwork within his living environment. The artwork he creates will function as part of his biological extension which represents his emotions and thoughts in a visible output with colours and lines on canvases or papers. It is like recycling what comes out of his mind and heart without any waste of his insight, dreams and intellectual representations of how he sees or how he visualises everything he has exposed to, from his angle. That's how Felix wants to build up his passion for his existence without getting lost within the bureaucratically complex labyrinth of a civil servant life as a barrister working in a courtroom trying to defend his client's legal rights against all the odds. For one second, Felix reconsiders whether he made a good decision to become a barrister. Wouldn't it be better to study art instead? He would feel freedom as an art student instead of law student. It isn't easy to make money out of art. At least, there will be a demand for his intellectual skill to exchange in the legal world. He wouldn't leave his future to the chance element for being discovered by others as a genius of art world. The art market has got its gate keepers to stop him from entering into global arena to be a celebrated artist like Picasso when Felix is still alive. Probably, he would have been turned into Van Gogh but not Picasso. They were both geniuses though. The later had eaten the cake of success with the joy of good appetite; the former one was left to starve to death without any mercy. Van Gogh couldn't sell a single work of art even though he had his art dealer brother Theo's support till the tragic end. The Dutch painter Vincent Van Gogh played the tragedy, the Spanish painter Pablo Picasso played the comedy within the same art market. That was the only difference they had as artist geniuses with full of creative energy for the new art forms which shocked the art world in their own time as they accomplished breakthrough in plastic reality of oil paintings. Van Gogh's paintings fetch the astronomic prices which are valued as expensive as Picasso's paintings in auction rooms of this century and are classified masterpieces on their own rights but they had no market value while Van Gogh was still alive.

Felix will be better off to get satisfied with the daily duties of a typical court barrister without taking the risk of starvation in the case of misfortune for not being able to sell his paintings like Van Gogh. Painting and drawing will stay Felix's passion for his luxurious habit in his life. His artwork is too precious to risk for making a living out of it. All he needs to do now is to take his mind off from his artistic ambition of producing art daily without getting distracted by the question of how I am going to survive financially. While Felix has been pondering around his future and present occupation with his academic studies, he remembers that he has got an appointment to see his support tutor Wonder in the afternoon. He changes quickly; he puts his beret on his head and thinks himself as an artist who has destined to study law instead of art. Felix leaves his council flat in rush and takes the DLR to Canary Wharf. He doesn't know the area. After getting off the train, he starts walking up and down, stops a stranger at random. He is directed to the correct address. The building is a luxury office block overlooking the River Thames. Felix presses the buzz of the intercom. The door is opened with an automatic reply 'please push the door'. He follows the instruction and takes the lift to the 3rd floor. Once the lift stops, Felix gets out of the lift. There is an office opposite the lift with the company logo on the door 'Three Dimension Dyslexia'. Felix rings the bell and the door is opened by Felix's *private support tutor Wonder. Felix is welcomed and asked to enter a room with slightly tinted colour. He was asked to sit in a special chair. The minute Felix sits in a chair, his whole body starts moving as the moving chair gives Felix a gentle massage while the calming music fills the room. Felix feels so good and surprised at the same time. Twenty minute massage therapy does the trick; Felix's stiff neck and shoulder loosen up without any tension. The support tutor asks Felix to close his eyes and remember how he felt in the therapy room.*

'How was the neck and shoulder therapy, Felix?'

'It was so good.'

'Could you describe how you felt before the therapy?'

'I was tensed. I had stiff neck and shoulder.'

'Before each support session, you'll be having 20 min massage therapy for your shoulder and neck in order to relieve your tension so that it'll be a lot easier for you to focus on your learning.'

'Thanks!'

''Let's go to the multisensory room in which you'll be experiencing aroma therapy to activate your brain with new associations

which will increase memory retention. Learning through aroma therapy has got the most powerful impact on your short-term memory. All the new terminology will be linked to certain aroma which will activate neurons of your brain to sustain the given information without erasing the details.'

'I'm rather surprised. I wasn't expected to try different therapies here. To tell you the truth, all these therapies are new to me.'

'The combination of therapies is a new concept I'm using as part of teaching strategies rather than complementary healing intervention.'

In the aroma therapy room, Felix is given tactile simulations with various scents. Felix starts squeezing each object during 10 min therapy session. Then, he is asked to use sunglasses with different colours. Each colour of a new object he squeezes turns into another colour. Felix's mind is distracted in a positive way which vitalizes his short-term memory. The experience of senses becomes tactile, aromatic and visual illusion. Felix enjoys being in another dimension which is sensed with emerging neurological pathways in his brain by going beyond his ordinary optical perceptions. Everything looks surreal and different than his customised visual codes in her visual memory. All those years, Felix didn't experience anything like that. Within 20 minutes, Felix's senses are empowered beyond his imagination. He feels completely relax and energetic and looks at his support tutor with a great satisfaction.

Wonder takes Felix to the next door which looks like a study room. It's a spacious room with the strong day light entering from the north. The study room is filled with ergonomic equipment such as 2 chairs, 2 desks, 2 PCs, 2 Macs with ergonomic input devices, mouse, mouse wrist rest and keyboard. There is a wobble board for back treatment on the floor. A flipchart, flipchart pens are placed near the stationary cupboard with plenty of notepads, pens, pencils, highlighters, rulers, scissors, sticky notes, paper folders and plastic pockets at the far end of the room. There is a large bookshelf with academic books and dictionaries. A large sofa and a coffee table with a beautiful plant on are displayed in the centre of the room. The abstract paintings on the walls complete the atmosphere with a sophisticated touch. A little fridge, a microwave, a coffee maker and a toaster appear in the half kitchen unit of a studio study room by the door. The interior of the study room looks pleasant and welcoming. There is no cluster to cause overcrowded feeling of the space.

Felix is given a learning agreement. He is asked to tick the boxes which are relevant to his needs. Felix ticks the boxes quickly and gives the paper back to his support tutor Wonder. Then, he is given another paper to fill out which has got learning style questionnaire.

Learning Style Questionnaire	
Questions	*Response*
1) *When you go to the new place which you have not been before, what do you do to find your way?*	*I ask other people for direction.*
2) *In the case of assembling a new machine which you are unfamiliar with, what do you do?*	*I figure out what needs to be done.*

3) When you need to follow instructions, how would you start reading the manual?	I skim through the manual.
4) What is your favourite leisure activity?	Drawing
5) How do you explore your strong emotions such as anger, distress, and agitation?	Through drawing
6) If you were given a choice to make a new start in life, where would you start from?	I'd start from the final part.
7) What makes you happy?	Not to worry about money.
8) What makes you unhappy?	To worry about money.
9) How do you describe yourself with one word only?	Content
10) How do others describe you with one word only?	Remote

Felix gives back the questionnaire to Wonder. In return, she smiles at Felix and gives him a book with academic texts this time. Then, she asks Felix to choose a topic to read it aloud.

Felix looks through the content page and chooses a topic from Maryanne Wolf.

Naming Colours and Developing Reading

Geschwind, one of the most influential neurologists of the latter half of this century, was the 1st person to see the link between the underlying requirement of naming and developing reading. Geschwind (1965) hypothesised that the best predictor of 'reading readiness' would be the young child's ability to name colours. The principle was that colour naming, like reading, requires all the cognitive linguistic and perceptual processes underlying the retrieval of a verbal label for an abstract visual symbol, yet doesn't require that the child knows letters.

Felix is stopped and asked to give the gist of the paragraph. Felix tries to remember the facts and answers Wonder's question.

'The paragraph is about young children's ability to name colours and how this ability affects acquiring their reading skills.'

'Who claimed that hypothesis, Felix?'

'I am not good at remembering names. I can't remember the name of the neurologist.'

'Please have a look at the text and tell me the name of the neurologist, Felix.'

'The name of neurologist is Geschwind.'

'That's correct. Could you remember when Geshwind mentioned his hypothesis, Felix?'

'I am useless remembering the dates. I think it's in 60s. I am not sure exactly what year though.'

'That's fine! Please read the text one more time and find the exact date for me, Felix.'

'It's in 1965.'

'That's correct. While I was asking you questions, you were practising reading strategy called scanning, Felix. Are you familiar with scanning?'

Yes, I am familiar with it.'

'What are the other reading strategies do you know, Felix?'

'Skimming'

'That's good. How about SQ3R? Have you practised detailed reading strategy before?'

'I think I did. However, I'll be happy to go over it with you, Wonder.'

'No problem! Time is up now. I'll book you in for next week. We'll practise SQ3R reading strategy next session. Please bring one of your academic texts with you. I've got another appointment to attend now. Shall I see you out now?'

'Thanks.'

Wonder leads Felix to the exit. The next student is waiting at the door. While Felix leaves, a female student with colourful jacket enters the premise. She smiles at Felix in a friendly way. Felix greets her while he is leaving the office building with a high spirit. The 1st time in his life, Felix feels so grateful to his dyslexia; otherwise, he wouldn't have an access to the special world of Wonder with multi sensory objects, aroma therapy, massage therapy and the beautiful study room. That young girl with a lovely smiling face must be another dyslexic. She looks so pretty. Dyslexic people are special. They greet you with a good smiling face. She is completely different than non-dyslexic students at university with moody and noisy characters. Felix feels like making friends with that attractive dyslexic girl, they must have something in common as they both have dyslexia. This is incredible. To meet another dyslexic person like him is awesome! Dyslexic people must have a special charisma to attract each other's attention like a magnet. Felix remembers his support sessions with Steve in prison. Although Steve has got such a wonderful personality and he is an excellent support tutor, having support session in a prison environment is totally different than being in a modern office environment with the exposure of modern technology and its benefit. All the way back home, Felix sees everything from a fresh angle. He is so happy that he'll be having an access to a 2 hours' support session in a comforting and welcoming environment with Wonder whose only concern seems to be Felix's achievement but nothing else. He is treated so well without being patronised. They had a pleasant conversation. The neck and shoulder therapy before starting each session will be extra bonus for increasing the feeling of being a special person with dignity and importance. Wonder treated Felix as if he was a VIP but not a person with a hidden disability. Felix doesn't like the word hidden disability; if he had a chance to alter the description, he could use the term 'hidden gift' like synaesthesia perhaps.

Felix visualises himself as an important person making significant decisions almost daily after graduation. No one will be able to overlook him any longer. He has got his developed personality with special characteristics. He carries a powerful visual memory in his brain. He could imagine every detail of his surroundings with a picturesque view, which is usually stored in his long-term memory so that he could reflect on the stored images whenever he wants to refresh his memory to vitalise his energy. He could go back to the years where he visited the River Thames once a week on foot, for example. He could remember the movements of the river when there was a boat passing by with high speed. He could remember the beautiful reflection of sun beams fallen on the river during the day time. He could remember how the trees look like by the Modern Tate Gallery in a sunny day and the flowers near the Bankside Gallery. Felix's visual memory captured every single moment of day light and its mysterious effect on the environment. When it rains, he could easily find a way back to the visual storage of sunny days by the river in his visual memory. That's how he could beat the winter blues until spring's arrival time. It's so good to be born as a dyslexic artist. His dyslexia enables him to utilise the right-hemisphere of his brain more efficiently than any other person who relies on his left-hemisphere of his brain most of the time. If Felix knew what he knows now years ago, he would have never seen himself inadequate among the people with left-brain approach. To be able to appreciate what gift one has got, one needs to know the art of self-discovery which doesn't come to you that easily. It could be learnt with an interaction of a skilled helper like Steve or Wonder. Felix predicts that he will be discovering himself and his strengths even more with the interactive process of one to one tutorial with Wonder. How misfortunate that Felix didn't have the luxury of self-discovery through the lenses of another person who facilitates the process years ago! He is at the peak of his self-gratification now with all the opportunities provided for him to take up for free of charge. Isn't it fabulous to be able to get the cake without even paying for it? All his life time, Felix worked so hard to make less than sufficient earning; he couldn't afford to rent an accommodation with his full time earning capacity in the factory. All he had during his lunch break was a simple sandwich with cheese only. Now, he can afford to have a proper meal regularly, he has got his own flat and plenty of time to go to university. He is able to have one to one tutorial at Wonder's office with all the luxury he has never been exposed to before. What a change! Felix will always be grateful to Justin, Jasmine and Steve for making all the positive things in his life possible for him to enjoy.

Felix pops into a supermarket near where he lives. He needs to buy food which should last a week to keep him going. He buys green vegetable, kale, courgettes, leeks, parsley, lettuce, carrots, garlic, a few limes, a dozen of eggs, honey, bread and tin fish. He pays for his groceries and comes back his flat with a great appetite to prepare his dinner. Felix grills the tin mackerel and eats it with green salad. He remembers Steve's words that he should have oily fish every day in order to increase his brain power as omega 3 helps to recall what he learns during the revision for exam preparation. Steve also recommended him that he should eat nuts every day to enhance his memory. Without feeding yourself properly, there is a danger of slowing down your brain power. It's like having a very expensive car without petrol to run it. Our brain works better if we nourish it with a balanced diet which is formulated by Felix in order to increase his energy throughout the day.

1 fish + 1 egg + a handful of nuts + 1 portion of green salad with carrots + 2 slices of wholemeal bread + an apple + a kiwi + a bunch of grapes + a handful of blueberries + soya milk + cereal + 2 litre of water + a teaspoonful of honey + green tea + rice or paste.

After having his dinner, Felix enters in his diary.

> 'I had a very pleasant afternoon. I visited my new support tutor Wonder in her office in Canary Wharf overlooking the River Thames. It was a wow moment for me to be there. It's a welcoming environment. It felt so good to be a dyslexic student. Otherwise, I would have never had a chance to experience what I experienced there. I am hoping that I'll be learning more about myself and how my brain works.
>
> I met another dyslexic person when I was about to leave Wonder's office. We greeted each other. She looks pretty. I'd like to know more about her and how

it feels to be dyslexic for her. I've never met a dyslexic person before. It'll be good to make friends with another dyslexic student especially when she looks like a model but not a person with low self-esteem as it is described by none dyslexic people.

I'm going to ask Wonder whether I could obtain her details so that we could meet up and talk about our common characteristics as dyslexic people. It'll increase our emotional intelligence through connecting each other and finding out more about how we see or how we look at things which will enable us to explore different points of view. She is a female dyslexic, I'm a male dyslexic. I wonder how dyslexia affects different gender. Is there any gender specific difference when it comes to dyslexia? I must find out what it is to be in a female dyslexic student's shoes. Jackie wasn't dyslexic and she didn't understand how I felt as a dyslexic person. Jackie was capable of offending me without even realising that. If she had dyslexic sensitivity even a bit, she would have left me alone when I wasn't in a mood to talk to her. Never mind, Jackie is out of my life now. I do not want to meet her again. Jackie will be out my sight and out of my thought.'

Felix feels sleepy and decides to go to bed. He puts his diary away and goes to the bathroom to take a quick shower. After having a warm shower, he goes to his bedroom and puts on his pyjamas. He turns on the tape recorder with the CD playing Heinrich Wilhelm Dove's bi-neural beats for relaxation and he immediately falls asleep. In his sleep, Felix finds himself in a heaven-like environment in which he experiences out-of-body feeling as a spirit without any limitation of bodily awareness. Felix walks on the surface of the boundless ocean without experiencing the law of gravity. He cuts out himself from the concept of mortality, time, money and fleshy limitations such as greed for money, fame, political power or any worries of materialistic kind. He feels inner peace as there is no fleshy sensation such as any irritation, pain, and the sense of burning, one may experience as a human being with flesh and blood. Felix thinks about infinity as there is no time concept in his mind. All his life when his spirit dwelt in his body, he worried about his mortality and how he was going to face his last minute on earth. Now, there isn't fear of any kind. He is immortal and time is infinite. There won't be the last stop of his journey. His spirit will be continuing his journey forever in the heavenly space without facing death or dying. Felix's spirit lands on the highest level of heaven without any need for a rocket or a spacecraft to fly in outer space. There is no one who could harm him in a physical way. He is an invisible spirit without any visible particulars of animated beings to be targeted by so-called human beings like it happens down there on earth. Felix escaped the limitation of human life and its threat of being harmed by the brutality of wild people with beastly characteristics who operate within the lowest level of human instinct to destroy anyone who doesn't look like them or approve their opinions.

Felix is in total control of his well-being. He is utterly in peace with his surroundings and his capability to move around without any need for a vehicle or a driver, or a pilot, or a captain to take him where he wants to go. Felix conquered the whole heaven with his spiritual existence. There is no evil spirit around him either. He is on the highest altitude of spiritual place. He doesn't even need a pair of wing to fly like a bird or an angel. His spirit moves around without any limitation. Felix's experience of heavenly existence makes him deliriously happy and he immediately stops thinking of himself as a human being. His spirit doesn't have the feeling of hot or cold either. Felix doesn't have 5 senses any longer. He is having his 7 senses as a spirit. Felix doesn't smell anything. All his 5 senses he used to have as a human being left him without leaving any trace of remembrance; he sees everything with his spiritual eye.

There is no optical illusion of a human eye. Felix looks at the 7 layers of the heaven and sees a luminous light which is as bright as the sun beams. It's a holy light which is warming up Felix's spirit. The warming up process of his spirit is completely different than bodily sensation of warming up. His spirit starts gaining more luminous power and becomes part of the light of the 7 layers of heaven. Felix realises that he became part of his surroundings; he is a heavenly spirit filling up the entire space of heaven. He is beyond the time limit of un-heavenly existence which is so far away now. Felix can't even remember how it felt to be in a flesh any longer.

While Felix in the depth of his dream, he is waken up beyond his deliberate intention; he looks around his room and the minute he remembers himself as a human being, his spiritual eye loses its sharpness; his vision is limited to the optical illusion only. Felix closes his eyes and wants to capture the same sensation of experiencing the out-of-body feeling without any success. It's useless to expect his body and mind to feel how he felt while he was in unconscious state of dream mode. Felix cannot find any logical explanation how he experienced beyond his flesh without any bodily sensations. How could this happen to someone without passing away. Each night looks like he experiences what a dead body might experience without any bodily sensation. The only difference between a living person in unconscious state of mind when they are in sleep and the dead person who never returns back into their body is the incomprehensible process of wakening up. When we are wakening up to the earthy reality, we lose our spiritual richness and become spiritually blind to our spiritual identity.

Felix feels thirsty. A few minutes ago, when he was asleep, he didn't have any of his 5 senses. Felix opens his eyes, goes to the kitchen, opens the fridge and gets a bottle of water. He drinks the water. It feels so good. Water is life. He is connected to this life with the water he has just drunk. Felix knows for sure that he is alive in a human form but not a spirit yet. Felix feels that dying wouldn't be that scary after all. When he loses the taste of water, he will be gaining spiritual freedom of fullness without any thirst for this life. That's the thing, the thirst for life keeps us occupied when we are alive in this side of our existence before entering into spiritual existence. Once the thirst of life is lost, we are almost there and our bodily function deteriorates without being restored by any medical interventions.

Felix meets Evelyn at University

After the lecture, Felix enters the university restaurant to get his lunch. He waits at the end of the queue. The dyslexic girl he met the other day at Three Dimension Dyslexia enters the restaurant and sits down at a table. She takes a sandwich out of her bag and starts eating her sandwich while reading her book. Felix leaves the queue and goes directly to the table where Evelyn sits.

'Hi, do you remember me? We met at Three Dimension Dyslexia the other day.'

'That's right! I remember seeing you with Wonder.'

'Can I join you for a quick chat?'

'Sure'

'Let me introduce myself to you first. I'm Felix. What's your name?'

'I'm Evelyn'

'Nice to meet you, Evelyn.'

'Nice to meet you, Felix.'

'What are you reading?'

'It's my text book.'

'What are you studying here, Evelyn?'

'Philosophy; how about you, Felix?'

'Civil Law.'

'You're going to be a legal person, then.'

'That's right. What are you going to do once you complete your degree in philosophy, Evelyn?'

'I might teach. I am not quite sure yet.'

'Are you dyslexic by any chance?'

'Yes, I am dyslexic. Yourself?'

'I am dyslexic. When were you diagnosed?'

'When I was 7 yrs old. What about you, Felix?'

'A few years ago.'

'Well, how comfortable are you with diagnosis?'

'That's what I wanted to talk to you about. I haven't met any other dyslexic person before. I'd like to find out how it feels to be dyslexic for you.'

'It's fine. It doesn't bother me at all. I've been living with my dyslexia since I was 7 years old. I'm comfortable with it. My both parents and my younger brother are all dyslexic. Somehow, I don't know how it feels not to be a dyslexic. It's part of my identity. How does dyslexia affects you, Felix?'

'I rather enjoy being dyslexic nowadays. I wasn't aware that I was dyslexic till I reach my twenty.'

'Is there anyone in your family dyslexic, Felix?'

'I am not sure about that.'

'Well, many dyslexic people aren't as lucky as we are. They are not diagnosed. Let's take my boyfriend Leo. I'm sure, he is dyslexic but he doesn't want to take the diagnostic test. He is not comfortable with the term dyslexia. In his family, there is no one dyslexic. He is the first dyslexic.'

'How do you know Leo is dyslexic?'

'We've got similar problems with time management. We are both disorganised.'

'You said you were diagnosed when you were 7 years old. Did you get one to one support immediately?'

'I've been having one to one support throughout my schooling.'

'How did you find support sessions?'

'If I stick to the strategies introduced to me, having regular support sessions could be very useful. You know the human nature. Sometimes, I'd like to forget about the problems I've got with time management. Then, things start going out of hand; I don't keep up with deadlines, for example. I find it so difficult to get any assignment done within the given timeframe.'

'I find it hard to prepare myself for exams. Too much information cramped into the last minute revision practice gets me down some time.'

'Tell me about it. I hate written exams. I can't cope with the factual information. I keep confusing with all the different concepts.'

'Do you like yourself despite having problems, Evelyn?'

'Not particularly. However, I don't hate myself either. I'm lucky that my boyfriend makes me feel I am a pleasant person. As long as he likes me, I don't care about loving myself.'

'How do you see your boyfriend's weaknesses?'

'I love Leo regardless his dyslexia. I don't think I would be happier if he didn't have dyslexia. Somehow, his dyslexia helps us to bond each other better than any other person without dyslexia. We don't judge each other for our weaknesses. I wish Leo was more comfortable in his skin with his dyslexia. He's a man. You must know how it feels to be a man. It's harder to come to terms with your weaknesses. In my case, it's a lot easier. I don't make fuss about my lack of time management skills. It only causes concern during my studies. Otherwise, I could cope with it. The people whom I care about are dyslexic. We all have the same problems with time management. We forgive one another's unreliability and have a good laugh about our forgetfulness. I mix up everyone's birthdays. My parents, my brother and Leo all get the dates wrong for birthdays. Who cares! We develop a home grown philosophy that we treat time as infinite. We don't have the limited concept of time, none-dyslexic people might have. We live beyond the present time which is irrelevant to our day-to-day existence. Our philosophy works rather well at weekends when we don't want to worry about time management until the beginning of the week. I start Mondays with Monday blues which last until the end of Friday. Then, I've got my freedom of not having any deadline to meet over the weekend. We have a meal whenever we want to eat; we go out for a walk whenever we feel like it. Nothing is pre-planned. Everything looks so informal and comfortable. It's blessing to forget about the limitation of 24 hrs concept.'

'It's good to hear your experience with dyslexia. Is it possible for us to make friends just to talk about how we feel about being dyslexic?'

'Sure, let's meet up at lunch breaks here in the canteen. How often do you come to university, Felix?'

'Every day. How about you?'

'I come here twice a week. I've got lectures all day long Mondays and Fridays. I'm a part time student here. I work part time.'

'What do you do?'

'I work as a child minder.'

'Is it enjoyable?'

'Yes, very much so. The kids I look after in a private crèche are autistic. They're so cute. There is a constant interaction with them on a one to one basis. It's very demanding and very rewarding at the same time. I feel so good at the end of each day.'

'Well, you'll tell me more about your work when I see you next time. Shall we meet here on Friday at lunch time?'

'Sure. I must go to afternoon lecture now. It's nice talking to you, Felix. See you later.'

'It's good talking to you, Evelyn. See you on Friday at lunch time.'

Felix realises that there isn't much food left. He goes to the counter and gets himself an egg sandwich with a bottle of water. Felix sits down by the window and eats his sandwich without any rush as there is plenty of time for the 2 o'clock lecture. He thinks about Evelyn and Leo. It'll be good to meet Leo as well. To spend some time with dyslexic people will enable him to find out more about how other dyslexic people experience dyslexia. Felix thinks about his whole life with ups and downs and the two years he spent in prison. When he tells Evelyn about his imprisonment and why he faced 2 years sentence before he enrolled on his university degree, how Evelyn will respond to his rather odd life circumstances without being judgemental. If Evelyn and Felix exchanged their social backgrounds, Felix would have felt apprehensive about meeting someone who spent two years in prison regardless she was completely innocent or not. Evelyn treated Felix at their first meeting without any misconception about his complicated history of misfortunes from birth to his prison life; judgements would usually follow once Felix or any other ex-offenders reveal their life circumstances to the people they meet recently. Consequently, things become more unpleasant which might even cause rejection. Even people as nice as Evelyn start treating him from completely different perspective with the history of conviction. Jackie was different than Evelyn. Despite the fact that Jackie wasn't dyslexic but she was O.K. about accepting Felix's rough upbringing and even being sentenced for several times didn't bother her. Jackie's non-judgemental approach to his conviction was only possible with her psychology degree. Nevertheless, she wouldn't consider getting married to Felix. How could she possibly accept the grim reality of being judged as an odd couple in the society by having an ex-offender husband who happened to be born out of wedlock at the same time? Life is too harsh on some people. No matter how hard Felix will try, some people will always treat him unfairly with judgemental approaches which wouldn't be overcome in any way. Felix will be condemned to be treated with contempt. Well, Felix is strong enough not to take any notice of others' low opinion about himself; who wants to make friends with prejudiced people even worst who wants to get married with a prejudiced person in the first place.

Felix's enthusiasm of meeting Evelyn didn't last long enough once he started projecting the possible misinterpretation of his bleak past. Before attending the lecture, he wanted to take a long walk by the River Thames. Actually, he didn't feel like attending the afternoon session. He thought it would do more good to take his mind off in the afternoon without thinking of all the possibilities of being judged by the people who have never experienced even 10% of his life circumstances. Felix leaves the canteen quickly without any feeling of guilt for not attending the afternoon session. He walks towards the gate in rush as if he is going to be discovered by the course lecturer that he doesn't want to attend the lecture in the afternoon. How on earth he could confess his lecturer that everything seemed too meaningless now; going through all the pain of studying and getting a university degree without any hope that he would be treated as a decent human being with dignity. What is the purpose of going through all the hassle if he is going to be discarded by so many judgemental people over and over again as though he was responsible for all his misfortune he has experienced in life! Felix takes the bus and gets off in Waterloo. He walks down to the River Thames. He immediately feels calm and doesn't care the less about prejudiced people's opinion. None of the judgemental people are around here in any case. He is on his own with the complete dignity of being himself without being disturbed by any unpleasant judgement. Felix considers himself luckier than being in prison now. While he was in prison, he only visualised being here. Now, he could physically walk by the river. Felix remembers his dream about being three people at the same time, the judge, the defence barrister and the convict. When his innocence was released, he wanted go to the River Thames and tell the river that he is completely free. At the current moment, he is living physical freedom he dreamt of years ago. The freedom he has got now shouldn't be blurred with the future worries. Everything needs to be dealt when we face it. There is no point in worrying about death until we face our mortality within the last minute of our lives. If we keep on worrying about how we are going to depart from life every single day, we might not live our moments as if there is no death or dying isn't a possible prospect to be experienced at some points of our lives. Felix goes to the cafe in the National Film Theatre. There is no one sitting outside. That's how he wants to experience his human existence without surrounded by a human crowd. There are a few pigeons around looking for left-over food from human consumers. Felix feels sorry for the pigeons without anything to eat. He goes to the cafe and buys another egg sandwich. He comes back to where he was sitting a few minutes ago. Out of the three pigeons, there are only two pigeons walking around with the hope of finding something to pick up for their late lunch. Felix starts feeding the two pigeons with the bread crumbs and pieces of the boiled egg. The third pigeon comes back and joins in the feast of bread and egg. The birds are happy so should Felix be. He looks at the second-hand book sellers at the distance with plenty of unsold books on their stalls without any browsers. It's raining. Book worms will come back to browse second-hand books early spring or summer when weather is more pleasant with warm sun shine. Felix leaves the cafe and takes a bus to take him back home which will be warm and cosy to comfort him without causing him any strange feeling of being an outsider in this big city where he was born and has spent most of his life time without any chance to discover how it feels somewhere else as a complete stranger without any attachment or hurt experienced whatsoever.

When Felix comes back home, he feels emotionally drained going through all the struggle of remembering his past experience of poverty and repetitive misfortunes he has experienced. Felix dries up his hair with the towel and changes his outfit. Felix switches on the kettle; he gets a slice of bread and spreads honey on it. Having a cup of tea with slice of bread and honey on top cheers him up again. Felix thinks about his next assignment. Whether he likes it or not, he has to get on with his written assignments. Otherwise, he will lose track on his law studies. Although Felix already feels that becoming a legal profession is not for him, he doesn't know what else he could study for gaining a new qualification in order to become a professional person to make a living without depending on social security. He guesses that he will never enjoy working as a barrister. Being stuck in an office for 9 to 5 working pattern is out of question. How on earth he enrolled on law studies. He was carried away with the life style of Justin and Jasmine. Felix starts worrying about his future. Studying two more years doesn't look that exciting any longer. He needs to talk to Justin. Felix feels a moral obligation not to let Justin and Jasmine down for quitting from his legal studies. Both of them committed themselves into Felix's studies. Telling Justin and Jasmine about his doubt that he wouldn't be able to enjoy working as a barrister makes Felix feel bad about himself. Nevertheless, he has to talk to Justin immediately. Felix calls Justin on his mobile phone; Justin answers Felix immediately.

'Hi Felix, is everything fine with you?'

'Not particularly! I'm sorry to call you. Is it convenient time to talk to you?'

'By no means. What is the problem, Felix?'

'Today, I didn't feel like attending the afternoon session.'

'Is something wrong with you, Felix?'

'Yes, this afternoon I felt that I do not want to be a barrister.'

'That's fine! You don't have to be a barrister. What would you like to be instead, Felix?'

'That's a good question. I don't have a slightest idea what I would like to study.'

'Don't worry about it. You need to speak to a career adviser as soon as possible and see what else you could study. You haven't lost your chance. You could switch to something else instead.'

'I thought you would be upset about my recent decision, Justin.'

'Why should I? It's your life and it's your decision. You need to be absolutely confident that the career path you have chosen is right for you. Otherwise, you'll suffer till the rest of your life. Working in an occupation which you hate will destroy your soul, Felix. It's never too late to find another path for yourself to be comfortable with.'

'I'll try my best. Do you think I should complete my first degree and make a second choice later on for the second degree?'

'It's entirely up to you, Felix. I don't want to influence you just in case you'll regret later on. Time is so precious in our lives. With another two years' commitment, you might be wasting your time which could be used for a new start in a totally new direction.'

'I wish I could be sure what I really want to do with my life.'

'Take your time now rather than making a wrong decision and wasting your two years without any possibility for you to enjoy your career as a barrister.'

'I'm sorry to interrupt you with my doubts about myself and what I want from my life.'

'Don't be impatient with you, Felix. We've all gone through what you have been going through now. It's a hard decision to make about what we would like to be in life. I worked as a bereavement therapist before I made up my mind to be a full time barrister.'

'Do you have any regret for that?'

'If I am honest with you, Felix; yes, I regret that I have left my previous career for good. I enjoyed working as a therapist. The legal life is tough. Sometimes, I feel I am not helping enough to the people who are in real need whereas as a therapist, I was more fulfilled at the end of each session with the client.'

'I thought you and Jasmine like having a legal career.'

'We have to like our occupation as we don't have any other option to choose from at present. It's too late to turn the clock back now. In an ideal world, I would have been happier if I didn't choose my second career for a living.'

'I feel so bad about reminding you that you are not hundred percent happy with your profession.'

'That's life, Felix! We can't have everything in our lives. We've been making more money from legal profession but we don't get enough job satisfaction. There are many people who go to work without being completely satisfied with their jobs as they do it for the sake of earning their living. They have got mortgage to pay, their bills and their children's expenses; you name the rest of it.'

'How awful it sounds working without getting enough job satisfaction!'

'It's not that bad. There is a time that I get some job satisfaction no matter how rare occasion it might be and doesn't change the reality that working as a barrister is a pretty dull profession as a matter of fact on the whole.'

'I'm terribly sorry to hear that.'

'Don't be sorry for me, Felix! Think about your future. Would you like to end up where I am now?'

'I am not sure. If I have no any other choice, I might carry on with my studies and see what happens.'

'As I said to you earlier on, it's entirely up to you. I don't want to influence you.'

'I know that. I'll figure out something else for myself perhaps. Are you going to tell Jasmine how I feel about my current law degree?'

'Yes, I'll tell her. I'm sure she wouldn't mind if you change your mind.'

'Thanks for all your support and effort.'

'It's our pleasure. We'll still support you whatever your final decision is. We'll be on your side as we'd like to see you a happy man without feeling like a failure.'

'Many thanks, Justin. I'll be talking through my concern about the future with my dyslexia tutor Wonder before I see the career adviser tomorrow.'

'That'll be a good idea!'

'Please give my regards to Jasmine.'

'I'll do that, Felix. Take care!'

'Thanks. I'll let you know once I know what to do next.'

'Thanks, Felix. Good night!'

'Good night, Justin!'

Felix feels confused without knowing what to do next as he has lost his interest in legal studies completely. How fool he has been to assume that Justin and Jasmine were happy with their professional career which has turned out to be an illusion only as they don't get enough job satisfaction. How distressing it is to face other people's realities besides your own! Felix goes to the kitchen and prepares his dinner with lack of interest in his future decision. Now, it's a meal time. He would like to enjoy his meal with the greatest satisfaction. Life is too short in any case. Whatever the career he will be choosing wouldn't make much difference. At the end of the limited life span, he will be leaving his career for good anyway. There is no point in spoiling the current time. Till tomorrow, he doesn't need to worry about his future at all. All he needs to do this evening is to have a grand meal to uplift his spirit. Then, he needs to sleep over his doubt about whether a legal career is for him or not.

When Felix wakes up at 10 am, he calls his support tutor Wonder and gets an appointment to see her urgently in the afternoon. Felix prepares his breakfast and enjoys his breakfast with the light guitar music playing in the background. He focuses on the rhythmical movements of the music to occupy his mind with and postpones worrying about what he is going to tell his support tutor Wonder this afternoon. Felix closes his eyes when he is chewing his last bite of bread with honey and sips from his mug for the last time. His favourite music Satie's Gymnopedie No.1 finishes at the same time. Felix puts the cutlery, plate and mug into the sink. He changes himself quickly. Then, he looks at his face in the mirror and realises how quickly his beard grew within a couple of days; yet, he can't make his mind whether he shaves his beard or just to ignore it. He can't be bothered as he is not in a good mood to look particularly good today. Felix leaves his home earlier than the actual appointment time. He wants to go for a long walk to clear his mind off. He gets on a bus towards Canary Wharf. The three stops before his actual destination, he gets off the bus and walks around the unfamiliar environment. He looks at the high rise buildings, shops and the passengers at the bus stops. While he is killing the time, he thinks how silly it is to waste his precious time doing literally nothing without any purpose whatsoever. While he gets bored with the aimless walk, he realises that he has already reached his destination and he is in front of the building where Wonder's office is. Felix is twenty minutes earlier than his appointment. He sits on a wooden bench overlooking the West India Docks. He sees the seagulls flying over the docks from one destination to another.

Felix thinks about life and other human beings living all around the world settling in one spot and spending significant part of their lives at the same spot without moving around. Home is where the bread is. The foreign porters in the West India Docks must have come from all over the world. Felix never dared to leave London for a new start. The idea of leaving the city he was born scared him. He can't understand how other people move to other countries and make foreign lands their home. It'll be adventure to go and live in another country though. Felix looks at his watch, time is just right to see his support tutor Wonder. He walks quickly and arrives at the building where Wonder's office Three Dimension Dyslexia is. The main door is opened automatically. He climbs up the stairs and finds himself in front of Wonder's office. Wonder opens her office's door and welcomes Felix.

'Hi Felix, it's good to see you.'

'Hi wonder, it's good to see you as well. Sorry about the last minute arrangement to see you today.'

'I'm happy to see you today rather than the end of the week as we arranged previously. What would you like to explore with me today, Felix?'

'I'm confused about the direction I've taken.'

'Tell me more about it please.'

'I've lost interest in legal studies. I don't feel like committing myself into two years' studies.'

'What would you like to study instead, Felix?'

'I am not sure what I want really. I'd like to make a living from a decent job. I can't figure out what type of job is the best for me to make money and enjoy at the same time.'

'How long have you had this feeling of not knowing what direction you would like to take?'

'For a short while I've been thinking about it; yesterday, I felt the urge to leave my legal studies.'

'You sound confused. How would you like to feel instead?'

'I'd like to feel happy, energetic and enjoy what I am studying.'

'What are your interests in your personal life?'

'I love painting, drawing and sculpting.'

'How would you utilise these interests in your future career?'

'I thought about studying art might be an answer. Then, I am concerned about the scarcity of job prospect after graduation.'

'How much research have you done in finding a new career which suits your interest?'

'I haven't done any research at all. I just guess that it'll be hard to get a job with an art degree.'

'What evidence do you have for your assumption?'

'I don't have any evidence apart from the fact that Van Gogh died penniless.'

'When did Van Gogh die penniless?'

'Long time ago, I think he died in 1890 if I am not mistaken.'

'What year are we in now?'

'2005'

'How realistic is it to compare the possibilities of making a living out of art in this century with Van Gogh's life circumstances in 1890?'

'There is no link between the century Van Gogh lived and the century I'm living. Van Gogh's circumstance doesn't apply to mine.'

'What is within your control in relation to your career choice, Felix?'

'Everything is within my control.'

'Such as?'

'I could choose whatever career I'd like to pursue.'

'What else?'

'I'm able to change my destiny.'

'How would you that?'

'I could create my own destiny with my actions.'

'Could you give me a few examples?'

'I could invent something that no one invented before and make money out of it that will make me happy. I'd like to use my imagination rather than applying legal systems into current situation when I am dealing with clients' cases. There isn't much creativity involved in working out what part of civil law is appropriate for me to use for supporting my argument at court. The civil law had already written by other people. Creativity is limited to how you defend your clients' rights. I cannot create new articles or change the legal system each time I encounter a difficulty of an error within the legal system.'

'I could hear an important observation coming from you. What does your insight tell you about your future, Felix?'

'Choosing a legal career doesn't suit my creative nature. I'd get bored and upset when I am confronted by the limitation of being stuck within the restrictive legal structure of civil law.'

'That's how you feel.'

'Yes, that's how I feel.'

'What could you do to find a new career which would suit your creative nature?'

'It must be definitely creative. I should be able to use my imagination. I'd like to be a decision maker, a problem solver and come up with authentic answers to problems.'

'That sounds great! How could you that?'

'I could use my creative skills in a creative environment that I'll be completely free to produce something new and make money out of it at the same time.'

'What type of creative outlets are you thinking about?'

'I could be a stage designer. I could paint, draw and do installation on the stage for theatre.'

'What else could you do?'

'I could make films in which I could use all my creative skills, visual and problem solving skills.'

'What else could you do?'

'I could be a programmer and design programmes which would be unusual and visually appealing. I could design software for animation, for example.'

'What else could you do?'

'I could produce public sculpture and install them in parks and empty spaces.'

'What else could you do?'

'I could become an interior designer.'

'What else could you do?'

'I could become a furniture designer.'

'What else could you do?

'I could design jewelleries.'

'I could see now that you don't have any limitation how you could use your creativity.'

'That's correct. I am only limited to my imagination. There are plenty of outlets in which I could utilise my creativity.'

'How would you select the specific area in which you could be more comfortable and make money at the same time?'

'I need to do some research about each area I would like to explore and see the statistical outcome of each market.'

'What is your intention behind your research in career options?'

'I need to find out where the skill shortage is and how my skills will fill the existing gap.'

'Awesome! When are you going to start your research, Felix?'

'As soon as possible.'

'How soon will that be?'

'After I leave here, I'll be going to the library and do online research.'

'Well, it's that quick.'

'I have to be quick.'

'If you delay your research, what would happen?'

'My career choice would take longer time to make.'

'What would be the possible consequences?'

'I would waste my time, money and energy.'

'What have you learned about yourself in this session, Felix?'

'I'm in control of my life and destiny. I know that nothing can stop me where I aim to reach in life.'

'I'm glad to hear your testimony about how powerful you are. You've got inner resources which cannot be leashed by anyone outside your permission. You're the only decision maker of your own destiny, Felix.'

'That's right! I feel that I'll be successful in finding the most suitable career for myself to take up and make money out of it.'

'Thanks for sharing your decision with me, Felix. On a scale 1 to 10, how committed are you to make things happen for you?'

'10 out of 10, I should say.'

'That's great! The next time I see you, what will it be accomplished?'

'I would definitely know what course I'd like to switch to.'

'What date would you like to see me, Felix?'

'Next Monday at the same time.'

'That's fine! I'll book you in now.'

'Thanks, Wonder. See you next week!'

'See you next week, Felix!'

Wonders sees Felix out, Felix leaves the apartment quickly with all the ideas rushing into his mind. He has got a lot of options now. The problem is what option would be the right one. To be able to select the most suitable and practical option wouldn't be that difficult once he could get the numbers right. He could be equally successful in different parts of creative job spectrum once he focuses all his energy into wherever his heart is. Nevertheless, his heart should be in line with his brain. His heart represents his passion for a particular aspect of creativity; his brain represents logic and tells him what opportunity would bring money. If his interest won't enable him to earn his livelihood, no matter how much he wants to engage with the creative skills he would like to learn, his ambition wouldn't lead him to a better place than where he started from. Felix doesn't want to work in a factory as a handy person to carry around scrap materials from one place to another for peanuts any longer. Felix walks down the street to the bus stop and gets on the bus. His brain doesn't stop questioning him about what profession will be determining his future career. Felix temporarily becomes visually blind to the sounds and images surround him on the bus. Felix doesn't perceive other passengers and scenery outside when he is sitting by the window. He turns back into his inner reality and tries hard to find his answer quickly what job prospect would be more pragmatic and enable him to reach his destination within a short time. He has no time to waste as he doesn't want to depend on Justin's generosity and needs to manage his living expenses by himself.

Felix's daydream is interrupted by the argument of a middle-aged female passenger with a shopping trolley about the driver's inefficiency for not stopping at the bus station she wants to get off just on time. The driver chooses to ignore her argument and carries on driving until he comes to the next stop. Felix gets up and looks out of the bus window. It's a familiar place where he has been living after he was released from his two year sentence in prison. He rings the bell in order to avoid missing his stop like the female passenger. Felix can't help wondering whether or not the driver hates his job. If he was a happy bus driver, perhaps, he would answer the passenger's cry for attention and apologise for the inconvenience caused to her. Perhaps, the driver is planning to find an exit plan to end his driving career he hates as he only does it for taking his earning to his family. What a complicated life! Felix starts reasoning all the odd things happening he witnesses in life as a result of lack of job satisfaction some other people suffer from. He realises that he had never thought there would be plenty of people at work experiencing lack of enthusiasm for their jobs which bring money but not job satisfaction alongside. Felix makes his mind up that he won't end up living like a miserable human being. The bus stops, Felix gets off the bus and walks toward his council flat in a hurry. He gets his library card from his flat and goes to the university library to do research on what subjects he wants to study next.

After spending the whole afternoon from 1 pm to 5 pm, Felix finds the subject he feels it will be suitable to his aspiration with innovative nature of his curious mind. The course lasts 2 years and it is called as 'Design Concepts for Animation'. Felix gets the details of the administrator to ask for an application form and arrange an informal meeting to see the course leader to discuss what topics the course module covers over 2 years' duration. This time, Felix is eager to meet the existing students on the course and find out about the course from the students asking their 1st hand experience whether or not the course contents are enjoyable to study. Felix also wants to meet the career advisor to find out some information about what employment opportunities are available in the employment market after the completion of the course. Felix sends an email to the administrator outlining his request for an application and an informal meeting with the course leader.

He sends another email to the career adviser for arranging a meeting to discuss his options for a career planning with her. It takes Felix 2 weeks to do intensive research about the course, how it is run and what progression routes are available afterwards. Felix is content with the outcome of his enquiry and enrols on the 'Design Concepts for Animation' course immediately. The only downside of changing the course is to wait for the next term as they take new students in autumn term. Felix has been half way through his law degree at the end of spring term. Felix decides to prepare himself for his new course at home doing a bit of research to learn how to use some of the software packages for animation. He enrols on a distant learning for a short term course in animated images online and starts experimenting with different functions. Felix feels so proud of his ability to pick up a new skill over his summer break. When he starts his course at university, he is already a component user of some of software packages available online. He even designed his first 5 min 3D sculptural animation. In his animation, Felix uses geometrical existence which is built with the concept of geometrical abstraction and geometrical figures with 3D appearance. The main characters are square, triangle and circle. They are named with their geometrical shapes. They all have emotional intelligence and connect to one another through geometrical conversations which resemble human intelligence at the same time. Felix felt so good while he was working on his 5 min animation which took him 3 months to build up the concept and its details at first on paper with sketching his brainstorming then on Mac using animation software with the help of the online tutorials. When Felix becomes an art student at university, he explores how to register his intellectual property for gaining its pattern right in order to sell it to the distributers as his own original concept. Felix also enters the competition for 5 min original animation. He wins the 1st price which brings him £40.000 financial reward and enables him to enter to the market place comfortably without much hassle. Felix's concept takes off and he is invited to give a talk on his original concept in the association of entrepreneurs for original concepts in 3D animations. Felix is offered joint venture partnership with an established 3D animation company. He is asked to design more 3D animations for creative advertisements online for new brands to increase their visibility in the global market. Felix is blown out with the idea of becoming the founder of the 3D geometrical animations. He develops series of concepts with his outstanding abstract images which become as recognisable as Walt Disney images within a year. Felix starts attracting multimillion investors' attention to invest his concept in 3D animation. When he finishes his 'Design Concepts for Animation course', Felix is already an established entrepreneur with an earning capacity of £100 million net profit. Felix buys himself a beautiful house and a separate digital studio of several Macs, and animation software packages. He employs other animators to work for him. His earning capacity increases from £100 million to £200 million through leveraging his value in global market. Felix doesn't need to work on his animation from scratch to the completion state or beyond the product design. The team of fellow animators work on his concept. The only part of his animation he produces is to define the concept. Then, he passes his concept on to his design team to bring his concept into life through motional, 3D geometrical animations. In the end, Felix is in charge of making a decision, which animation is distributed and given a new brand identity among other brands. Felix becomes a public speaker and travels all around the world to give a talk about his animated images and how his first concept came about. He is given the title of the best 3D Animator Artist. His brand is associated with the unique selling point of its originality which has no competition. He is the market leader of the animation for the mass advertisement in the 21st century in 2008.

Felix's success in his professional life brings him supporters, followers and admirers of his unique talents. He is welcomed warmly wherever he appears either giving public speech or attending as a delegate to take part in symposium run for entrepreneurs and academic community globally.

Chapter 6

Felix reflects on his life as a successful entrepreneur - Jan 2015

How Felix fulfilled his potential wasn't a mystery but it was a well deserved success through carefully defined objectives he set for himself to achieve as a dyslexic person. Felix goes back to his beginning where he was and comes back to the present time where he is now. The largest gap between the two poles of his life is enormous; the pole of failure was full of excuses which justified his weaknesses by hiding himself what he couldn't do without trying to change the things where he was repeating for years. Now, at the peak of his career, the pole of success as the wealthiest entrepreneur with dyslexia and ADD, he found all the answers for each weakness he had years ago. Felix worked on his weaknesses without letting them to conquer him or defeat him in life. Felix confronted his weaknesses with the conscious decision to overcome all the obstacles in his life. Lack of organisational skills and insufficient time management were the most detrimental weaknesses Felix suffered from. Now, Felix is a very well organised entrepreneur with the excellent time management. Without time management, he wouldn't be in control of his life or his business. No one could temp Felix to waste his precious time doing silly things like watching TV or chatting without any purpose for the sake of killing time. Felix's consciousness for time has been increased over the years. He doesn't waste even a single minute without gaining capital return. Felix smiles with contentment based on his inner peace. He's fully aware of the fact that how much his self-esteem has been improved from hating himself to accepting his new identity better than his broken image of the past. Yes, he acknowledges the grim reality that he had a rough start in life. Still, he made it in the end. If he didn't take up the several offers came to his way when he met Justin, Jasmine and Steve in his early twenties, he wouldn't end up where he is now at the age of thirty five. He remembers how he pushed Jackie out of his life when Jackie was there to support him. It was Felix's pride which made Jackie redundant from his life. His relationship with Justin, Jasmine and Steve was completely different than suffocating relationship he had with Jackie. Neither Justin nor Steve had interfered with Felix's life. Their offer wasn't intimidating. It was welcoming, gentle and healing gesture for Felix to take up without any doubt of their good will to support him which put him in charge of his own life. He could have mistaken their offer with Jackie's offer to change him completely. That would have been resulted with disastrous end by making him vulnerable without building up his own confidence in his ability to make things happen in the way he aimed for. Felix didn't want to be changed in order to be loved by Jackie. All he wanted was to be accepted and loved as he was with all his weaknesses. Each criticism Jackie came up with, irritated Felix whereas the tactful criticism of Justin, Jasmine and Steve enabled Felix to accept his weaknesses and work on them one by one without being offended.

Felix enters his diary a new paragraph with the description of zebra which he associates himself with. The strips he carries within his invisible self represent the misery of his past, his shortcomings and vulnerability he carried over to his new self in the present time.

...in a country near the Himalayas, there was a zebra lived with freedom without any inhibition of fear from anything or anyone. The zebra was named 'Freedom' lived his life with the wisdom of turtle when he walked, ran and flew without stopping at the time zone he was locked into. One day 'Freedom' reached the highest point of the Himalayas and looked over the place where he started his journey. He realised how much he has enjoyed the travel from the long distance coming to the point where he is now. Zebra won't have the fear of being oppressed by anybody as he wouldn't be locked into the little cell for squatting. Zebra

is a powerful person with the financial freedom he eventually gained with his own stamina and unstoppable desire to be successful which could not be destroyed by any human being.

Felix opens the window and looks over his picturesque garden. The 1st beautiful garden he gazed was 13 years ago and made him long for a home with the same garden. That was his starting point to make an important decision to be a wealthy person. It was the first transformational experience in his mindset to imagine that he could make it if he really wanted to own a house with a beautiful garden. No matter where he came from, how much he struggled with his early misfortune in life, he knew that he could increase his life expectation from bare existence to comfortable living conditions. However, his luck enabled him to find himself even in a better place than he originally imagined while he was spending the most welcoming week with Justin and Jasmine as a convict who would be spending 2 years in prison later on. Felix's garden looks more splendid than his defence barrister Justin's garden now. He has got his own sculptures in his garden with a beautiful water fountain for the birds and wild habitat to drink water from. Felix feels the urge to go downstairs and walk in his garden to breathe the air of freedom. He leaves his study room and goes down the stairs quickly as if he is going to meet his destiny of being freed from the captivity for the first time. The sense of freedom is Felix's only obsession in life. He doesn't want to lose his freedom. When he is indoors, he gets the illusion of being locked again, perhaps not in a prison he spent 2 long years but being locked in the most beautiful house surrounded with the most expensive and elegant furniture this time. How unfortunate it would have been if he couldn't go downstairs and walk in his big garden freely without being observed by the prison warden or any other person who might have taken over the same role of controlling his life by depriving him from enjoyment of every single breath he takes in and out from his nostrils while the fragrance of the flowers empowers his vision to be fully alive.

Felix sits down in the deckchair near the water fountain and looks at the beautiful sparrows and robins enjoying their drinking ceremony without any rush. They don't mind his presence at very close proximity as they sense that he is a harmless soul. The birds are happy and know how to enjoy the water from the fountain. Then, they are washing themselves together in the same water fountain. It is a joy to watch the birds seeing them in tune with life! This must be the heaven on this earth! That's how Felix experiences the heavenly feeling of peace with himself and environment while he is sitting in his beautiful garden, watching the wild life without any concern for today or tomorrow. Time stops in this garden. Felix spends 2 hrs in the garden watching the birds, insects, butterflies, frogs, squirrels, turtles, cats and dogs surrounding him like a very big family. Felix doesn't want to leave the garden. His cook Peacock enters his garden and interrupts his communication with the nature.

'Shall I bring your lunch here, sir?'

'Hi, Peacock. You're as quiet as my inner peace. I haven't heard you entering the garden.'

'I didn't want to scare you, sir. I've walked on tiptoe.'

'What an excellent thought! What do we have for lunch, Peacock?'

'Your favourite food!'

'Which one?'

'The most favourite one you told me once.'

'All the foods you cook are my favourites, Peacock. How lucky I'm to have you around. I don't know what I could do without you. I was fed up feeding myself with convenient food before your arrival.'

'I am lucky to be employed by you, sir. Living in this beautiful house with splendid garden would be beyond my means.'

'You work hard to get what you deserve. I'm glad that you appreciate the surroundings as much as I do, Peacock.'

'Very much so, sir.'

'I'd like to remind you that you don't need to call me sir any longer. Call me Felix, please.'

'I am afraid I can't. This is not possible. I'm used to call gentleman like yourself as sir.'

'You remind me of my stubbiness. I did the same thing years ago. I called the person who was very dear to me as sir. He is a barrister and a very good friend of mine now. It took me quite while to practise calling him with his first name. I hope you'll be getting rid of the unnecessary formality. I'd like you to feel at home here. Tell me about yourself Peacock. I haven't had a chance to make enquiries about your nature or where you come from. I don't know who you are. Could you tell me a bit of yourself, please?'

'I don't think my existence will be a matter of importance neither to you nor anyone else, sir.'

'How do you reason like that? You are important part of my life; you feed me with your delicious meals. I'm entitled to get to know you a bit more. Please don't make me feel unease for asking about your origin.'

'I don't know my origin, sir. That's why I told you that I am not important.'

'Well, you're important to me. You said you don't know your origin. What does that mean actually?'

'I was brought up in an orphanage. I didn't know who my parents were. I don't have any blood connection with anyone. I was put into a monastery when I was 16. I got out of the monastery which was run by nuns. I didn't fit into a missionary duty. I looked for a job. I was hired as a chef assistant in a big restaurant and worked there for about 3 yrs. Then, you hired me as a cook that is my story, sir. I'm completely different than you are or anyone else from your class. I come from a humble background.'

'That's what I like about you, Peacock. I'll tell you about my life story when we have got a bit of time for that. Let me have my lunch now.'

'Certainly, sir.'

'What am I going to have for lunch today?'

'Scallops with steamed vegetables and yoghurt sauce to go with home-made bread and beetroot salad.'

'How awesome it sounds! What do we have for desert?'

'Chocolate pudding with nuts.'

'That's great! Please bring my lunch here. Have we got a freshly squeezed juice?'

'I've squeezed blueberries and carrots.'

'That'll complement my delight for lunch. Thank you, Peacock.'

'I'd better fetch the meal, sir.'

'Would you like to join me for lunch, Peacock?'

'I'll be visiting the temple for prayers.'

'That's fine! When you've time to dine with me here in the garden, please let me know, Peacock. By the way, I've decided to have a garden party for my close friends on Easter day. You're invited as well. Shall we hire another cook for that day?'

'I'll be honoured to be asked to be in charge of the garden party myself.'

'I don't want you to get tired and not being able to enjoy the garden party. I'd like you to be part of the occasion which may provide good memories of sharing my life in this place. I haven't been looked after in the same way you've been looking after me during the last 3 months. It'll be a small gesture of my appreciation about your commitment to make me feel so good without having any doubt about your values for integrity and reliability. I don't want to lose you. Without you, I cannot manage, Peacock.'

'Thank you, sir. I'll never leave you as long as you need me. I'm happy to serve you here till the rest of my life.'

'I don't think I'll have that long expectation from you. You're young and beautiful. One day will come and you'll leave me for another life. However, I don't want to think about your leaving at present. Let me enjoy what I've got now. You're here and cooking for me to appreciate your excellent skills. How fortunate I'm that no one else has discovered your talent yet.'

'That's very kind of you, sir. Thank you ever so much for your complement.'

'It isn't a complement. I enjoy your cooking and your presence in my home.'

'Thanks, sir. I'll get your meal.'

'Thank you, Peacock.'

Felix is delighted with Peacock's disclosure of her unusual origin which reminds him who he is. Peacock is the first person in his present life without a natural family upbringing like himself. Although Felix became a prominent figure with substantial amount of wealth, he finds it difficult to relate to other people who have got ordinary upbringings in life. Felix always felt as an outsider within any society he had been so far. Apart from Justin, Jasmine and Steve, no one knows that he was brought up by a foster family. Poor Peacock assumes that he comes from a high class origin as she insists on addressing him sir. The acquired wealth and the status attached to it as a consequence of being a wealthy person doesn't change anyone's past history. Felix is still a person without any legal status of his biological parents to associate with him neither in his past nor the current time; this reality will never be changed in the future either. He was born to face the void of his biological identity through a lack of blood connection.

What a strange world it is. Felix assumed that Peacock comes from a middle class family background with her good nature and well manners. It has never occurred to Felix that Peacock was brought up within the strong discipline of a monastery life with nuns as her teachers. She must have been under the influence of the prayers she was taught there. Who could possibly imagine a lovely young woman like Peacock taking her spiritual existence so seriously by going to temple for regular prayers instead of mixing with her age group and risking the possibility of losing her natural spiritual identity?

How we perceive others at first instance and how we pick up more clues about the same people's identities over a longer period are completely different than what we assume while we are going through the conditioning process of social norms, which could easily mislead us if we don't question our assumptions with our personal observations of those individuals and their value systems. At the short interview, what Felix asked Peacock had nothing to do with her nature or her family background and even her upbringing; all he was interested in finding about Peacock's cooking skills. Nothing mattered much outside her ability to cook for him when he offered Peacock a very well paid employment with an opportunity to receive free board and lodging in his luxurious house. All he got from her was that an excellent reference from the restaurant chef whom Peacock worked for 3 yrs. In the reference, it has been noted that Peacock possesses all the skills and talent for the highest quality of cooking matters with examples of her speciality such as authentic vegetarian meals, whole-meal baking style without preservatives and freshly made juices of original taste. What else could possibly Felix want to know about Peacock. The job was to find the most appropriate cook who was able to cook for him. Felix had the bad luck with the previous cook who didn't know how to cook. Felix had no choice but to ask him to leave on his probation. Then, Felix couldn't fill the vacancy for a while. Peacock's application form looked outstanding among 250 applicants when he advertised the vacancy in the professional cooks' journal. Felix selected Peacock to invite for an interview as he wanted to take a chance and give her an opportunity for a week before making his decision to employ her for good. Peacock had exceedingly fulfilled Felix's expectation from a cook within an initial period of her probation. There was nothing to mourn about Peacock or her cooking for a dismissal. Felix had drawn a proper contract of employee and given it to Peacock to keep it in safe as he didn't want her to feel that he was going to exploit her in any way. How could he exploit another human being in life? He was the one who knew what exploitation meant from his early experience working without any contract in a factory as a handy man carrying scraps from one place to another. When his boss said he didn't need him any longer; that was it. He had no choice but to leave without any legal right to appeal against his employer's wish to get rid of him when he wanted to chuck him out like a scrap metal which Felix used to carry around for a living in that awful factory.

Life has been transformed from a nightmare to a beautiful dream which Felix daily experiences with the unlimited joy and gratitude to his Creator. Felix has got everything he has dreamt of when he was poor and needy. The most important possession Felix has ever owned is his freedom without any doubt; the freedom of choice in life is the most precious asset he has generated from scratch. He could live comfortably even he hits his 100 years without any need to work. He could do whatever he wants to do with his life. He could travel all around the world for several times if that is what he wants. He has got plenty of passive income coming regularly each month. He is the only decision maker to make up his mind what to do next, to stay in London or to move to another county of his choice is within his control. No one could stop him what he wants to do with his life. There is no daily worry for a struggle of finding a job. Felix doesn't need to be employable or be a best candidate for someone else to employ him for a certain period of time for making a living. His time is too precious to be sold to someone else. His time is limited to his own ambition how well he wants to prosper within the power of his own vision. He knows what is best for him. He knows when to explore his leisure activities without any time restriction. There is nothing to bore him. His surroundings, even his meal times are all full of enjoyment and fun. He feels he is making up his losses when he had a poor life which limited his choice to cheese sandwich only for his lunch. Every day is a new day with delicious and healthy meals for 3 times a day as a treat for a healthy individual who happens to be the wealthiest entrepreneur within his field. He could afford to spend 2 or 3 hrs in his heavenly garden enjoying the wild habitat with peaceful fulfilment. He could walk in the privacy of his garden without being exposed to the curiosity of paparazzi to interrupt his inner peace for making unusual demands to pose them for making money. He doesn't need to bother with publicity any longer. He has got plenty of contacts thorough social media in any case.

Felix felt so good to be born as himself but not someone else. All the agony of not knowing his biological parents has immediately lost its saddening effect on his current mood. He doesn't care the less any longer for being disowned as soon as he was born. He is more than happy to be given birth in the first place. Whoever his mother was he should be grateful to her for bearing him for 9 months and bringing him into this world without getting rid of his foetus in her womb. If his biological mother didn't take all the hassle of giving birth to him, he wouldn't be here and wouldn't enjoy what he has got in his current life in abundance. The first time in his life, Felix feels that he loves his mum and his dad. They both facilitated his emergence from nothingness. Penguins care for their off springs till they are old enough to survive and leave them behind forever without worrying about them. The parentship of the adult penguins is seasonal but not life-long. Felix's parents must have acted like a couple of penguins once they caused the reason of his existence, the job was done and they thought they weren't needed. Yes, Felix's biological parents must have similarity with other mammals who are not concerned about their off springs' survival with longer commitments. Felix decides not to hate his biological parents any longer. After all, he carries their genes. Meeting Peacock who doesn't know her biological parents makes Felix understand that there are some occasions in the history of human kind that not all children are cared for by their own biological parents. This fact should be accepted. Felix realises that being a wealthy person enables him to be less judgemental in life. When he was struggling to make the *ends meet or find an accommodation to live, he couldn't help hating his parents not to be around to support him during his struggle. Now, Felix's circumstances are completely different than his early years in poverty. Once he forgives his parents' negligence, all the burden of his sorrow for being left alone vanishes. Felix overcomes his human limitation of not being able to forgive his parents for their insensitivity for such a long time. There is nothing to be sorry about and there is no one to forgive any longer. Felix's unease to come to terms with his untraceable existence is over. He is content with his new identity as he is certain that no one could take it away from him. This thought facilitates his final conclusion that he is not only a successful man from financial point of view but he is a successful man from emotional point of view at the same time.*

Peacock brings Felix's lunch to the garden and leaves Felix with his contentment of being a strong person who is completely in charge of his own life once again. Felix spends the whole afternoon in the garden taking his time to enjoy being surrounded with wild animals, gazing at his flowers and the water fountain. Life is a splendid dream and he is the most realistic dreamer of the modern age as far as he is aware of. His past fantasies became his dream reality in the present time. Felix possesses an amazing capacity of imagination which produced unlimited realms of beautiful narratives by transforming the impossible into the possibility of his dream garden. He is the creator of his destiny. Felix feels a great appetite for life and wants to live till the age of 100 at least. He could settle for more if only his opinion is asked by the divine Creator. Felix imagines himself as a 100-year-old man sitting in the same spot and reflecting his past successes with the same contentment without yearning to go back to his younger ages even for a short visit. The prison cell left behind years ago and there is no a valid reason to go back there as he doesn't want to remember the humiliation of being locked for 2 years even though the prison cell provided the most valuable years for him to learn English, maths and law. That was the only good thing about being in prison. He had plenty of time to do revision and to receive regular support provided by Steve, Justin and Jasmine. Without their support, he couldn't survive his captivity within the 4 walls of his cell. He imagined the freedom and painted it when he was a prisoner lacking the freedom of movement from one place to another. Yet, he was free in his mind when he was painting relentlessly.

Felix remembers how he met Justin and how he kindly offered to spend a week in their home while he had nowhere to go before moving to prison to serve his 2 years sentence. Justin and Jasmine have never left him alone over the years. They are already retired now. Their dream came true after they hit their retirement age as they travel all over the world without any restriction of time. They were ahead of the game when Felix had zero existence financially. Years later, Felix's financial success achieved enormous capacity to buy him time to enjoy his life without any need to wait for the state retirement age and he is ahead of the game now. Felix is financially free for life at the age of 35. The starting point of any existence below zero can't necessarily hinder one's direction if a person has got a clear aim to reach with a plan designed for. The rest will be achieved within relatively shorter time span than many people don't have enough knowledge to access. Felix couldn't read and write when he first met Justin and Jasmine. He didn't even have any qualification. He dropped out of his 1st degree in law. It was all trial and error he found his way through success which didn't come to him that easily. Nevertheless, it didn't take him far too long to figure out the fast track to the route which he could speed up his race to finish the marathon as a first class athlete.

Life has been turned out to be a joyful race with the speed Felix set for himself and no one seemed to compete with him. The last came the first like in a stack for a computer language a programmer creates. Felix walks up and down in his garden to think his brand in the global market place. He has got plenty of ideas to merge his brand even further not for the sake of making more billions but for the sake of seeing how far he could still travel from where he is now. That makes him curious and motivates him to continue growing. There is no limitation in creativity. One could carry on for years without getting bored or running out of steam. Every single day brings its inspiration. When Felix walks around his garden, there are plenty of materials around to activate his imagination. All the plants, animals, textures of the rocks, the surfaces of the trees, the pebbles, the colours of sunset, sun rise, kaleidoscope, rain, snow, every single element of the nature generates many images for Felix to create his animations until he reaches his 100 years. Felix walks down the garden by the little pathway leading him to his glass studio; opens the door and enters his enormous studio space with plenty of drawings on his desk, on the floor and on the glass walls hung from yesterday's working hours spent in his studio. He loves working on many different drawings at the same time. A day could be spent all day long without doing nothing but drawing only. That's how he mostly spends his life in his London home. During his long journeys to other countries, he has no time to draw. He misses the process of divine mystery before he produces the end product of a drawing which puzzles him most of the time as he has no control over his drawings. Something happens during his drawing, the lines are composed beyond his wish almost. There is an automated hand movement which happens outside his will. Nothing is within his control in abstract drawings where coincidence takes part so inexplicably without any error involved. Once he becomes conscious about the drawing process, he can't draw and loses his fluency it's like touch typing perhaps. If a typist with touch typing skills, start worrying about what key he is going to touch next, the automation of typing process disappears and the typist loses his spontaneity to type without looking at the keyboard.

Felix reclines on his couch and looks at his large abstract drawing done with various colour inks and paint brushes two days ago. It has got a calligraphic quality. One could gaze the drawing for hours and interprets its lines with their own narrative attached to. Felix could see his vitality in this drawing, a life without any intimidation. His lines with different thickness and lengths are the symbol of his unleashed creativity. He is at the peak of his creative energy. Felix visualises his next master piece he is going to draw in a minute. He closes his eyes and sees the empty canvas with his inner eye. He takes his brush and starts drawing on the canvas. The drawing he captures in his visual eye looks almost impossible to create in the real life. He opens his eyes and walks far end of his cube studio. He takes the vast canvas from the piles of other large canvases. He carries the canvas which is taller than his height and puts it on canvas holder which he made from the wood in his garden as he couldn't find a life-size easel to buy. All the easels in the art material warehouse store are for small size paintings only. Felix's large canvases don't fit into commercially produced easel sizes. A typical large canvas Felix uses, looks like a wall in which Felix spends hours with bodily movements of his drawing through large brush strokes standing on top of a wooden ladder. His drawings on the enormous size canvases are sold for the large buildings of several international banks to make their space less intimidating to their customers. According to the surveys, Felix's drawings have increased the bank customers' transactions. Art dealers, the business people with unique taste for high art appreciate Felix's large drawings done on enormous canvasses. The art film made with Felix's large drawings hanging on the large windows of the several global banks has increased not only Felix's artwork's value but the image of the global banks at the same time. It'll be hard to find a suitable storage if Felix's large canvases didn't find the right market to be sold. The minute his drawing finishes on a large canvas, there is a public collector to take away his canvas with a very handsome price. The buyers are on the waiting list to purchase Felix's drawings which Felix hasn't even produced yet. The transition from miniature size canvases to the enormous size canvases has made a lot of impact on Felix's artistic development and financial stability. Within a small size canvas, Felix's drawing was limited to its tiny space. Now, Felix's reputation has been increased enormously so does the size of his canvases. There is a parallel between his artistic reputation and the size of his artwork. There is juxtaposition between the drawings he produced in prison when he was only 20 years old and the drawings he has been producing as an established artist in his 30s. The complete transformation from the unknown artist existence to the well-known celebrated artist status has been massive and couldn't be predicted 15 years ago.

Felix feels the creative energy filling his body as he is familiar with this extra ordinary state of mind while he picks up the red paint and squeezes it on his palette carefully. He gets his medium size brush and dips it into the red acrylic paint. Then, he starts his drawing from the middle of the canvas. Once the abstract drawing is completed within the centre of the canvas with the same size of red lines, he changes his brush size and gets a thinner brush this time. He starts drawing the rest of the canvas with thinner red lines. After an hour of automated drawing, Felix gets the thickest brush and slashes with the thickest remarks all over the thinner and medium sizes of red lines. There is a variety of line thicknesses on the canvas within reddish monochromatic hue of the paint. Felix gets the blue paint out of his paint box. He squeezes the blue paint on his palette and dips the thinnest brush into the blue paint. He starts drawing contours all around the red lines. Then, he gets yellow paint, squeezes on his palette and gets his palette knife to spread the yellow paint on top of the empty spaces of the canvas. The drawing with the 3 strong colours has been completed within 3 hrs this time. He looks at his watch. Time is 8 o'clock. Peacock must be preparing his supper. It's better to *have his dinner indoors. He looks at his drawing with affection as if it is a living organism. Felix smiles at his thought and nods his head, yes each painting is a living organism for him. He has created this painting which didn't have any artistic quality as an empty canvas 3 hrs ago. All his artwork carries his gene in the same fashion a human foetus might have. That's why he feels attached to each piece of his artwork. He has overcome the sad feeling of being departed from his creation. He accepted the fact that all his creation needs to be accommodated within different spaces and environment as they have got their own life cycle which he has no control over. The only record of his creation is the photos of his artwork which has been archived for him to remember the details of each creation with its unique identifier of title and its particulars like the medium he used, the width and the height and the date it has been created. His archive reminds him the registry office for new born human beings. Each artwork has been acknowledged as his own off spring within the history of art movements. He is the only copyright holder of his concepts in visual art form. He locks up his cube studio and walks from the same pathway he came here 3 and a ½ hrs ago.*

The bird on a tall tree next to the cube studio starts chirping with joy as if the bird is celebrating his fulfilled day with a creative action he deliberately chosen to accomplish. Felix walks in haste taking in the natural perfume of the evening primroses and gazes at the misty twinkle of the early evening with a delight. He wonders how he is going to entertain himself after supper. He could compose a poem or write his diary by recording his daily pleasures with satisfaction. Felix has no intention of publishing either his poetry or his reflective dairies. They are all created for the sake of his private enjoyment. How good it is to feel that there is a long life ahead of him. He is not going to die tomorrow. If he lives another 70 years like this it'll be splendid. Living without any financial worries at an old age must be heavenly blessing on its own. Let's hope the worst day of my life will be like today that's what he wishes.

This means I deserve to have even better life condition than the one I've at present. I'm Felix Worthful with no trace of past misery. I'm a completely free human being with a vision for the prosperity of future dreams.

Felix enters the cosiness of his world he built for himself in this gorgeous house. He goes to the kitchen and let Peacock know about his return for supper. Peacock is familiar with Felix's frequent visits to the kitchen without causing her any surprise.

> *'Good evening, Peacock.'*

> *'Good evening, sir. Are you ready for your supper?'*

> *'That's right. I'll have my supper in the dining room please.'*

> *'I'll bring your dinner to the dining room, sir.'*

> *'Thanks, Peacock.'*

Felix leaves the kitchen and climbs up the stairs. He visits the bathroom, takes a warm shower. He puts on his evening suit as if he is going out for a meal in a decent restaurant. This is what he learned from Justin and Jasmine while he was staying with them. To be able to feel good, they both dress up even indoors. Felix likes being casual while he is in the garden or working in his studio but not in his rather formal dining room which is an occasion for him to dine even without any guess around. Felix takes delight in living the luxury of fitting each occasion with the flexibility of his private dressing code he created for him to follow. He enters his huge dining room overlooking the beautiful garden. He turns on the contemporary crystal chandelier which lightens up his dining room immediately. He turns on the antique gramophone which is based on Edison's Amberol cylinder mechanism he introduced in 1909 with a minimum playing time of 4 minutes at 160 rpm. While the gramophone brings the nostalgic feeling of past which was unfamiliar to him, Felix remembers of Thomas Edison's memorable quotes which summarised his determination to succeed in life as a dyslexic person.

I have not failed. I've just found 10,000 ways that won't work.

Many of life's failures are people who did not realize how close they were to success when they gave up.

There's a way to do it better - find it.

Felix sits in his antique chair and leans over the long wood table, places his hands on the surface of the antique table. Another quote from Thomas Edison enters his short term memory suddenly;

'You can't realize your dreams unless you have one to begin with.'

Felix hums the quote with a cheerful tune he has just created and taps his fingers on the wooden table like a tap dancer. His current life is his dream which was created by him. This is a momentous experience of his life waiting for an extravagant supper in his dining room overlooking the beautiful garden which is lightened by the garden lamps while he is listening to the old music from Edison gramophone in his elegant suit. He doesn't feel arrogant of any sort. He knows that he deserves the best of everything. All the deprivation of his early years had been buried in his past memories. He stops humming as he hears the opening of the electrical home lift. Peacock must have brought his meal. Peacock enters the dining room with a moving service table which carries all the repertoire of his supper from the starter, the 3 course meals to the dessert to finish up his supper in a joyful mood. Peacock lays the table with silver cutlery, porcelain dinner set and crystal drinking glass. She pours the water from the crystal jug. Peacock serves Felix's dinner with a professional manner without dropping any food on the surface of table. Peacock repeats the same good wish for him to hear;

'Enjoy your dinner, sir.'

'Thanks, Peacock. Everything looks perfect.'

Peacock leaves the dining room quietly in a humble gesture of keeping her head down. Felix knows what her body language means. Peacock must have learned to stay humble even when she produces the most extraordinary meals Felix had ever eaten before; she doesn't like to make noise about her high ability and her excellent cooking skills. What a shame though! If Felix didn't offer Peacock the position as a house cook, she could have been easily ignored by others because of her painfully humble nature. She doesn't aware of the reality which is to say that your importance needs to be acknowledged by yourself first before the arrivals of others' approval within the market place. Making or producing something of high quality is not enough on its own. Marketing your skills what makes a person outstanding among others. Peacock is so naive to figure out this. She doesn't care the less, perhaps, because of her value for humility which is always in contradiction with the demand of the modern market place for shouting out what you are good at. It took some time for Felix to overcome the uncomfortable feeling of talking about what he is good at. He remembers the 1st talk he had given to the handful of academic students about his animation at university campus. It was such a struggle to admit that he hated to reveal his embarrassment for highlighting the importance of evolutionary stages of his work. To use the words such as creativity, invention even naming his animation as his artwork sounded too alien to him in those days as an emerging artist coming from nowhere. He was scared to be misunderstood like a pretentious idiot. Nevertheless, he has learned how to promote his creation without appearing insignificant due to his humility. Felix is able to deliver a speech with assertiveness by emphasising on his strengths. His strength looks even better while he reveals his weaknesses. He discloses his dyslexia without any discomfort attached to it. Everyone he is in contact with him knows that he is dyslexic. Felix positions himself with all the well-known dyslexic artists, scientist, writers, entrepreneur and boxer such as Leonardo da Vinci, Pablo Picasso, Thomas Edison, Albert Einstein, Hans Christian Anderson, Agatha Christie, W.B. Yeats, Henry Ford and Muhammad Ali. What an important circle of dyslexic people to be related to as a dyslexic artist!

Felix enjoys the delicious lentil soup with peas and carrots in it. He looks at the aubergine salad which is mixed with pomegranates, globe artichokes and grilled red pepper. It looks mouth watering. Oyster mushrooms are roasted with baby tomatoes as a side dish. Dried roasted shirataki noodles are presented with toasted tofu cubes and exotic herbs. According to Peacock, shirataki noodles contain low calorie, a water-soluble dietary fiber and are healthier than pasta or ordinary noodles. Felix moves on to the main dishes as soon as he finishes his soup while he is enjoying his supper like a child who is spoiled with the plenty of choices for home-made cooking prepared by an affectionate mother. It was a good job that Felix hired Peacock to cook for him regularly as her cooking is always interesting with diverse varieties of taste from all over the world. When he puts the slice of the roasted tomato into his mouth, he remembers reading about the nutritious value of tomatoes as they contain substances which fight against cancer and prevent Alzheimer's disease. He eats his meal slowly without any rush. He drinks plenty of water which aids his digestion. Felix makes sure that he drinks 8 glasses of water throughout the day for ultra natural detox diet. All of a sudden, Felix eye catches his dessert with fresh grapes & berries on top of natural yoghurt with honey and nuts. It'll be a heavenly experience of finishing off his dinner with his favourite dessert. Felix loves fresh grapes and berries which are also good for his brain functioning and reduced the risk of Alzheimer's disease. Knowing the nutritious value of his food intake makes him lead a healthy life style that increases his vitality and enables him to manage his energy without getting rundown. Felix's eating habit maximises his brain power for his creative activities. He eliminates tea and coffee during his supper time as he wants to have a good sleep without being kept awake. Having healthy sleeping pattern is as important as having healthy eating pattern which prevents us from going into depression especially during the winter days when there is lack of sun light which could easily cause depression such as 'Seasonal Affective Disorder'. Generally speaking, many people feel better once summer arrives with plenty of sun shine as the warmth of sun beams uplifts our moods; colours of the nature look more beautiful and much brighter. Felix likes taking a break for a week during the Christmas time by going away to sunny countries to boost his morale and avoid falling into winter blues. Before starting his dessert, Peacock comes back and makes enquiries whether he needs 2nd helping of food.

'Would you like to have some more food, sir?'

'No, thanks, Peacock. I've had more than enough. I've enjoyed the supper thoroughly. Have you eaten your supper, Peacock?'

'Not yet, sir.'

'When are you going to have your supper, Peacock?'

'After I do clearing up in the kitchen.'

'You should have your supper before clearing up. I don't want you to get tired. You need to feed yourself well in the same way you feed me well.'

'I feed myself well, sir. Thanks for your concern.'

'I had days in my past I didn't have enough food, Peacock. When I have got plenty of good food, I can't help being grateful to our Creator and you, of course, for producing all the delicious food for me. I cannot bear the possibility of depriving you from a decent mealtime. I realised that you left home for praying without having your lunch after serving me in the garden at lunch time. I hope you didn't starve yourself till very late.'

'I will never starve in this household. There is plenty to eat. Thanks for thinking of me, sir.'

'Will it be easier for you if we get an assistant to help you in the kitchen?'

'Honestly, I am fine, sir. I don't need any assistant. The cooking is limited to two of us. We don't have many guesses on ordinary day. It's a joy for me to cook daily for you and for myself. I love eating a variety of food.'

'It's good to hear that, Peacock. I can't afford to see you fallen ill. You're an asset to me. I need to look after you as much as you look after me. How are you getting on with the cleaner who comes to clean the house every other day?'

'She is very quiet.'

'Do you feed her while she is here?'

'Yes, sir. I always give her lunch. She seems to appreciate the hot meal.'

'That's good to hear. The gardener comes here every other week to look after the garden. How do you find him?'

'He is a fine block, sir. He is as quiet as Alison.'

'Do you feed him as well?'

'No, sir. I give him tea and scones at 5 o'clock when he is around.'

'He works hard. Please be generous to him as well. I'd like him to have a hot meal during his lunch time when he works in the garden.'

'From now on, I'll feed the gardener as you've instructed, sir. I was only worrying about the cost.'

'Please don't worry about the cost. I can afford to feed the people who work for me. I don't want any of you to suffer from hardship. As long as you work for me, I'm responsible for your well-beings. I'd like you all feel good when you are under my protection.'

'Thank you, sir. I could only talk for myself. I am exceedingly content to serve you and I'm grateful to you how you have been treating me. I don't think I would have been happier than I am now living in your household and having an access to the food, the accommodation and to the garden at the same time.'

'I'm glad to hear that you're satisfied with your life here. If you don't take me wrong, I'd like to ask you a private question now. You don't have to answer if you feel I'm breaching your privacy.'

'Go on, sir. Ask me what you would like to know.'

'Apart from cooking, what do you do to pass your time, here?'

'To pass my time?'

'Yes, after you finish cooking and doing clearing up, you must have plenty of time left to occupy yourself.'

'That's right, sir. I've got plenty of time left to utilise for which I'm also grateful to you. I read during my spare time.'

'Are you a book worm like me, Peacock?'

'Yes, sir. I like reading.'

'That's good. You know that you are more than welcome to borrow my books in the library if you wish to read my collection of literature books.'

'Thank you, sir. I'll definitely make use of your offer.'

'Is there anything else that makes you occupied apart from reading, Peacock?'

'I keep a diary, sir. It takes a bit of time to record my daily life.'

'How good to hear that! I'd loved to have an access to your diary. I'm sure it wouldn't be possible, will it?'

'Reading about my daily life could bore you, sir.'

'Each person's diary is exciting for others to browse as our lives completely different than one another.'

'My diary is a cook's diary, sir. I record what ingredients I use daily and how they taste when I experiment with different combinations. The colour spectrum of the food, the aroma of the food, how long it could be preserved without wasting and some other details of cooking which are classified in different sections of my diary. Then, I look at them to refresh my memory for further cooking experiments.'

'It'll be fun to read them. Will you be interested in sharing of your cooking experience through getting published as a cook expert?'

'I haven't thought about publishing my diary. Keeping a diary is for my development as a cook. It might have been a good idea to pass my experience on to others though.'

'Just think about it and let me know your answer later on. A very good friend of mine is a publisher. I could ask him to have a look at your diaries for the possibility of publishing them. I'm sure there will be a niche for a good cook diary book out there in the market place. You'll get a bit of passive income besides your salary.'

'I'll give a good thought about your offer, sir.'

'The dessert is delicious. Thanks for the splendid supper, Peacock. I'll be in my library for 3 hrs. You could have your supper and enjoy the rest of your evening. Good night, Peacock.'

'Good night, sir.'

Felix leaves the dining room with the pleasant feeling of having a good supper and getting to know a bit more about Peacock's personal life. Each time he talks to Peacock, there is more to learn about her distinctive qualities. She looks like she knows how to preoccupy herself to increase her virtue. It'll be good to help Peacock stretch her abilities outside cooking skills. She could be an accomplished writer. Felix walks down the corridor and enters his grand library with the rare books of his collection on the shelves. He turns the light on. He gazes his 3.000 rare books collections under his possession. When he enters the library, he feels how wealthy he is. The worth of his rare book collection is priceless. Felix doesn't collect the rare books for investment but his distinct taste for the rare books of quality. He goes directly to his library catalogue. He looks at the title of the book he wants to read. He points at its classification number. He pushes the ladder with the wheels towards the highest shelf where the book is placed. He finds the book on the shelf with ease. He puts a bookmark to the point he removes the book in order to find the same spot without difficulty when he finishes reading. Felix takes the book down and leaves the ladder in the same place. He carries the book all the way to his corner where he loves sitting in his antique chair by the fireplace next to the statute of a reading man. He opens the book with a warm affection as if it is a holly book.

He opens the first page and reads the title 'Think and Grow Rich' by Napoleon Hill'. He skims through the book. He decides to read the Chapter about 'Persistence'. He reads the several pages within a minute. He stretches himself to reach his notepad and pen on the coffee table next to him. He jots down the causes of persistence the author defines in his notepad. Felix puts his pen and notepad down; he closes the book for 5 minutes. He closes his eyes and visualises each point he jotted down in his notepad. He visualises all his actions he took since he left university.

He was 100 percent sure of his purpose before he emerged as an entrepreneur. His purpose in his life was to fulfil his potential in the best possible way and make a good living out of his talent, his skills and knowledge.

The burning desire of becoming an established artist in visual art kept him to be determined with the persistence for the greatest success in his field.

He learned to be self-reliant throughout his personal and professional journey without putting too much hope in others when things didn't look like promising or within anyone's control except God alone. Once Felix decided to make a living entirely out of his artwork but nothing else, he had no one to turn to for even a brief comfort of encouragement that he was in the right direction. In the rainy days of his start up, he was the only person to blame if things didn't turn up in the way he planned for.

Felix had always plans to make things happen for him. He planned all his routes to success in his enterprise from scratch. He loves giving himself detailed directions with plenty of sketches using mind map.

Felix accumulated his knowledge not only through academic education but his private studies of reading other people's success stories for years. He is almost self-made and self-thought man as far as he is concerned. No one taught him how to be a successful entrepreneur. It was a hard work to find out his way around to success on his own without meeting any role model as an entrepreneur to start with. Justin, Jasmine, Steve and Wonder are all good at passing on theoretical knowledge to him but had no practical experience of entrepreneurship. They couldn't direct him to the fast lane which he needed to find out as quickly as possible.

Felix mastered the skills of co-operation throughout his one to one support sessions with all the support tuition given to him. Whatever was expected of him, he took the pain of producing it; he did all his homework, revision and practical assignments over and over again without giving up until he refined his academic writing style. That was why he made such a progress in his intellectual development. He remembers the date Justin discovered the most disappointing fact about his inability to read newspapers. He was completely illiterate to start with. Now, he enjoys reading the books which stimulate his high level thinking skills. Felix spends minimum 3 hrs a day reading and educating himself through private research on great thinkers' way of thinking.

Without will-power, Felix would have never reached out success. His determination was kept alive with his unlimited will-power to overcome all the hurdles in his way without compromising with his original plans he designed to accomplish.

Felix has developed the good habits of reflecting on his past mistakes and learning from them without giving up. He has mastered the fear of failure. There isn't such a thing as failure for Felix. There is a learning curve to achieve out of each shortfall during his development programme as he sees it. All his endeavours from art to educating himself through reading, travelling, making observations of the nature, human beings and wild life taught him how to thrive with the good habits of acquiring new concepts in order to advance himself further. There is no limit how much we could learn in life.

As Napoleon Hill suggests in his book:

'A quitter never wins, a winner never quits.'

Felix owes his success to his persistence with all the definitive causes he possesses in his refined nature as a civilised man of wisdom. Felix opens his eyes after assimilating the given knowledge in the book and picks up the book gently from the coffee table. He opens the book, skims through the chapters. He chooses the chapter on 'Imagination' and reads it carefully. He is intrigued by each expression the author uses about the two types of imagination as he names them Synthetic

Imagination and Creative Imagination. He rereads the same passage and jots down the distinctive difference between them.

Felix closes the book and visualises his experience with the two different types of imagination. He remembers how he memorised the factual information during his law study. He felt it was too difficult to keep the factual information in his working memory. He needed to do several revisions in order to retain the information without forgetting. At that time, he didn't know the difference between synthetic imagination and creative imagination. He felt so inadequate not being able to absorb the facts in legal studies immediately. That was why he decided to drop out from his 1st degree in Civil Law. When he enrolled on art course, he didn't have any difficulty writing his assignments as he could choose the topic of his interest which made writing more enjoyable as though he was creating his practical artwork. Although Felix is capable of using his synthetic imagination with technical staff and often reads technical instruction written in manuals while he uses different software packages for his animation, he is still more comfortable with creative imagination.

What a shame that I've just learned the fact that creative imagination versus synthetic imagination. At university, while I was doing my law degree, I had the impression that my imagination lacked the power of superiority and I felt inferior to the non-dyslexic fellow students who seemed to have the power of synthetic imagination. In comparison with the creative imagination, synthetic imagination has not got much originality apart from storing all the facts in your brain and making connection with them without losing track. That's named sequential order in academic writing style. I wish I knew the difference between the two types of imagination. I might have completed my law degree before moving on to art degree. Never mind, it is too late to change the course of my decision. Thankfully, I make more money out of my artwork; I enjoy my profession as I depend on my creative imagination 90 % of time. It's a joy to be an artist. It's not a duty one could do for the sake of making a living out of it. I cannot imagine myself as happy as I am now if I chose to work in legal profession. It would have been a hard work to prepare legal cases using all the factual information in a sequential order.

Felix opens the book and skims through the chapters. This time, his curiosity stops him in Chapter 14 which is entitled 'The Sixth Sense -The Door to the Temple of Wisdom.' He starts reading the chapter quickly first. Then, he stops at the place where the author mentions about how the sixth sense has been obtained.

Felix thinks about his experience with sixth sense. Although he is 35 years old at present and this age doesn't qualify him mature enough to get into touch with sixth sense according to the author's statement, Felix believes that he reached the spiritual maturity earlier than the individuals from the same age group. Since he discovered the void in his past for not knowing his biological parents enabled him to question his origin, the purpose of his life, how he emerged, how he met certain individuals at certain point of time and how his life transferred from zero existence to the highest point within the wealth spectrum could only be understood through the sixth sense experience but not from other channels of understanding.

Felix goes back to his reading and stops when he comes to the sentence which deals with human understanding. Felix likes the author's statement more than anything written on human understanding. Yes, without any desire to understand who we are, our feelings such as happiness, the nature of origin, and other human kinds, human knowledge couldn't be advanced. When we think about it, the human intellect is based on the accumulation of what we understand from our observations which might be internal or external. In terms of understanding our deeds, our aims, our human emotions, we must observe ourselves internally. Self observation couldn't be achieved without any desire to get to know who we are and what we want from our lives. Similarly, nobody is able to acquire the knowledge of others, if they don't have any desire to get to know other people as much as ourselves. The former way of acquiring knowledge is called intrinsic, the later form of acquiring knowledge is named extrinsic which could be achieved through observation of other fellow human beings either directly or reading the books about human behaviour based on authors' intrinsic or extrinsic knowledge of human nature.

Felix feels he has learned a lot within 3 hrs while he has been reading the book written by Napoleon Hill. It was like talking to the author each time he stopped and responded to the author's statements. It took 20 years for Napoleon Hill to accumulate the knowledge he recorded in his book. He was employed by a wealthy philharmonic business man Andrew Carnegie who was born broke like Felix and made fortune over the years as a self-made entrepreneur. Felix visited Carnegie's birth place in Dunfermline which is a small town in Scotland in 2012. It was such a surprise for Felix to find out how poor Carnegie's living conditions were when he was born. Carnegie and his parents lived, slept and ate in the same room. They were that poor. He was an uneducated man to start with; yet, he became the first class scholar of his time and funded 3,000 libraries, in USA, Canada, Ireland, Australia, New Zealand, the West Indies, and Fiji. When Carnegie died at the age of 83 in 1919, his net worth was $75 billion which classified him as the wealthiest philanthropist of his time. Carnegie had given away 90 percent of his wealth in the amount of $350 million to charities when he was alive. He is a legend with the burning desire of human development through education and perseverance for success. Felix sees the similarities of his life with Andrew Carnegie and Napoleon Hill as he persevered to reach where he is now without quitting in life. Felix places the book on the coffee table and leaves his library with the quote from Napoleon Hill in his mind.

> 'A quitter never wins, a winner never quits.'

Felix aims to adopt Carnegie's philosophy for the legend he is going to leave behind.

To spend the next third of his life by acquiring wealth.

To spend the last third of his life by donating substantial amount of his wealth to appropriate charities.

Felix closes the door of the library quietly. He feels the healing power of charitable nature a philanthropist already. Felix reaffirms his gratitude to his supporters Justin, Jasmine, Steve and Wonder once more. It'll be good to help out the most misfortunes. He was helped out when he was in need as a homeless soul, as a convict, as an ex-offender, as a university student and as a small business owner. Even now, as a successful and wealthy entrepreneur, Felix still needs the selfless people's continuous moral support. It's time to hold a small gathering and inviting all his supporters to his garden party during his Easter break.

Time is midnight. Felix's usual day always ends at midnight. Tomorrow will be another day to catch up with his drawing and private study. In between, he'll be enjoying Peacock's cooking. Felix thinks about Peacock and her existence in his dwelling place. She must have been fast asleep by now. There is no soul in his big house apart from Peacock and himself. Yet, he doesn't feel strange to live in a large cottage with plenty of rooms unoccupied by either guests or tenants. He couldn't start a family life which has been delayed up until now as he didn't enough time to look for someone suitable who could be compatible with his hectic life style. It isn't ideal to be responsible for a wife and kids when his life is so unpredictable.

He often travels around the world. When he is in London, there are a lot of things he needs to do in order to increase his personal and professional developments. He passes the long corridor and walks up to the top floor where his bedroom is. Felix prefers occupying his attic room to go to sleep. There are 3 master bedrooms on the 2nd and 3rd floor. However, the attic room looks so cosy with a large glass ceiling on top so that he could watch the sky, stars and the moon before he falls asleep. It's good for the imagination to wonder about the cosmos and not to limit oneself to the earth orbit only. In the master bedrooms, there is no possibility of gazing the starry nights or milky way when the moon is below the horizon. In his attic bedroom, it is possible to observe the sky by his Skylight 6 Observatory Class telescope. Felix remembers French futurist science fiction novelist, Jules Verne. Felix read Jules Verne's *"From the Earth to the Moon"* with a joyful delight. How strange it is that the French novelist could predict the future with his sixth sense while he was writing his science fiction novel when no one could imagine sending any spacecraft to the moon during his life time. Jules Verne died in 1828. His legendary influence on space scientists came to fruition 63 years after his death when the Apollo 8 human spaceflight left earth orbit and landed at moon orbit in 1968. It has been a long day. Felix feels exhausted. He goes to shower cabinet in his bedroom and turns on the tap; the warm water takes away his exhaustion. He puts on his pyjamas and goes to bed. He looks at the sky from his bed. Ending his day by gazing at the sky enables Felix to remind himself how small his human existence in the universe is. He is as small as a tiny dot perhaps, in the divine canvas of his Creator. He closes his eyes and mediates for the end of day clearance. After a short while, he falls asleep. He dreams of Jules Verne as an aged man with the satisfaction of completing his journey on this earth. They both have a conversation about creative writing.

'Hi, Jules Verne. I have been thinking of your book "From the Earth to the Moon" quite recently. How did you write such an ingenious novel when no one could imagine sending a spacecraft to the moon when you were alive?'

'Hi, Felix. My fantasy allowed me to go to the moon when I was writing my novel. Everything starts with fantasy before it becomes reality.'

'How did you generate ideas for your writing?'

'I travelled a lot to generate ideas for my writing. It is not possible to produce work from fantasy if you are stuck in one place without having an access to different environments.'

'How far did you travel, Jules Verne?'

'I bought a small ship in 1867 and named the ship, Saint-Michel. I replaced the Saint- Michel 3 times. I sailed around Europe with the Saint-Michell III. That was how I fed my imagination for my writing.'

'What is the secret of your success, Jules Verne?'

'Having an adventures life with plenty of voyages was my success, Felix.'

'What was your objective in your life?'

'My objective has been to depict the earth, and not the earth alone, but the universe...'

'I travel a lot. I've been all over the places in Europe. Is travelling widely sufficient enough for me to be a successful writer, Jules Verne?'

'There are a lot of travellers but only a handful of successful writers, Felix. Travelling on its own wouldn't make you a great writer. You need to combine the experience of being in different places with your imagination. That's how you could produce something out of ordinary. Otherwise, you would be only a travel writer by recording the details of your journey without making any art out of it which will be limited to the non-fiction functionality most of the time.'

'What do I need to do in order to be as good as you in science fiction, Jules Verne?'

'What do you do in your real life, Felix?'

'I am an artist.'

'What type of art do you produce?'

'Mainly abstract drawings and I also produce 3D sculptural animations from geometrical figures whose intelligence resembles human intelligence.'

'Here we are, Felix. You already know how to create out of nothingness for which you must be using your imagination. You don't need me to answer your question now. You've already got your own answer for creativity. You could apply your visual imagination to science fiction writing if you wish. That's all you need to do. All the people with creative energy have got their own patterns of creativity. No one could teach anyone to be a creative artist or a writer of originality. All the art schools are there to inform students about the technical aspects of drawing, painting whatever the medium they want to master. The teachers could only equip you with technical perfection but cannot teach you how to be original that comes from your nature. You need to trust your own ability to bring out something which belongs you only; it's like having a blue print of your genius but you cannot repeat someone else's genius. That's why I state that everyone is unique. In art, nothing could be duplicable. The originality could exist when an artist produces non-repeatable creation even the originator of the creation cannot repeat his product twice. If he does, he loses his originality.'

'That's what I thought so. Thanks for the affirmation, Jules Verne.'

'You're very welcome, Felix. Let me leave you with yourself. You're an artist. You're in charge of your creativity. I cannot teach you what you already posses in you.'

'I understand. It's been very helpful talking to you, Jules Verne. I'll never ask others to advise me on how to be original any longer. You taught me that it is not possible. Whether we are born with creative power or not determines the nature of our products we produce.'

'That's what I meant, Felix. Trust your own ability when it comes to creativity. Follow your instincts. You'll be always producing something with the same stamp of your own uniqueness. Art critics name that uniqueness as individual style.'

'Many thanks, Jules Verne. I'll remember your wisdom and how you passed it on to me.'

'Thanks for your appreciation, Felix. All the best with your creation!'

Felix opens his eyes and realises that he had a beautiful dream. How dreams come about in our lives is a mystery to us. There is a life when we fall asleep. We start understanding some of the concepts like creativity much clearly when we are half unconscious or cut off from the external reality. Truth is attached in Jules Verne's statement about the nature of originality. No one is capable of teaching someone to be original which comes to us as divine revelation and it's a gift from God like our lives. How we come to this earth and how we depart from it is within our destiny which is defined beyond our will. In between our birth and death, we're given an opportunity to make difference without being limited to the scarcity of the beginning if we experience such deprivation. Felix remembers the poem he has read about destiny from Firdevs Dede and recites the whole poem while his eyes are closed.

DESTINY

Our destiny is not known by any of us

We cannot plan our birth or the final episode of our lives

We all taste the life and death which are planned beyond our wish
most of the time

There is nothing to be scared of

There is nothing to be proud of

We're all vulnerable while we face our birth or death
at some point of our lives

There is nothing to be planned by us for the better or the worst in life

Everything will happen within our destiny, somehow.

Felix falls asleep and dreams about his destiny to turn all his dreams into reality. An artist is the creator of his destiny while he is living his dreams day by day without any fear of his mortality as all the creators are immortal in reality. To be born as an artist with dyslexia was within his destiny and he has been blessed with the gift he was born with. There is nothing to be ashamed of and there is nothing to be proud of either. He is a great artist with the additional gift of having dyslexia as his blueprint. He likes himself as he is; after all, dyslexia isn't an Obstacle. It's been a rewarding experience of living with it and being recognised as a dyslexic artist like Leonardo da Vinci or Pablo Picasso, perhaps, that has been a great bonus in Felix's life!

Lightning Source UK Ltd.
Milton Keynes UK
UKOW04n0313140815

256916UK00001B/7/P